LITTLE WALKERS CREEK

A History of the Land
and
Its People

By
Rebecca Cox Sowers

© 2005

By

Rebecca Cox Sowers

All rights reserved. No portion of this book may be reproduced or transmitted in any form or by any means electronic, mechanical or otherwise using devices now existing or yet to be invented, without written permission from the publisher, except for brief quotations for review purposes.

Published by

American History Imprints
Franklin Tennessee

Visit us on the Internet and explore our online store - thousands of titles of interest to the genealogist and historian.

www.Americanhistoryimprints.com
www.genealogyinprint.com

Iinternational Standard Book Number 0-9753667-4-2

Printed in the United States of America on acid-free paper

This Book is lovingly dedicated to my Mother
Elsie Irene Davis
May 21, 1932-February 16, 2001

"Not to know what happened before we were born is to remain
perpetually a child. For what is the worth of a human life unless it
is woven into the life of our ancestors by the records of history?"
--Marcus Tullius Cicero, 106-43 B.C.

Acknowledgements

One of the most enjoyable parts of writing a book like this one is meeting and becoming friends with all those who were willing to help with the book. Many people volunteered their time and effort in either sending information or pictures. They also supplied the encouragement and excitement which kept me focused on the research and writing
of the book. I have made many dear friends.

I want to thank Juanita Cox Bentley for her patience and help. I called on her often. She supplied much of the Henry Davis information; I am indebted to her.

I an also indebted to Sara Melton Sumner; she was a great help in sending pictures and information on the Millirons and Meadows families. Thanks Sara.

Reba and Jack Crawford, thanks so much for the encouragement, help and pictures.

Christine Hamblin Distelhorst sent tons of pictures which made the book come to life. She is a dear friend. Thanks Christine for the Hamblin and Millirons pictures and information.

A dear childhood friend, Milton Davis took the time from his busy life sending pictures and information. Again, making the book come alive. He graciously sent information from the King and Brunk Family Bibles and many pictures.

Bobbie Lee, a Ritter descendent helped with the Ritter Family. Thanks Bobbie. I hope to meet you one day.

Loretta Hancock Patterson and Karen Fallin helped with the Hancock Family. Karen also helped with the Pauley Family. Thanks to both of you.

I have to add Suella Wolfe and Kay Robinson Welch for their help with photographs. I must thank them for having patience with my never ending questions about the King family. Thanks, Suella and Kay.

To everyone who let me know they were interested in the book, thank you. I appreciate the interest and hope no one will be disappointed.

If I have unintentionally left anyone out, forgive me. There have been many others who offered encouragement which helped a lot when things were a little slow. Thanks to everyone.

TABLE OF CONTENTS

VIRGINIA LAND HISTORY ... 2
EARLY YEARS ... 2
COLONIAL LAND OFFICE PATENTS, 1623–1774 ... 3
LAND OFFICE GRANTS, 1779–1993 ... 4
HISTORICAL OVERVIEW OF THE NEW RIVER VALLEY ... 4
BIOGRAPHY ... 5
Dr. Thomas Walker (1715-1794) ... 5
SOUTHWEST VIRGINIA COUNTY FORMATION ... 5
Lines of Pulaski County ... 6
LITTLE WALKERS CREEK ORIGINAL LAND GRANTS ... 7
Montgomery and Pulaski Counties, Virginia ... 7
Wythe and Bland Counties, Virginia ... 14
    Long Spur Branch ... 18
        The Draper Tract ... 19
            Mustard Family ... 20
        The Hounshell Tract ... 22
            Brawley Family ... 22
                Hutsell Family ... 23
        The Patterson Tract ... 24

DISEASES AND EPIDEMICS ... 25
EPIDEMICS ... 25
DISEASES—EARLY YEARS ... 26

FIRST FAMILIES ... 28
FOREWORD ... 28
AKERS FAMILY ... 29
Moses Akers Sr. Family ... 29
Moses Akers Jr. Family ... 33
ALLEN FAMILY ... 39
AUSTIN FAMILY ... 42
BANES FAMILY ... 43
BRUNK FAMILY ... 52
CHANDLER FAMILY ... 56
Biography ... 57
    Robert Lee Chandler ... 57
Biography ... 58
    Emma Louella Millirons ... 58
COMBS FAMILY ... 60
COLLINS FAMILY ... 65
CORDER FAMILY ... 67
DAVIS ... 71
Henry Davis Family ... 71
Samuel Caddell Davis Family ... 85
FAW FAMILY ... 103
Biography ... 103
    Wiley Henderson Faw ... 103

v

- Hamblin Family 105
- Hancock Family 112
- Harrell Family 120
- Hunter Family 127
  - *Riley Harrison Hunt* *127*
- Johnston/Johnson Family 130
- King Family 133
- Kitts Family 146
- Lambert Family 148
  - *Elizabeth Jane Lambert* *150*
- Meadows Family 151
- Millirons Family 155
- Montgomery Family 158
- Moody Family 160
- Morris Family 161
- Parcell-Parsell Family 164
- Pauley Family 167
- Pegram Family 170
- Ritter Family 175
- Tickle Family 177
- Underwood Family 179
- White Family 181

MISCELLANEOUS PHOTOGRAPHS 187
- Davis School 187
- Spur Branch School 187
- Pulaski County Little Walkers Creek School 188
- Goshen Church 188
- Henry Davis' Sawmill 189
- Emmett Davis 189
- Spur Branch--Possibly School Children 190
- A Family Reunion/Church Gathering 190

BIBLIOGRAPHY 191
- Books 191
- Census Records 191
- Court Records 191
- Published Manuscripts 192
- Nonpublished Family Manuscripts 192
- Websites and Online Databases 192
- Government Documents 193

ABOUT THE AUTHOR 195
INDEX 196

VIRGINIA LAND HISTORY
From the Library of Virginia
Richmond, VA

EARLY YEARS

Land was not granted in any consistent fashion during the earliest years of the colony when the Virginia Company of London had the rights to settle the land. In 1624 the Company's charter was terminated and the colony became part of the manorial holdings of the King. (This is rather unusual. The King did not govern Virginia as sovereign of England, but as a feudal lord).

In 1627 Governor George Yeardley began the headright system of granting land to those who brought people into the colony. Land could be taken out at the rate of 50 acres per imported person. Grantees had to pay annual quitrents (a kind of real estate tax), and "plant and seat" the land in order to keep it.

In 1649 exiled King Charles II gave the "Northern Neck", the area between the Potomac and Rappahannock Rivers, to seven of his supporters including Thomas Lord Culpeper. Over the years Culpepper purchased the shares of the others. By 1690 it became associated with Thomas Lord Fairfax, and grants in this huge (over 5 million acre) proprietorship were begun. Because of the proprietorship, grants in the Northern Neck are not found at the Virginia archives. There were basically two separate colonies operating in Virginia from the point of view of land grants. For example, head rights were never recognized in the Northern Neck.

There was substantial disagreement over the boundaries of the Northern Neck Proprietary. In 1730 Fairfax's son, also named Thomas, got into a legal wrangle with Virginia over the extent of his domain, its size being defined by the location of two rivers whose sources were unknown at the time Charles had made his grant. Fairfax argued that the Rapidan River was the real Rappahannock, thus enlarging the proprietorship. Incredibly, he won his case in 1745, throwing into tumult the legal status of land granted by Virginia in the fork of the Rappahannock. Many residents repatented under Fairfax. Others ended up in court.

In 1699 a new system of treasury rights (or treasury warrants) came into being, and it effectively did away with the headright system. Anyone could purchase rights for 5 shillings for each 50 acres. As before they were liable for quitrent and settling the property. Otherwise the land would revert to the Crown.

A law of 1705 forbade the granting of patents in excess of 4000 acres, but a number of companies and individuals were occasionally given permission to take out large tracts. Land companies and speculators played an important role in facilitating the settlement of the land because it was easier for immigrants to buy from the company (which had already purchased the treasury rights) than to go to Williamsburg. John Vanmeter, Robert Beverley, and Benjamin Borden obtained large grants of approximately 100,000 acres starting in the 1730's.

A map of the most inhabited part of Virginia containing the whole province of Maryland with part of Pennsylvania, New Jersey and North Carolina was drawn by Joshua Fry and Peter Jefferson in 1751.

The Loyal Land Company was granted 800,000 acres in 1749, the Greenbrier Company got 100,000 acres in 1751, both in the western part of the colony. They were given four years to survey the tract and purchase treasury rights but this time limit was extended up to the

Revolution. There were numerous lawsuits relating to conflicting claims with early settlers and land awarded for military service.

During the Revolution it was not possible to obtain land patents. A state Land Office was created in 1779 by the new state government and it set about the business of approving land claims that had languished since 1775, and processing military service warrants.

Even though Lord Fairfax was English, his proprietary was not seized during the war because he was such a long time resident. But his heirs were British subjects, and when Fairfax died in 1781 it was decided to go after his lands and collect taxes on them. Needless to say, a lengthy series of legal cases began. The family finally sold their last interest in the estate in 1808.

With the creation of the Federal Government, Virginia and other states were asked to cede their western lands to the fledgling government, which used them to create the Northwest and Southwest Territories. In 1781 Virginia relinquished its claim to lands in the Northwest Territories in exchange for being able to award bounty lands in the Virginia Military District in what is now south-central Ohio. Virginia proceeded to award its military bounty lands in the Kentucky territory (until Kentucky became a state in 1792), and then in the Military District (after 1792 and before Ohio achieved statehood in 1803.)

COLONIAL LAND OFFICE PATENTS, 1623–1774

With the abolition of the charter of the Virginia Company of London in 1624, the administration of the colony was placed directly under the crown. As this included the disposal of land, it fell to the governor to use his broad powers to issue land patents. In 1634 the Privy Council authorized the patenting of lands under the principle of granting patents to any person who qualified as a planter. In practice, the acreage was awarded to the person who paid the transportation cost of the emigrant and not to the settler himself. This method, called the headright system, was employed as the major means of distributing virgin lands in the 17th century.

The office of the Secretary of the Colony was key to the process, and it remained in place until the Revolution. This office issued patents after all the steps were approved. First, the patentee was required to appear before a county court and present proof that a stated number of persons had been imported to the colony at his expense. The certificate of importation rights issued by the courts was taken to the Secretary of the Colony in the capital, where a "right" was issued that, when presented to a county surveyor, authorized him to survey the tract located by the patentee. Once the survey was completed, it and all supporting papers were returned to the office of the Secretary, and, if no discrepancies existed, two copies of the patent were made. One copy was signed by the governor, sealed, and delivered to the patentee, and the other was retained by the Secretary. No Land Office surveys are extant prior to 1779 although some county court records include survey books. Also, none of the supporting papers mentioned above are extant prior to 1779.

Another method of land distribution authorized during the 17th century was the military right granted to persons who would settle in hostile territory, but this was seldom used. In the 18th century the treasury right was established whereby land could be purchased. The office of the Secretary of the Colony continued to act as the official channel for the legal distribution of land until the establishment of the Virginia Land Office on June 22, 1779. This collection consists of the patents as recorded by the office of the Secretary of the Colony. These copies were hung on strings in the office and, as time was available, they were recorded in bound volumes. A random method of selection of documents to be entered accounts for the haphazard dating in the early volumes, and the method of hanging the patent on string accounts for loss of documents. The system of recording was improved in the 18th century. Rather than having duplicate copies made and entered in a bound volume at intervals, the patents were recorded when issued. All other accompanying documents including surveys were annually destroyed.

LAND OFFICE GRANTS, 1779–1993

The Virginia Land Office was established in 1779 by the General Assembly and was headed by a Register "appointed from time to time, by joint ballot of both houses of assembly. . . . " It was the responsibility of the Register to carry out the very carefully structured legislation that provided the procedure for obtaining waste and unapproriated lands. Under the act, any person could purchase as much land as desired upon payment to the Treasurer of a fee of forty pounds for one hundred acres. In return the purchaser was given a receipt, that was then given to the Auditor of Public Accounts, who issued a certificate noting the amount of land to which the person was entitled. The certificate was taken to the Land Office where the Register entered a warrant authorizing a surveyor to lay off the land. The warrantee entered a claim to the land by depositing the warrant with the surveyor of the county in which the land was located.

Once the survey had been completed, it and the warrant on which it was based were returned to the warrantee whose responsibility it was to deliver the papers to the Land Office. The documents were examined by the Register, and, if correctly executed, were filed for a period of not less than six months. If, within that time, no caveat (A formal notice filed by an interested party with a court or officer, requesting the postponement of a proceeding until the filer is heard.) was entered on the survey, the plat and certificate of survey were recorded and the grant was issued by the Register. Once written, the grant was signed by the governor, sealed, recorded, and delivered to the grantee.

HISTORICAL OVERVIEW OF THE NEW RIVER VALLEY

The earliest documented European exploration of the New River and its valley was a 1671 expedition sponsored by Abraham Wood, Commander of Fort Henry at the falls of the Appomattox River of Virginia (Petersburg area). The cartographer for the expedition named it Wood's River the adoption of "New" is unclear). Notable expeditions were made by Henry Batte, Thomas Batte, John Sailing and Dr. Thomas Walker between 1671 and 1748.

It was opportunist and adventurer, Colonel James Patton that obtained the original grant, The Wood's River Grant, in 1745 and commenced surveying and the solicitation for settlers. There had been numerous claims in the area, but it is now generally believed that the original settlement was in 1748 near present day Blacksburg and Drapers Meadows by George Draper, John, Thomas and William Ingles. A competing grant of 800,000 acres in 1749 was made to Dr. Thomas Walker and others as the Loyal Company of Virginia in 1749.

In the intervening years, the French, to protect its exploration interests from current Canada, and the Cherokee and Shawnee tribes, became more alarmed regarding the English intrusion of these hunting grounds. This would result in numerous skirmishes and bloodshed in the next few years which would retard settlement.

BIOGRAPHY
Dr. Thomas Walker (1715-1794)

The Walkers Mountain chain, Big Walkers Creek and Little Walkers Creek were named for Dr. Thomas Walker. Dr. Walker was born on 25 January 1715 in King and Queen County, Virginia, to Thomas and Susan Preachy Walker. Walker's ancestors came to America in 1650 from Staffordshire, England, and settled in Tidewater, Virginia, where the family prospered as respectable plantation owners. Thomas was educated at the College of William and Mary and then studied medicine under his brother-in-law, Dr. George Gilmer of Williamsburg, a medical graduate of Edinburgh University. In 1741, he married Mildred Thornton Meriwether, widow of Nicholas Meriwether. Mildred was also a second cousin to George Washington. Walker erected their home, Castle Hill, on Mildred's 15,000-acre estate in Albemarle County, east of Charlottesville. The couple had 12 children.

Walker was physician to Thomas Jefferson's father, Peter Jefferson. After Peter's death, Walker became Thomas Jefferson's guardian. Peter Jefferson, like many of the wealthy Virginia gentlemen of the time, had spent much of his life exploring and surveying. It was perhaps through this long association with the elder Jefferson that Thomas Walker acquired his love for exploration, a fondness that he shared with the young Thomas Jefferson.

Walker developed great skill and reputation as an explorer and surveyor and in 1743 led an expedition as far west as present-day Kingsport, Tennessee. In March 1750, he led another expedition through present-day Kentucky that lasted four months. In 1752 he became the head of the Loyal Land Company, a position he held until his death. Thomas Walker was a physician, planter, trader, surveyor, cartographer, and explorer. He also served in the House of Burgesses, in local government, and in the Fredericksville Parish. He was an executor of the estates of Meriwether Lewis's grandfather and Peter Jefferson. In 1779 he served, along with Daniel Smith, as a Virginia Commissioner responsible for extending the Virginia-North Carolina border to the Mississippi River. He died at his home 09 November 1794.

SOUTHWEST VIRGINIA COUNTY FORMATION

The County of Augusta governed the New River Valley from 1745-1769. The county seat was Staunton and was far removed from the frontier settlements of the New River Valley.

In 1769, the new county of Botetourt was formed with the county seat being in Fincastle.

Because of more remote settlements west and along the New River and due to the great difficulties of reaching the Botetourt county seat; the residents of these areas petitioned the Virginia legislature for the formation of a new county. The county of Fincastle was formed in 1772 from parts of Botetourt. Fincastle remained the county seat for Botetourt while the Fincastle County seat was in the area of the Lead Mines in what is now Wythe County. This was a short lived county being abolished in 1776. All records for Fincastle are located at the Montgomery County Courthouse in Christiansburg.

Formed from the now extinct Fincastle County was Montgomery, Kentucky and Washington Counties. Named for Richard Montgomery, killed at Quebec in 1775, the county seat for Montgomery was Fort Chiswell now in Wythe County [later moved to Christiansburg]. Montgomery County covered 12,000 square miles and more than 25 counties were taken from it over the years.

Wythe was formed in 1790 from Montgomery County. Wythe County was named for George Wythe, the first Virginia signer of the Declaration of Independence. A place near the middle of the county was chosen as the place for the county seat, and was then called Evansham, although it eventually became Wytheville. The original boundary lines for Wythe County included all of Carroll and Grayson Counties, part of Smyth County, most of Tazewell County, parts of Bland and Buchanan Counties, a small portion of Giles County, part of Pulaski County, McDowell County, parts of Mercer, Wyoming, Boone, Logan, and Mingo Counties. The latter six counties are now in West Virginia.

Giles was formed the 1st day of May 1806 from Montgomery, Tazewell, Wythe, and Monroe Counties. It was named for William Branch Giles, United States Senator from Virginia at that time.

Pulaski was formed in 1839 from Montgomery and Wythe, named for Casimir Pulaski who paid the ultimate price, having sustained a mortal wound while fighting for American independence at the battle of Savannah in 1779.

Bland was formed in 1861 from Wythe, Giles counties and part of Tazewell county after 1870. Named in honor of Richard Bland the prominent Revolutionary period Virginia patriot.

Lines of Pulaski County

"To the honorable the members of the County Courts of the Counties of Montgomery, Wythe and Pulaski
Greetings We your Commissioners appointed by act of the General assembly of Virginia passed the 30th day of March 1839 appointing us to run and mark the lines between the counties of Montgomery and Pulaski on the one side and the counties of Wythe and Pulaski on the other side as designated by said act we met agreeable to appointment on the 23rd day of June 1839 and proceeded to the top of the Gap mountain to the line dividing the counties of Montgomery and Giles and commencing our operations from said line in a low gap of said mountain at the head of a hollow leading down to Hiram Davis's upper place little Walkers creek and running as follows Beginning at a white oak and red oak in the gap of a mountain and running S 20 E 2096 poles crossing little Walkers creek and the brush mountain and Peak creek to 3 chestnut oaks, 2 black oaks and chestnut on the top of a mountain thence S 45 E 1660 poles crossing Peppers ferry road to the mouth of a lane between John S. Sayers and Harvey Shepherd on the South side of the stage road thence S 41 E 960 poles to the mouth of pine run thence S 37 E 1280 poles crossing New River and little reed Island to the Grayson County line, here your Commissioners considered their labors at an end as the Grayson and Floyd County lines have been run and marked heretofore and lines between Giles and Pulaski are natural boundaries your Commissioners thought it not necessary to be run at this time. We have the honor to submit the above report to your honorable bodies assuring you that we did perform our duty to the best of our skill and judgment. Given under our hands Viz the first day of July 1839."[1]

Note**When Bland was formed in 1861, Pulaski gained land. The first Pulaski County line was in the area of land owned by the Chandlers. This would be about a mile east of the present line. Hiram Davis mentioned above once owned much of the land in that area and I think part of it was also in what is now Bland County. The first Pulaski County line has been referred to as the "old

---

[1] Wythe County, Virginia Deed Book 14, p. 289

Pulaski County line" or as the " the Foote line". Sylvanus Foote was a surveyor during the period of Pulaski's formation.

LITTLE WALKERS CREEK ORIGINAL LAND GRANTS
Virginia Land Office Patents and Grants and Northern Neck Grants and Surveys; Library of Virginia.

Montgomery and Pulaski Counties, Virginia

Thomas Shannon, Montgomery County, 208 acres, 2 January 1788. Grants # 17, pg. 390.
On Walkers Creek at the mouth of Little Walkers Creek. Beginning about 400 yards above the mouth of Little Walkers Creek. [most of this land is probably in Giles County in the Poplar Hill area, as this is where the Shannon family settled.] This is most likely Thomas Shannon who married Agnes Crow in Montgomery County, Virginia as the younger Thomas was not born until 1797.

Elijah Shofflebarrier [Shufflebarger], Montgomery County, 315 acres, 21 July 1788. Grants # 17, pg. 502. On Little Walkers Creek in a place known as Meadows.

Abraham Shufflebarger listed in the 1815 Wythe County, Virginia tax list with "one farm on Little Walkers Creek, having one cabben, one stable, one smoke house and corn crib. Valued at $150.[1]

Robert McCulloh, Montgomery County, 14,500 acres, 29 September 1795. Grants # 33, pg. 189.
On Big Walkers, Little Walkers, some waters of Back Creek adjoining Saml. Hollinsworth's survey. Crossing Little Walkers Creek to a red oak marked **M**…by the Waggon Road…crossing little Walkers Creek and Big Walkers Creek to the beginning.

Samuel Shannon, Montgomery County, 465 acres on Little Walkers Creek., 3 February 1799, Grants # 42, pg. 193.

Samuel Shannon, Montgomery County, 74 acres, 3 September 1800. Grants # 46, pg 49.
On Little Walker Creek in a place called Baiery Bottom.

Samuel Shannon, Montgomery County, 50 acres, 3 September 1800. Grants # 47, pg. 150.
On Little Walkers Creek.

Thomas Shannon, Montgomery County, 100 acres, 11 May 1808. Grants # 56, pg. 333
On the south side of Walkers big mountain on the waters of Walkers Little Creek adjoining Samuel Shannon.

Daniel Howe, Montgomery County, 100 acres, 11 December 1798. Grants # 42, pg. 17.
On Little Walkers Creek adjoining own land.

On November 6, 1851, John D. Howe and Joseph Howe executors of Daniel Howe's will conveyed 100 acres to William Miller on the waters of Walkers Creek…corner to Zachariah Cecil[2]

---

[1] 1815 Wythe County, VA Tax List.
[2] Pulaski County, VA Deed Book 2, p. 138.

Thomas Shannon, Montgomery County, 80 acres, 20 November 1817. Grants # 67, pg. 93. On Walkers Little Creek adjoining Samuel Shannon. Most likely Thomas Shannon son of elder Thomas married Juliet Allen in Giles County. Two of his children, James King Shannon and Mary Haven Shannon wife of William Miller owned land on Little Walkers Creek.

Thomas S. and Juliet H. Shannon conveyed for love and affection to their son James K. Shannon. Land on the north side of Walkers Little Mountain…with the old road with James Cloyd's inclusive survey. Dated March 19, 1867.[1] Located around the area of Cloyd's Mountain and land …near the "Gap". James King Shannon married Betty Bush. The Shannon family is buried in the Shannon Cemetery, Poplar Hill, Giles County, Virginia.

Two of James K. Shannon's children conveyed land on Little Walkers Creek to William L. Hunter…Bettie Shannon Lula Shannon Weaver and husband Walter M. Weaver 750 acres running on old Robinson line corner to William Miller. Dated February 6, 1904.[2]

On April 15, 1911, W. M. and B. J. Weaver conveyed 800 acres to Oscar Laugon…being the James K. Shannon estate.[3]

Oscar Laugon conveyed the same land to D. K. Shinault on August 18, 1915.[4]

On July 1, 1919, D. K. Shinault and Nancy Mary conveyed the land to T. T. Dulaney.[5]

Hiram H. Davis, Wythe County, 50 acres, 25 August 1835. Grants # 85, pg. 144.
On Walkers Little Creek corner to his own land. [now Pulaski County]

John Shufflebarger of Montgomery County conveyed 74 acres to Hiram Davis on September 24, 1817…" said John Shufflebarger & Margaret his wife for and in consideration of the sum of three hundred dollars in hand paid by the said Hiram Davis to Abram Shufflebarger & the further sum of one dollar to him in hand paid the receipt whereof is acknowledged, do give, grant, bargain and sell unto the said Hiram Davis and his heirs and assigns one certain tract of land containing Seventy four acres be the same more or less, as surveyed for Samuel Shannon the 27th day of February 1783 lying in the County of Wythe upon little Walkers creek a branch of New River…".[6]

William Davis, Wythe County, 134 acres, 25 August, 1835. Grants # 85, pg. 161.
On Walkers Little Creek corner to his own land…at the mouth of Harman's Lick hollow.

William sold two tracts of land to his two daughters and their children Catherine King and Sarah Banes.[7]

John Shufflebarger conveyed 50 acres to William Davis on March 2, 1818 "…in consideration of the sum of two hundred dollars to the said John S Barger in hand paid by him the said William Davis the receipt thereof he doeth hereby acknowledge hath given, granted, bargained and sold,

---

[1] Pulaski County, VA Deed Book 4, p. 122.
[2] Pulaski County, VA Deed Book 23, p. 145.
[3] Pulaski County, VA Deed Book 30, p. 356.
[4] Pulaski County, VA Deed Book 37, p. 216.
[5] Pulaski County, VA Deed Book 41, p. 106.
[6] Wythe County, VA Deed Book 7, p. 154.
[7] Pulaski County, VA Deed Book 2, p. 214; Pulaski County, VA Deed Book 2, p.173.

and by these presents doeth give, grant, bargain, sell and confirm to him the said William Davis his heirs and assigns forever a tract or parcel of land containing fifty acres, be the same more or less, lying in the county of Wythe and state of Virginia on little Walkers creek, the waters of New River…".[1]

John Shufflebarger bought land from George Helm on October 9, 1811 "…lying and being in Wythe County on little Walkers creek the water of New River being part of a survey of 75,000 acres, sold by Hugh McGavock collector of the Direct Tax, for the taxes due thereon and unpaid & William Patterson became a purchaser who sold the same or an interest therein to the said Helm … on the line of a parcel of 100 acres of the same tract laid off for Daniel Howe, besides the quantity now conveyed, two tracts of land, the property of the said John Shufflebarger and containing 74 acres other 50 acres…"[2]

The above mentioned 75,000 acres was granted to Robert Pollard on October 1, 1794 in the county of Wythe on the waters of East river, Bluestone River, Clinch River and Wolf Creek. Mentions James Shannon, William Patterson, Akalis Fanning, John Crockett, Robert Adams, Hugh McGavock. He was also awarded another grant for 150, 000 acres dated September 8, 1794.

<u>Hiram H. Davis</u>, Wythe County, 110 acres, 21 April 1837. Grants # 86, pg. 675.
Both sides of Walkers Little Creek beginning at a stake to his own patent land.

On October 18, 1846 the Hiram H. Davis heirs "…Elizabeth Davis widow and relict of Heirman H. Davis, deceased, Sally Davis, Juliet Davis, Lucien B. Davis and Martha his wife, Nehemiah Henderson and Amy his wife of the one part and Addison Davis of the other part all of the county of Giles…two certain tracts or parcels of land containing by survey one tract of one hundred and ten acres more or less and one other of seventy four acres more or less, it being the land which the late Hiram H. Davis decd. sold in his life to David & John Millirons and executed his title bond to said John and D. Millirons and by them assigned to the said Addison Davis, the land lying and being in the county of Pulaski on Walkers little creek…".[3]

On January 12, 1848 the Davis heirs conveyed land to Joshua Mustard "…Elizabeth Davis widow and relict of Hiram H. Davis, Nehemiah Henderson and Amy his wife, and Sally E. Davis, Lucien B. Davis and Martha his wife, and Juliet G. Davis of the one part and Joshua Mustard of the other part, all of the county of Giles and state of Virginia (except Lucian B. Davis and Martha his wife of the County of Fayette)…a certain tract or parcel of land containing sixty acres more or less lying and being in the county of Pulaski on Walkers little Creek, it being the same that was sold by a decree of the Circuit Supr Court of Wythe for the benefit of Leonard Straw and sold by him to James Overstreet and by said Overstreet to Hiram H. Davis…".[4] (This was the eastern part of the Draper survey.)

On April 19, 1850 Addison Davis conveyed a tract of land to "…David Millirons and John J. Millirons lying and being in the county of Pulaski state of Virginia on the waters of Walkers Little Creek and bounded as follows to wit…corner of survey that the said Addison Davis got of his Father…".[5]

---

[1] Wythe County, VA Deed Book 7, p. 153.
[2] Wythe County, VA Deed Book 5, p. 194.
[3] Pulaski County, VA Deed Book 2, p. 36.
[4] Pulaski County, VA Deed Book 2, p. 180.
[5] Pulaski County, VA Deed Book 2, Pg. 320

In January of 1852 "…by and between Addison Davis of the County of Giles and state of Virginia of the one part and William Mustard of the second and last part of the state and county aforesaid…sum of five hundred dollars…in trust for the benefit of Martha Johnston (wife of Lewis Johnston)and her heirs three several tracts or parcels of land situate, lying and being in the county of Pulaski in the state of Virginia on the waters of little walkers creek the first part of which contains one hundred and ten acres and is bounded as follows to wit Beginning at a stake corner to the 74 acre tract the original corner down with the lines thereof…the second tract 74 acres…Beginning at two black oaks on the banks of the creek…the third contains 53 acres and was patented to said Addison Davis in the year 1848…".[1]

In October, 1871 William Mustard, trustee and Martha Johnston conveyed about 1 acre to William Miller corner to Lewis Johnson's land.[2]

Joshua Mustard and wife Betsey… of the County of Wythe…conveyed three parcels of land to John Mustard on the waters of Walkers little creek known as the Kinion Place containing sixty three acres… taken off the Hoge farm twenty acres…also an entry containing ninety six acres adjoining the same tracts…a special Deed…with the buildings and appurtenances…sum of five hundred and fifty dollars…".[3]

John Mustard and Lavica his wife conveyed two tracts of land to Hickman Powers on May 28, 1850; the 20 and 96 acre tract.[4]

Powers sold the same tract of land to Harvey R. Mustard.[5]

Mariah Mustard (wife of Harvey R.) sold the same land to Chas W. Fletcher on April 5, 1902… two pieces of land…first piece…corner of land of William Davis…Second piece…with a line of the Thurston land…with a line of Henry Davis equals 116 acres…[6]

On October 16, 1908 Charles W. Fletcher sold the same land to Ollie E. Davis and J. E. Davis her husband.[7]

<u>Zachariah Cecil</u>, Pulaski County, 807 acres, 30 September 1844. Grants # 96, pg. 18.
On the waters of Little Walkers Creek on a line of a survey of 14,500 acres made by Robert McCulloh …on a line of a survey of 75,000 acres made by Robert Pollard…corner of the land of Charles King.

<u>James C. Ingram</u>, Pulaski County, 188 acres, 30 September 1848. Grants # 99. pg. 765.
On Walkers Little Creek…by the Banes branch… corner to Wm. Davises land.
James B. Caddall bought the above tract of land from James C. Ingram in 1849.[8]

<u>Henry Honaker, Sr.</u>, Pulaski County, 9 ½ aces, 30 September 1848. Grants # 100, pg. 685.

---

[1] Pulaski County, VA Deed Book 2, p. 416.
[2] Pulaski County, VA Deed Book 5, p. 135.
[3] Pulaski County, VA Deed Book 2, p. 633.
[4] Pulaski County, VA Deed Book 3, p. 60.
[5] Pulaski County, VA Deed Book 10, p. 372.
[6] Pulaski County, VA Deed Book 21, p. 51.
[7] Pulaski County, VA Deed Book 27, p. 439.
[8] Pulaski County, VA Deed Book 2, p. 204.

On Walkers Little Creek corner of James Sayers's land…with a line to his own land.

Lewis Jones, Pulaski County, 97 acres, 30 September 1848. Grants # 100, pg. 738.
On Little Walkers Creek…corner to land of William Davis…on a line of Addison Davis's land. Jeremiah Banes bought this land. *See Banes Family.

Addison Davis, Pulaski County, 83 acres, 26 April 1850. Grants # 103, pg. 716.
On the south side of Walkers big mountain near the top including the Ferrin spring.

Addison sold this land to W. H. Woodyard on November 30, 1901.[1]

Addison Davis, Pulaski County, 53 acres, 1 October 1850. Grants # 104, pg. 114.
On Walkers Little Creek…corner to his own land.

Solomon King, Pulaski County, 122 acres, 2 October 1854. Grants # 110, pg. 420.
On Walkers Little Creek…corner to own land…corner to Lewis Jones's land.

Addison Davis, Pulaski County, 83 acres, 1 August 1856. Grants # 112, pg. 716.
On the south side of Walkers big mountain east of the spring.

William Miller, Pulaski County, 646 acres, 1 January 1862. Grants No. 118, 1860-1874, p. 157
646 acres in the valley of Little Walker's Creek (inclusive grant).

William Miller was married to Mary Haven Shannon. On March 4, 1847 Jacob Peck conveyed to William M. Miller and Sebastian W. Miller 190 acres of the south side of Walkers Mountain corner to the McCulloh survey.[2]

John D. and Joseph Howe conveyed 100 acres to William Miller recorded on November 6, 1851.[3]

William Miller leased the above mentioned 100 acres to John and James W. White recorded October 25, 1848.[4]

From various census years, land records and William Miller's will, it appears that he did not actually live on Little Walkers Creek nor did his children. Up until 1880, the census listed value of real estate owned. There were several families living on Little Walkers Creek listed with no land. I suspect William Miller either rented this land or had some type of agreement such as sharecropping. Also, his children did not marry into any of the Little Walker Creek families. Taking into account that neighbors usually married neighbors throughout the 1800's, I find there is significant evidence that William Miller was not a resident of Little Walkers Creek.

Miller wrote his will on February 17, 1871 mentioning his sons, daughter and grandchildren. 1) I have already, some years ago, made distribution of part of my land to my children as I thought would be equal. 2) Give beloved wife all household, kitchen embracing contents of springhouse and cellar. 3) Sale of personal property, selected by wife, divided equally; that which is not sold (except that given to wife) to be divided equally. 4) 1/5 of land to son James A. Miller, 1/5 to granddaughters Mary K. Darst and Elizabeth M. Darst; 1/5 to son John K. Miller, 1/5 to daughter

---

[1] Pulaski County, VA Deed Book 21, p. 275.
[2] Pulaski County, VA Deed Book 2., p. 63.
[3] Pulaski County, VA Deed Book 2, p. 406.
[4] Pulaski County, VA Deed Book 2, p. 240.

Mary M. Glendy and 1/5 to daughter Henrietta Trolinger,. John K. got the lands of Walkers Little Mountain corner to the Hoge survey. Remainder of lands on south side of Cloyd's Mountain and lands of Walkers Little Creek dealt with by executors. Executors were James A. and John K. Miller. Wish executors employ John B. Baskerville as their attorney. William Miller added a codicil on October 24, 1882…Since death of James A. Miller, I make change giving his first wife Orlena Miller, Hattie Miller and Thomas Miller children their equal share…Orlena not being capable of taking care of her part—have put in the hands of John M. Glendy. The children of Thomas Miller by Mary an equal share. James A. Miller children with last wife five in number will received equal share as children with first wife. I give John K. Miller the homestead by willing it to Nancy Glendy and Henrietta Trolinger, 284 acres. The graveyard to be enlarged 2 feet on either side. My old clock, desk and 2 old chests to Nancy Glendy and Henrietta Trolinger. My Hoge land—to John G. Miller—90 acres. On Walkers Little Creek 700 acres and land on Cloyd's Mountain bounded by McCulloch survey, I put in the executors hands. Named executors William J. Glendy, Henry C. Trolinger as executors. William died sometime between 1889 and 1891 as his heirs had several law suits pertaining to partitioning of his land.

There are two men mentioned in many conveyances in Bland and Pulaski Counties:
One being Phineas Thurston who conveyed land in Pulaski, Wythe, Giles and Bland Counties. In 1866, in Bland County, Phineas Thurston of "Roane County, Tennessee" appointed James Wygal and Joseph Wygal as his attorneys to transact all business relative to the recovery of a tract of land lying in the counties of Pulaski, Wythe, Giles and Bland, containing 7,500 acres and known as the Robert Morris survey.

Found at the Library of Virginia for Robert Morris grant for 75,000 acres in Wythe County March 19, 1795 on the waters of Reed Creek, Peak Creek and Walkers Creek.[1] The above mentioned entry in the Bland County Deed Book 1 may have been in error. In looking at the entry description, this land was also partially located in the Crockett's Cove area of Wythe County.

Another name mentioned in many Bland County deeds is Max Grief (of Baltimore, Maryland) bought land from Franklin Sterns and wife of the City of Richmond…" which said tract was surveyed for James M. Gibboney…two separate tracts…containing 14,100 acres in Bland and Wythe counties. Dated May 12, 1890.[2]

The only land entry found for a James M. Gibboney was in 1895 in Wythe for 95 acres on the north side of Draper's Mountain.[3]

Jacob Peck appears in Pulaski County in the 1850 Pulaski County census as 80 years old with wife Eve. Jacob married Eve Wysor 5 January 1796 in Montgomery County. He does not appear to have lived on Little Walkers Creek. Just as William Miller, he may have rented the land. The only land grants found for him were in Giles County on Walkers Creek. Jacob's will was probated in Pulaski County on February 9, 1854. His will was written May 12, 1853 and mentions the following: "…$1900 in cash to Augustus and Elizabeth Martin for taking care of me while I live…my daughter Louisa Robinson to have the tract of land she now lives on Little Walkers Creek, 85 acres…"$500 to be divided equally between Robert Weeks' children which he had by his wife Catherine, my daughter…all other be divided between Christopher Peck, William

---

[1] Library of Virginia, Richmond, VA; Land Office Grants No. 31, 1793-1795, p. 379 (Reel 97).
[2] Bland County, VA Deed Book 5, 687.
[3] Library of Virginia, Richmond, VA; Land Office Grants No. 120, 1883-1887, p. 454 (Reel 186).

Peck, Mary Brookman, Nancy Burton, Fradela Burton, Louisa Robinson, and Catherine Brookman, my granddaughter.[1]

Christopher Peck had moved to Wisconsin by 1855 as he appointed a lawyer in Pulaski on October 11, 1855 for the purpose of …"getting my share of the estate of J. Peck…"[2]

Russell H. Cecil was conveyed a tract of land on July 4, 1842 by James Bane, John Carr, John Bane, William C. Carr and Jesse Bane, all of the county of Giles. The tract of land being part of a survey of 14,500 acres patented to Robert McCullough located Little Walkers Creek and Cloyd's Mountain. No acreage was given.[3]

Russell H. Cecil and Zachariah W. Cecil were brothers, sons of Zachariah White Cecil, Sr. Zachariah, Sr. married Julia Howe on 02 October 1814 in Montgomery County. Zachariah, Sr. most likely received his land through his wife, Julia as she was the daughter of the above mentioned Daniel Howe. Zachariah, Jr. was the only member of the Cecil family who lived on Little Walkers Creek.

Zachariah W. Cecil, Sr. conveyed two tracts of land to Russell H. Cecil and Zachariah W. Cecil, Jr. on September 2, 1841. Lying adjoining each other on Little Walkers Creek and adjoining Millirons, Simpkins and other others.[4]

In April, 1843 John Simpkins conveyed to Giles S. Cecil in trust for the purpose of securing to Russell H. Cecil the sum of one hundred and eleven dollars a parcel of land he now lives on containing 115 acres on Little Walkers Creek and adjoins the land of Jacob Peck and Russell H. Cecil it being the land conveyed to said Simpkins by David Miller and on May 20, 1844 the Giles S. Cecil acting in conformity of the trust deed did at the front door of the courthouse of Pulaski County sold the land at public sale to Russell H. Cecil, he being the highest bidder…adjoining Jacob Peck and Russell H. Cecil…[5]

On May 20, 1844 between Russell H. Cecil and Zachariah Cecil, Jr. for consideration of an equal division of lands between the said parties. Russell conveyed to Zachariah two certain tracts of land adjoining each other and adjoining Jacob Peck, Russell Cecil and his own and others.[6]

On September 14, 1852 Russell Cecil and Lucy A. his wife of Wayne County, Kentucky conveyed to Zachariah Cecil, Jr. of Pulaski their entire interest in the Alum Spring and that portion of 1 ½ acres of land that is included.[7]

Zachariah Cecil Jr. wrote his will on April 12, 1878: "…To Mary Ann my beloved wife my whole real estate and half personalty except what is hereafter devised…what is left after her death is to be equally divided between Nancy Jane Boyd, James T. Cecil, Estelle Ann Cecil, Julia E. Lachy, Irene E. Holbrook and Charles W. Cecil…" After death of wife 2/3 of real estate goes to son Zachariah S. Cecil. Interest in the Pulaski Alum Springs to be equally divided.[8]

---

[1] Pulaski County, VA Will Book 1, p. 319.
[2] Pulaski County Deed Book 2, p. 531.
[3] Pulaski County Deed Book 1, p. 239.
[4] Pulaski County, VA Deed Book 1, p. 169.
[5] Pulaski County, VA Deed Book 1, p. 404.
[6] Pulaski County, VA Deed Book 1, p. 407.
[7] Pulaski County, VA Deed Book 2. p. 454.
[8] Pulaski County, VA Will Book 3, p. 229.

Probated in August 1878.[1] Zachariah White Cecil, Jr. was married to Mary Ann Henderson on 10 June 1839 in Montgomery County.

Wythe and Bland Counties, Virginia

<u>John Crockett</u> Wythe County, 350 acres, 5 June 1799. Grants # 41, pg. 290.
On both sides of Walkers Little Creek.

John Crockett, Wythe County, 250 acres, 4 June 1799. Grant # 41, pg. 264.
On Walkers Little Creek.
"...a military warrant number one thousand and twenty two issued the twentieth day of May 1780 under the King of Great Britain Proclamation of 1763 and an exchange Preemption Warrant number 145 issued the 18th day of April 1782..."

"John Crockett appears to have served in the French and Indian War, as he is listed as a sergeant on the frontier in 1763/1764. He is also mentioned as a member of William Christians' Company in 1764, and as a claimant for 200 acres of land in 1780, for service in that war." He served as lieutenant in the Revolutionary War.[2]

John Crockett was the son of Samuel Crockett and Ester Thompson born 1737 in Lancaster, Pennsylvania and died in 1799 in Wythe County. He is buried in the old Crockett Cemetery in Crockett's Cove. John married Elizabeth Martha Montgomery in 1768.[3]

In 1808, Samuel and John Crockett, sons of John, were holding the land inherited from their father as tenants in common. There were three tracts, two being on Walkers Little Creek.[4]

Samuel Crockett wrote his will on September 4, 1808 and it was probated on March 14, 1809. The executors were to sell the 350 acre tract on Walkers Creek and divide the money equally among the three daughters.[5]
Evidently, the executors did not sell the 350 acre survey because Samuel Crockett's daughter and grandson sold it on August 16, 1872. Margaret Crockett and Robert H. Gleaves sold 408 acres in Bland County to Abraham Wampler located on Walkers Little Creek. "...been owned jointly by the said Margaret T. Crockett and Malvina Gleaves...".[6] Robert H. Gleaves was the son of James T. Gleaves and Malvina Crockett.

A contract was made between Abraham Wampler and Mary Wampler his wife and Robert S. King on December 27, 1879. It was agreed that Robert King would build a house on the Wampler property and reside there and shall furnish to the parties of the first part a good and comfortable support and sustenance during their natural lives; the said party of the second part shall faithfully perform the conditions above set forth in this contract then at the death of the survivor of the said parties of the first part the said Robert S. King to be the full and complete owner in fee of all the

---

[1] Pulaski County, VA Will Book 3, p. 229.
[2] Kegley, *Western Waters, Volume III, Part 2*, p. 623; J. D. Crockett, Crockett Family History, Unpublished.
[3] J. D. Crockett, Crockett Family History.
[4] Kegley, Western Waters, Volume III, Part 2, p. 627.
[5] Wythe County, VA Will Book 1, p. 44.
[6] Bland County, VA Deed Book 3, p. 68.

lands now owned by said Wampler in said tract being the residue of the tract conveyed to said Abraham Wampler by Margaret Crockett and Robert H. Gleaves.[1]

Evidently Robert King did not comply with the contract as Abraham Wampler and wife made another contract with Sarah C. Srader [Shrader] and her 6 children as above written with Robert S. King, to wit: "James Brown, Samuel Gleaves, Eliza J., Mary J., and Joseph, Henry".[2]

On August 8, 1881, Abram Wampler and Mary Wampler his wife, Joseph Shrader and Sarah C. Shrader his wife conveyed land to Wm. N. Mustard, J. Henderson Bruce and A. N. Thompson school trustees for Seddon school District in Bland County, Va. "...doth hereby grant unto said parties of the second part and their survivors to be held, used, enjoyed and verified as and for public free school purposes to erect a Public free schoolhouse...Beginning at a dead stump corner to the lands of George Hancock and others."[3]

On the 14th day of August 1884 Abram Wampler and Polly his wife and Joseph Shrader and Sarah C. Shrader his wife conveyed land to George W. Hancock, Jr. a certain tract of land lying on waters of Walkers Little Creek adjoining the lands upon which the said Wampler now lives & being a part of the tract bought by said Wampler known as the John Crockett entry.[4]

In 1812, John Crockett (son of the elder John) sold 250 acres of land on Little Walkers Creek to John Leedy.[5] John Leedy is listed in the 1815 Wythe County tax list as follows:
"one farm lying on Little Walkers Creek, 575 acres having thereon one "cabben," one loom house, valued at $300. Part mountain land".[6]

In 1825, John Leedy and wife Polly sold 250 acres on Little Walkers Creek to Isaac Baker.[7]
In 1831, the same land was conveyed to James Overstreet by Isaac Baker and wife Sally.[8]

In 1832, James Overstreet and wife Sally of Montgomery County sold the land back to the Crockett family..."James Crockett and John Crockett..."[9] This may be James Overstreet who married Sarah Caddall 10 February 1817 in Montgomery County.

In 1850, the same land was conveyed to John C. Crockett "...Joseph N., William G. and Thompson S. Crockett of the one part and John C. Crockett of the other part... Being the same land conveyed from James Overstreet unto James and John Crockett by deed bearing date the 15th day of August 1832"[10]

John C. Crockett, Wythe County, 70 72/116 acres, 31 August 1846, Grants # 98, pg. 126. On Walkers Little Creek.

William Hounshell, Wythe County, 605 acres, 30 June 1843. Grants # 94, pg. 271.

---

[1] Bland County, VA Deed Book 4, p. 34.
[2] Bland County, VA Deed Book 4, p. 236.
[3] Bland County, VA Deed Book 4, p. 347.
[4] Bland County, VA Deed Book5, p. 225.
[5] Wythe County, VA Deed Book 6, p. 450.
[6] Kegley, *Southwest Virginia Tax* Assessments, 1815, p. 134.
[7] Wythe County, VA Deed Book 10, p. 106
[8] Wythe County, VA Deed Book 12, p. 180.
[9] Wythe County, VA Deed Book 12, p. 653
[10] Wythe County, VA Deed Book 19, p. 486

On Walkers Creek…corner to James T. Gleaves and Margaret Crockett…crossing Dunn's road .

In 1876, Nancy Hounshell sold 100 acres to Martin Hill being part of a grant of 605 acres and 112 perches "…bounded on west by the Turnpike…".[1] The Turnpike refers to the Raleigh Grayson Turnpike which ran from Grayson County into Wytheville through Smith Hollow and Little Walkers Creek. then into Raleigh County.

On January 29, 1906, Martin Hill and wife Elizabeth conveyed their land to Newton Pauley with the condition that he (Newton) would care for and maintain the Hills in sickness and health during their natural lives, provide a comfortable home at their dwelling house where Hill now resides—provide clothing, food, medical attention and a Christian burial. The land was located between Poplar Spring Branch to the east and the Raleigh Grayson Turnpike to the west.[2]

On January 26, 1876, Nancy Hounshell sold 100 acres to G. W. Hancock being the east end of the 605 acre grant for William Hounshell.[3]

Isaac Patterson, Wythe County, 124 acres, 30 November 1844. Grants # 96, pg. 59.
On the waters of Walkers Creek on the north bank of Little Creek adjoining John Crockett, decd…East of James Patterson's path…in a draught near Draper's path. No other land records found. May have reverted to National Forest.

John Leedy's land was an interesting case for research because the original land grant belonged to Robert Pollard. It is not listed here because the grant was for 75,000 acres covering a great deal of the Southwest Virginia area. Robert Pollard was awarded a grant in Wythe County on October 1, 1794 "…by virtue of a Land Office Treasury Warrant Number eight hundred and five, a certain tract or parcel of land containing seventy-five thousand acres by survey bearing the date the twenty sixth day of November one thousand seventeen hundred and ninety four, lying and being in the county of Wythe on the waters of East River, Bluestone River, Clinch River and Wolf Creek…". Apparently, some of the 75,000 acres included parts of Little Walkers Creek..[4]

On January 14, 1806, William Patterson of Wythe County sold to George Helm of Montgomery County 60, 000 acres of land "…being part of a survey made by Robert Pollard containing 75,000 acres bearing date by survey August the first one thousand seven hundred and ninety four…".[5]

George Helm sold part of this land to John Shufflebarger on October 9, 1809. "…containing seven hundred acres…lying and being in Wythe county on little Walkers creek the waters of New River being part of a survey of 75,000 acres, sold by Hugh McGavock collector of the Direct Tax, for the taxes due thence and unpaid and William Patterson became a purchaser who sold the same or an interest therein to the said Helm…"[6] This tract of land would later become part of Pulaski County.

Helm sold a total of 350 acres to John Leedy on December 4, 1813; the land lying south of where John Leedy lived…"that of which bought of John Crockett it ran a course with Leedy's land…and was corner to Allford's land".

---

[1] Bland County, VA Deed Book 3, p. 514.
[2] Bland County, VA Deed Book 9, p. 288.
[3] Bland County, VA Deed Book 4, p. 15.
[4] Virginia Land Office Patents and Grants and Northern Neck Grants and Surveys; Library of Virginia.
[5] Wythe County, VA Deed Book 4, p. 321.
[6] Wythe County, VA Deed Book 5, p. 194.

In 1844, "John Leedy of the County of Wythe and State of Virginia of the one part and Casper Yost high Sheriff of Wythe County and State aforesaid of the other part Witnesseth that whereas the said John Leedy has been taken and is now in the custody of the high Sheriff of Wythe County on a Writ of Capias and [illegible] suit out of the Clerks Office of the County Court of Wythe in the name of John A. Simmerman for the sum of $3.75 with interest from the 4th day of April 1824 till paid and $1.34 costs and whereas the said John Leedy being unable to discharge the debt aforesaid; and wishing to avail himself of the benefit of an insolvent Debtor. Beginning at or upon the partition line between the said Leedy land and the land of Samuel Crockett Decd… a corner of Alford's and Leedy's land and with his line to the beginning. Twenty-five acres as above named to be laid off on the north side bot. of John Crockett and after the special direction of said Leedy but neverless to include the house and part of a field in which the said Leedy lived at the time he purchased said land of one George Helm…".[1]

Casper Yost late high Sheriff of the County of Wythe and State of Virginia to Samuel Cassell the 16th day of June 1849. "…which said tracts of land was advertised and the said Samuel Cassell became the purchaser thereof…".[2]

James H. Hounshell, Wythe County, 431 acres, 30 August 1845. Grants # 97, pg. 57.
On Spur branch, waters of Walkers Creek on the north side of Long Spur…with a line of James Patterson's survey.

John, John A. and James Jones, Wythe County, 182 acres, 19 February 1845. Grants # 99, pg. 594. On the waters of Walkers little creek…crossing Hearns old path…corner to a survey of 359 acres made by John Crockett.

John A. Jones and Nancy his wife to Margaret Crockett 23 June 1847 in Wythe County, 182 acres on Walkers little creek…crossing Hearns old path…corner to a survey of 350 acres made by John Crockett.[3]

Madison Shelton, Wythe County, 180 1/8 acres, 30 November 1850. Grants # 104, pg. 403. On Walkers Little Creek corner to the Jones survey; also a corner to a 350 acre survey made by John Crockett.

Madison Shelton and wife Elsey his wife sold this land to James Collins in 1859.[4]

Madison Shelton married Elizabeth Ann Halsey on March 14, 1841 in Wythe County. She was the daughter of Stephen Halsey and Margaret Walraven.[5] Madison Shelton supposedly murdered his brother-in-law, John Trigg Halsey.[6] There is no evidence of this murder in any Wythe County court record. The Shelton family later moved to Knox County, Kentucky.[7]

Bennett King, Sr., Wythe County, 175 acres, 30 June 1846. Grants # 97, pg. 282.
On Walkers Little Creek, corner to John Crockett's land.

---

[1] Wythe County, VA Deed Book 16, p. 364.
[2] Wythe County, VA Deed Book 18, p. 68.
[3] Wythe County, VA Deed Book 17, p. 657.
[4] Wythe County, VA Deed Book 21, p. 511.
[5] Rebecca Sowers' Research.
[6] Halsey, Richard Jay, *One Branch of the Halsey Family*.
[7] Rebecca Sowers' Research.

Bennett King, Sr., Wythe County, 64 acres, 30 June 1847, Grants # 110, pg. 149.
On Walkers Little Creek near Ravens Cliff and top of the Spur.

Bennett King wrote his will September 1, 1857. It was probated Monday, December 14, 1857. Mentions sons David, James W., William G, Bennett and Solomon. Daughters Hannah Ritter, Nancy Davis and Mary Sublett. Grandson James, infant son of James W. and wife Sarah.

John Sutton, Wythe County, 64 acres, 30 June 1848. Grants # 100, pg. 288.
On Walkers Little Creek.
No other records found.

Allen T. Newberry, Wythe County, 100 acres, 1 December 1857. Grants # 114, pg. 372.
On the south side of Walkers Little Creek.

John M. Leedy, Wythe County, 220 acres, 2 August 1858. Grants # 115, pg. 242.
On Walkers Little Creek… corner of Crockett's land.
No other records found.

Moses Akers, Bland County, 96 ½ acres, 15 November 1879. Grants # 119, pg. 428.
On Walkers Little Creek to his own corner and line to Abram Wampler's land…corner to the "old Crockett survey".

John G. Pauley and John Havens, Bland County, 200 acres, 5 July 1881. Grants # 119, pg. 610.
On the south side of Walkers big mountain and the waters of Walkers Little Creek corner of lands of Robert Wyrick…crossing Newberry's corner.

W. N. Harman, Bland County, 2,832 acres, 7 July 1890. Grants # 121, pg. 499.
On the waters of Walkers Little Creek …south side of Walkers big mountain…above the house of Addison Davis and a corner of the Pulaski County line…corner to the lands of Henry Davis on north hill opposite Charles Parsell's house…with the Brally lines…crossing the Crockett path…down the north side of the mountain…with line of W. C. Newberry corner to A. Z. Harman's line.

Long Spur Branch

Spur Branch is a branch of Little Walkers Creek entering "Little Creek" about one half mile west of the Bland/Pulaski County line. The Spur Branch community is a long, narrow valley separated from the Little Walkers Creek community by the Long Spur Ridge. Several families still reside there.

Land Grants from the *Virginia Land Office Patents and Grants,* Library of Virginia, Richmond, Virginia:

John Draper, Jr., Wythe County, 340 acres, 29 March 1800. Grants # 43, pg. 536.
Walkers Little Creek…a corner to Shannon's survey…south side of the long spur…by Draper's path. (This land is located on Spur Branch and Little Walkers Creek and located what is now Pulaski and Bland Counties, Virginia.)

James H. Hounshell, Wythe County, 227 acres, 5 June 1844. Grants # 96, pg. 58. On the Spur branch, waters of Walkers Creek beginning at four white oaks at Draper's path…above the Big Spring…crossing Little Hiram Davis's path.

James Patterson, Wythe County, 77 acres, 30 November 1844. Grants # 96, pg. 60. On Spur Branch, waters of Walkers Creek.

James H. Hounshell, Wythe County, 431 acres, 30 August
1845. Grants # 97, pg. 57.
On Spur branch, waters of Walkers Creek on the north side of Long Spur…with a line of James Patterson's survey.

The Draper Tract

John Draper's survey was located in what is now Pulaski and Bland Counties. It contained approximately 306 actual acres even though the grant specified 340 acres "more or less". Surveying during the 1800's was not very precise. As surveying techniques became more precise, acreage and boundary descriptions changed in the deeds describing more exact locations and listing adjoining land owners.

John Draper and wife Jane sold their Little Walker Creek land to John Alford on November 12, 1811. This may be John Draper, Jr. who married Jane Crockett. Jane Crockett was the daughter of Samuel and Jean Armstrong Crockett. Jane Crockett Draper died about 1815.[1]

John Alford is listed in the 1815 Wythe County tax list as follows:
"One farm on Little Walkers Creek, 340 acres having thereon one "cabben," one blacksmith shop, one loom house, smoke house, corn crib, valued at $800".[2]

John Alford and his wife Peggy of Giles County sold part of this land to James Davis in 1829 "…containing two hundred and eighty acres more or less…".[3]

James Davis and wife Rachel sold to Isaac Patterson in 1833 "…Walkers Little Creek containing one hundred acres…".[4]

James Davis and wife Rachel sold to James C. Overstreet "…both of the county of Giles… containing one hundred and eighty three acres, and being the lower end of the tract of two hundred and eighty three acres, which I bought from John Alford…".[5]

On Thursday September the 18th 1845, a court case arose involving James Davis, Hiram Davis, Isaac Patterson and James Overstreet, John Alford & James Hoge complainants–vs–Hiram Davis & others defendants.
"This cause comes on this 18th day of September 1845 to be heard upon the bill and amended bills. The answer of James Overstreet the exhibits filed & examination of witnesses the exception thereto which are overruled by the court. It being of the opinion that the interest of said witness is equal between the parties and it appearing that the subpoena has been returned executed more than two months on the defendants James Davis, Hiram Davis and Isaac Patterson, and they still failing to appear & answer the bills the same as to them is taken for confessed, and it appearing to the satisfaction of the court that the order of publication against the defendant John Alford has been duly posted and published and he still failing to appear & answer the amended bill as for

---

[1] J. D. Crockett, Unpublished, Crockett Family History.
[2] Kegley, Southwest Virginia Tax Assessments, 1815, p. 112.
[3] Wythe County, VA Deed Book 11, p. 349.
[4] Wythe County, VA Deed Book 12, p. 650.
[5] Wythe County, VA Deed Book 12, p. 650.

confessed as to him. It is herefore adjudged, ordered and decreed that the complainant James Hoge recover against the Defendants Hiram Davis and James Davis two hundred dollars with interest from the first day of September 1832 until paid and the costs of this suit. And it appearing to the satisfaction of the Court that the said sum of two hundred dollars is part of the purchase money of the land in the bill mentioned. And the court being satisfied that the defendants Overstreet and Patterson were purchasers with full notice that the said two hundred dollars constituted a part of the purchase money of said land and that it had been paid. It is therefore adjudged, ordered and decreed that unless the said sum of money with its interest and the costs of this suit be paid on or before the first day of January 1846. Charles A. Bowyer who is hereby appointed a commissioner for that purpose do sell the land mentioned or so much thereof as shall sufficient to pay the said sum of two hundred dollars with interest as aforesaid and the costs of this suit to the highest bidder upon a credit of six months taking bond with good security for the payment of the purchase money having first advertised the time and place of sale for four weeks at the front door of Wythe Court house, and for the same length of time in a newspaper published at Wytheville, and that he make a report of his proceedings to the next term of this Circuit Court."[1]

Hiram Davis lived in Giles County on Walkers Creek, Mechanicsburg area. He died before 1844 as his estate was appraised January 22, 1844 in Giles County.[2]

James Davis and wife Rachel lived in both Wythe and Giles according to the deeds filed at the Wythe and Giles Courthouses. The only James Davis found in Giles is in the 1810 Giles census. There were several James Davis's listed in Wythe before 1850. Since the early censuses [before 1850) only list heads of household, it is difficult to determine if one of these James's were the same as mentioned above. James Davis evidently died before 1850 as his wife, Rachel Kennison Davis, is listed with their son, Hiram Davis in the 1850 Daviess County, Missouri census.

Hiram Davis married Nancy Bateman on 23 October 1817 in Montgomery County, Virginia. They migrated to Missouri in the mid 1840's.

On the 13th day of May 1846 between "...Charles A. Bowyer commissioner of the County of Wythe and State of Virginia of the one part and James Hoge of the County of Pulaski...And whereas by another decree of the said Court pronounced on the 17th day of April 1846 the said Bowyer having made a report his proceedings the same was affirmed a commissioner to make a conveyance of the said land to the said James Hoge... doth hereby grant, bargain, sell and convey unto the said James Hoge the said tract or parcel of land to wit: a tract of land containing two hundred and eighty acres more or less lying & being in the County of Wythe & State of Virginia on little walkers Creek and is the same conveyed by John Alford & wife to James Davis by deed bearing date the 3rd day of October 1829... purchaser at the price of four hundred and fifty dollars that being the highest and best bid offered for the same."[3]

Mustard Family

On the 24th day of June 1848 James Hoge sold to Joshua Mustard the same tract of land "...it being the same which was conveyed to the said James Hoge by deed bearing date the 13th day of

---

[1] Wythe County, VA Chancery Book 2; 1835-1853, p. 389.
[2] Giles County, VA Will Book B, p. 415
[3] Wythe County, VA Deed Book 17, p. 118.

May 1846... containing two hundred and eighty acres be the same more or less, lying & being on little Walkers creek the whole or the greater part being thereof in the county of Wythe..."[1]

This land was located in the area of what is now the intersection of Little Walker's Creek Road and the Spur Branch Road and it extended into what is now Pulaski County.

In 1857, Joshua Mustard and Elizabeth his wife sold part of the above tract to Samuel C. Davis, no acreage listed, but estimated at about 110 acres.[2]

Joshua Mustard was the son of James Mustard and Sarah Munsey. He was born about 1796 in Montgomery County, Virginia. He married Elizabeth "Betsey" Davis on 15 November 1824 in Giles County. Elizabeth was born about 1806 to William and Lovica Davis. Joshua is said to have died 07 March 1862 in Bland. The estate appraisement and sale bill were recorded on August 1, 1862. The appraisers were Anselm Brawley, John Mustard and Samuel C. Davis. Buyers at the sale were Russell Patton, W. G. Crockett, David King, Col. Crockett, Nick Wynn, James W. White, W. Mustard, John Mustard, Claib Curtice, Tim Hamilton, J. B. Rutherford, Samuel C. Davis, Lewis Johnston, W. T. Rorrer, A. Brawley, David Millirons, David Kent, Z. Cecil, M. Hunter, William Hunter, James H. Mustard, J. B. C. Rutherford and John C. Crockett.[3]

Joshua and Elizabeth's children were:
1. William Thomas born about 1830 married Paulina Tynes. William joined the CSA Army Company F, 45th Regiment. Died in Confederate Prison, Camp Morton, Indiana on 19 February 1865.
2. John born about 1834 married Mary Parsons.
3. Lavica born about 1837.
4. James Harvey born about 1839
5. Sarah born 20 August 1843 married Thomas B. Wygal.
6. Minerva Jane born 30 January 1845. Never married but had six children.
7. Katherine born about 1848 married Obadiah Jones, son of James J. Jones and Charlotte Hancock.
8. Joshua Nye born October 1852 married Mary Elizabeth Jones, daughter of James J. Jones and Charlotte Hancock.

From court and land documents, Joshua Mustard did not live on Spur Branch but probably used the Spur Branch land for farming or possibly rented it out. It is important to note that Henry Davis later bought the Mustard tract and did live on Spur Branch as did some of his children.

On June 26, 1875 Elizabeth Mustard conveyed to James H. Mustard and John J. Mustard..." all her right, title, interest and privilege in and to a certain tract or parcel of land being her dower in the estate of her late husband Joshua Mustard, lying on Walkers Little Creek... in consideration of one mare in hand paid and twenty five dollars per annum during her natural life..."[4]

Elizabeth Davis Mustard is said to have died in Pulaski County on 15 September 1881. She is listed in the 1880 Pulaski County census with her daughter and son-in-law, Tom B. Wygal.

---

[1] Wythe County, VA Deed Book 17, p. 624.
[2] Wythe County, VA Deed Book 20, p. 809.
[3] Bland County, VA Will Book 1, pg 86-87.
[4] Bland County, VA Deed Book 3, p. 368

The Hounshell Tract

The Hounshell surveys contained approximately 763 acres encompassing most of the Spur Branch area. The land grants listed a total of 658 acres "more or less".

In 1849, "James H. Hounshell of Carroll County sold to John Smith of Wythe County land granted to said Hounshell one for 227 acres the other for 431 acres making in all an aggregate of 658 acres...".[1]

On May 13, 1854, John Smith and wife Sarah to Anselm Brawley the same land.[2]

Brawley Family
(often spelled Bralley/Brally)

John Brawley was born about 1740 in Cecil County, Maryland. He married Mary Guy about 1764 in Cecil County. John died about 1798 in Wythe County, Virginia. John and Mary had six known children: James married Hannah Smyth; Barbara married Joseph Hoge 09 November 1790 in Montgomery County, Virginia; Martha. Married Benjamin Rogers 24 March 1788 in Montgomery County; John married Martha Hoge 08 February 1793 in Montgomery County; Mary married John Rogers 19 August 1793 in Wythe County, Virginia; Elizabeth married John Wooden 02 March 1797 in Greenbrier County, Virginia.

James and Hannah Smyth Brawley had eight children: James, John Smyth; Anselm, Jonathan; Louisa Adams, Elizabeth, Samuel Guy and Julia.

Anselm married Susannah Hutsell 22 March 1831 in Wythe County, Virginia.[3] She was the daughter of Jacob and Elizabeth Hutsell. From the 1850 Giles County census, he and Susannah had eight children:
1. George T. born about 1832 married Emma Griffith on 27 September 1868 in Pike County, Missouri. Listed in the 1870 and 1880 Pike County, Missouri as a physician. No children listed.
2. Elizabeth H. born about 1834 married Thompson H. Bussey on 13 May 1852 in Giles County. Children:
    2.1. Hester Ann married John Stinson 04 March 1874 in Bland County.
    2.2. George.
    2.3. James.
    2.4. Sarah F.
3. Julia Ann born about 1836 married John Bogle, Jr. on 03 September 1857 in Wythe County. Children:
    3.1. Margaret Susanna.
    3.2. Sarah Elizabeth
    3.3. Victoria Jane.
    3.4. Luemma Isobel.
    3.5. Lucinda Catherine.
    3.6. Joseph Longstreet.
    3.7. George William.
    3.8. John Lockhart

---

[1] Wythe County, VA Deed Book 18, p. 388.
[2] Wythe County, VA Deed Book 19, p. 667.
[3] Wythe County, Virginia Marriage Book 1.

4. <u>James</u> born about 1838, enlisted in Company D, 45th Infantry Regiment as a Sergeant on 29 May 1861 in Wytheville, Virginia and died of wounds on 06 October 1864.[1]
5. <u>Sarah P.</u> born on 29 May 1843 married Moses Akers on 19 October 1859 in Wythe County.
6. <u>Susannah</u> born about 1847 married George Newton Pegram.
7. <u>Ariminta</u> born about 1849.
8. <u>Margaret Emily</u> born on 19 October 1855 in Wythe County.[2]

Anselm Brawley was born in about 1800[3] and died before 25 January 1868 as his estate was appraised then.

Appraisal Bill of personal estate of Anselm Bralley, deceased, by Samuel C. Davis, J. T. Mustard & J. H. Mustard, dated January 25, 1868. Sale bill of estate of Anselm Bralley, deceased. Buyers were: Solomon King, James H. Mustard, Harvey R. Mustard, Washington King, Stanford Melvin, [illegible] Hendrick, Moses Akers Sr., Moses Akers, Jr., Thomas Mustard, Susan Bralley, Dandridge Akers, Stephen Halsey, Allen W. Sublett, John Bogle, David King, John Harman, John T. Mustard, Henry Mustard, & George W. Suiter. Certified by John Bogle and Moses Akers, administrators of Anselm Brawley, deceased. Recorded February 13, 1868.[4]

Susannah Hutsell Brawley died between 1870-1880.[5] They are probably buried somewhere on Spur Branch in unmarked graves.

Anselm Brawley's heirs [did not list names] eventually sold Anselm's land to John Pegram, David Y. Hamblin and John Parsell. Evidently, Pegram, Hamblin and Parsell had some difficulty getting the titles from the Brawley heirs. In the Bland County, Virginia Deed Book 3, three deeds were recorded on June 14, 1876 for the three men above. "…Between Samuel W. Williams Special Commissioner of the first part and John H. Pegram of the second part. Witnesseth that whereas by a decree rendered on the [blank] Day of May 1876 by the Circuit court of Bland County, Virginia in the chancery cause therein pending in the name of A. Bralleys Administrators and A. Bralley's heirs amongst other things… convey to said party of the second part that part of the real estate in the bill and proceedings mentioned described in statement in writing signed by George N. Pegram and referred to in said decree as having been sold by said George N. to said John H. Pegram… this deed witnesseth that for and in consideration of the premises aforesaid doth hereby grant and convey unto said party of the second part that part of that certain tract or parcel of land lying and being on the Spur Branch waters of Walkers Little Creek known as the Bralley tract, the part hereby conveyed contains 300 acres more or less on the west end of said tract…".[6]

Hutsell Family

Johann George Hutsell was born 04 October 1711 in Pfaffenhofen, Germany. He married Anna Maria Magdalena Schweinhardt 17 June 1739 in Maryland. The marriage was recorded by Reverend John Casper Stoever as George Hutzel of Monocacy, Maryland and Anna Maria Magdalena Schweinhardt. Johann Georg Hutzel's name varies on documents: Joh. Georg, Johann Georg, John George, Hans George, and George. Arrived in Philadelphia, Pennsylvania on August

---

[1] The Virginia Regimental Histories Series. 45 vols. Lynchburg: Howard, 1987.
[2] Wythe County, VA Births and Deaths, Wythe County Courthouse.
[3] 1850 Giles County, VA Census.
[4] Bland County, VA Will Book 1, p. 158-159
[5] 1880 Bland County, VA Census
[6] Bland County, VA Deed Book 3, p. 444.

29, 1730 on the ship "Thistle" from the Palatinate with his older brother Ludwig. Johann died 2 May 1778 in Frederick County, Maryland buried in the Churchyard of the Evangelical Lutheran Church in Frederick County, Maryland. Johann and Anna had 12 children: Margaret, Susanna, George, Johannes, Johann Peter, Johann Matthaus; Ludwig, Jacob, Anna Maria, Michael and Gabriel. Ludwig (often called Lewis) Hutsell born 15 July 1753 in Frederick County, Maryland. He accompanied his two older brothers through the Shenandoah Valley in his late teens. Ludwig married Eva Davis, daughter of John Davis and Mary (many Hutsell/Davis researchers believe her maiden name was Hutsell). John Davis also accompanied the three brothers into Virginia. John was instrumental in forming the town of Evansham (now Wytheville), Wythe County, Virginia. Ludwig had ten children and many moved on to Tennessee and Kentucky. Jacob was the third child born to Ludwig and Eva Davis Hutsell. Jacob died between 1832 and 11 March 1833; his will was probated 11 March 1833 in Wythe County.

The Patterson Tract

James Patterson was from Crockett's Cove, Wythe County, Virginia. His will stated "...Son James Harvey had already received a horse, bridle, saddle, and gun, but his father devised to him 77 acres on Little Walker Creek...".[1]

Land Grant description exactly as written (The Library of Virginia):
James McDowell Esquire, Governor of the Commonwealth of Virginia
To All To Whom these Presents shall come—Greetings: Know Ye, That in Conformity with a Survey made on the 15th day of May one thousand eight hundred and forty four by virtue of a Land Treasury Warrant. N: 15308 there is granted by the said Commonwealth, unto James Patterson a certain tract or parcel of land containing seventy seven acres lying and being in Wythe County on the Spur Branch waters of Walkers Creek and bounded as follows viz: Beginning at two chestnut oaks and a chestnut on the north side of a ridge corner to a survey for James H. Hounshell thence with a line thereof N 10 east 156 poles to hickory ssplings near the head of a drain on the south side of a spur thence S 5 W 80 poles to two red oaks and a maple on the north side of a spur thence S 89 W 132 poles to the beginning with appurtenances.
To have and to hold said tract or parcel of Land, with all its appurtenances, to the said James Patterson And his heirs forever.
In witness whereof, the said James McDowell Esquire Governor of the Commonwealth of Virginia, hath hereonto set his hand, and caused the Lesser Seal of the said Commonwealth to be affixed, at Richmond, on the thirteenth day of November in the year of our Lord one thousand eight hundred and forty four and of the Commonwealth the sixty ninth. Ja McDowell

---

[1] Wythe County, VA Will Book 7, p. 217.

DISEASES AND EPIDEMICS

EPIDEMICS

In case you ever wondered why a large number of your ancestors disappeared during a certain period in history, this might help.

Epidemics have always had a great influence on people—and thus influencing, as well, the genealogists trying to trace them. Many cases of people disappearing from records can be traced to dying during an epidemic or moving away from the affected area. Some of the major epidemics in the United States are listed below:
- 1732-3—Worldwide—Influenza.
- 1759—North America [areas inhabited by white people]—Measles.
- 1761—North America and West Indies—Influenza.
- 1772—North America—Measles.
- 1775-6—Worldwide [one of the worst epidemics]—Influenza.
- 1793—Virginia [killed 500 in 5 counties in 4 weeks]—Influenza.
- 1820-3—Nationwide [starts-Schuylkill River and spreads]—"Fever".
- 1831-2—Nationwide [brought by English emigrants]—Asiatic Cholera .
- 1841—Nationwide [especially severe in the south]—Yellow Fever.
- 1847-8—Worldwide—Influenza.
- 1848-9—North America—Cholera.
- 1850—Nationwide—Yellow Fever.
- 1850-1—North America—Influenza.
- 1852—Nationwide [New Orleans-8,000 die in summer]—Yellow Fever.
- 1855—Nationwide [many parts]—Yellow Fever.
- 1857-9—Worldwide—Influenza.
- 1873-5—North America and Europe—Influenza.
- 1918—Worldwide [high point year]—Influenza.

More people were hospitalized in WWI from this epidemic than wounds. US Army training camps became death camps, with 80% death rate in some camps.[1]

The influenza pandemic (epidemic over a wide geographic area and affecting a large proportion of the population) of 1918-1919 killed more people than the Great War, known today as World War I (WWI), at somewhere between 20 and 40 million people. It has been cited as the most devastating epidemic in recorded world history. More people died of influenza in a single year than in four-years of the Black Death Bubonic Plague from 1347 to 1351. Known as "Spanish Flu" or "La Grippe" the influenza of 1918-1919 was a global disaster.

The Spanish Influenza pandemic is the catastrophe against which all modern pandemics are measured. It is estimated that approximately 20 to 40 percent of the worldwide population became ill and that over 20 million people died. Between September 1918 and April 1919, approximately 500,000 deaths from the flu occurred in the U.S. alone. Many people died from this very quickly. Some people who felt well in the morning became sick by noon and were dead by nightfall. Those who did not succumb to the disease within the first few days often died of complications from the flu (such as pneumonia) caused by bacteria.

---

[1] The USGenWeb Project. *Epidemics*. http://www.usgenweb.org/researchers/epidemics.html.

One of the most unusual aspects of the Spanish flu was its ability to kill young adults. The reasons for this remain uncertain. With the Spanish flu, mortality rates were high among healthy adults as well as the usual high-risk groups. The attack rate and mortality was highest among adults 20 to 50 years old.

DISEASES—EARLY YEARS

From outbreaks of diarrhea that claimed countless infants to the dreaded cholera that destroyed the flesh, the lives of children and adults were endangered with each new epidemic.

In the nineteenth century more young people succumbed to consumption, or tuberculosis, than all other diseases. A disease that destroyed the lungs, consumption was transmitted by sprays from the respiratory tracts of infected people or from infected cows. Affecting those between ages five and thirty, it often occurred in urban areas after extended contact with an infected person. Symptoms included fever, weight loss, night sweats, and fatigue. Its hallmarks were a persistent cough, chest pain, and, later, coughing up blood. Those in the early stages could be cured with rest, fresh air, and sunshine. Consumption was originally blamed on short sleeves and low-necked clothing.

Another major killer was whooping cough, the most deadly of the infectious diseases. An acute disease that usually affected children, it involved an inflamed respiratory tract and prolonged coughing spasms that end in violent gasping as the victims attempt to catch their breath—hence the whoop.

One of the most hideous diseases was cholera. Usually fatal, cholera resulted in violent diarrhea and vomiting with muscular cramps, chills, pain, fever, and circulatory failure ending in collapse. Striking infants and young children as well as adults, the disease worsened in sultry weather. Victims often died within hours from diarrhea and dehydration. The body would swell and decay so rapidly after death that burial was often immediate. Cholera outbreaks affected America in 1832, 1849, 1866, and 1873, with many smaller outbreaks throughout the century. Asiatic cholera in Boston in 1854 left many dead in a very short period.

Typhoid fever was an acute infectious disease acquired by drinking infected milk or water. Symptoms included high lingering fever and intestinal discomfort, chills, diarrhea, and prostration. At the end of the first week rosy spots appeared on the chest and abdomen. During the Spanish-American War in 1898 one-fifth of American troops developed typhoid fever.

Deadly and highly infectious, diphtheria affected children especially, striking the upper respiratory system. It was spread through saliva and through touch, with bacilli entering the body by the mouth and nose. Bacteria attacked the walls of the nose and throat five days after exposure. Those who survived might be temporarily paralyzed in the eyes, legs, or one side of the body.

Acute and contagious, scarlet fever also attacked through the nose or mouth. It was transmitted by direct contact, through utensils used by an infected person, or by infected milk. Common in children aged two through ten, it occurred in winter or late spring mostly to fair-skinned people. Symptoms included headache, sore throat, and vomiting, followed by a tongue rash and high fever. It subsided after five days, after which the skin peeled.

The hallmark of smallpox was a skin eruption that left permanent scarring. Caused by a virus, smallpox left its victims with severe chills, pain in the back and limbs, intense headache, vomiting, and fever. On the third day a rash began on the face.

Measles was deadly in the nineteenth century. Also caused by a virus, it was characterized by small red spots on the skin, an aversion to light, nasal discharge, coughing, and a high fever.

Yellow fever, also called the black vomit or the miasmas, was spread by mosquitoes. It destroyed the liver and kidneys, its telltale mark being jaundiced skin. An outbreak hit Philadelphia in 1793 and New Orleans in 1853. When 5,000 died in Memphis in 1878, more than half its residents left the city.

For most of these diseases, no cause was discovered or vaccine developed until the 1880s at the earliest. Taking a closer look at your ancestors might help you uncover unexpected causes of death.

FIRST FAMILIES

FOREWORD

Information on the families of Little Walkers Creek was taken from many sources, which include records from the Wythe, Bland, Pulaski Counties Courthouses, the Wythe, Bland and Pulaski Counties censuses and other various state and county censuses. Family members have contributed information and many pictures. Birth and death dates are from various Little Walkers Creek Cemeteries. The source of information will be noted in each specific family. I welcome any comments, additions, corrections or questions.

It must be noted that indiscretions did occur in the past just they do today. Several couples had children before they married. Some women never married but had several children. Although these are exceptions to the rule, these indiscretions did occur. This book is not written to hide the truth but to examine the complete history of these families determined from the many County records and censuses. This book presents the evidence. The final decision is left to the reader.

This book is a history of Little Walker's Creek and the families who lived and died there. Enough information is included (if the information is available) so the reader can possibly discover a link to the Little Walkers Creek community. I have not included information about living family members because of privacy issues. All families are listed in alphabetical order.

AKERS FAMILY

English, meaning "on a plot of one acre", referring to men who could be addressed by the particularly well-known farm or piece of land on or near which they lived, size or shape of the plot of land observed.[1]

William Akers was born about 1640 in Virginia and died in 1702; his will was probated in Essex County the 10th day of August 1702. William was married to Katherine. His will mentioned two children, William and Ann.

William II was born about 1675 and was married to Ann. They had a son William born about 1700 in Buckingham County, Virginia.

William III died about 1790 in Montgomery County, Virginia. He was married to Susanna Blackburn. William III and Susanna had Blackburn born about 1730 in Albemarle County, Virginia.

Blackburn married 1st Elizabeth Blackburn. He married 2nd Susannah Scaggs. He was sworn to the American cause on 13 September 1777 in Montgomery County. Blackburn was placed on the unfit-for-duty list of the militia company of Captain Daniel Trigg, indicating he was 50 or more years of age. Blackburn and Susannah Scaggs had William B. born about 1765 in Buckingham County, Virginia.[2]

William married 1st Lydia Elkins and 2nd Nancy Sowers. on 02 July 1811 in Montgomery County. William and Lydia had three known children, one being Moses Sr.

Moses Akers Sr. Family

Moses Akers, was the son of William B. Akers and Lydia Elkins. He was born about 1808 in Montgomery County, Virginia and died between 12 April 1872 and 05 April 1875 in Bland County, Virginia. He married Catherine Altizer 24 December 1828 in Montgomery County. She was born about 1808; the daughter of John Altizer and Elizabeth Elkins. Catherine died sometime between 1876-1880.[3] Moses Akers moved to Little Walkers Creek, Bland County from Pulaski County by 1869 having bought two tracts of land on Little Walkers Creek from John C. Crockett on 10 February 1869 totaling 272 acres "more or less".[4]

Moses Akers, Sr. wrote his will April 12, 1872:
"To my wife I leave all my land and appurtenances; after her death to be divided among my children as follows: To my son John $1; son Davis $1; son Amos $1; my daughter Elizabeth $1; daughter Octava $1; my son Dandridge $1; son Moses $1; daughter Mary Catherine $1.
To my son William D. Akers 100 acres of land off the upper end of my farm square across from mountain to mountain…the balance of my land to be divided equally by and between my daughters Fransina, Emeline and Mildred Ann. My personal property to be divided equally between son William D. and daughters Fransina, Emeline and Mildred Ann…".[5] Moses' will was

---

[1] *What is in Your Name?* Vitalog.net. website http://www.vitalog.net/cgi-bin/select_name.cgi
[2] *The Akers Family,* by: Henry B. Brackin, Jr., MD (c) 2000, Privately Published.
[3] Montgomery County, VA Marriage Records; Bland County, VA Deed Book 3, p. 405; 1880 Bland County, VA Census.
[4] 1850 & 1860 Pulaski County, VA Census; Bland County, VA Deed Book 1, p. 379.
[5] Bland County, VA Will Book 1, p. 389.

presented to the court on April 5, 1875 and proven by the oath of Samuel C. Davis, one of the subscribing witnesses. W. B. Akers, the other witness, not present.[1]

Moses Akers, Sr. and wife Catherine sold land to the Bland County board of Trustees on October 18, 1872: "...a lot of land lying on the waters of Little Walkers Creek... The said Moses Akers and wife doth warrant generally the said lot of land, the house upon the land to be open to Church privileges with the understanding that the Class at that place takes care that the School property and furniture is not abused in that it is taken care of... ".[2] Note—this was probably in the area of where the Davis school was built.

Moses and Catherine Akers are probably buried (unmarked graves) in the old "Davis" Cemetery on Little Walkers Creek. The "Davis" Cemetery is named so because it is now on Davis property which once belonged to Moses Akers.

Moses and Catherine had 15 children; several lived in Pulaski County while others lived in Bland County and later in Wythe County.
Children:
1. John born about 1830 married Martha Becklehimer 28 February 1850 in Pulaski. John and Martha lived in Pulaski.[3]
2. Davidson born October 23, 1831 married Rachel Graham 23 October 1851 in Pulaski County. Davidson and Rachel lived in Pulaski.[4]
3. Amos born October 18, 1833 married Missouri Kelly 06 July 1853 in Pulaski. Amos and Missouri lived in Pulaski.[5]
4. Elizabeth born about 1834 married John Becklehimer.[6]
5. Octava born about 18355 married Jackson Holiday 25 December 1853 in Pulaski County. Jackson and Octava were living on Walkers Creek, Giles County in 1880.[7]
6. Dandridge born about 1836 married Parthena Farmer 13 January 1859 in Pulaski County. They lived in Pulaski and Bland counties.[8]
7. Moses was born 03 October 1839 married Sarah Brawley 13 October 1859 in Wythe County. Sarah was born 29 May 1843, the daughter of Anselm Brawley and Susannah Hutsell. Moses and Sarah lived on Little Walker's Creek.[9]
8. Mary Catherine born about 1840 married George White.[10]
9. Francina Julia born about 1841 married Joseph H. Lefler. Joseph was the son of Aaron Maize Lefler and Mildred Butler. Joseph enlisted in the 54th Infantry Regiment, Company F on September 9, 1861 in Newbern, Pulaski County and was wounded in Bentonville, North Carolina. He applied for a Confederate pension on May 12, 1899 at the age of 64 years.[11] In 1880, Joseph and Francina were living in Wythe County; living with them was William D. Akers.[12]

---

[1] Bland County, VA Order Book 1872-1877, p.371.
[2] Bland County, VA Deed Book 2, p. 362.
[3] Various Pulaski County, VA Censuses, Pulaski County, VA Marriage Records.
[4] Various Pulaski County, VA Censuses, Pulaski County, VA Marriage Records.
[5] Various Pulaski County, VA Censuses, Pulaski County, VA Marriage Records.
[6] Bland County, VA Deed Book 3, p. 405.
[7] 1880 Giles County, VA Census.
[8] Various Pulaski and Bland Counties, VA Censuses, Pulaski and Bland Counties, VA Marriage Records.
[9] Wythe County, VA Marriage Records, Various Pulaski and Bland Censuses; Library of Virginia, Richmond, VA, *Confederate Pension Rolls, Veterans & Widows*.
[10] Bland County, VA Deed Book 3, p. 405.
[11] Library of Virginia, Richmond, VA, Confederate Pension Rolls, Veterans & Widows.
[12] 1880 Wythe County, VA Census.

Joseph and Francina's children were:
- 9.1. <u>James M.</u>
- 9.2. <u>Lucy M.</u>
- 9.3. <u>Leila A.</u>
- 9.4. <u>Henry Sidney</u> married Dora Alice Akers 21 November 1894 in Bland County. They were living in Clearfork, Tazewell County, Virginia in 1920.[1]
- 9.5. <u>Joseph E.</u>
- 9.6. <u>Mary L.</u>

Joseph H. Lefler and Fransina J. conveyed land to John T. Davis on December 4, 1885. "…To east bounded by Jacob Kitts…west by Peter Tickle…32 ½ acres…".[2]

10. <u>Emeline</u> born about 1845[3] married Isaac Maize Lefler. Isaac was the son of Aaron Maize Lefler and Mildred Butler. Isaac enlisted in the 54th Infantry Regiment, Company F on September 9, 1861 in Newbern, Pulaski County. He was wounded at Chickamauga Creek, Georgia. He applied for a Confederate pension on May 18, 1900 at the age of 69 years. Emeline [gave her name as Ellen C. Leffler] applied for a widows pension on May 4, 1920. The application gave Isaac's date of death as 22 March 1920, 7 miles from Rural Retreat. He died of heart problems. Emeline was 75 years old and explained her husband was 78 years old when he died. They were married in Pulaski County in 1865 by Red Swinney. She had lived in Wythe County for 36 years.[4] Isaac and Emeline later moved to Rural Retreat, Wythe County. Their children were:
    - 10.1. <u>Thomas Reed</u> married Mary Jane Kitts Their children:
        - 10.1.1. <u>Bessie.</u>
        - 10.1.2. <u>Harvey Kent</u>
        - 10.1.3. <u>Issac Maize</u> married Ruth Kid.
        - 10.1.4. <u>Luther Green</u> married Amelia E. Fortner.
        - 10.1.5. <u>Ella</u> married Charles S. Bowles.
        - 10.1.6. <u>Claude William</u> married Ina Augusta Davis.
        - 10.1.7. <u>Garland.</u>
        - 10.1.8. <u>Leslie Brown</u> married Gussie Ring.
        - 10.1.9. <u>Ida Gray</u> married George B. Allison.
        - 10.1.10. <u>Sherman.</u>
        - 10.1.11. <u>George P.</u>
        - 10.1.12. <u>Ada.</u>
    - 10.2. <u>William J.</u> married Viola Kitts.
    - 10.3. <u>Stuart.</u>
    - 10.4. <u>Ollie G.</u> married William Gullion.
    - 10.5. <u>David Houston</u> married Larnie Belle Cameron.
    - 10.6. <u>Mary Lou.</u>

On February 2, 1888, Isaac Lefler and wife Emeline conveyed 30 acres to William T. King "…adjoining own land on the east, Jacob Kitts on the west and the Big Survey on the north and south…".[5]

11. <u>Gordon F.</u> born about 1846[6] [not mentioned in will, may have died young].

---

[1] 1920 Tazewell County, VA Census.
[2] Bland County, VA Deed Book 5, p. 65.
[3] 1850 Pulaski County, VA Census.
[4] Library of Virginia, Richmond, VA, Confederate Pension Rolls, Veterans & Widows.
[5] Bland County, Virginia Deed Book 5, p. 367.
[6] 1850 Pulaski County, VA Census.

12. William D. born about 1848[1] married Jennie Robinson 24 February 1886 in Wythe County.
13. Margaret Melvina born about 1850[2] married Christopher P. Collins 12 November 1874 in Bland County. He was born about 1852, the son of Edmond and Elizabeth Collins[3]. Christopher and Margaret were living in Crockett's Cove, Wythe County in 1880. From the 1880 Wythe census, they had the following children:
    13.1. John.
    13.2. William.
    13.3. Charles.

Christopher P. Collins and Margaret M. his wife of Wythe County conveyed to William L. Collins "all the right, title and interest of said Margaret M. of her father Moses Akers…31 ½ acres…" on November 24 1882.[4]

14. Madison R. born about 1852; died June 1853 in Pulaski at age 8 months.[5]
15. Mildred Ann born 18 January 1853 married William L. Collins 22 August 1874 in Bland. William was the son of James and Mary Ann Collins. William and Mildred lived in Crockett's Cove, Wythe County. Mildred Ann died 19 October 1932 and William died 20 August 1938. William and Mildred are buried in the St. Luke's Lutheran Church Cemetery in Wythe County. Children from the Bland and Wythe census:
    15.1. James.
    15.2. Harvey.
    15.3. Walter.
    15.4. Nancy.
    15.5. Mildred.
    15.6. Cynthia Lou married Joseph Shannon Bowles 27 January 1897 in Wythe County.
    15.7. Estell.
    15.8. Crockett.
    15.9. Callie.
    15.10. Emma.
    15.11. Bertha.

William L. Collins and wife Mildred conveyed 62 acres to Jacob Kitts on February 10, 1888 adjoining the lands of William King, John Davis and others.[6]

On February 11, 1876, Moses Akers, Sr. heirs conveyed land to William T. and Nancy L. King: "…John Akers and Martha Akers his wife, John Becklehimer and Elizabeth his wife, Davis Akers and Rachel his wife, Amos Akers and Missouri his wife, Dandridge Akers and Parthena his wife, Moses Akers and Sallie P. his wife, Jackson Holiday and Octavia his wife, George White and Mary C. his wife, Joseph Lefler and Francina his wife, Isaac Lefler and Emeline his wife, William L. Collins and Mildred C. Collins his wife, Christopher P. Collins and Margaret M. his wife, Wm. D. Akers and Catherine Akers (widow)…one tract…containing forty acres…".[7]

---

[1] 1850 Pulaski County, VA Census.
[2] 1860 Pulaski County, VA Census.
[3] Bland County, VA Marriage Records.
[4] Bland County, VA Deed Book 4, p. 463
[5] Pulaski County, VA Death Records, Pulaski County Courthouse.
[6] Bland County, VA Deed Book 5, p. 556.
[7] Bland County, VA Deed Book 3, p. 405.

Moses Akers Jr. Family

Moses Akers, Jr. married Sarah P. Brawley 13 October 1859 on Spur Branch, Wythe County. She was the daughter of Anselm Brawley and Susannah Hutsell. Moses was born 03 October 1839 in Montgomery County and died 10 July 1916 on Little Walkers Creek, Bland County, buried in the old "Davis" Cemetery on Little Walkers Creek. Sarah was born 29 May 1843 in Wythe County and died 25 March 1940 in Bland and is buried in the "Davis" Cemetery.[1]

Moses Akers Jr.

On February 12, 1876, Moses Akers, Sr. heirs conveyed land to Moses Akers, Jr. "…Catherine Akers widow of Moses Akers, Sr. decd, Davis Akers and Rachel his wife, Amos Akers and Missouri his wife, Dandridge Akers and Parthena his wife, Joseph Lefler and Fransina his wife, Isaac Lefler and Emeline his wife, Christopher P. Collins and Melvina his wife, George White and Mary his wife, Wm. L. Collins and Mildred his wife and Wm. D. Akers children and heirs at law of Moses Akers, Sr. decd. of the first part and Moses Akers, Jr. of the second part. Witnesseth that whereas the parties of the second part did on the 14th day of August 1874 purchase of the said Moses Akers Sr. a certain tract or boundary of land off the farm on which said Moses Akers, Jr.. then resided…". This was a 60-acre tract.[2]

On November 15, 1879, Moses Akers, Jr. received a land grant for 96 ½ acres "…to his own corner and line to Abram Wampler's land…corner to the "old Crockett survey…".[3]

On the 12th day of June 1897, Samuel W. Williams and wife Maggie conveyed 56 acres to Moses Akers"…adjoining the lands of Moses Akers and others…being all the land said Williams embraced in what is known as the old Crockett survey which lies between the tract of land recently conveyed to John H. Collins…[4]

Moses Akers and wife Sarah P. conveyed three tracts of land to R. Lee Millirons the first containing 4/5 acre on August 6, 1890 and on December 1, 1897; one for 50 acres and another for 8 acres.[5]

Moses Akers Jr. and Sarah P. Brawley's children:
1. Gillie B. born April 1860 in Pulaski County married John H. Collins on 14 April 1885 in Bland County. John was born in June 1858. He was the son of James Collins and Mary Ann. John H. Collins and Gillie B. Akers had the following children:[6]
    1.1. William C. born January 1886 married Hester (maiden name unknown) .Children:[7]
        1.1.1. Thelma born about 1910.
        1.1.2. Cary born about 1912.
        1.1.3. Martha born about 1918.

---

[1] 1850 Giles and Pulaski Census; Tombstones, Davis Cemetery, Little Walkers Creek, Bland County, VA; Library of Virginia, Richmond, Virginia, *Confederate Pension Rolls, Veterans & Widows*.
[2] Bland County, VA Deed Book 3, p. 392.
[3] Library of Virginia, Richmond, VA, *Virginia Land Office Patents and Grants*, Grants # 119, p. 428.
[4] Bland County, VA Deed Book 8, p. 305.
[5] Bland County, VA Deed Book 7, p. 136; Bland County, VA Deed Book 10, p. 232.
[6] 1900 Bland County, VA Census
[7] 1920 Bland County, VA Census.

1.2. Sheffey Margaret Frances born January 1887 married David Henry Carl Pauley on 31 December 1907. He was the son of Gratton Crockett Pauley and Mary Geneva Kitts in Bland County. Children from the 1920 Bland census:
- 1.2.1. Vivian G. born about 1910.
- 1.2.2. Garnet C. born about 1911.
- 1.2.3. Cleo S. born about 1914.
- 1.2.4. Margaret born about 1916.

1.3. Harvey Lee born June 1888.
1.4. Kelley J. L. born March 1890.
1.5. Sarah born 06 August 1892.
1.6. Hugh C. born December 1893, died in World War I on 03 March 1919 of disease while Prisoner of War.[1]
1.7. Nellie A. born 16 October 1895 married Tobias King born 22 September 1891, son of John Nye King and Martha Taylor Children from the 1920 Bland census:
- 1.7.1. Irene.
- 1.7.2. Roy Elmer.
- 1.7.3. Seagle
- 1.7.4. Nina.
- 1.7.5. Ernest Chaffin.
- 1.7.6. Joseph Sidney born 24 April 1897.

1.8. Berta M. born January 1899 married Thomas W. Ogle 20 October 1919 in Bland.
1.9. Mary J. born about 1901.
1.10. Charles E. born about 1903.
1.11. Frank Estell born 24 May 1905 married Rose Catherine Hancock on 19 April 1929 in Bland. She was the daughter of Saunders Helton Hancock and Carrie Nellie Louisa Hancock. Children:
- 1.11.1. Nina.
- 1.11.2. Frances.
- 1.11.3. Della Geraldine.

1.12. David H. born about 1907.[2]
1.13. John H. born about 1912.[3]

2. Julian Missouri born July 1867[4] married Jacob Hines Davis about 1887. Jacob was born about 1860 in Giles or Tazewell; he was the son of Isaac Newton Davis and Martha Esther Sands. They later moved to Giles County.[5] Children:[6]
- 2.1. George M. born 06 February 1888.
- 2.2. Sallie S. born 08 February 1890.
- 2.3. Mary L. born 21 May 1891.
- 2.4. John W. born 26 June 1892.
- 2.5. Miller Daniel born 09 November 1898. Served in World War I.
- 2.6. Terry Chaffin born 23 August 1900 married Julia Rose Millirons.[7] Children:
  - 2.6.1. Terry C., Jr.
  - 2.6.2. Christine.

---

[1] *Virginia Military Dead:* Library of Virginia, Richmond, Virginia.
[2] 1910 Bland County, VA Census.
[3] 1920 Bland County, VA Census.
[4] 1900 Bland County, VA Census.
[5] Bland County, VA Deed Book 12, p. 7.
[6] Bland County, VA Births: 1861-96; Tombstones, Birtchlawn Cemetery, Giles Co, VA; 1910 Giles County, VA Census.
[7] Bland County, VA Marriage Records.

    2.6.3. Loretta.
 2.7. Charley b. about 1902 married Hazel Fleeman

On March 18, 1889, Moses Akers gave Julian Davis, wife of Jacob, 7 ½ acres of the 96 ½ survey and another tract for 40-50 acres "…for love and affection".[1]

Jacob Davis and wife Julia conveyed 50 acres to Walter Brunk on June 9, 1913.[2]

3. Emily Elizabeth was born December 1871 in Bland married Marcus Walker Hancock on 13 December 1910 in Bland. He was born about 1855 in Wythe County the son of George Washington Hancock and Julia Wyrick. She married second John Chrisman Helvey on 04 August 1931 in Bland.
4. Dora Alice born about 1873 married Henry Sidney Lefler 21 November 1894 in Bland. He was born about 1873 in Wythe County. Henry was the son of Joseph H. Lefler and Francina Julia Akers. Henry and Dora were living in Tazewell County in 1920.[3] Children:
    4.1. Sallie F. born about 1899.
    4.2. Bowen C. born about 1901.
    4.3. Genoa B. born about 1905.
    4.4. Henry S. born about 1907.
    4.5. Mary M. born about 1910.
    4.6. Edward S. born about 1913.
    4.7. James O. born about 1915.
5. Ella Augusta born 19 July 1879 in Bland; died 16 September 1941 in Bland. She married Estell Hoge Millirons, born 31 January 1881 in Pulaski County, died 07 February 1946 in Bland. They married in Bland on 24 December 1902. Estell Hoge was the son of William Millirons and Julia Rose Banes. Both are buried in the "Davis" Cemetery, Bland County

**Estell Hoge Millirons & Ella Augusta Akers
Submitted by Reba & Jack Crawford**

Moses gave Ella A. Millirons a tract of land for love and affection on January 28, 1911 [acreage not given].[4]

Estell and Ella's children:
    5.1. Meek Gordon born 23 October 1903 and died 15 January 1963 buried in the Millirons Methodist Church Cemetery.
    5.2. Howard Preston born 06 April 1905 and died 26 May 1981 buried in the Millirons Methodist Church Cemetery. Howard married Annie Elizabeth Hancock daughter of Elexander Stinson Hancock and Emily Lea Corder. Howard and Annie's children:[5]
        5.2.1. Howard Paul married Florence Farmer and had two children.
        5.2.2. Estil Stinson married Miss Dewey and had three children.
        5.2.3. George William married Beatrice Havens and had seven children.
        5.2.4. Emma Lee married Leonard Hensley Hamblin and had the following children:

---
[1] Bland County, VA Deed Book 6, p. 211.
[2] Bland County, VA Deed Book 12, p. 7.
[3] 1920 Tazewell County, VA Census.
[4] Bland County, VA Deed Book 10, p. 537.
[5] Courtesy of Lena Christine Hamblin Distelhorst.

5.2.4.1. Annie Mae.
5.2.4.2. John Crockett.
5.2.4.3. Vanessa Gail.
5.2.4.4. Augusta Gray.
5.2.5. Malcolm "Mac" married twice and had two children.

5.3. Clarence Hicks was born 19 November 1906. He married Waucella Mae Coburn. Children:
5.3.1. Douglas.
5.3.2. James Hicks.
5.3.3. Harry Zelmer.

5.4. William Moses was born 15 September 1908 and died 19 August 1938. William is buried in the Davis Cemetery, Little Walker's Creek. He married Frances King on 12 August 1930 in Bland. She was born on 15 September 1906, the daughter of Joseph S. King and Emily Etta Pegram. One daughter:
5.4.1. Delphine.

5.5. Emma Louella was born 10 September 1910. She married Robert Lee Chandler on 28 July 1943 in Bland County; son of Hannah Chandler. Robert was the mail carried for many years on Little Walkers Creek. Robert and Emma "Louella" lived about a mile from the Bland/Pulaski line. Robert and Emma's children:
5.5.1. Reba Lee married 1ˢᵗ Larry Warren Rigney and 2ⁿᵈ Jack Crawford.
5.5.2. James William married Judith Elaine Davis

5.6. Lelia Pearl born 23 January 1913 and died 10 April 1987. Lelia married Alvie Garland Corder son of Benjamin Larkin Corder and Frances Bell Davis. Both are buried in the Grandview Memory Gardens, Bluefield, West Virginia.
5.6.1. Edna Augusta.
5.6.2. Ruth Elizabeth.
5.6.3. Robert Wiley.
5.6.4. Garland Lee.
5.6.5. Roger Allen.
5.6.6. Dewey Wayne.

This is the wedding picture of Lelia Pearl Millirons and Alvie Garland Corder, taken in front of Howard Millirons' homeplace on Little Creek. This was one of the sweetest couples I ever knew. Uncle Alvie gave me a beautiful wooden bowl he made when I was around 9 yrs old. He said take this in the living room and ask your Mommy if you can have it. Boy, when I ask that question I thought I was going to get the spanking of my life. Uncle Alvie stepped in and said, "I gave her that bowl and you keep it for her." Today that bowl is a main part of my home. My Mother kept it until she felt I was old enough to hang on to it— Submitted by Christine Hamblin Distelhorst.

Lelia Millirons & Alvie Corder

5.7 Walter "Pug" Vance was born 27 April 1915 and died 28 April 1985. He married Rosa "Rosie" Evelyn Millirons 18 January 1936 in Bland County. She was the daughter of Lelia Pearl Millirons. Walter and Rosa are buried in the Millirons Church Cemetery. Children:
5.7.1 Mason Vance married Wilma Beatrice Phipps.
5.7.2 Augusta Delphine married Edgar Albert Banes.

5.7.3 <u>Norman Thomas</u> married Carolyn Aileen Banes.
5.7.4 <u>Dolly Marie</u> married Ernest Dreyton Banes
5.7.5 <u>Donnie Sue</u> married Thomas Rhea Phipps.

On June 6, 1941, Ella A. Millirons conveyed 125 acres to Howard P.. and Louella Millirons which had been conveyed to Ella by her father, Moses Akers. The deed contained stipulations: It was understood that Howard and Louella would retain control and possession of the real estate so long as she [Ella] lives and she was to be looked after, cared for and maintained in her old age in a manner to which she was accustomed. It was also understood that Gordon M. Millirons would have a home there and receive support from the real estate as long as he lives. If the land was to be partitioned, Louella was to have the dwelling, out buildings, garden and all household and kitchen furniture.[1]

Howard and Louella later sold the above tract of land in two parcels. James L. Corder bought 93.9 acres of the tract and Marvin Davis bought 31.1 acres.[2]

Moses Akers, Jr. enlisted in the 54th Infantry Regiment, Company F on September 9, 1861 in Newbern, Pulaski County. Captain William J. Jordan's Company enlisted on September 9, 1861, from Pulaski County men, for one year. Jordan and 82 other men cast their fate with the Confederacy at Newbern at the regiment's formation. A total of 217 men eventually served in this company, making it the largest in the regiment. Moses may have served in the following engagements: December 25, 1861—Floyd County, KY; August 31, 1862—Rocky Gap, VA; January 30, 1863—Kelley's Store, VA; November 11, 1863—Ringgold, GA; and of course, the two engagements where he was wounded. The 54th fought for the last time in Bentonville, North Carolina on March 17-19, 1865.

Moses was wounded on February 25, 1864 at Rocky Face Ridge, Georgia and again July 4, 1864 in Atlanta, Georgia. Moses applied for a Confederate pension in Bland County at the age of 49; explaining that he had received a wound from a musket ball "…shot into the main bone of my left leg below the knee…the bullet entered my left leg and embedded itself in the bone. The bone had to be split and the bullet extracted". He also states that his disability is so great "…so far as manual labor is concerned, is equivalent to the loss of a limb". He stated that he was unable "to obtain a livelihood by manual labor". He was entitled to fifteen dollars annually. In 1907, Moses was re-rated and placed on the pension rolls as totally disabled "due to the infirmities of age being now in my 69th year". He was then entitled to thirty dollars annually. Both documents were signed by Moses Akers.[3]

Moses served in the 54th Company F with his brothers, Amos and Dandridge.

In 1917, Sallie P. Akers applied for a Confederate Widows pension[4]. She was required to answer several questions in the application:
1. Name: Sallie P. Akers
2. Age: 73
3. Place of birth: Wythe County
4. How long have you resided in Virginia: All my life
5. How long have you resided in the City or County of you permanent residence: 40 years

---

[1] Bland County, VA Deed Book 25, p. 49.
[2] Bland County, VA Deed Book 39, p 555.
[3] Library of Virginia, Richmond, Virginia, Confederate Pension Rolls, Veterans & Widows
[4] Library of Virginia, Richmond, Virginia, Confederate Pension Rolls, Veterans & Widows

6. Where do you reside? If in city give street address, post office: Long Spur, County of Bland, Virginia
7. With who do you reside? E. H. Millirons
8. What was your husband full name? Moses Akers
9. When, where and by whom were you married?
10. When? Oct 13, 1859
11. Where? On Spur Branch, Bland County, VA
12. By whom? Rev Curtis
13. When and where did your husband die? July 10, 1916. Long Spur, Bland County, Va.
14. What was the cause of his death? Stomach trouble
15. Give name and address of physician who attended your husband at the time of his death. Dr. J. A. Wagner, Bland, Va.
16. Have you married since the death of your husband? If yes, give the particulars. Have not married
17. In what branch of the army did your husband serve? 54 regiment, F Company
18. Who were his immediate superior officers? Colonel R. C. Trigg and Captain W. F. Eaton
19. Give the names and addresses of two comrades who served in the same command as your husband during the war. William Millirons, Poplar Hill, VA. Adison Jordan, Pulaski, VA
20. Give the name and addresses of two persons who are familiar with the circumstances of your husband's service and death. William Millirons, Poplar Hill, Va. W. H. Brunk, Long Spur, Va.
21. What assistance do you receive and what income do you have from all sources? Not any.
22. How much property do you own? Real estate? None Personal Property? None
23. Was your husband on the pension rolls of Virginia? If yes, in what county or city was his pension allowed? Bland Co, Va.
24. Have you ever applied for a pension in Virginia before? If yes, why are you not drawing one at this time? I have not applied before.
25. Is there a camp of Confederate Veterans in your city or county? Yes
26. Give here any other information you may possess relating to the service of your husband or the cause of his death which support the justice of your claim. Served through the war from first to last and was wounded in one leg. Stomach trouble and general [illegible].

Signed:
Sallie P. Akers
C. C. Davis signed as Justice of the Peace for Bland County, Va.

ALLEN FAMILY

Allen is a poplar English surname meaning originally dwelt near the Allen or "green plain."[1]

William Allen was born before 1770 (based on the 1820 Grayson County, VA census) He purchased 400 acres in 1791 in Grayson County. William married Ann Stuart. William died between 12 July 1823 (date of will) and September 1823 (will probated). His wife Ann was found in the 1830 Logan County, Virginia (now West Virginia) census. William and Ann had eleven documented children. One being Carr Allen born about 1786 in Grayson County.

Carr Allen married Temperance Daniel on 10 March 1815 in Patrick County, Virginia. Carr was living in Carroll County, Virginia in 1850. By 1860, he was in Raleigh County, Virginia and he may have died there. Carr and Temperance had eight known children, one being John Allen born 29 January 1817 in Grayson County.

John Allen married Sarah Johnson 26 November 1840 in Mount Airy, North Carolina. John was listed in the 1870 Raleigh County, West Virginia census which included his wife Sarah and four of his children. Evidently, John moved to the Alum Spring area of Little Walkers Creek, Pulaski County shortly after 1870. From Dr. R. A. Brock's book, *Virginia and Virginians* (1888), "John Allen served in Pulaski County as the district clerk from 1871-1875 and was constable from 1876-1880". John Allen wife Sarah and daughter Margaret were listed in the 1880 Raleigh County, West Virginia census, Clearfork District, page 129; son John was living next door. [Even though Dr. Brock says John Allen lived in Pulaski, no land records have been found to validate this information.] John and Sarah Johnson Allen had eight children, one being William Carr Allen.

William "W. C." Carr Allen was born 07 February 1845 in Carroll County, Virginia. He was married three times. He first married Eliza J. Combs on 28 October 1866 in Raleigh County, West Virginia. Eliza's father was John Combs and Peninah Beller. Like the Allen family, John Combs moved from Carroll County to Raleigh County and on to Pulaski County. After the death of wife Eliza, W. C. married Lucy J. Morris 12 February 1885, daughter of Samuel and Rachel. Lucy died 05 February 1886. W. C. married third Susan S. Morris 22 May 1886. She was the daughter of Jesse Morris and Caroline Beller. W. C. died 21 April 1906.[2]

On November 10, 1879, the J. W. White heirs conveyed a tract of land on Little Walkers Creek to William C. Allen. It was located between the lands of Nancy Johnson and William Miller. Acreage not given.[3]

W. C. Allen bought land from M. J. and H. E. Combs. The land was conveyed December 6, 1888 and contained 55 acres. Bounded on the east John Combs which he had bought of James Johnson and bounded on the west of David Millirons. Known as the Johnson tract.[4]

John Combs and wife Phebe R. conveyed to William C. Allen a tract of land which was located at the corner of the original corner to Hiram Davis patent land. Dated October 25, 1889.[5]

---

[1] *What is in Your Name?* Vitalog.net. website http://www.vitalog.net/cgi-bin/select_name.cgi
[2] The Allen Family of Little Creek (A Genealogy of the Family of John Allen, Son of Carr, resident of the Little Creek Area of Northern Pulaski County, Virginia). Hamann, Lee. February 1992. [Courtesy of George Allen.]
[3] Pulaski County, VA Deed Book 7, p. 387.
[4] Pulaski County, VA Deed Book 12, p. 117.
[5] Pulaski County, VA Deed Book 18, p. 185.

On February 19, 1898 Bertha Mineral Company conveyed 67.82 acres to William C. Allen..."corners to the Shannon grant and Davis grants to a corner of William Millirons...".[1]

On November 25, 1903, William C. and Susan S. sold 67 acres of land to Mary J. Tynes of Wythe County bounded on the east by William Miller; by the west Nancy Johnson; north and south by the Bertha Mineral Company and known as the Isaac Johnson tract.[2]

W. C. and Susan conveyed 3 tracts of land, a total of 152 acres, to W. J. Allen on January 9, 1904. The first conveyed to W. C. by M. J. Combs and wife, 55 acres. The second was conveyed to W. C. by John Combs, 45 ¼ acres. The third tract was conveyed by Bertha Mineral Company, 67. 82 acres. W. C. further transfers the following personal property: "...2 horses, 4 cows, 1 yoke of oxen, 6 yearlings, 4 calves, 20 sheep, 1 wagon and gears, 2 buggies and gears, 2 mowing machines, 1 rake, 3 plows, 7 stakes of hay, 100 bushel of corn, 9 head of hogs, 1 organ, 1 sewing machine, 1 cooking stove and utensils, and all beds and bedding, bureaus, chairs, tables and all other personal property and all household or kitchen furniture, fixtures and appliances.[3]

On March 11, 1913, Ms. Launia Suthers wife of Charles R. of Wytheville conveyed 67 acres to Susan S. Allen; it being the same land Ms. Suthers bought of Mary J. Tynes unmarried of Bluefield, West Virginia on January 5, 1911.[4]

Near the lower end of the Allen property is a house which once served as a parsonage for the pastor of the Millirons Methodist Church (located about half a mile up the road). Next to this home is the Allen Cemetery, with about fifteen tombstones. Included are the markers for W. C. Allen, his third wife Susan, and his son James H. Also there, although without a tombstone, is the grave of Benjamin Franklin Allen, father of Jack—Submitted by George Allen

Children of William and Eliza:[5]
1. Benjamin Franklin "Frank" born 22 October 1867 in Raleigh County, West Virginia married Mary Ella Blackwell on 21 December 1893 in Fayette County, West Virginia. He died in Pulaski County on 07 April 1903. Frank died four months after his youngest son was born; his son were reared by various relatives.[6] He was living in Pulaski in 1900 with wife and children:
    1.1. Charles Edward born August 1894.[7]
    1.2. James Franklin born about 1897 and died before 1900.
    1.3. William Carson born April 1898.[8]
2. Joseph L. born 06 March 1869 in Raleigh County; died 26 February 1885 in Pulaski County.
3. Mary Magdalene born 06 March 1871 in Raleigh County married 1st John D. Runions and 2nd John Quincy Barton. She died 02 November 1935 in Fayette County, West Virginia.
4. Sarah A. born 21 March 1873 in Raleigh County; died 13 September 1884 in Pulaski County.

---

[1] Pulaski County, VA Deed Book 19, p.562.
[2] Pulaski County, VA Deed Book 23, p. 24.
[3] Pulaski County, VA Deed Book 23, p. 59.
[4] Pulaski County, VA Deed Book 33, p. 299; Pulaski County, VA Deed Book 33, p. 300.
[5] *The Allen Family of Little Creek* (*A Genealogy of the Family of John Allen, Son of Carr, resident of the Little Creek Area of Northern Pulaski County, Virginia*). Hamann, Lee. February 1992. [Courtesy of George Allen.]
[6] *The Allen Family of Little Creek* (*A Genealogy of the Family of John Allen, Son of Carr, resident of the Little Creek Area of Northern Pulaski County, Virginia*). Hamann, Lee. February 1992. [Courtesy of George Allen.]
[7] 1900 Pulaski County, VA 1900 Census.
[8] 1900 Pulaski County, VA 1900 Census.

5. Ida Catherine born 30 April 1875 married first George Fletcher, son of Madison Allen Fletcher and Martha Esther Sands. Ida and George divorced. She married second, George's brother Joseph Walford.
6. John A. born 09 April 1877 in Pulaski County married Flora L. Stafford on 12 September 1894 in Giles County, Virginia. He died 08 April 1915.
7. James H. born 09 March 1879 in Pulaski; died 06 July 1945.
8. William Jackson born 29 November 1881 married Cherrie Elizabeth Musser. He died 11 February 1959 in Richlands, Virginia.

Child of William and Lucy:
9. Margaret May born 27 November 1885 in Pulaski married Floyd Newton Hamblin on 06 September 1902 in Pulaski. He was the son of John M. Stafford Hamblin and Sarah Catherine Croy. She died 29 May 1978 in Albany, Georgia. *See Hamblin Family.

Children of William and Susan:
10. Martha Alice born 06 April 1887 in Pulaski married John Frank Smith 28 October 1902 in Bristol, Sullivan County, Tennessee. She died 14 December 1961 in Wythe County.
11. Samuel Walice born 01 June 1889 in Pulaski; died 21 March 1891 in Pulaski.
12. Albert Asa born 14 September 1894 in Pulaski married Bessie Owens Woodyard 03 March 1918 in Pulaski. She was the daughter of Andrew Grayson Woodyard and Mary Jane Morris. Bessie was born 17 September 1898 and died 22 February 1972 in Dayton Ohio. Albert died 16 January 1974 in Mercer County, West Virginia. Albert and Bessie are buried in the Hunter Cemetery, Little Walkers Creek, Pulaski County, Virginia.
13. Jesse McKinley born 06 November 1896 married 1st Gertrude Spackner; married 2nd Gladys Shewey. Jesse died 16 December 1981.
14. Hubert Troy born 17 September 1899 in Pulaski married Gladys Elizabeth King 10 July 1910 in Pulaski. Gladys was the daughter of Isaac Henry King and Bessie May LeFew. Hubert died 04 Oct 1995 in Pulaski.[1]

---

[1] Social Security Death Index.

AUSTIN FAMILY

A vernacular (the standard native language of a country or locality). form from Old French Aoustin, ultimately derived from Ausustine "majestic".[1]

The Austin family is one of the African-American families who lived and bought land on Little Walkers Creek in Pulaski County. James Young Austin bought land from the Z. W. Cecil heirs. It was conveyed on November 5, 1897 from Z. S. Cecil and Sallie, Mrs. Mary A. Cecil, Mrs. Julia Lackey of Wytheville, Virginia; Mrs. Lou N. Cecil of Norfolk, Virginia; Irene Holbrook and G. L. Holbrook of Bluefield, Virginia; Nannie C. Boyd and Thomas I. Boyd of Florida No acreage listed.[2]

James Young Austin was born October 1847[3]; he was married to Mary (maiden name unknown) born May 1850[4]. Their children were:
1. Lucy born 29 September 1874 in Pulaski County.[5]
2. Martha born 29 August 1876 in Pulaski County.[6]
3. Mollie born 04 May 1878 in Pulaski County.[7]
4. James born 17 February 1880 in Pulaski County.[8]
5. Isaac born 10 November 1881[9] married Fannie Brown They had children:
    5.1. Percy Lee.
    5.2. Sarah Peggy.
    5.3. Lillie Mae.
    5.4. Mollie.
    5.5. Kate.[10]
6. Isabella born 13 May 1885 in Pulaski County.[11]
7. Willie born 31 May 1889 in Pulaski County.[12]
8. Malinda born 17 February 1891 in Pulaski County.[13] She married a Mr. Dyer.[14]

---

[1] *What is in Your Name?* Vitalog.net. website http://www.vitalog.net/cgi-bin/select_name.cgi
[2] Pulaski County, VA Deed Book 22, p. 87.
[3] 1900 Pulaski County, VA Census
[4] 1900 Pulaski County, VA Census.
[5] Pulaski County, VA Births, Pulaski County Courthouse.
[6] Pulaski County, VA Births, Pulaski County Courthouse.
[7] Pulaski County, VA Births, Pulaski County Courthouse.
[8] Pulaski County, VA Births, Pulaski County Courthouse.
[9] World War I Draft Registration Cards, 1917-1918 > Virginia >Pulaski County.
[10] Isaac's children found in obituary of Lillie Mae Austin Morris, Published on September 7, 2003; © The Roanoke Times.
[11] Pulaski County, VA Births, Pulaski County Courthouse.
[12] Pulaski County, VA Births, Pulaski County Courthouse.
[13] Pulaski County, VA Births, Pulaski County Courthouse.
[14] World War I Draft Registration Cards, 1917-1918 > Virginia >Pulaski County.

BANES FAMILY

Scottish, most often refers to a person with an unusually light complexion.[1]

Jeremiah Banes was born on 25 January 1825 in North Carolina which the county of birth was probably Orange. His parents were George Banes and Nancy Cook who married 05 January 1820 in Orange County, North Carolina. Jeremiah had a sister named Elizabeth who married William Roberts and lived in Pulaski and Giles County. The surname Banes has often been spelled Bane, Bains, Baynes[2]

A George Banes was listed in the 1820 Orange County, North Carolina census with one male under 10, 1 male of 18 but under 26, 1 female under 10, 1 female of 16 but under 26. In 1830; a Nancy Banes was listed in 1830 Orange County, NC census with one male under 5, 1 male age 5 and under 10, 1 female under 5, 1 female of 5 and under 10, 1 female of 40 and under 50. In 1840, Nancy Bains was again listed in Orange County, NC with 1 male of 10 and under 15, 1 male of 20 and under 30, 1 female of 10 and under 15 and 1 female of 40 and under 50. George and Nancy had two known children. Both Elizabeth Banes and William Roberts were born in North Carolina.

Jeremiah Banes married Sarah Davis on 19 September 1846 in Giles County. She was the daughter of William Davis and Lovica [maiden name unknown]. William Davis married 2nd, Jeremiah's mother, Nancy Cook Banes 16 October 1849 in Giles County.[3] Jeremiah married 2nd M. Ann Wiggington Gibbs on 26 June 1882 in Pulaski County. Both were listed as widowed.

On April 25, 1849 William Davis of Giles sold to Sarah Banes and children 46 acres of land for $500 "to insure the said William Davis a comfortable support in his old age…if money owed after death of said William…will become null and void…".[4]

William Davis's last will and testament:[5]
In the name of God Amen I William Davis of the County of Giles and State of Virginia advanced in life and frail in body but of sound mind and disposing memory and mind that it is appointed unto all men once to dye make and constitute a last will and testament revoking all other wills heretofore made by me first that after my decease so soon as convenient my executor named pay all of my just debts and funeral expenses secondly I give and bequeath to my wife Nancy Davis thirty three acres of land it being the part of land patented to me and which patent is in the hands of [*] Harrison the above thirty three acres to be laid off on the upper end to Robt. G. Davis. I also give to my said wife all of my perishable property consisting of one horse, three cows and three calves all of my hogs all of my household furniture all my sheep my still and all the fixtures belonging to the same above property together with any money that may be on hand or in the hands of the executor after paying to my daughter Elizabeth Mustard… which sum is to be paid by my said executor as soon as convenient is…to my wife and to be hers and at her disposal at her death. The above the residue which will be 100 acres I will to William Roberts by Roberts paying to my estate at the end of four years the amount of one hundred dollars if the land above named should be taken by any prior claim Before that the said Roberts to be released from the payment of the above named hundred dollars. I also give to my wife my entire interest in all my

---

[1] *What is in Your Name?* Vitalog.net. website http://www.vitalog.net/cgi-bin/select_name.cgi
[2] Giles County, VA Marriage Records, Orange County, NC Marriage Records.
[3] Giles County, VA Marriage Records.
[4] Pulaski County, VA Deed Book 2, p. 214.
[5] Giles County, VA Will Book 4, pgs. 7 & 8.

growing crops of corn wheat and rye. I give to my daughter Polly Burgess all the property which she has heretofore received of me also one dollar. I give to Amanda Patterson all the property she has received of me heretofore also one dollar. I give to Peggy Harmon all the property she has received of me also one dollar. I give to my daughter Katherine King all the property received of me also one dollar. I give to my daughter Sally Bane all the property she received of me together with one loom and its fixtures. I give to my son Isaac J. Davis all the property which he has received of me heretofore also one dollar. I give to James W. Bane my grand son my smyth tools, if there should be any property or any money from any debt dues to me not heretoforenamed by me I desire that the same be sold or collected and after paying the several devises to my several heirs should there be a surplus my wife is to be the sole heir and lastly I do appoint William Mustard as my executor in witness I hereunto set my hand and seal in presents of 26 day of May 1856.

Signed in presents of   William X Davis (SEAL)
Madison Allen mark
Ralph A. Shifford

Solomon King and wife Caty conveyed 122 acres to Jeremiah Bane on June 3, 1856; being the same Solomon received as a land grant on October 2, 1854.[1]

Jeremiah bought land from Lewis Jones which was conveyed on November 5, 1853 in Pulaski County. Lewis Jones had received this tract as a land grant on September 30, 1848 containing 96 acres…"adjoining William and Hiram Davis…Beginning at a corner to William Davis and with line…" It also ran on a line of Addison Davis's land.[2]

Jeremiah bought 60 acres of land from Phineas Thurston on February 20, 1871 on the Big Mountain.[3]

Jeremiah wrote his will on July 26, 1887:
"…I give and bequeath to my son James W. and daughters Sarah Bane, Elizabeth A. Bane and Nancy C. Bane…all of my real estate…" included land lying on the Spurs of the "big Mountain" containing about 61 acres known as the Thurston tract, another lying where James W. Bane now lives, the Jones tract all to be equally divided. Witnessed by Samuel C. Davis and John W. King. Probated on Monday, September 5th 1887.[4] Jeremiah is buried in the Banes/Leeson Cemetery on Little Walkers Creek, Pulaski County. Most likely, Sarah Davis Banes is also buried in the Banes/Leeson Cemetery but there is no marker for her.

Jeremiah Banes and Sarah Davis's children:
1. <u>Edna Jane</u> born about 1848, Giles or Pulaski.[5] Not listed after the 1850 census; most likely died young.
2. <u>Elizabeth A. "Bettie"</u> born February 1850.6 She had one daughter:
    2.1. <u>Ann May "Annie"</u> was born 22 July 1893; died 27 November 1992 married Thomas J. Leeson 30 August 1911 in Pulaski. Thomas was born 20 March 1892 and died 05 February 1951. Thomas and Annie are buried in the Banes/Leeson Cemetery. Children:
        2.1.1. <u>Vance G.</u>
        2.1.2. <u>Garnett.</u>

---

[1] Pulaski County, VA Deed Book 3, p. 87.
[2] Pulaski County, VA Deed Book 2, p. 632.
[3] Pulaski County, VA Deed Book 5, pg. 57.
[4] Pulaski County, VA Will Book 4, pg. 186.
[5] 1850 Pulaski County, VA Census.

- 2.1.3. Freda.
- 2.1.4. Violet.
- 2.1.5. Alma Mildred.
3. James William "Bill" was born 11 March 1851 on Little Walkers Creek, Pulaski Co, Virginia, and died 21 March 1915 buried in the Banes/Leeson Family Cemetery, Little Walker's Creek, Pulaski County. He married Margaret Ann Tickle 24 October 1876 in Bland County, daughter of Peter Conrad Tickle and Mary Ann Journell. She was born 11 March 1856 in Bland County and died 1924 buried in the Goshen Methodist Church Cemetery, Little Walker's Creek, Bland County.7[1] *See Tickle Family.

James William Banes and Margaret Ann Tickle's children:

- 3.1. Willie Missouri was born 1876, Little Walker's Creek, Pulaski County and died 1934. She is buried in the Goshen Methodist Church Cemetery, Little Walker's Creek, Bland County. She married Mitchell M. Burton born 1863 in Pulaski County. He was the son of Levi S. Burton and Margaret Bateman. Mitchell died 1942 and was buried in the Goshen Methodist Church Cemetery, Little Walker's Creek, Bland County. Children:[2]
  - 3.1.1. William born about 1894.
  - 3.1.2. Della born about 1897.
  - 3.1.3. John born about 1899.
  - 3.1.4. Charles Calvin born 25 October 1900. He died 03 June 1949. Charles married Bertha Jane Brunk born 07 April 1900 and died 09 September 1970. They are buried in the Goshen Methodist Church Cemetery.
  - 3.1.5. David born about 1903.
  - 3.1.6. Daisy born about 1905 married Robert T. Tickle on 07 July 1921.
  - 3.1.7. Vernie born about 1909.
  - 3.1.8. Jerry born about 1912.
  - 3.1.9. Robert born about 1916.
  - 3.1.10. Frank born about 1919.
- 3.2. Cynthia Jane was born 12 August 1879, Little Walker's Creek, Pulaski County, died 23 October 1960 in Pulaski County. She is buried in the Sifford Cemetery, Parrott, Pulaski County. She married 1st David Cloyd Carden 07 September 1898 in Pulaski. He was born 20 October 1875 in Pulaski County the son of Robert Andrew Carden and Mary Bell Runyan. David died 29 August 1915, Pulaski and is buried in the Sifford Cemetery, Parrott, Pulaski. Cynthia married 2nd John Monroe Hypes on 02 February 1918 in Pulaski. Lived in the Belspring/Parrot area of Pulaski County. David and Cynthia's children:[3]
  - 3.2.1. Vergie Bell born 25 Sep 1901, married 1st James Vernon Ledford, 2nd James Harvey Sifford and 3rd Earl Kenneth Sifford.
  - 3.2.2. Everett Oral born 15 Sep 1907, married on 18 March 1927 Sarah Gertrude Warf.
  - 3.2.3. Willie A. born 07 Jun 1908, died 4 December 1913.
  - 3.2.4. Robert Cloyd born 20 May 1910, married on 23 Dec 1929 Callie Jeanette Overstreet. She was the daughter of Robert Lee Overstreet and Mary Belle Carden.
  - 3.2.5. Lottie Jane born 06 Aug 1912, married Lenza Farley.
  - 3.2.6. Lillian Helena born 06 Feb 1916, married on 16 Dec 1933 Emmett Granville Hungate.

John Hypes and Cynthia's children:

---

[1] Tombstones, above named cemeteries, Bland County, VA Marriage Book.
[2] Various Pulaski County, VA Censuses; Goshen Methodist Church Cemetery.
[3] Various Pulaski County Census and information from Tickle Family.

- 3.2.7. <u>Frank Montgomery</u> born 10 July 1924 married Dorothy Jenett Hylton.
- 3.2.8. <u>Rachael Magelene</u> married Buford Marion McCoy.

3.2 <u>John Harvey. Sr.</u> was born 25 December 1880, Little Walkers Creek, Pulaski County; died 02 August 1961. He is buried in the Sifford Cemetery, Parrott, Pulaski. He married Virginia Bell Carden 25 December 1899 in Pulaski County; she was born 09 July 1882 in Pulaski, the daughter of Robert Andrew Carden and Mary Bell Runyan. She died 11 July 1960 in Pulaski. She is buried in the Sifford Cemetery, Parrott, Pulaski. Spelled surname as Bane. Children:[1]

- 3.2.1. <u>Alice Bell</u> born 11 November 1901 married Rufus Ward on 06 February 1919.
- 3.2.2. <u>Robert Andrew</u> born 03 August 1902 married Virginia Bessie Mabel Vaught on 25 April 1923.
- 3.2.3. <u>Lillie Sue</u> born 05 March 1905 married Robert Lee Purdy on 20 Jan 1920.
- 3.2.4. <u>John Harvey, Jr.</u> born 26 July 1907 married Virginia Catron.
- 3.2.5. <u>Lottie Ellen</u> born about 1910 married Leonard Moxley on 16 January 1928.
- 3.2.6. <u>Carl William</u> born 11 February 1913 married Agnes May Brunk on 19 January 1934. She was the daughter of George Thomas Brunk and Ellen Lee Carden
- 3.2.7. <u>Rachel Madeline</u>.
- 3.2.8. <u>Frances Nellie</u>.
- 3.2.9. <u>Hubert Lee</u> born 07 May 1921 married Madelene Drummand.
- 3.2.10. <u>Brady Edward</u> born 03 June 1915 married Virginia Elizabeth King on 18 March 1936.
- 3.2.11. <u>Nettie Frances</u> born 01 September 1913 married Otis Roy Brunk, son of George Thomas Brunk and Ellen Lee Carden

John Harvey moved from Little Walkers Creek to Parrott, Pulaski County, Virginia and remained there until his death. Parrott was a mining town for many years and John worked as a miner for a time. He also worked as a carpenter and mason, having done a lot of work in the Parrott area, and at one time he ran his own little general store in Parrott.

3.3. <u>Daisy</u> born 18 March 1883; died 18 March 1883 (Pulaski County Births-1853-1893 lists her born 15 August 1883).

3.4. <u>Harrison L.</u> born 14 August 1884 in Pulaski; died 05 November 1941 in Pulaski County. He married Anna B. "Bessie" Hoback. Harrison and Anna "Bessie" are buried in the Sifford Cemetery, Parrott, Pulaski County. Spelled as Bane. Their children:

- 3.4.1. <u>Ellen M.</u> born about 1908 married Bandy Matherly on 04 April 1934.
- 3.4.2. <u>Ethel D.</u> born about 1910 married Carl Matherly on 18 June 1931.
- 3.4.3. <u>Arthur Clifford</u> 27 October 1912 married Verland R. Sifford on 01 July 1933. They are buried in the Sifford Cemetery.
- 3.4.4. <u>Earl</u> born about 1915 married Mary Kimbleton.
- 3.4.5. <u>Harrison L.</u> born 16 November 1916 married Bertha Goad on 16 January 1935. They are buried in the Sifford Cemetery.

Other Bane's in the Sifford Cemetery are Dorothy S. Bain—1932, J. Walter Bain—1924; George Harrison Bane—26 February 1938-30 January 1994-SP4 US Army, John Robert Bane—20 April 1924-10 May 1972-Virginia PFC US Army World War II, Mabel V. Bane—1903-1967, Robert A. Bane—1902-1959 (son of John Harvey)

---

[1] Various Pulaski County, VA Censuses and Tickle Family.

3.5. Charles J. "Jerry" born 29 March 1885, Little Walker's Creek, Pulaski married Nettie Ann Willis 13 July 1906 in Pulaski County. She was born about 1891. Charles "Jerry" and Nettie was living in Pulaski in 1910[1]. Charles died before 28 February 1913. One daughter, Margaret born about 1908.[2] Nettie remarried on 30 December 1913 to Charles L. Tickle, son of John H. Tickle and Sarah Caves.

3.6. Nancy Cathern born 22 June 1886, Little Walker's Creek, Pulaski; died 29 September 1951, Little Walker's Creek, Bland; married Walter Herbert Brunk 22 August 1903 in Pulaski County. Walter was born 29 March 1886 to William Steven Brunk and Eliza Allen in Montgomery County, Virginia. Walter died 27 February 1962 in Bland. Nancy and Walter are buried in the Goshen Methodist Church Cemetery. Children:

    3.6.1. Albert born 06 June 1904 married Dorothy M. Davis, daughter of Charles William Davis and Louisa Virginia Davis. Had eight children. Albert and Dorothy died in Athens, Mercer County, West Virginia.

    3.6.2. Charles Neal born 01 July 1905 married Nellie May Davis on 22 June 1927 in Bland County. She was the daughter of Stuart P. Davis and Ethel Murray.

    3.6.3. Clarence Herbert born 13 March 1908; died 14 October 1935; buried in the Goshen Methodist Church Cemetery.

    3.6.4. Francis Catherine born 12 February 1910 married John Gorden Leslie on 02 November 1925 in Bland.

    3.6.5. Eva Ann born 15 November 1913 married Elmer Lawrence Davis on 16 September 1931 in Bland. He was the son of Emmett Milton Davis and Willie Jane Parsell. Eva married 2nd Mr. Stanley.

    3.6.6. Floyd..

    3.6.7. Genoa Bell born 04 December 1919 married George Lewis Millirons son of Rufus Lee Millirons and Annie Kate King.

    3.6.8. Thomas Repass born 20 November 1921 married Mary Crockett.

    3.6.9. Clara Elizabeth married Fayette Francis Corder on 09 August 1944 in Bland. He was the son of Benjamin Larkin Corder and Frances Bell Davis.

    3.6.10. Beulah Virginia married George Lewis Sink.

    3.6.11. George.

3.7. Andrew born 10 September 1889 in Pulaski.[3]

3.8. Nellie Gray born August 1891 married Silas D. Mason 25 March 1907 in Pulaski. Silas and Nellie were living in Pulaski County in 1910 and 1920.[4] Silas died sometime between 1927 and 1930. Nellie was in Cumberland County, Virginia; Randolph District in 1930. Living with her were her children: Leonard born about 1908 with wife, Susie; children Lillie and Robert. Silas and Nellie's other children were Mary born about 1910, Lula D. born about 1912, Ida born about 1915, Hazel V.. born about 1918 and Annie L. born about 1927.[5]

3.9. William "Joe" Dreyton born 18 March 1893 married 1st to Minnie [maiden name unknown]. One daughter Ethel.[6] Married 2nd Lucreasey Carver 14 January 1931 in Bland County. Joe died April 1976; buried in the Goshen Methodist Church Cemetery. Joe and Lucreasey's children:

    3.9.1. Edith Virgie married Fred Hensley Roope.

    3.9.2. William David married Betty Estep.

---

[1] 1910 Pulaski County, VA Census.
[2] 1910 Pulaski County, VA Census.
[3] Pulaski County, VA Births-1853-1893.
[4] 1910 and 1920 Pulaski County, VA Census.
[5] 1930 Cumberland County, VA Census.
[6] 1900 Pulaski County, VA Census.

- 3.9.3. <u>Edgar Albert</u> married Augusta Delphine Millirons.
- 3.9.4. <u>Ernest Dreyton</u> married Dolly Marie Millirons.
- 3.9.5. <u>Ellis Wilber</u>.
- 3.10. <u>Josephine Alice "Josie"</u> born May 18954 married Calvin Gleve Thompson 20 August 1912 in Pulaski.
- 3.11. <u>Edgar Albert</u> born 04 June 1897 married Jessie L. Bond on 16 January 1923 in Pulaski. Jessie was the daughter of James R. Bond and Martha Jane Johnston. Edgar died 06 January 1976 and Jessie died 16 October 1973. They are buried in the Goshen Methodist Church Cemetery. Edgar and Jessie had sons:
  - 3.11.1. <u>Bernard</u> born 17 June 1924 in Pulaski; died 13 February 1997 in Junction City, Geary County, Kansas.
  - 3.11.2. <u>Wayne Kenneth</u> born 20 September 1925 married Colleen Noal Davis on 17 June 1947 in Bland. Colleen was the daughter of Albert Terry Davis and Annie Kate King. Wayne died on 18 December 1968 and Colleen died 30 May 1969. They are buried in the Goshen Methodist Church Cemetery.
  - 3.11.3. <u>Oakley Neal</u> born 07 May 1928 married Francis Irene Davis on 23 December 1948 in Bland. Francis was the daughter of Albert Terry Davis and Annie Kate King. Oakley died on 24 April 1995 and Francis on 27 May 1994.
- 3.12. <u>Lula</u> born December 18995 married Thomas Masfield on 03 July 1920 in Pulaski.

James William Banes wrote his will on February 28, 1913:
1st All just debts be paid.
2nd To my wife, Margaret all personal property and real estate during the remainder of her life and at her death to be divided as follows:
To daughter Willie M. Burton $1
To daughter Nancy Brunk $1
To son Harrison Banes $1
To daughter Josie Thompson $1
To daughter Nellie Mason $1
To heirs of Jerry Banes $1
To heirs of Shurley Banes $1
To son John $1
To my youngest daughter Lula $50.
To Drayton and Edgar, the balance of my estate to be divided equally.
3rd I appoint W. N. Millirons as my executor.
4th I appoint W. N. Millirons guardian of any of my children under 21.
Probated on April 19, 1913.[1]

There are three handmade stones in the Goshen Methodist Church Cemetery: Charley, Mary and Chester Banes; no dates.

4. <u>Sarah</u> born 31 May 1855; died March 1934. Buried in the Banes/Leeson Cemetery. She never married..
5. <u>Julia Rose</u> born 1850 died 1898 married William Millirons on 24 December 1873 in Pulaski County. Julia and William are buried in the old Millirons/Allen Cemetery, Little Walkers Creek, Pulaski County.

William served with the 54th Virginia Infantry Company F On 20 April 1888, he applied for a Confederate pension. He explained that he was injured while in prison in on detail carrying

---

[1] Pulaski County, VA Will Book 6, p. 480.

water, slipped on ice and broke left leg at the hip joint. Left leg is two to three inches shorter than the right leg. Am partially disabled. Prisoner at Camp Douglas, Chicago.

Camp Douglas, originally constructed at Thirty-first Street and Cottage Grove Avenue as a Union Army training post, served as a Confederate prisoner-of-war camp. Between 1862 and 1865, the camp housed about twenty-six thousand prisoners in temporary, wooden barracks. As a result of harsh conditions, some four thousand men died at the camp; they were buried in unmarked paupers' graves in Chicago's City Cemetery, located at the southeast corner of what is now Lincoln Park. In 1867, the remains were reburied at Oak Woods Cemetery, about five miles south of the camp.

William and Julia's children:
5.1. Rufus Lee "R. Lee" married Annie Kate King 29 August 1894 in Bland. He was born 12 September1875 in Pulaski and died 09 February 1933. Annie was the daughter of William Thompson King and Nancy Lovica King. She was born 30 May 1872 in Bland County and died 17 November 1944. They are buried in the "Davis Cemetery.

From the book, *History of Bland County (Virginia)* by the Bland County Centennial Corporation, Bland County Historical Society:
R. Lee Millirons, a teacher and certified surveyor, was born in Pulaski County and

moved to Long Spur in Bland County around the turn of the century. His formal education was procured in Pulaski grade schools and through study of his own he became well-qualified in many subjects.
He was influential in the establishment of the post office at the head of Little Walkers Creek in 1916, and named that post office Carnot after the French president whom he admired greatly.

R. Lee Millirons & wife Annie Kate King with children Vicey, Louis, Annie, Edgar, and Laura. Submitted by Sara Melton-Sumner.

R. Lee and Annie's children:
5.1.1. Edgar Hampton born 06 June 1896 and died 06 November 1966. He married Cecil Thelma Davis 20 November 1919 in Bland. She was the daughter of Charles Clinton Davis and Willie Floyd Davis. Cecil was born on 17 February 1899 and died 27 May 1977. *See Davis Families.
5.1.2. Laura Emily born 03 April 1898 married Albert Terry Meadows 25 November 1915 in Bland. He was the son of James William Allen Meadows and Ida Belle Parsell *See Pegram/Meadows Family.
5.1.3. Sarah "Vicey" Lavica married Charles William Davis 29 October 1919 in Bland. He was the son of Samuel Caddell Davis and Elizabeth Agnes Patterson. "Vicey" was Charles's second wife. *See Samuel C. Davis Family.
5.1.4. George Lewis married Genoa Bell Brunk. She was the daughter of Walter Herbert Brunk and Nancy Cathern Banes. *See Brunk Family.

5.1.5. Annie Kate married Samuel Roosevelt Hancock 15 July 1925 in Bland. He was the son of George Washington Hancock and Isabelle Shrader. Samuel and Annie's children:
    5.1.5.1. Larry M.
    5.1.5.2. Naomi Isabell.
    5.1.5.3. James Lewis.

5.1.6. Julia Rose married Terry Chaffin Davis 30 January 1929 in Bland. He was the son of Jacob H. Davis and Julia M. Akers. *See Akers Family

5.1.7. Robert Lee Jr. married Ruby Mathews.

5.1.8. John Daniel married Gladys Cannaday.

5.2. George Edward [twin] born 20 March 1877 in Pulaski; died 1894 of tuberculosis.

5.3. Joseph Hampton [twin] born 20 March 1877 in Pulaski died about 1898 of tuberculosis.

5.4. Olive Virginia born 14 September 1879 married Edward L. Hamblin 22 August 1903 in Bland. He was the son of William J. S. Hamblin and Oleva E. Tabor. Olive died 08 May 1961 and Edward died 31 January 1969. They are buried in Hamblin Cemetery, Spur Branch, Little Walker's Creek. Their children:

5.4.1. Glenord C.. married Margaret Stephens 29 April 1926 in Bland.

5.4.2. Maggie Leona born 22 August 1905 married Orsen Wylie Chewning.

5.4.3. Roxie M. born 22 April 1907; died 19 March 1916. She is buried in the Hamblin Cemetery.

5.4.4. Dorothy married first Wiley Vincent Meadows and second Jerome Walter Greene. One son:
    5.4.4.1. Allen Lee Meadows married Mary Catherine Brunk.

5.4.5. Genoa Thelma married Raymond Earl Davis 01 October 1928 in Bland. He was the son of Henry Hampton Davis and Victoria Agnes Davis. Children:
    5.4.5.1. Clyde.
    5.4.5.2. Raymond Elwood.
    5.4.5.3. Louise Alberta.
    5.4.5.4. Rosaline.
    5.4.5.5. Daniel.

5.4.6. Garnett Lee married Janie Elizabeth Chewning.

5.4.7. Govan Thedmer married Martha Levell Davis, daughter of Robert Lee Davis and Josephine Elizabeth Burton. Children:
    5.4.7.1. Judas.
    5.4.7.2. Barbara.
    5.4.7.3. Yvonne.
    5.4.7.4. Polly.
    5.4.7.5. Sylvia.
    5.4.7.6. Carlos M.

5.4.8. Charles W. born 11 January 1916 and died 21 March 1916. Buried in the Hamblin Cemetery.

5.4.9. Hobert born about 1919.[1] No other information.

5.4.10. Arthur Edward born 09 February 1922 and died 11 May 1955. Buried in the Hamblin Cemetery.

5.4.11. Ernest born about 1924[2] married Mary Etta Hancock daughter of Sidney Edward Hancock and Bessie Pearl King.

---

[1] 1920 Bland County, VA Census.
[2] 1930 Bland County, VA Census.

- 5.5. <u>Estell Hoge</u> born 31 January 1881 married Ella Augusta Akers 24 December 1902 in Bland. *See Akers family.
- 5.6. <u>Wythe Monroe</u> born 15 December 1883.
- 5.7. <u>Thomas Martin Luther</u> born 29 May 1885.
- 5.8. <u>Hugh Lagner</u> born 01 January 1888 married 1st Rebecca Louise Raines 17 May 1906 in Pulaski. They had seven children. Hugh married 2nd Mary Tarter Lambert 10 March 1922 in Bland. Mary was the daughter of James Edward Lambert and Cynthia E. Stowers. Hugh and Mary are buried in the Thornspring Cemetery in Pulaski County.
- 5.9. <u>Lelia Pearl</u> born August 1890 had one daughter, Rosa Evelyn. Lelia married William H. Washington 15 March 1921 in Pulaski.
- 5.10. <u>Elizabeth Ellen</u> born 08 December 1893 married Samuel Joseph Yonce 28 November 1923 in Bland. Four children. They are buried in the Thornspring Methodist Church Cemetery, Pulaski County.
- 5.11. <u>John</u> born January 1897.[1] No other information.
6. <u>Nancy "Nannie" Catherine</u> born 21 June 1858 married William Steven Brunk on 09 May 1889 in Pulaski. William's parents were Jacob Brunk and Elizabeth W. Keffer. He was born 03 October 1848 in Montgomery Country. William died 21 August 1922; Nancy died 24 June 1909. They are buried in the Goshen Methodist Church Cemetery, Bland County. *See Brunk Family

---

[1] 1910 Bland County, VA Census.

BRUNK FAMILY

German, a similar form of the English Bruns, Bronson, Brown, and Brownel; all derived from the Anglo-Saxon name and name element Brun "brown".[1]

Jacob Brunk was born about 1734 in Germany, migrated to America by 1759 when he married Anna Maria Stouffer in Dauphin County, Pennsylvania. Jacob died in 1787 in Washington County, Maryland They had a son John born about 1760 in Dauphin County, Pennsylvania.

John married Mary Magdalene [maiden name unknown]. John died before 1811 in Botetourt County, Virginia. They had a son, Jacob born about 1785 in Virginia.

Jacob married Nancy Ann Shank on 10 October 1806 in Montgomery County. They had son Jacob born about 1818 in Montgomery County; married Elizabeth W. Keffer on 07 June 1841 in Montgomery. Elizabeth's parents were George Washington Keffer and Hannah Ruth Caldwell. They had children George Washington., Nancy Ann, Christopher, Hannah M., William Steven, Sara Lavina, John Griffith and Mary Louisa.[2]

William Steven Brunk was born 03 October 1848 in Montgomery County and died 21 August 1922 in Bland County. He is buried in the Goshen Methodist Church Cemetery, Spur Branch, Little Walker's Creek, Bland County. He married 1st Eliza Allen on 17 February 1876 in Montgomery County. Eliza died 02 February 1889 in Cox's Hollow, Pulaski County.[3] William remarried to Nancy Catherine Banes on 09 May 1889 in Pulaski County. She was the daughter of Jeremiah Banes and Sarah Davis. Nancy "Nannie" was born 21 June 1858 and died 24 June 1909 and is buried in the Goshen Methodist Church Cemetery.

William S. bought 124 acres on Spur Branch from Joseph E. Stafford on May 25, 1887. Joseph had died and had not conveyed the land to William. On May 20, 1890, James B. Peck Commissioner of the Circuit Court of Giles County conveyed this land to William S. Brunk pending a lawsuit between Brunk and Stafford's heirs. Stafford's heirs were claiming Brunk had not paid for the land. It was shown to the satisfaction of the court that Brunk had paid the entire $450.00 amount. A decree was entered into court on May 8, 1890.[4]

William and his wife Nancy C. conveyed 50 acres to David S. Ritter on October 7, 1893.[5]

William was living in Montgomery County in 1880 per the 1880 Montgomery County census. It is unknown where he lived in 1890 as most of the 1890 U. S. Census was destroyed by fire.

William Stephen Brunk and Eliza Allen's children:
1. <u>Elizabeth "Lizzie" Cora</u> was born 11 January 1877 in Montgomery County and died 21 April 1950. "Lizzie" is buried in the Goshen Methodist Church Cemetery on Spur Branch. She never married.
2. <u>Eugene Edward</u> was born December 1878 in Montgomery County. He married Allie Ann Ritter, daughter of David Spencer Ritter and Hettie Locritta Shufflebarger. Allie was born

---

[1] *What is in Your Name?* Vitalog.net. website http://www.vitalog.net/cgi-bin/select_name.cgi
[2] Jacob's Ladder: A Supplement to The Progeny of Jacob Brunk I, The Will-maker, by Ivan W. Brunk, 1982, Sarasota, FL.
[3] Brunk Family Bible, Courtesy of Milton Davis.
[4] Bland County, VA Deed Book 6, pg. 392.
[5] Bland County Deed Book 6, pg. 548.

February 18, 1884 in Pulaski County. Eugene died in 1918 of influenza. Allie was living in Augusta County, Virginia in 1920. Allie later married Robert Peery and moved to Richmond, Virginia. Children from the 1920 Augusta County census:
- 2.1. Nellie L.
- 2.2. Ernest B.
- 2.3. Eugene B.
- 2.4. Raymond E.
- 2.5. Linda
- 2.6. Ralph C.
- 2.7. Irene E.

3. John William born 13 February 1882 and died 04 May 1882 in Montgomery County.[1]
4. George Thomas born 30 August 1883 and died 29 June 1956 in Pulaski County. George married Ellen Lee Carden on 19 January 1904 in Pulaski County. Ellen was born 30 June 1885 in Pulaski County and died 08 November 1955 in Pulaski County. She was the daughter of Charles W. Carden and Cynthia Victoria Tickle. They are buried in the Church Of Jesus Cemetery-Highland Road, Pulaski County. George and Ellen lived in the area of Belspring, Pulaski County. Children from the 1920 Pulaski census:
   - 4.1. Bertie L.
   - 4.2. Dorothy M.
   - 4.3. Otis Roy married Nettie Frances Bane, daughter of John Harvey Bane, Sr. and Virginia Bell Carden.
   - 4.4. Agnes May married Carl William Bane son of John Harvey Bane, Sr.. and Virginia Bell Carden.
5. Walter Herbert born March 29, 1886 and died February 27, 1962 in Bland County. He married Nancy Catherine Banes on August 22, 1902 in Pulaski County. *See Banes Family

   On November 15, 1951, Walter Brunk, widower, sold 50 acres to Buford R. Martin. "…situated on the waters of Walker's Little Creek…being bounded on the East by the Moses Akers Home Place, on the South by Max Grief's land, on the West by the lines of R. L. Milliron's land, and on the North by Max Greif's big survey (now owned by the United States Government)…being the same property which was conveyed to the said Walter Brunk by deed from Jacob H. Davis and Julia A. Davis, his wife, of date June 9, 1913…".[2]

6. Robert Kelley born July 21, 1887 and died May 4, 1971 in Wythe County. Robert married Effie Ethel Davis on September 17, 1913 in Bland County. Effie was born July 14, 1892 in Bland County and died August 15, 1974 in Wythe County. She was the daughter of Charles William Davis and Louisa Virginia Davis. Robert and Effie are buried in the Hidden Valley Cemetery #2 on Little Walker's Creek, Bland County. Children:
   - 6.1. William.
   - 6.2. Samuel Neal married Irene Robertson.
   - 6.3. Elizabeth married Mr. Leslie.
   - 6.4. Edith married Mr. Duncan.
   - 6.5. John T.
   - 6.6. Ethel married Henry Newton Jones.
   - 6.7. Robert Kelley, Jr.
   - 6.8. Edna
   - 6.9. Louise C.

---

[1] *Jacob's Ladder: A Supplement to The Progeny of Jacob Brunk I, The Will-maker*, by Ivan W. Brunk, 1982, Sarasota, FL.
[2] Bland County Deed Book 34, pg. 561.

6.10. Edward.
7. Vernie Eliza born 11 January 1889 and died 02 November 1957 in Bland County. She married Richard Floyd Davis December 29, 1915 in Bland County. Richard was born 14 January 1886 to James Whitten Davis and Nancy Jane King. Richard died 25 September 1971 in Bland County. Both are buried in the Hidden Valley Cemetery #2 on Little Walker's Creek. Children:
   7.1. Trinkle Whitten born 13 October 1916 and died 1994. He married Vivian G. Chandler daughter of John Robert Chandler and Wilma Lou Ritter.
   7.2. Floyd Clayton was born 12 October 1919 and died 25 September 1971 buried in the Hidden Valley Cemetery #2.
   7.3. James William was born 15 March 1924; died 16 September 1978. He married 1st Ima Cox and 2nd Virginia Magdalene Spencer. He is buried in the Hidden Valley Cemetery #2

William Steven also had a stepdaughter named Laura Ellen Allen born 24 January 1869.

Children of William Steven and Nancy Catherine Banes:
8. Houston Neel born 06 February 1896 in Bland County and died August 1979 in Bland County. He married Genoa Agnes Davis September 16, 1917 in Bland County. Genoa was born January 24, 1901 in Bland County and died December 1987 in Bland County. She was the daughter of Charles William Davis and Louisa Virginia Davis. Huston was a World War I veteran. Houston and Genoa are buried in the Goshen Methodist Church Cemetery. Children:
   8.1. Robert Bruce married Irene Burton. She was the daughter of Charles Calvin Burton and Bertha Jane Brunk.
   8.2. Lavina Elizabeth married John Trenton Meadows. He was the son of Wiley Vincent Meadows and Dana Rhoena Hamblin.
   8.3. Lola Grace married Raymond Alton Hamblin. He was the son of William Hoge Hamblin and Virgie Ethel Bond.
   8.4. Marvel.
   8.5. Junior Neel married Hazel Davidson Wolfe. She was the daughter of Everett C. Wolfe and Nannie Belle Shrader.
   8.6. Vance Clayton married Naomi Katherine Davis.
   8.7. Betty Marie married Hoge Harvey Wolfe.
   8.8. Hazel Naomi married Luther Vivian Vaughn.
   8.9. Mary Catherine married Allen Lee Meadows.
   8.10. Viola Agnes married Luther Hubert Wilson.
   8.11. Opal Belle [Opal born 06 June 1940; died 15 April 1941; buried in the Goshen Cemetery].

On March 10, 1909, W. S. Brunk conveyed 68 ¼ acres to Houston N. Brunk.[1]

Junior N. Brunk bought the David Ritter land in 1950 from the Ritter heirs which contained 100 acres…"being the same land as conveyed to David S. Ritter by two deeds from William S. Brunk and J. H. Overstreet…50 acres each…".[2]

9. Lula Ann was born 06 July 1907 in Bland County and died 26 April 1926. She married William Edward Corder on 02 August 1922 in Bland County. He was the son of Benjamin Larkin Corder and Frances Bell Davis. Lula is buried in the Goshen Church Cemetery.

---
[1] Bland County, VA Deed Book 13, pg. 544.
[2] Bland County, VA Deed Book 33, pg. 168.

10. <u>Bertha Jane</u> was born 07 April 1900 in Bland and died 09 September 1970. She married Charles Calvin Burton. He was born 25 October 1900 to Mitchell M. Burton and Willie Missouri Banes. He died 03 June 1949. Charles and Bertha are buried in the Goshen Methodist Church Cemetery.

CHANDLER FAMILY

Almost all Chandler families can trace their ancestry back to one of two ancient lineages. After arriving in the American colonies, one line migrated through Pennsylvania, the other through Virginia, North Carolina, South Carolina and then Tennessee where they stayed for many generations. Because of the route followed by those families, it is easily believed that this is our line of Chandler ancestry. The earliest ancestor is Nicholas, born in 1540 at Oare, Wiltshire, England. While both Chandler lineages come from England, a common ancestor has never been identified that would connect the two branches.

Chandler is an occupational name, meaning "the Chandler", a candle maker, the official who attended to the lights in his lordships household. The family is of English extraction and most of the pioneer Chandlers in the American Colonies came directly from England.

The first evidence found is in Wythe County, Virginia and in the Wythe and Bland County censuses. Found were three early Chandler marriage records in Wythe County. The first was Richard married Catherine Porter on 13 February 1798. The second being George and Peggy Tade married 07 December 1815. The third James H. married Mary Norris 18 November 1841. Each one of these Chandler men are of a different generation and so I theorize that the first was the father of the second, ect. Maybe not so, but I did come to the conclusion that George was the father of James H. Chandler.

There was only one Chandler listed in the 1850 Wythe census and that was James H. Chandler age 28 with wife Mary age 31. Most likely children: George W. age 7, Margaret age 5, Ellen age 3. Also listed in the 1860 Wythe census. Mary had died, evidently, she was not listed with the family. There was an additional child, Hannah born about 1851. During my research in Wythe, I found one additional child born and died on 14 October 1853, a female unnamed. Mary may have died during childbirth. James H. Chandler lived in the area of Wythe which became Bland in 1861; he was found in Bland in the 1870 Bland census with children. James and Mary's children where George born about 1843; Margaret born about 1845; Ellen born about 1847 and Hannah C. born about 1851. Hannah never married but had several children out of wedlock. One being Mr. Robert Lee Chandler who would later moved to Little Walkers Creek and become one of the most respected men in the area.

Robert Lee Chandler 1st married Lucy Augusta "Gussie" Davis and 2nd Emma "Louella" Millirons. He and Gussie first lived in McDowell County, West Virginia where his first four children were born. Robert had a total of six children. He moved to Little Walkers Creek sometime in 1919 buying land from James Edward Davis and his wife[1], Tobias King[2] and Morrison Vandergrift[3]. Later, his twin sons bought the rest of James Davis's land from James Davis' heirs.[4]

Robert and Lucy Augusta Chandler's children:
1. <u>John Robert</u> born 13 July 1905 married Wilma Lou Ritter 23 June 1924 in Pulaski County. Wilma was the daughter of Thomas Fenton Ritter and Martha Jane N. Johnston Bond. John died 07 November 1960; Wilma was born 15 November 1907 and died 26 December 1970. They are in the Millirons Methodist Church Cemetery.

---

[1] Pulaski County, VA Deed Book 40, p. 599.
[2] Pulaski County, VA Deed Book 43, p. 467.
[3] Pulaski County, VA Deed Book 41. p. 19.
[4] Pulaski County, VA Deed Book 81, p. 493.

2. Mary Ada was born 17 August 1908 married William Robert Morris King 15 May 1929 in Pulaski. William was the son of William Davis King and Olivia Virginia Thompson, born 16 May 1905. Mary Ada died 28 March 1987 and Morris died 04 March 1987. They are buried in the Millirons Methodist Church Cemetery.
3. Carl Davis born 19 March 1913 married Ola Faw 06 August 1937 in Pulaski. Ola was the daughter of Wiley Henderson Faw and Effie Goodman.
4. Ralph Scott born 19 March 1913 married Georgia Mabel Faw 06 August 1937 in Pulaski. Georgia's parents were Wiley Henderson Faw and Effie Goodman.

Robert and Emma Louella Chandler's children:
5. Reba Lee married 1st Larry Warren Rigney and 2nd Jack Crawford.
6. James William married Judith "Elaine" Davis. Elaine is the daughter of Lewis Baxter Davis and Clarice Neely.

Biography
Robert Lee Chandler
Submitted by Reba Chandler and Jack Crawford

Robert Lee Chandler was born November 29, 1879 in Bland County, VA. He was living with Judge Kegley in Bland County, Virginia at age twelve, in 1891. As a child, he would go to Bland County Courthouse and listen to court cases. He had no formal education, but managed to make a good living for his family. He was an avid reader, and read anytime he had the opportunity. He was a kind person, and well liked by everyone.

He married Lucy Augusta Davis on May 25, 1904. They had four children - John Robert, Mary Ada, Carl Davis, and Ralph Scott Chandler. His wife, Lucy Augusta died March 9, 1938 from heart problems. After she died, he married Emma Louella Millirons on July 20, 1943. They had two children - Reba Lee, and James William Chandler. Robert had 40 descendants from his first marriage to Lucy, and 4 descendants from his marriage to Emma.

He moved from Bland County, VA to Ashland, McDowell County, WV in 1904. His first four children were born there. In 1908 he ran a steam engine at Algoma, West Virginia. Around 1913 he was a tipple boss at Ashland, West Virginia. In 1919, Robert purchased a house and land in the Little Walkers Creek section of Pulaski County, VA, and his wife, Lucy, returned to Virginia in 1920. Robert remained in West Virginia, due to his work, and in 1921, was working at Crumpler, West Virginia rebuilding wooden mine cars. He returned to Pulaski County, Virginia in 1922 and went to work for Spur Branch Lumber Co, where he operated their sawmill. He went to work for the U S Postal Service as a mail carrier in Bland and Pulaski Counties, Virginia from 1925 –1929. He lost the bid for the next four years, and won the bid again in 1934, and carried the mail continuously until 1957.

He retired from the U S Postal Service in 1957, after 27 years of service. He enjoyed two years of retirement before his death. He suffered a stroke on December 24, 1958, and died a week later on January 1, 1959, at age 79 years, 1 month, and 3 days. He is buried in the Millirons Church Cemetery, Little Walkers Creek, Pulaski County, Virginia.

Biography
Emma Louella Millirons
Submitted by Reba Chandler and Jack Crawford

Emma was born on Sept 10, 1910 in the Little Creek section of Bland County, Virginia. She was the fifth of seven children born to Estil Hoge and Ella Akers Millirons. Her siblings were Gordon, Howard, Clarence, Moses, Pearl and Vance Millirons. The Hoge Millirons home, where Emma grew up, was a two story frame dwelling and is located on Little Creek Road about two miles from the current Fire House. Emma walked about two miles to attend school in a log schoolhouse located near her parents home. Her teachers were R L Millirons, Edgar Millirons, Sinclair Brown and Lucille Havens. The log schoolhouse was torn down around 1932, and a new one built, and that school later became the building that currently houses The Little Creek Fire Department, Established in 1951. (*Note: The school house is now a Community Center; the Fire House built beside it—RS).

Much of Emma's early life was dedicated to the role of caregiver. She left school at the age of twelve to help take care of her grandmother, Sally Akers, who had broken her hip. About 1934, her brother, Howard, was divorced and moved his family into the home of his parents, and she helped to care for his family until the children grew into adulthood. Her brother, Gordon, also lived in the household, and she helped to care for him too.

When Emma was sixteen she had a childhood sweetheart. They almost got married. He told someone they were getting married, and when her father became aware of it, he would not let her see him anymore. He said she was too young to be married. Emma continued to live in the home of her parents, and did not marry until age 32. She met and married Robert Lee Chandler, who had become a widower in 1938, when his wife Lucy, had died from heart problems. Emma and Robert were married July 20, 1943 in Bland, VA, in the parsonage of Methodist minister Rev. Ernest Dugan, Jr.

When Emma and Robert were married she moved into his house. Their first child, Reba Lee Chandler was born on May 14, 1945, and exactly one year later their second child, James William Chandler was born on May 14, 1946. Emma enjoyed her life as wife and mother. Her husband, Robert, carried mail in Bland and Pulaski County for many years. He retired in 1957.

Emma continued to live in the house she shared with Robert and their children until 1974. It was then that she came to Pulaski, and lived with both her children. After that, she moved into the homes of Mrs. Ruth Moore and Mrs. Margaret Keister, and helped to care for them in their old age. In 1980, she moved into an apartment on 10th St, in Pulaski, Virginia, and lived there until 1986. Then she lived with her daughter, Reba, until the fall of 1987, when she moved to Randolph House. She remained there until May 1996, then moving to Pulaski Health Care, where she currently resides (July 2003).

COMBS FAMILY

Combs; originally designated a dweller in a valley, dale, glen, deep hollow, pit, ravine, or bottom land.[1]

John Combs, born in Grayson County, Virginia 10 December 1815, was the son of Zedekiah (often called "Zadoc") Combs and Elizabeth Johnson. Zedekiah was born about 1775 probably in North Carolina and died in Grayson County before August 1821 (date of estate inventory. He was the father of seven children: Joseph born 1802, Sarah born 1804, Jeremiah born 1806, William born 1810, Nancy born 1811, John 1815 and Melinda 1820. Zedekiah lived in Paul's Creek and Crooked Creek area of Grayson, same as the Allen family.

Just as the Allen family, John Combs left Grayson County and moved to Raleigh County, Virginia (now West Virginia). John Combs 1st married Penninah Jane Beller. She was born 24 April 1822 in Grayson County and died 02 May 1883 in Pulaski County. Her parents were Elias Beller and Nancy Wills. John Combs married 2nd Phoebe R. Wills on 02 November 1883 in Pulaski County.

On June 16 1873, John Combs bought 45 ¼ acres from James M. Johnson and wife Hester—corner to Hiram Davis's patent land.[2]

John bought 700 acres of land in the area of Alum Springs on Little Walkers Creek from William L. Hunter on January 26, 1876. This deed was not recorded until May 12, 1905.[3]

On June 7, 1877, Jesse Morris was conveyed 300 acres by John Combs and wife Peniah "…near a line between Hunter and said Combs…".[4]

John Combs and Phebe his wife conveyed 125 acres "…between John Morris and said John Combs…" to Joseph W. Combs for "natural love and affection" on February 27, 1888.[5]

John and Phebe conveyed 125 acres to the children of John W. Combs for "…natural love and affection…" on February 27, 1888.6 and to John W. Combs "for natural love and affection…" 125 acres between William Hunter and John Combs.[6]

John Combs wrote his will on September 6, 1889:
"1st I request to be decently buried; after death, my executors may have my burial expense and all debts paid out of my estate.
2nd I bequeath to my 3 daughters, Nettie M., Georgiana and Vergie Bell my tract of land and wife Phebe to share jointly with them her lifetime; also to daughters-one bond worth $600 held against John D. and Allen Hall.
3rd To wife and 3 daughters all my household and kitchen furniture, my gray mare, 2 cows and my mowing machine and rake—Joe W. Combs holding equal share in machine and rake. Unto daughter Nettie, my watch.

---

[1] *What is in Your Name?* Vitalog.net. website http://www.vitalog.net/cgi-bin/select_name.cgi
[2] Pulaski County, VA Deed Book 6, p. 357.
[3] Pulaski County, VA Deed Book 24, p. 267.
[4] Pulaski County, VA Deed Book 9, p. 182.
[5] Pulaski County, VA Deed Book 12, p. 63.
[6] Pulaski County, VA Deed Book 12, p. 137.

4th To son Joe W. all my blacksmith tools he may select and request that he does blacksmith for my wife and the 3 children—balance of said tools to be sold.
5th I request my executors sell all personal property not before mentioned at public auction all things not necessary for the place.
6th I request my executors collect all debts owed to me.
7th To my son M. J.. I have already paid his part.
8th To daughter Nancy Combs I have already paid her part.
9th To granddaughter Madona Cook $75 of Raleigh County, West Virginia.
10th To Liza Allen deceased her children $88.25 as they become of age.
11th To Son John W. I have already paid his part.
12th To son Joe W.. I have already paid his part.
13th To daughter Mary White $25 plus what I have already paid.
14th Paulina Akers and children $65 plus what I have already given.
15th To son William R.. my love and affection
16th I request executors to use the money left from the estate and use to best advantage for my wife and daughters.
17th I appoint Joe W. Combs as my executor.
Witnesses were R. M. T. Hunter and S. M. B Morris

John Combs added on September 8, 1889 "J. W. Combs made guardian of children Nettie, Georgiana and Virgie Bell" Witnesses R. M. T. Hunter and J. B. King.

John added on March 3, 1890 "Request and will that should any more children be born unto my wife during my life or within nine months after my death, they should share equally with my daughters. Witnesses were R. M. T. Hunter and William A. Morris. John Combs' will was probated on January 4, 1892.[1] He is, most likely, buried in the Hunter Cemetery, Pulaski County, Virginia.

John Combs and Penninah Jane Beller's children:
1. <u>Mandeville Jackson</u> born 06 April 1841 married Henrietta E. Martin on 27 July 1871 in Giles County, Virginia. Children:[2]
    1.1. <u>John W.</u> born about 1872.
    1.2. <u>William J</u>. born 31 December 1875.[3]
    1.3. <u>Lizzie J</u>. born about 1878.
    1.4. <u>Charles C</u>. born 25 January 1880.[4]
    1.5. <u>Everett</u> born 10 August 1884.[5]
    1.6. <u>James</u> born 05 October 1886.[6]

Mandeville disappeared from Pulaski after 1880. He may have died between 1880 and 1900.

Mandeville Jackson served with the 36th Infantry Regiment Virginia, Company C; enlisted on October 6, 1862. Promoted to Full Corporal on August 10, 1864. He was paroled on June 12, 1865.[7]

---

[1] Pulaski County, VA Will Book 4, p. 309.
[2] 1880 Pulaski County, VA Census.
[3] Pulaski County Births-1853-1893.
[4] Pulaski County Births-1853-1893.
[5] Pulaski County Births-1853-1893.
[6] Pulaski County Births-1853-1893.
[7] The Virginia Regimental Histories Series. 45 vols. Lynchburg: Howard, 1987.

2. <u>Nancy Ann</u> born 22 August 1842 married Jeremiah Combs on 3 April 1860 probably in Raleigh County, Virginia.
3. <u>Eliza J. C.</u> married William Carr Allen. *See Allen Family.
4. <u>John W.</u> born about 1848 married Mary J. T. Williams on 30 January 1879 in Pulaski. He married 2nd in Raleigh County, West Virginia, Mary Ann Combs on 24 March 1904. John and Mary Williams' children from Pulaski County Births-1853-1893:
   - 4.1. <u>John</u> born 29 December 1872.
   - 4.2. <u>James</u> born 22 February 1880.
   - 4.3. <u>William "Cam" Cameron</u> born 21 March 1884 married Bertha Haga and had the following children from the 1930 Pulaski County census:
     - 4.3.1. <u>Lena</u> born about 1921.
     - 4.3.2. <u>Virginia</u> born about 1923.
     - 4.3.3. <u>Mary E.</u> born about 1925.
     - 4.3.4. <u>William Victor</u> born about 1927 married Violet Virginia Davis.
     - 4.3.5. <u>Herbert D.</u> born about 1928.
   - 4.4. <u>Creed Frank</u> born 30 March 1887[1] married Lula E. Harrell on 29 January 1913 in Pulaski.

On June 14, 1905 J. W. Combs and wife Mary Ann of Raleigh County, West Virginia conveyed all interest in his father's land to W. C. Combs and C. F. Combs of Pulaski…bounded by lines of P. R. Combs and children—west of R. M. T. Hunter and North of Ballard Harrell. 125 acres.[2]

5. <u>Joseph W.</u> born 12 January 1851, married Matilda K. Robertson on 17 September 1874 in Giles County. Joseph died on 06 May 1902. Matilda was born January 1856 and died 25 July 1946. They are buried in the Hunter Cemetery, Little Walkers Creek, Pulaski County. Children:
   - 5.1. <u>Infant female</u> born 15 May 1875.[3]
   - 5.2. <u>William Hix</u> born 30 March 1877[4], never married. His mother was living with him in 1930.[5] William died 30 October 1954, buried in the Hunter Cemetery, Pulaski County.
   - 5.3. <u>Nannie Della</u> born 12 June 1879, married John Bell Morris on 19 September 1896 in Pulaski County. Nannie died 19 July 1966, buried in the Hunter Cemetery. John was born 29 April 1874 to Joseph Johnson Morris and Sarah Shinault. He died on 28 March 1958, buried in the Hunter Cemetery. Their children:[6]
     - 5.3.1. <u>Delia B.</u> born December 1897 in Pulaski.
     - 5.3.2. <u>Harris H.</u> born April 1900 in Pulaski.
     - 5.3.3. <u>Fanny</u> born about 1902.
     - 5.3.4. <u>Mary</u> born about 1906.
     - 5.3.5. <u>Glen</u> born about 1909.
     - 5.3.6. <u>Myrtle M.</u> born about 1911 married Jackson Vest on 13 March 1937 in Pulaski. Jackson was the son of William Vest and Ettie Woodyard.
     - 5.3.7. <u>Lelia</u> born about 1914 married Robert Woodyard on 01 January 1937 in Pulaski. Robert was the son of Sidney Woodyard and Rhoda White.
     - 5.3.8. <u>Edith</u> born about 1915 married Cecil Woodyard on 28 June 1934. He was the son of Sidney Woodyard and Rhoda White.

---

[1] Pulaski County Births-1853-1893.
[2] Pulaski County, VA Deed Book 25, p. 155
[3] Pulaski County Births-1853-1893.
[4] Pulaski County Births-1853-1893.
[5] 1930 Pulaski County, VA Census.
[6] 1900, 1910, 1920 and 1930 Pulaski County, VA Census.

- 5.3.9. John Bell, Jr. born about 1921.
- 5.4. Robert V. born February 1880 married Agnes Underwood on 19 November 1899 in Pulaski; the daughter of Andrew Joshua Underwood and Sarah Jane Kennedy. Agnes is listed as widowed in the 1920 and 1930 Pulaski County census. Children:
  - 5.4.1. Jessie Savella born 09 March 1900 in Pulaski married Edward Luther Haynes Stafford.[1]
  - 5.4.2. Mary Alva born about 1903.[2]
  - 5.4.3. Lee Roy born about 1907.
  - 5.4.4. Harry Genett.[3]
- 5.5. Myrtle born 26 February 1881 married Robert L. Underwood on 07 October 1902 in Pulaski. Robert was the son of Andrew Joshua Underwood and Sarah Jane Kennedy. Robert died 23 July 1905; Myrtle died 19 February 1912. They are buried in the Hunter Cemetery. Children:[4]
  - 5.5.1. Herbert born about 1903.
  - 5.5.2. Stella born about 1905.
- 5.6. George Edward born about 1882 married Lucinda Motley on 17 January 1903 in Pulaski County.

  On August 1, 1905 G. E. Combs and Lucinda his wife of Pulaski and Robert Combs and Aggie his wife of Bluefield, Mercer County, West Virginia conveyed to Cam Combs and Frank Combs of Pulaski all their interest in their father's land 125 acres.[5]

- 5.7. Nellie G. born 01 October 18837 married John Milton Underwood 29 November 1904 in Pulaski. John was the son of Andrew Joshua Underwood and Sarah Jane Kennedy. Nellie died in 1914, buried in the Hunter Cemetery. John was born 28 July 1880 and died 11 April 1957, also buried in the Hunter Cemetery. They had two daughters:
  - 5.7.1. Jennie.
  - 5.7.2. Lucille.
- 5.8. Foy Crockett born about 1886 married Alice Stone on 20 February 1915 in Pulaski County. Children from the 1920 and 1930 Pulaski County census:
  - 5.8.1. Robert Wesley born 09 October 1915 married Lela Hazel Woodyard. She was the daughter of Albert Sidney Woodyard and Rhoda P. White. Robert died 09 November 1985. Robert served in World War II.
  - 5.8.2. Evelyn born about 1918.
  - 5.8.3. Dorothy born about 1920.
  - 5.8.4. Dicie born about 1922.
  - 5.8.5. Foy Crockett, Jr. born 02 March 1924 and died 21 December 1956; buried in the Hunter Cemetery. Served in World War II.
  - 5.8.6. Joseph W. born about 1926.
  - 5.8.7. Mary E. born about 1930.
- 5.9. Frank.
- 5.10. Charles W. born 22 March 1888 married Ethel Vest on 22 June 1921 in Pulaski.
- 5.11. Mabel B. born November 1893 married Oscar Leroy Millirons on 14 September 1914 in Pulaski County. Children:
  - 5.11.1. Franklin Hicks.

---

[1] Bobby Talbert, Underwood Family.
[2] 1900 Pulaski County, VA Census.
[3] Bobby Talbert, Underwood Family.
[4] 1910 Pulaski County, VA Census.
[5] Pulaski County, VA Deed Book 25, p. 156.

       5.11.2. <u>Glenn.</u>
       5.11.3. <u>Opal.</u>
       5.11.4. <u>Raymond.</u>
6. <u>Mary Arabella</u> born 07 April 1854 married Turner Bascom Wheeler 01 February 1877 in Giles County.
7. <u>Paulina C.</u> born 03 October 1858 married David Crockett Akers on 31 January 1874 in Pulaski County. He was the son of Davidson Akers and Rachel Graham. Their children:[1]
    7.1. <u>Mary Lizzie</u> born 04 July 1876 in Pulaski.
    7.2. <u>Willie</u> born 11 February 1878 in Pulaski.
    7.3. <u>Emma V.</u> born December 1879 in Pulaski.
    7.4. <u>William C.</u> born 03 November 1881 in Pulaski.
    7.5. <u>Pearl R.</u> born August 1883 in Pulaski.
    7.6. <u>Maggie L</u>. born 28 August 1891 in Pulaski.
    7.7. <u>William</u> McKinley born June 1897.[2]

John Combs and Phoebe R. Wills' children:

8. <u>Neta Morgan</u> born August 1884 in Pulaski[3] married George Julian Allen on 02 May 1913. *See Allen Family.
9. <u>Georgiana</u> born 10 February 1886 in Pulaski.[4]
10. <u>Argie Bell</u> born 18 February 1888 in Pulaski.[5]
11. <u>Henry</u> born about 1890.[6]

---

[1] Pulaski County, VA Births-1853-1893.
[2] 1900 Pulaski County, VA Census.
[3] Pulaski County, VA Births 1853-1893.
[4] Pulaski County, VA Births 1853-1893.
[5] Pulaski County, VA Births 1853-1893.
[6] 1900 Pulaski County, VA Census.

COLLINS FAMILY

English; patronymic derived from the middle and last part of the Biblical name Nicholas "people's victory", a very popular saint's name known throughout the Western World due to St. Nicholas, the fourth century Bishop of Myra, patron saint of children.[1]

James Collins was born in NC in about 1821 and was married to Mary Ann who was born about 1823 in NC. Mary Ann's maiden name is unknown. James and Mary Ann were listed in the 1850 Giles County census, the 1860 Wythe County census and the 1870 Bland County Census. Their birthplace and ages were taken from the above censuses.

On August 9, 1859 James Collins bought 186 acres of land from Madison Shelton and wife Elsey; "being in the county of Wythe on little Walkers Creek".[2] From deed records in Wythe, Madison and wife were living on Little Walkers Creek between 1851 and the time they sold the land to Collins. Shelton put up his land and personal belongings for money owed to Stephen Halsey, Junior…"also twelve head of sheep, three head of cattle, fourteen head of hogs and all the household & kitchen furniture of said Shelton, crops of corn now in the field, one sorrel mare & one rifle gun. In trust to secure Stephen Halsey, Jr. the sum of three hundred dollars by note bearing even date with this deed and due on day after date. Now if the said Shelton shall fail to pay to the said Stephen Halsey, Jr. the said sum of three hundred dollars with the interest thereon accruing on or before the 23rd day of September 1852 then it shall be lawful for the said Michael Moyer to proceed to sell aforesaid tract of land & personal property or so much thereof as will be sufficient to pay the debt & interest due said Halsey & the surplus if any, pay over to said Shelton, having previously given reasonable notice by advertisement of the time & place of said sale".[3]

It can be assumed there was a cabin or house located on this land. It can also be assumed that Madison paid the loan since he sold the land to James Collins in 1859.

Children of James and Mary Ann Collins:
1. Sarah J. born about 1848 married Robert P. Hancock on 08 December 1872 in Bland. Robert was born about 1852. From the Bland County Marriage Book 1, Robert's mother was Eliza A. Hancock. There was a Robert King listed with David King and Eliza A. King in the 1860 Wythe County and 1870 Bland County census. There is a Robert and Sarah King living next door to James and Mary Ann in the 1880 Bland County census. There is no other information available for this couple.
2. William L. born on 12 October 1852 and died 28 August 1938 in Wythe County. He married Mildred Ann Akers on 22 August 1874 in Bland County. Mildred was the daughter of Moses Akers and Catherine Altizer. *See Moses Akers, Sr. Family
3. Elizabeth born October 1854[4] married James Collins on 25 February 1890. James was born May 1850[5] in Wisconsin. He was the son of Edmond and Elizabeth Collins. James was listed as a widower. A comment must be made on the children of James and Elizabeth; some of them were born before their marriage date. Minnie Caldonia was listed in the Bland County Marriage Book as James and Lizzie's daughter but she was born about 1876 and was listed with James and Mary Ann Collins in the 1880 Bland census as their granddaughter. The children must be examined closely to determine exactly which wife they belong to. From the 1880 Pulaski County census, the children of James Collins and first wife: Louisa J. born

---
[1] *What is in Your Name?* Vitalog.net. website http://www.vitalog.net/cgi-bin/select_name.cgi
[2] Wythe County, VA Deed Book 21, pg. 511.
[3] Wythe County, VA Deed Book 21, pg. 511.

about 1873, Dolly B. born about 1876, James C. born about 1877, William P. born about 1879. The 1900 Bland census lists the following for James and Elizabeth: Mary J. born about 1889 and Stuart M. born about 1892. There may one other, Josie Collins born 1883 who married Kelly Orson Hamilton in Bland on 15 September 1909 and lists James and Lizzie as her parents. James C. Collins (age 60) remarried on 04 July1909 in Bland to Elizabeth Anderson. Both were listed as widowed. James was listed in the 1910 Bland census with son Stuart and listed as widowed.

4. John H. born June 1858[1] in Bland and married Gillie B. Akers on 14 April 1885 in Bland County. Gillie was born April 1860 to Moses Akers and Sarah Brawley. *See Moses Akers, Jr. Family

5. Nancy was born January 1860[2] and married Maxwell Hill on 01 January 1880 in Bland County. Maxwell was born October 1859[3] and was the son of Martin and Elizabeth Hill. Maxwell and Nancy were living in Raleigh County, West Virginia in 1920. Children from Bland County, Virginia Births: 1861-1896, the1900 Bland census and 1920 Raleigh Co, WV census:
   - 5.1. Jenny.
   - 5.2. Charles J.
   - 5.3. Lucy E.
   - 5.4. Mary.
   - 5.5. Cora J.
   - 5.6. Stephen.

6. Rosa born about 1862[4] in Bland and married Peter H. Tickle on 10 September 1884 in Bland County. Peter was born about 1862 in Bland to Peter Conrad Tickle and Mary Ann Journell. Bland County births lists children:
   - 6.1. William born April 1885.
   - 6.2. James born 01 April 1887.

A contract was made between John H. Collins and James Collins on October 6, 1886. John and James mutually agreed that John H would take care of and comfortably maintain James and his wife during their natural lives. In return, John H. would have as his own the portion of land on Walkers Little Creek where James Collins lived. If John did not abide by the agreement, he would get nothing. The paper was to be treated as James' last will and testament. It was presented and recorded as a will, as James Collins was dead, in December 1890.[4]

In 1909, John Collins and Gillie, his wife sold to Elizabeth J. Clark, part of the Madison Shelton survey 1 ½ acres.[5]

---

[1] 1900 Bland County, VA Census.
[2] 1900 Bland County, VA Census.
[3] 1900 Bland County, VA Census.
[4] Bland County, VA Will Book 1, p. 475-476.
[5] Bland County, VA Deed Book 10, pg 172.

CORDER FAMILY

English, originally referred to a craftsman who made and sold cords and ropes.[1]

Edward Corder I was born about 1700 in England and died about 1770 in Frederick County, Virginia. He emigrated from England in 1722 aboard the ship "Gilbert", captained by Darby Lux. He was an English convict transportee and former inmate of Newgate Prison, who later accompanied George Washington in his early years as a surveyor. His wife's name is unknown at this time. He had a son Edward born about 1730.

Edward II was married to Susannah. On Sept. 6, 1777, Edward Corder took oath of allegiance sworn to state in Captain McCorkles Company of Montgomery County by Stephen Trigg. In April 1781 he was listed in a company of Montgomery County Militia. Edward Corder was on the Montgomery County tax lists from 1787 through 1801. He was on the Wythe County personal property tax lists in 1802 with one tithable over 16 (himself). From 1803 to 1806 there were two Edward Corders taxed, then just one through 1811. He died about 1810. Edward and Susannah had nine children. One being Benjamin born about 1769.

Benjamin Corder married Rebecca Runyon 07 April 1798 in Montgomery County. Rebecca was the daughter of Isaac Runyon and Geertje Charity Haganan. Benjamin died 28 August 1851, age 87, interred in St. John Cemetery, Union township, Ohio. Benjamin and Rebecca had ten children.

COURT OF PROBATE OF THE COUNTY OF AUGLAIZE, OHIO : The said decedent died seized in few simple___ of the following real estate, situate in the town of St. John in the said county of Auglaize. In lots, #1,10- 27 & 29 in said town, the following persons are the heirs, having the next estate of inheritance in the premises above declared from said decedent, namely: John Corder, Elias Corder and Rebecca Barber residing in County of Auglaize aforesaid: John Lusk and Mary his wife, and James Corder residing in the State of Missouri, Jacob Bowls and his wife Susannah residing in the State of Ohio; William Corder residing in the State of Virginia; John Wellman residing in the state of Kentucky, and his wife Hannah Wellman. Petition of Robert C. Layton, Adm. of Estate of Benjamin Corder, decd. Dated 07 July 1853 William Corder was born about 1808 in Montgomery County.[2]

William married Rebecca Runyon 27 September 1825 in Montgomery County. She was the daughter of Richard Runyon and Hannah Carden. They had four children. One being Benjamin F. born about 1828, married Julian B. Hammonds 20 January 1849 in Giles County. They had five children: Mary J.. married James H. Bird; William B., James Larkin; Samuel Snow married Mary Lucy Hudgins; Sallie A. married J. G. Cassell.

James Larkin Corder married Minerva Pauley on 16 June 1874 in Bland County. He married 2nd Sarah Elizabeth Davis on 28 March 1889 in Bland. James married 3rd Mary Elizabeth Hancock on 04 March 1914 in Bland

Children of James Larkin and Minerva from the 1880 Bland County census and Bland marriage records:

---

[1] *What is in Your Name?* Vitalog.net. website http://www.vitalog.net/cgi-bin/select_name.cgi
[2] Courtesy of Estelle Corder Txcorder@aol.com.

1. <u>Ida Josephine</u> born about 1873 in Bland married John Henry Epperson on 31 January 1901 in Bland. John Henry was born about 1862 and was the son of Edward Elisha Epperson, Sr. and Drucilla P. Epperson.
2. <u>Cora Ethel</u> was born 23 June 1875 in Bland and died 11 July 1907. She is buried in the Burton Cemetery, Little Walkers Creek, Bland County. She married James Andrew Burton on 22 December 1892. He was born 17 January 1868 in Bland and died 08 September 1909. James was the son of James Thomas Burton and Mary Elizabeth Muncy. He is buried in the Muncy Cemetery in Bland. Children from the 1900 Bland census:
    2.1. <u>Samuel Vance</u> born 08 October 1896; died 10 April 1956. Buried in the Bland Cemetery in Bland.
    2.2. <u>Miller T.</u> born 16 May 1894; died 04 October 1918. Killed in WW I. Buried in the Muncy Cemetery, Bland.
    2.3. <u>Mary J.</u> born July 1895.[1]
    2.4. <u>Ida L.</u> born April 1898.[2]
    2.5. <u>Nannie L.</u> born August 1899.[3]
3. <u>Benjamin Larkin</u> was born 06 March 1877 and died 19 March 1952. He married Frances Bell Davis on 10 August 1899 in Bland. She was born 19 November 1879 and died 25 February 1956. Frances' parents were James Whitten Davis and Nancy Jane King. Benjamin and Frances are buried in the Hidden Valley Cemetery #1, Little Walkers Creek, Bland.

Benjamin Larkin bought land from Meek Hoge Davis; it was conveyed to Benjamin on June 12, 1903 "…known as the R. S. King land estimated to contain 40 acres…described in the Bland County Deed Book 4, p. 377…".[4] This land was part of the Bennett King survey conveyed to Robert King by James Washington King wife Sarah and sons, James D., William S. and Allen A. King. This conveyance was dated 18 March 1881.

Francis Bell Davis Corder was the second Post Master of the Carnot Post Office. She was confirmed as Post Master on June 2, 1929 and assumed charge on July 29, 1929.[5]

Benjamin Larkin Corder and Frances Bell Davis's children:
   3.1. <u>William Edward</u> born about 1901. *See Banes/Davis Family
   3.2. <u>Benjamin Victor</u> born 09 June 1902 married Ivan Hope Davidson.
   3.3. <u>Edna Bell</u> born 03 September 1904 and died 08 February 1911; buried in the Hidden Valley Cemetery #1, Little Walkers Creek.
   3.4. <u>Samuel Richard</u> born 16 October 1906 married Beulah Virginia Clemons. He died 09 September 1979, buried in the Hidden Valley Cemetery #1.
   3.5. <u>Archie C.</u> born 11 November 1908 married Mamie Montgomery. He died 11 February 1990; buried in the Hidden Valley Cemetery #1.
   3.6. <u>James Larkin</u> born 07 August 1911 and died 15 April 1998. He married Agnes Ruth Davis. She was born 04 January 1919 and died 11 February 1996. Ruth was the daughter of Charles Calvin Davis and Lucy Clara Davis. Jim and Ruth are buried in the Goshen Methodist Church Cemetery.
   3.7. <u>Alvie Garland</u> born 14 May 1913 and died 05 March 1998. He married Lelia Pearl Millirons, daughter of Estell Hoge Millirons and Ella Augusta Akers. Lelia was born

---

[1] 1900 Bland County, VA Census.
[2] 1900 Bland County, VA Census.
[3] 1900 Bland County, VA Census.
[4] Bland County, VA Deed Book 8, pg. 161.
[5] National Archives and Record Administration, Washington, DC, RG 68, Site Location Reports, Carnot Post Office.

23 January 1913 and died 10 April 1987. Alvie and Lelia are buried in the Grandview Memory Gardens, Bluefield, West Virginia.
- 3.8. Meek D. was born 16 June 1915 and died January 1988 in Botetourt County, Virginia
- 3.9. Amy Ruth was born 30 May 1917 and died 06 September 1917. She is buried in the Hidden Valley Cemetery #1
- 3.10. Fayette Francis was born 10 August 1918 and died 02 May 2000 in Pulaski County. He married Clara Elizabeth Brunk in Bland. Clara is the daughter of Walter Herbert Brunk and Nancy Cathern Banes. Fayette is buried in Highland Memory Gardens, Dublin, Pulaski County.
- 3.11. Louella
4. James born about 1879.
5. Samuel Madison born about 1881 married Effie Pearl Hancock on 23 January 1902 in Bland. Effie was born 21 March 1878 and died 12 February 1934 in West Virginia. Her parents were Marcus L. Hancock and Margaret Virginia Wyrick.
6. Emily Lea born 17 March 1885 and died 20 May 1911. She married Elexander Stinson Hancock on 21 May 1903 in Bland. He was born 21 December 1878 and died 01 June 1951. Elex was the son of George Washington Hancock and Sarah J. Pauley. Children:
   - 6.1. Wilbur Weeden born 12 September 1904 married Carrie Belle McMeans. Wilber died October 1986. He is buried in the West End Cemetery, Wythe County.

     Mrs. Carrie Bell Hancock was the third Post Master of Carnot having been approved on April 28, 1939.[1]

     Wilber W. Hancock was the fourth Post Master of Carnot having assumed charge of the post office on January 1, 1945; confirmed on May 22, 1945. The Carnot Post Office was closed on July 19, 1950; all mail sent to the Long Spur Post Office.[2]

   - 6.2. George Larkin born 21 May 1906 married Helen Nester.
   - 6.3. Annie Elizabeth born 29 February 1908 married Howard Preston Millirons. She married 2nd Lewis Peyton Hoback. Annie died 25 April 1994 in Wythe County. She is buried in the West End Cemetery, Wythe County. *See Akers Family
   - 6.4. Albert Mitchell born 02 September 1910.

Sometime between 1900-1910 [they were listed in the 1900 Bland census] James and Sarah Davis Corder moved to Pierce County, South Dakota. Sarah supposedly died there in 1908.

Children of James Larkin and Sarah Elizabeth Davis from Bland County, Virginia Births: 1861-96 and the 1900 Bland census
7. Virgie D. born January 1890.
8. Walter T. born May 1891.
9. Mollie N. born 21 May 1893.
10. Vance S. born July 1895.
11. John Roach born April 1897 married Gladys Brown Burton 20 June 1931 in Bland.
12. Sallie E. born September 1899.

---

[1] National Archives and Record Administration, Washington, DC, RG 68, Postal Records, Site Location Reports.
[2] National Archives and Record Administration, Washington, DC, RG 68, Postal Records, Site Location Reports.

Children of James Larkin and Mary Elizabeth Hancock from the 1920 and 1930 Bland census and Bland County Marriage Book:
13. George born about 1919.
14. Mary Elizabeth born about 1920 married Robert Luther Hancock on 16 July 1933 in Bland. He was born 21 April 1915 and was the son of Saunders Helton Hancock and Carrie Nellie Louisa Hancock.
15. Grace born about 1922.

DAVIS

English, patronymic (of, relating to, or derived from the name of one's father or a paternal ancestor) derived from the Old Testament name David "beloved", the patron saint of Wales.[1]

Henry Davis Family

William Davis was born about 1781 in Virginia.[2]. He died between 1850 and 1860 as he was not listed in the 1860 Carroll County, Virginia census. William married Judith; her maiden name is unknown. She was born about 1803 in Virginia.[3] She died 28 February 1865 in Carroll County. William and Judith had four known children: Angelina born about 1831 married Andrew J. Franklin; James born about 1842; Susan Elizabeth born about 1843 married William Anderson Smythers and Henry.

Henry Davis was born in Carroll County, Virginia on 05 May 1844. He died on 15 February 1906 in Wytheville, Wythe County. On 28 February 1863, he married Margaret Fowler in Carroll County. She was the daughter of Samuel L. Fowler and Margaret Stoots. Margaret was born 05 March 1841 in Carroll County and died 02 May 1905 in Bland. Henry and Margaret are buried in the Goshen Methodist Church Cemetery.[4]

Henry Davis Margaret Fowler
Submitted by Juanita Bentley

It is not known why Henry moved to Bland County. From the 1870 Bland census, page 380, Henry was living in the Mechanicsburg district but not on Little Walkers Creek. Neighbors included the following families: Almarine Woodyard, Letitia Raines, William P. Mustard, A. J. Nye and J. H. Hoiliman. Henry was listed as not owning real estate.

Henry Davis bought land from the Joshua Mustard heirs sometime between 1870 and 1880. The land was not conveyed until after Henry had died. On September 10, 1906, the land was conveyed to "…C. A. Davis, J. E. Davis, F. V. Davis, Mrs. L. V. Davis, C. C. Davis, Mrs. B. J. Kitts, Mrs. T.. B. Parcell, Mrs. A. J. Ritter, H. H. Davis, J. J. Davis, who are the children and heirs at law of Henry Davis deceased…" by Arthur J. Porterfield, special commissioner of Bland County. "That whereas by decree of the Circuit Court of Bland County, Virginia duly rendered by

---

[1] *What is in Your Name?* Vitalog.net. website http://www.vitalog.net/cgi-bin/select_name.cgi
[2] 1850 Carroll County, VA Census.
[3] 1850 Carroll County, VA Census.
[4] Juanita Cox Bentley kindly donated much of the Henry Davis family information.

the Judge thereof in vacation as prescribed by law in the Chancery cause therein pending in the name of Henry Davis v. Nye Mustard et. als. and which after the death of said Henry Davis by decree therein rendered on the 15th day of March 1906 was duly revived in the name of the said parties of the second part as the heirs at law of said Henry Davis Dec'd., and in which cause amended and supplemental bill was filed and duly matured against all the defendants therein including the heirs at law of Nye Mustard deceased and J. H. Mustard deceased and in said cause amongst other things it was adjudged, ordered and decreed that the said Henry Davis in his lifetime had fully paid the purchase money for the lands in the bill and proceedings mentioned which he bought of J. J. Mustard and J. H. Mustard and which the said J. J. Mustard and J. H. Mustard had purchased from the Court's Comr. In the Chancery suit of Sol. B. King v. Joshua Mustard's heirs and others that the said Henry Davis in his lifetime was entitled to a deed conveying to him the legal title to the said land and all interest therein and it was further decreed that the said A. H. Porterfield as the Court's Commissioner should by proper deed with covenants or special warranty should convey the said land in said Chancery causes mentioned to the said parties of the second part as the heirs at law of Henry Davis Deceased. Now therefore this deed witnesseth that in consideration of the premises aforesaid and by virtue of the decree aforesaid the said party of the first part as Commissioner as aforesaid doth hereby grant and convey of special warranty unto the said parties of the second part that certain tract or parcel of land in said Chancery causes mentioned and being what is known as the old Joshua Mustard tract of land and which lies on the waters of Walker's Little Creek in Bland County, Virginia near the Pulaski County line and adjoins the lands owned or formerly owned by Saml. C. Davis and others and being the same lands owned by Joshua Mustard Deceased and the same lands owned and occupied by the said Henry Davis in his lifetime and now owned and occupied by his heirs. It being the intention and effect to convey all the land in said tract as fully to all intents and purposes as if the land was specifically described by metes and bounds".[1]

On November 4, 1884, W. J. Lambert and wife Sarah E. conveyed 7 acres to Henry Davis being the same land bought of David Y. Hamblin.[2]

W. N. Harman and wife Orlevia conveyed 8 acres to Henry Davis... corner of land sold to W. Hamblin and to Wm Lambert, thence with said Hamblin's line to said Davis old patent line and thence with the calls of said patent line to where the same intersects the said Harman's line of the 2832 acre patent at the county line...".[3]

Henry Davis applied to the Post Office Department in Washington, DC on May 4, 1891 for the establishment of a post office at Long Spur, Bland County, Virginia. The application was sent to Mr. Henry Davis care of the Post Master of Bland C. H. [Court House]. The Long Spur Post Office was to be located in the Township of Mechanicsburg; which would be carried from Long Spur to Wytheville, Virginia, on which no mail was then being carried on Route number 11725 [postal route number]. The mail would be carried once per week. The names of the nearest post offices: Mechanicsburg, six miles to the north; Pulaski City, fifteen miles to the south; Point Pleasant, 8 miles to the northwest. The nearest creek was Walkers Little Creek and the post office would be located ¼ mile on the north side of it. The number of residents supplied by the new post office was two hundred. A map was supplied by Henry Davis drawn at random and without

---

[1] Bland County, VA Deed Book 9, pg. 344.
[2] Bland County, VA Deed Book 5, pg. 33.
[3] Bland County, VA Deed Book 6, pg. 137.

instruments by W. A. Harman of Point Pleasant, Virginia. At the same time, a new post office was opened in Crockett's Cove, Wythe County.[1]

From Minnie Davis Parsell's articles: "There had never been a Post Office on Little Creek or a mail route. Daddy told Mother he was going to get up a petition for a post office. He went out with a paper and come back and said everyone had signed it . He sent it off and it soon came back and he had the Post Office. A 2c stamp sent a letter and a postal was 1c. He needed a Postmaster and a place for the Post Office. He went to his mill and upstairs to the store at the end of the counter he set up his Post Office. It was very private. This was in 1865." Also, "Jack Carr worked the year around for Daddy for 25c a day and his board. He made him the mail carrier. There was just mail on Saturday. He had to carry it on his shoulder. He walked about two miles up Spur Branch, then across Big Walkers Mountain. There wasn't any road across the mountain, just a walking path. The mail was carried to Mechanicsburg and back. This post office was named Larton. The mail was carried like this for several years. They changed the mail route to go down the creek to Poplar Hill and the name was changed to Long Spur, Virginia. This route had five fords to cross. My brother, Coma took the mail on horseback a long while and then he used a horse buggy until the cars came in. Even then they still had to ford the water." Later, Comie's son, Jasper Hampton carried the mail for many years.

On Tuesday, March 12, 1907, a suit was brought before the Circuit Court of Bland County between J. E. Davis et als [meaning "and others"] Complainants versus C. C. Davis et als. Defendants "...whereof it is adjudged, ordered, and decreed that the Complainants and Defendants as the heirs at law and devisees of Henry Davis deceased, are entitled to partition of the lands in the bill and proceedings mentioned and to have the same partitioned in kind, it is therefore adjudged, ordered and decreed that S. C. Chumbley, Jno. C. Mustard and L. D. Repass be, and they are hereby appointed Commissioners for the purpose, and are directed, at as early a day as possible to go upon the lands of which the said Henry Davis died seized and possessed and which lies on Walker's Little Creek in Bland County, Virginia, and is the same lands set forth in Complainant's bill and the same land devised by the will of the said Henry Davis as stated in the bill, and said commissioners will divide and partition said land amongst the children and devisees of said Henry Davis...". It further reads "some of the heirs of Henry Davis have sold their shares to some of the other heirs...that Henry Davis in his lifetime sold to Elizabeth Carr who is now the wife of C. A. Davis, a small parcel of land set forth in a contract in writing signed by the said Henry Davis dated on the 15th of May 1897, and which is filed with the records of this suit..." it goes on to say Elizabeth Carr now Elizabeth Davis land will be laid off first. This partition lists the following:

Lot No.1—assigned to Coma A. Davis, it being 3/11 in value of the whole tract...2/11 bought of J. J. Davis and Mrs. Alice Ritter. It contained a total of 108 acres and 60 square rods.

Lot No.2—assigned to Charles C. Davis being 3/11 in value of the whole tract...2/11 bought of W. T. Davis and H.H. Davis. It contained 86 acres and 122 square rods.

Lot No.3—assigned to Robert H. Kitts and Mrs. Bertha J. Kitts being 4/11 in value of the whole tract...purchased from J. E. Davis, Louisa V. Davis and F. V. Davis. It contained 130 acres and 70 square rods.

Lot No.4—assigned to Ms. T. D. Parsell, being her share containing 32 acres and 125 square rods.

---

[1] National Archives and Record Administration, Washington, DC, RG 68, Site Location Reports, Long Spur Post Office.

Henry and Margaret Fowler Davis's children:
1. <u>James Edward</u> born 01 May 1864 in Carroll County and died 24 October 1934. James married Ollie E. Byrd on 27 May 1886 in Bland. Ollie was born 02 April 1866 in Bland and died on 27 October 1934. Her parents were John and Susan Byrd. James and Ollie are buried in the Goshen Methodist Church Cemetery. James and Ollie lived on the Pulaski side of Little Walker's Creek about three miles from the Bland County line in the same house Walter "Pug" Vance Millirons lived in later years.

On October 16, 1908 Charles W. Fletcher and Aldora Fletcher, his wife conveyed land to Ollie E. Davis and J. E. Davis her husband two tracts of land on Little Walkers Creek. The first containing 20 acres and the second tract 96 acres. The two tracts are the same that was conveyed to Charles Fletcher from Mariah Mustard by deed bearing date the 5th day of April, 1902.[1]

John S. Draper, special commissioner of the Circuit Court of Pulaski County in Chancery cause of J. M. LeFew, Guardian -vs- Beatrice and Gladys King 1913 was directed to sell at public auction 16 ½ acres the property of said Kings. Draper sold the land to J. E. Davis and wife, he being the highest bidder. J. E. Davis directed the deed be made to Morrison Vandergrift. This was the same land conveyed to Bessie King by M. N. King and wife April 7, 1907…refer to Deed Book 27, page 148.[2] This land was actually conveyed to Bessie King by F. V. Davis and wife. *Note (Bessie was the wife of Isaac Henry King; her maiden name was LeFew; Isaac was called Harvey in all records, he died on 13 April 1911).

In September 1914, James and Ollie Davis conveyed 27 ¾ acres to Morrison Vandergrift.[3]

Morrison Vandergrift (bachelor) of Keystone, McDowell County, West Virginia conveyed to R. L. Chandler 27 ¾ acres on January 3, 1919.[4]
James E. and Ollie to R. L. Chandler 12 ½ acres in May 1919.[5]

Ollie E. and husband J. E. Davis to R. L. Chandler 16.6 acres …"corner to T. B. King…" in September 1926.[6]

James Edward Davis's heirs sold the remainder of his land to Carl and Ralph Chandler sons of Robert Lee Chandler.[7]
James and Ollie's children:
1.1. <u>Wise L.</u> born 18 November 1888; he married Martha Ethel Parsell on 26 November 1913 in Bland County. Martha was born in July 1896 to Calvin "Kelly" Parsell and Cynthia Margaret Pegram. Clayton Parcell of Giles County believes Martha Parsell Davis died in Maryland.
1.2. <u>Susan</u> born 19 November 1889; she married John William Patton on 22 April 1908 in Bland County. He was born about 1876 and was the son of J. R. and Mary Patton. They were living in Pulaski in 1910. John and Susan are buried in the Mechanicsburg Cemetery, Bland County. James Edward Davis built the future "Chandler" house for his

---

[1] Pulaski County, VA Deed Book 27, p. 439.
[2] Pulaski County, VA Deed Book 35, p. 283.
[3] Pulaski County, VA Deed Book 35, p. 285
[4] Pulaski County, VA Deed Book 41, p. 19.
[5] Pulaski County, VA Deed Book 40, p. 599.
[6] Pulaski County, VA Deed Book 54, p. 317.
[7] Pulaski County, VA Deed Book 81, p. 493.

daughter and son-in-law Susan and John Patton in 1901. The house burned down in February 1979. Susan and John Patton are buried in the Mechanicsburg Cemetery, Bland Co, VA. Their children:
- 1.2.1. <u>Flossie</u>.
- 1.2.2. <u>Hubert</u>.
- 1.2.3. <u>Henshell</u>.
- 1.2.4. <u>Ellis</u>.
- 1.2.5. <u>Margaret</u>.

1.3. <u>Ada Ann</u> was born about 1896 married Preston S. Amburn on 03 January 1912 in Pulaski County. They were living in Pulaski in 1920. Children from the 1920 Pulaski census; in the 1930 census they were in Bluefield, Tazewell County, Virginia. Children were:
- 1.3.1. <u>W. E.</u>
- 1.3.2. <u>Preston S. Jr.</u>
- 1.3.3. <u>Katherine</u>.
- 1.3.4. <u>Ada Mary</u>.
- 1.3.5. <u>David</u>.
- 1.3.6. <u>Edward</u>.
- 1.3.7. <u>Doris</u>.

1.4. <u>Estel Vance</u> was born 20 May 1903; he married Aryce Selma Davis on 28 March 1924 in Pulaski. Arcie was born 10 April 1905 to Fabious Victor Davis and Susannah Holloway. Children:
- 1.4.1. <u>Zelda Mae</u>.
- 1.4.2. <u>Daniel</u>.
- 1.4.3. <u>David</u>.
- 1.4.4. <u>Linda Jane</u>.

2. <u>William Thomas</u> born 23 November 1865 in Carroll County and died 30 December 1951 in Wythe County. He married Permelia Ann "Nellie" Davis on 30 October 1889 in Bland County. She was the daughter of Samuel Caddell Davis and Elizabeth Agnes Patterson. Permelia was born 04 October 1871 in Bland County and died 07 January 1928 in Wythe County. William and Permelia are buried in the Fairview Methodist Church Cemetery in Wythe County. They lived in Pulaski and later moved to Smith Hollow, Wythe County.
William Thomas and Permelia Ann's children are:

2.1 <u>Roxie Mae</u> never married, was born 30 January 1891 in Pulaski and died 20 August 1961 in Wythe County. She is buried in the Fairview Methodist Church Cemetery in Wythe County.

2.2 <u>Millard Floyd</u> born 31 August 1893 in Pulaski and died 27 December 1973 in Springfield, Clark County, Ohio. He married Ethel Virginia Bowles daughter of Marcus Lafayette Bowles and Mary Etta Tickle. Ethel was born July 1899 and died 12 November 1966. Millard was a World War I veteran. Millard and Ethel are buried in the Glen Haven Memorial Gardens, Clark County, Ohio. Children:
- 2.2.1 <u>Agnes</u> married William Hunt.
- 2.2.2 <u>Lucille</u> married Thomas Rife.
- 2.2.3 <u>Mary Ann</u> married Robert Winegardner.
- 2.2.4 <u>Julia</u> married Charles Richard Meranda.
- 2.2.5 <u>Martin L.</u> married Carolyn Davis

2.3 <u>Edna Margaret</u> was born 08 January 1896 in Pulaski and died 05 February 1984 in Wythe. She married Robert E. Buchanan 16 April 1924 in Wythe. He was born 13 September 1893 and died May 1967. They are buried in the St. Luke's Lutheran Church Cemetery, Wythe. Children:
- 2.3.1 <u>Raymond</u>.

2.3.2 Victor.
2.4 William B. was born 10 January 1898 in Pulaski married Ruth Trent. He died 03 January 1980 in Richmond, Wayne County, Indiana. Children:
2.4.1 Gregory.
2.4.2 Debbie.
2.4.3 Ronald W.
2.5 Florence was born 18 October 1900 in Pulaski and died 26 July 1990. She is buried in the St. Luke Church Cemetery, Wythe County. She married Carl Cecil Halsey, son of Thomas Reed Halsey and Ella M. Bowles. He was born 05 September 1904 and died 25 September 1948. Carl and Florence are buried in the St. Luke's Lutheran Church Cemetery, Wythe County. Children:
2.5.1 James William.
2.5.2 Thomas.
2.5.3 Helen Genevieve.
2.5.4 Carl Cecil, Jr.
2.5.5 Gladys Louise.
2.5.6 Thelma Irene.
2.6 Russell James was born 03 June 1904 in Pulaski and died 24 October 1984 in Springfield, Clark County, Ohio. He married Annie Bowles, daughter of Marcus Lafayette Bowles and Mary Etta Tickle. Russell married 2nd Mary Derr. Russell and Annie are buried in the Glen Haven Memorial Gardens. Russell and Annie's children
2.6.1 Betty Lou.
2.6.2 Russell James, Jr.
2.7 Edith Virginia was born 16 November 1906 in Wythe and died 16 January 1937. She married Robinette Brown Blankenship born to H. J. Blankenship and Mary Hounshell on 28 September 1905. Robinette and Edith are buried in the in the Fairview Methodist Church Cemetery in Wythe County. He died 04 June 1977. Children:
2.7.1 Robinette Brown, Jr.
2.7.2 Donald L.
2.8 Nellie P. was born 29 March 1909 in Wythe and died 27 January 1991. She married William Odell Hoback.
2.9 Bessie A. was born 07 December 1910 in Wythe and died 03 October 1997. She married Martin Luther Felty. Children:
2.9.1 Lois.
2.9.2 Mary Ellen.
2.10 Henry Samuel "Little Henry" never married, was born 22 May 1913 and died 21 December 1985. He is buried in the Fairview Methodist Church Cemetery in Wythe.

3 Fabious Victor was born 13 December 1868 in Bland and died 17 December 1957. He married Susannah Holloway; she was born 25 May 1880 in Butler County, Tennessee and died 04 November 1921 in Pulaski County. Fabious married 2nd Nela Tickle on 07 August 1951 in Pulaski County. Fabious and Susannah are buried in the Goshen Methodist Church Cemetery. Fabious lived in Pulaski County less than ½ mile from the Bland County line on Little Walkers Creek. Fabious served in the Spanish American War, the 2nd Tennessee Volunteer Infantry USA Company M.

Fabious Davis and Susannah Holloway. Submitted by Juanita Bentley.

Fabious and Susannah's children:
- 3.1 Infant (2) 1898/1901 buried in Tennessee.
- 3.2 Fred Pierce was born 05 April 1903 and died 27 October 1982. He married Martha Lawson. Fred and Martha's children were:
    - 3.2.1 Kathleen.
    - 3.2.2 Garland Pierce.
    - 3.2.3 Clifford.
    - 3.2.4 Eugene.
    - 3.2.5 Lockie L.
    - 3.2.6 Peggy Jane.
- 3.3 Aryce Selma was born 10 April 1905 and died 10 March 1971. She married Estel Vance Davis.
- 3.4 Lee Earl, Sr. was born 27 September 1906 and died 04 April 1966. He married Virginia Myrenthia "Vergie' Roark. Children:
    - 3.4.1 Lee Earl, Jr.
    - 3.4.2 Aileen Gayle.
    - 3.4.3 Joseph Donald.
- 3.5 Therman O. was born 07 April 1909 and died 23 May 1981. He married Vergie Gleason. Children:
    - 3.5.1 David.
    - 3.5.2 Irene.
    - 3.5.3 Michael.
- 3.6 Alvin Howard was born 23 December 1910 and died 16 September 1996. He married Dollie Cox. Children:
    - 3.6.1 Clevell.
    - 3.6.2 Donald Alvin Mauyer.
    - 3.6.3 Sharon.
- 3.7 Eavie E. born 03 August 1912 and died 23 May 1946. She married William G. Gleason. Children:
    - 3.7.1 Thomas W.
    - 3.7.2 Rosalee.
    - 3.7.3 Evelyn.
- 3.8 Cora Lee born 01 July 1914; married William Walker Cox. Children:
    - 3.8.1 William Edward.
    - 3.8.2 Juanita B.
    - 3.8.3 Wilma May
- 3.9 Elwood was born 10 September 1915 and died 11 November 1978. He married Hazel Maxine Shell. Children:
    - 3.9.1 Robert Elwood.
    - 3.9.2 Shelby Jean.
    - 3.9.3 Alicia.
- 3.10 Darce Benjamin was born 12 March 1918 and died 18 August 1985. He married Minnie Harris. Children:
    - 3.10.1 Larry Benjamin.
    - 3.10.2 Carol Jean.
- 3.11 Ruby V. born 18 April 1920 and died 26 November 1920.

4 Louisa Virginia was born on 03 February 1870 in Bland County and died 22 March 1917 in Bland County. She married Charles William Davis on 29 September 1891 in Bland. He was born on 17 May 1865 and died 15 October 1950 and was the son of Samuel Caddell Davis and Elizabeth Agnes Patterson. Charles William and Louisa Virginia are buried in the old "Davis" Cemetery, Little Walker's Creek. From Minnie Davis Parsell's articles, "My sister,

Louisa, married Charles Davis. They lived on a farm on Little Creek and had several children. Louisa had a stroke and didn't live long." Charles and Louisa's children:

- 4.1 Effie Ethel married Robert Kelley Brunk. *See Brunk Family.
- 4.2 Andrew W. married Mary Francis Parsell on 23 March 1915 in Bland County. He was born 11 March 1894 and died 29 December 1961 in Giles County. Mary Francis was the daughter of Calvin "Kelly" Parsell and Cynthia Margaret Pegram. She was born on 14 October 1893 in Bland and died 25 August 1980 in Giles County. Andrew and Mary are buried in the Birtchlawn Cemetery, Giles County. Children:
  - 4.2.1 Hubert C.
  - 4.2.2 Frank
  - 4.2.3 Wayne William.
  - 4.2.4 Macie.
  - 4.2.5 Margaret.
  - 4.2.6 Doris.
  - 4.2.7 Charles C.
- 4.3 Genoa Agnes married Houston Neel Brunk. *See Brunk Family.
- 4.4 Ina Augusta married Claude William Lefler on 27 October 1920 in Bland County. She was born 13 March 1902 and died 29 August 1994 in Pulaski. Claude was born 28 February 1900 and died 1969 in Pulaski. He was the son of Thomas Reed Lefler and Mary Jane Kitts. Ina and Claude are buried in the Thornspring Methodist Church Cemetery, Pulaski County. Ina and Claude's children:
  - 4.4.1 Damon Cassell.
  - 4.4.2 Helen Virginia.
  - 4.4.3 Mary Beatrice.
  - 4.4.4 Raymond Isaac.
  - 4.4.5 Claude, Jr.
  - 4.4.6 Margaret Irene.
  - 4.4.7 James Thomas.
  - 4.4.8 Alma Marie.
  - 4.4.9 Beulah Mae.
  - 4.4.10 William Dennis.
- 4.5 Dorothy M. married Albert Brunk *See Brunk Family
- 4.6 Minnie Alberta married Woodrow Wilson Collins. She was born 10 April 1915 in Bland and died 24 December 1992 in Pulaski. Children:
  - 4.6.1 Betty.
  - 4.6.2 Lucille.
  - 4.6.3 Douglas W.
- 4.7 Arthur Adam married Curtis Andrews. He was born 21 October 1916 and died February 1985. Arthur served in the 121st Squadron, F Company, 106th Calvary Group, WWII and received a Bronze Star.

5 Comie Albert married Elizabeth "Nannie" Ellen Carr on 13 July 1893 in Bland County. He was born on 04 February 1872 in Bland and died 17 March 1945 in Bland. Nannie was born 29 November 1876 and died 07 December 1912. She was the daughter of John J. and Elizabeth Carr. Comie married 2nd Edna C. Davis; she was the daughter of James Whitten Davis and Nancy Jane King, Edna was born on 15 September 1891 and died 12 October 1973. Comie, Nannie and Edna are buried in Goshen Methodist Church Cemetery.

On November 7, 1898, Max Grief conveyed 53 acres and 87 ½ rods to C. A. Davis…"beginning on a corner to S. C. Davis…reserving right for wagon road across said land…"[1]

On October 21, 1926 C. A. Davis sold to E. M. Davis 6.8 acres.[2]

Comie and Nannie's children:
5.1   Lucy Clara married Charles Calvin Davis on 24 January 1911 in Bland. She was born in August 1893 and died in 1938. Charles was the son of John Troy Davis and Mary D. Bowles. He was born on 25 September 1887 and died in 1929. Lucy married 2nd Garnett Terry on 25 July 1934 in Pulaski. Garnett was the son of William Saunders Terry and Eugenia Thomas King. He was born 25 June 1904 and died 03 January 1960. Lucy and Charles are buried in the Goshen Methodist Church Cemetery; Garnett in the Hidden Valley Cemetery #1, Bland. Charles and Lucy had children:
       5.1.1   Charlie Ray married Ethel Mae Collins, daughter of George William Collins and Bessie L. Hancock.
       5.1.2   Vance Calvin married Ethel Letha Kitts, daughter of Robert Hutsel Kitts and Bertha J. Davis. They had one son:
             5.1.2.1   Duane Calvin
       5.1.3   Phillip Astor married Violet Etta King on 11 April 1934. Violet was the daughter of Joseph S. King and Emily Etta Pegram.
       5.1.4   Carl Brown married Ida Kate Terry on 11 April 1936 in Bland. Kate was the daughter of William Saunders Terry and Eugenia Thomas King.
       5.1.5   Ruth Agnes married James Larkin Corder, son of Benjamin Larkin Corder and Frances Bell Davis. *See Corder Family.
5.1   Emily Jane married Walter Wirt Hall on 12 February 1917 in Bland. Emily was born 04 January 1896 and died 24 January 1982. Walter was born in 1897 and died in 1967. Walter and Emily are buried in the Bland Cemetery, Bland County. Two sons were listed in the 1920 Bland County census, Walter age one year and eleven months and Ervin age one month. Ervin Blake married Lois Katherine Davis; daughter of Claude Swanson Davis and Gladys C. Davis.
5.2   Allie Belle married Edgar Carpenter on 23 June 1919 in Bland. Allie was born on 24 February 1897 and died 06 April 1968. Edgar was born on 27 June 1897 in Carroll County and died 28 October 1958. They are buried in the Goshen Church Cemetery. One daughter is buried in the Goshen Cemetery: Lorene M. born 1927 and died 1927. Other children from the 1930 Wythe County Census:
       5.2.1   Comie.
       5.2.2   Raymond.
       5.2.3   Ruby.
       5.2.4   Ernest.
       5.2.5   Geraldine
5.3   Albert Jackson married Nannie Virginia Davis on 11 February 1918 in Bland. Albert was born April 1898. Nannie was born 25 March 1899. She was the daughter of James Whitten Davis and Nancy Jane King. Albert and Nannie were living in the city of Bluefield, Mercer County, West Virginia in 1920 with daughter Beulah who was 1½ years old. Sister-in-law, Amie Davis was living with them. In 1930, Nannie was listed

---

[1] Bland County, VA Deed Book 7, p. 272.
[2] Bland County, VA Deed Book 16, p. 201.

with sister Amy and her son David Martin and her own two daughters, Beulah and Helen.[1]

5.4 Miranda Elizabeth married Adam McKinley Crisco on 06 September 1923 in Pulaski County. She was born 28 September 1900 and died 13 October 1988. Children:
    5.4.1 Calvin Orrin.
    5.4.2 Andrew Wayne.
    5.4.3 McKinley Adam.
    5.4.4 Donald.

5.5 Lena Gray married Estell Crockett Hamblin on 22 July 1925 in Bland. Lena was born on 04 May 1902 and died 21 October 1952. Estell was born 11 December 1893 and died 23 March 1970. Estell was the son of John M. Stafford Hamblin and Sarah Catherine Croy. Children:
    5.5.1 Leonard Hensley.
    5.5.2 Kenneth Stafford.
    5.5.3 Arnold Wade.
    5.5.4 Naomi Adeline.
    5.5.5 Edgar Albert.
    5.5.6 Alma Mae.
    5.5.7 Estell Lewis.
    5.5.8 Eleanor.
    5.5.9 Clinton born 1942; died 1942.
    5.5.10 Lena Bell.

5.6 Clarence L. was born 1905 and died 1962.

5.7 Glen Caudell married Lucy Alberta Meadows. Lucy was the daughter of Wiley Vincent Meadows and Dana Rhoena Hamblin. Glen was born on 31 August 1907 and died 19 May 1984 in Wythe County. Lucy was born on 11 November 1909 and died 21 July 1981 in Wythe County. They are buried in the Beasley Cemetery, Austinville, Wythe County. Children:
    5.7.1 Cadwell.
    5.7.2 Ellen.
    5.7.3 Wesley.
    5.7.4 Carlton Albert.

5.8 Gladys C. married Claude Swanson Davis. Claude was born on 12 May 1905 and died 25 December 1975. He was the son of Hiram Newton Davis and Elizabeth Catherine Farmer. Gladys was born 07 February 1910 and died 26 July 1952. Claude and Gladys are buried in the Goshen Methodist Church Cemetery. Children:
    5.8.1 Lois Katherine.
    5.8.2 Franklin.
    5.8.3 Marie.
    5.8.4 Loraine.
    5.8.5 Edith Jane.
    5.8.6 Aletta.
    5.8.7 Gerald.

Comie and Edna's children:

5.9 Norman married Ruby Irene Meadows. He was born on 16 May 1916 and died 09 November 1961. Ruby was the daughter of Albert Terry Meadows and Laura Emily Millirons. They are buried in the Goshen Methodist Church Cemetery

5.10 Gilbert Frazier married Ola Belle Meadows. He was born in 1919 and died in 1951. Ola was the daughter of John Jesse Meadows and Mary Alberta Davis. She was born

---

[1] 1920 and 1930 Mercer County, West Virginia Census.

21 July 1920 and died in 1984. An infant son born and died 30 April 1940 is buried at the Goshen Methodist Church Cemetery.
- 5.11 Jasper Hampton married Mary Edith Meadows. Mary is the daughter of John Jesse Meadows and Mary Alberta Davis. Jasper was born on 26 February 1920 and died 29 February 2000. He is buried in the Goshen Methodist Church Cemetery.
- 5.12 Violet Virginia married William Victor Combs.
- 5.13 Margaret Naomi married Raymond Linkous.
- 5.14 Ranald Lee married Alma Mildred Leeson. She is the daughter of Thomas J. Leeson and Annie Banes.
- 5.15 Earl Bowman born 19 December 1931.

6 Charles Clinton married Willie Floyd Davis on 29 June 1898 in Bland. Charles was born on 27 June 1875 in Bland and died 15 June 1932. Willie was the daughter of John Troy Davis and Mary D. Bowles. She was born 17 September 1877 in Bland and died 18 April 1942. Charles and Willie are buried in the Goshen Methodist Church Cemetery.
- 6.1 Infant son buried Goshen Methodist Church Cemetery.
- 6.2 Infant son buried Goshen Methodist Church Cemetery.
- 6.3 Cecil Thelma was born 17 February 1899 and died 27 May 1977. She married Edgar Hampton Millirons 20 November 1919 in Bland. Edgar was born 06 June 1896 and died 06 November 1966. He was the son of Rufus Lee Millirons and Annie Kate King. Edgar and Cecil are buried in the Thornspring Methodist Church Cemetery, Pulaski County. Cecil Thelma and Edgar's children:
  - 6.3.1 Geraldine married Robert Lloyd Mathews.
  - 6.3.2 Marie Gertrude married Edward L. Gilbert.
  - 6.3.3 Owen Hampton married Doris Mabe.
- 6.4 Lilia M. was born 23 June 1901 and died 28 March 1977. She married Elmer C. Eversole 31 December 1927 in Pulaski County. Elmer was born 26 June 1905 and died 31 December 1962. Elmer and Lilia are buried in the Thornspring Methodist Church Cemetery, Pulaski County.
- 6.5 Kyle C. was born 06 September 1903. He married Sally Smith.
- 6.6 Wilma was born 23 December 1904 and died March 12 March 1919. She is buried in the Goshen Methodist Church Cemetery.
- 6.7 Hazel Irene was born 03 April 1909. She married Gomez Dalton.
- 6.8 Paul Preston was born 24 July 1914.
- 6.9 Wallace Green was born 25 March 1920 and died 18 January 1973. He married Aileen Hale.

7 Minnie Bell was born 19 December 1877 and died 03 August 1982 in Chapel Hill, North Carolina. She married Tobias "Tobe" Daniel Parsell on 16 June 1891 in Bland. Tobias was the son of John Parsell and Mary Ann Coleman. He was born 26 May 1869 in Franklin County, Virginia and died 21 December 1940 in Giles County. Tobias and Minnie are buried in the Wesley's Chapel Cemetery, Giles County

Minnie Bell Davis Parsell wrote a series of articles rewritten by Minnie's niece, Mrs. Jessie D. Felty of Wytheville for publication in the Bland Messenger and Southwest Virginia Enterprise. Minnie wrote this before her 100th birthday, 19 December 1976. The series of articles were called *A Hundred Years of Livin*. There were sixteen articles in this series. Minnie Bell was truly an amazing woman. She begins, "In my sunset years I have decided to write this history of my life, family, and Bland County." I am quoting some of her writings throughout this book.

Minnie writes of her husband, "Some people ask me how I met my husband. We grew up together in the same neighborhood. His parents lived about five miles from my parents. He was Tobias Parsell. After we were married, he told me when I was a child, he made up his mind to marry me when I grew up, and that's just what happened." She goes on with the story later, "I have heard from my mother say that Tobe's mother, Mrs. Parsell, came and delivered me. Some people say marriages were made in heaven. It seems ours was almost made there."

Tobias and Minnie later sold her father's land to Charles Lee Parsell. On August 24, 1907, Minnie Parsell and husband conveyed 32 acres and 125 square rods to C. L. Parsell.[1]

Tobias and Minnie's children:
- 7.1 Visa Alma was born 01 August 1893. She married Clarence Johnston.
- 7.2 Nina Leecester was born 09 January 1895. She married Kenny Web.
- 7.3 Ernest Victor was born 30 November 1896. He married Verna Darnell Fuqua.
- 7.4 Elsie Virginia was born 27 February 1899 and died 17 December 1903. She is buried in the Wesley's Chapel Cemetery.
- 7.5 Zular Bell was born 30 August 1899 and died 23 September 1903. She is buried in the Wesley's Chapel Cemetery.
- 7.6 Lester Guy was born 30 July 1901.
- 7.7 Laura Elizabeth was born 21 August 1903 and died 09 December 1903. She is buried in the Wesley's Chapel Cemetery.
- 7.8 John Henry was born 19 August 1909 and died in 1962. He married Elizabeth Watts.
- 7.9 William Dailey was born 01 July 1912. He married Rhoda Loutta Brown.
- 7.10 Lewis Russell was born 16 September 1913. He married Lebran Poff.
- 7.11 Tobias Daniel, Jr. was born 20 January 1917. He married Salatha Brown.
- 7.12 Paul Mason was born 01 April 1923. He married Daisy Virginia Caldwell.

8. Bertha J. was born 22 December 1879 and died 24 May 1938. She married Robert Hutsel Kitts 26 December 1900 in Bland; he was born on 10 September 1874 and died 05 December 1964. Robert was the son of Jacob Franklin Kitts and Cynthia Wyrick. Robert and Bertha are buried in the Goshen Methodist Church Cemetery.

Robert was the second Postmaster at the Long Spur Post Office confirmed on March 15, 1906. He retired on January 31, 1945.[2]

From Minnie Davis Parsell's articles, "My Father hired a young man by the month. His name was Robert Kitts. After a year or two, he and my younger sister, Bertha, were married about 1899. He worked on for my Daddy as long as Daddy lived. He must have been a very reliable man because in 1906 Daddy made him Assistant Postmaster and clerk in the store. Robert and Bertha lived in a house near the mill and store, and he became the wealthiest man on Little Creek at one time."

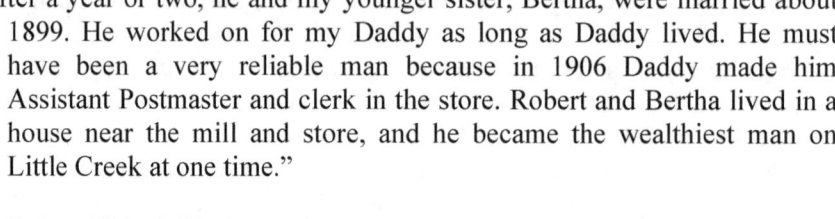

Robert Kitts & Bertha Davis
Submitted by Juanita Bentley

Robert and Bertha's children:
- 8.1 Lute married Mr. Harrington.
- 8.2 Ethel Letha married 1st Hugh David Hamblin on September 12 September 1919 in Bland. Hugh was the son of John M.

---
[1] Bland County, VA Deed Book 9, p. 534.
[2] National Archives and Record Administration, Washington, DC, RG 68, Site Location Reports, Long Spur Post Office.

Stafford Hamblin and Sarah Catherine Croy. Hugh was born 18 March 1892; died on 22 December 1920; buried in the Goshen Church Cemetery. She married 2nd Chester Setliff on 12 March 1923 in Pulaski County. Ethel married 3rd Vance Calvin Davis. He was the son of Charles Calvin Davis and Lucy Clara Davis. Ethel was born on 05 December 1901 and died 01 October 1978. Vance was born on 03 December 1911 and died 30 December 1960. Vance and Ethel are buried in the Goshen Methodist Church Cemetery. Ethel and Hugh had one son:

8.2.1 John Robert born 06 August 1920 married Clemens Robertson.

Ethel and Vance had one son:

8.2.2 Duane Calvin married Betty Newberry.

8.3 Clora married Dewey B. Millirons on 25 November 1926 in Pulaski County. He was the son of William Newton Millirons and Mary Morgan. Lived in Pontiac, Michigan. One son

    8.3.1 Edward.

8.4 Eunice A. 1st married Rome Hancock on 11 November 1924 in Wythe County; she married 2nd Mr. Lucas.

8.5 Alford R. married Ora Lee King. She was the daughter of Joseph S. King and Emily Etta Pegram. Alford was born on 10 August 1908 and died in a logging accident on 13 August 1936. Alford is buried in the Goshen Methodist Church Cemetery. Children:

    8.5.1 Madeline.
    8.5.2 Geneva.

From Minnie Davis Parsell's articles, "I have written before of my sister, Bertha, and her husband, Robert Kitts. They had a terrible tragedy in their family. Born to them were nine girls and one boy. Two of the girls died when they were small. Alfred, their only son was 28 years old. He was married and had two children. He was logging, dragging logs to the sawmill out of the mountain, when the horse ran off. Alfred fell and got his feet and legs tangled in the chains, and the horse dragged him to his death. This was a very sad occasion. This was in 1936."

8.6 Mabel Gertrude married John Thomas Davis. He was the son of Stuart P. Davis and Ethel Murray. He was born on 02 September 1906 and died on 20 April 1970. Mabel was born on 01 March 1910 and died 19 April 1998. They are buried in the Hidden Valley Cemetery #2. Children:

    8.6.1 Euvada.
    8.6.2 Thomas Dayton.
    8.6.3 Mildred.

8.7 Beatrice married Gilford Lafayette Davis. He was the son of Samuel David Davis and Della Rose King. He was born 25 November 1905 and died 05 July 1966. Beatrice was born on 25 August 1911 and died 19 March 1983. Guilford and Beatrice are buried in the Hidden Valley Cemetery #2. Children:

    8.7.1 Clarina.
    8.7.2 Della.
    8.7.3 Gilford David.
    8.7.4 Peggy.
    8.7.5 James Robert.
    8.7.6 Naomi Katherine.
    8.7.7 Judy.

8.8 Ruth married Carl Miller Newberry on 04 February 1937 in Pulaski County.

8.9 Viola E. Lee was born on 02 January 1916 and died 16 March 1916. She is buried in the Goshen Cemetery.

8.10   Fay Rena was born on 22 December 1919 and died 24 December 1924. She is buried in the Goshen Church Cemetery.

9   Alice Gray was born 14 November 1881. She married Edward Ritter on 14 April 1901 in Bland. Edward was born 01 August 1881 and died on 15 April 1946. He was the son of David Spencer Ritter and Hettie Locritta Shufflebarger. Alice died 21 August 1959. They are buried in the Sifford Cemetery, Parrott, Pulaski County. Children:
- 9.1   Howard.
- 9.2   Lawson.
- 9.3   Wendell H.
- 9.4   Richard.
- 9.5   Macy V.
- 9.6   Wilber S.
- 9.7   James.

10   Henry Hampton was born on 12 March 1884 and died 30 December 1962 in Wythe. He married 1st Victoria Agnes Davis Vandergrift on 14 November 1906 in Bland County. She was born 15 September 1875 and died 29 September 1928 of a heart condition. Victoria's parents were John Troy Davis and Mary D. Bowles.

From Minnie Parsell's articles "Brother Henry, the twin, lived in West Virginia and worked there for several years. He married a widow who had twin sons. She was Victoria Vandergrift. She and Henry had two sons of their own. They moved to Wythe County, bought a farm in the head of the Cove. She had heart trouble and was not able to do much. Henry could make the best biscuits of anyone."

Henry and Victoria's children:
- 10.1   Raymond Earl married Genoa Thelma Hamblin on 01 October 1928 in Bland County. Genoa was the daughter of Edward L. Hamblin and Olive Virginia Millirons.
- 10.2   Audrey Hampton married Myrtle Thelma Davis on 08 March 1930 in Bland County. Myrtle was the daughter of Stuart P. Davis and Ethel Murray.

Henry Hampton married 2nd Ida Augusta Parsell on 23 November 1929. Ida was born 14 September 1891 and died 26 July 1957 in Wythe. Her parents were Charles Lee Parsell and Martha Jane Davis.

Henry and Victoria are buried in the Patterson Cemetery in Crockett's Cove, Wythe County. Ida is buried in the Goshen Methodist Church Cemetery. Henry and Ida had no children.

11   John Jasper was born 12 March 1884 and married Julian Bell. King on 14 January 1907 in Pulaski County. She was the daughter of William Davis King and Olivia Virginia Thompson. Julian was born 08 February 1888.[1] One daughter found: Pansy F. born about 1908.[2]
From Minnie Davis Parsell's articles, "John, one of the twins, married Julia Bell King and they made their home in Beckley, West Virginia. He had six children. He worked with mines there."

---

[1] Pulaski County, VA Births, Pulaski County Courthouse.
[2] 1910 Pulaski County, VA Census.

Samuel Caddell Davis Family

William Davis born sometime before 1765 per the 1810 Giles County, Virginia census married Priscilla Grimes probably sometime around mid to late 1770's in unknown place. They had eight known children: Mary born about 1780 married James Drinnon 12 May 1797 in Bath County, Virginia; James born in the 1780's married Rachel Kennison 12 May 1797 in Bath County; Hiram H. born about 1779-80 married Elizabeth "Betsey" Burk 21 July 1808 in Giles; William born about 1781[1] in North Carolina married 1st Lovica (maiden name unknown) and 2nd Nancy Cook Banes; Nancy born about 1793[2] married Mark Kennison in or around Bath County. Later moved to Elkhart County, Indiana; Abraham born about 1791 in Virginia[3] married Sarah Moore 17 March 1817 in Giles; Isaac born between 1790-1800 married Jane Patterson 24 December 1818 in Wythe County, Virginia; Archibald born about 1798 in Virginia[4] married Elizabeth Caddall 16 July 1823 in Giles County.

Archibald and Elizabeth had ten known children: Permelia born about 1824[5] married John Williams 10 January 1845 in Wythe; Samuel Caddell born 21 February 1826 in Giles[6]; Hiram Green born 1827 married Cosby Jane King 22 June 1848 in Wythe County, lived in Bland; Jerome Bonaparte born about 1828, never married, died in Pulaski County sometime between 1880 - 21 May 1887.[7]; Nancy Jane born about 1830 married James Harvey Patterson on 12 December 1850 in Pulaski, lived in Crockett's Cove, Wythe County; Rush F. born about 1831 married Julian M. Morehead on 16 February 1865 in Pulaski; John born about 1833 (no other information); Isaac Newton born 12 January 1834 married Saphronia Surface 17 March 1868 in Giles County; Martha born about 1836 (no other information); Elizabeth born about 1838 (no other information).

Samuel Caddell Davis was born on 21 February 1826 in Giles County and died 23 October 1906 in Bland County. He was the son of Archibald Davis and Elizabeth Caddall. Samuel married 1st Elizabeth "Eliza" Agnes Patterson on 09 September 1851 in Wythe County. Eliza was the daughter of James Patterson and Sarah Halsey. She was born on 25 January 1832 in Wythe and died 08 January 1882 in Bland of consumption. Samuel married 2nd Mary C. Hayes on 02 June 1885 in Wythe. Mary was the daughter of Samuel C. Hayes and Cornelia Chandler. She was born April 1846 in Wythe County and died in 1924 in Wythe County. She is buried in the Mountain View Methodist Church Cemetery, Smith Hollow, Wythe County. There were no children born of this union. Samuel and Eliza are buried in the Patterson Cemetery in Crockett's Cove, Wythe County.

Samuel was listed in the 1850 Pulaski County census living with his parents, Archibald and Elizabeth. Oddly, Samuel was listed as owning the land. No deeds are available before 1853. On February 16, 1853, Samuel bought land from the Summers family which was on the waters of Peak Creek.[8] Samuel conveyed this land to John Wygal on March 31, 1857. On April 5, 1857,[9]

---

[1] 1850 Giles County, VA Census.
[2] 1850 Elkhart County, Indiana Census.
[3] 1850 Giles County, VA Census.
[4] 1850 Pulaski County, VA Census.
[5] 1850 Giles County, VA Census.
[6] Marriage record for Samuel and Mary Hayes, Wythe County, VA Marriage Records.
[7] Pulaski County, VA Will Book 4, p. 204, settlement.
[8] Pulaski County, VA Deed Book 2, p. 561.
[9] Pulaski County, VA Deed Book 3, p. 96.

Samuel was conveyed land on Little Walkers Creek by Joshua Mustard.[1] Samuel's mother, Elizabeth died in Pulaski on 06 July 1856[2] and it seems, he decided to move after her death.

Samuel also bought land on Little Walkers Creek from John C. Crockett, conveyed on February 10, 1869 containing 50 acres.[3]

On September 30, 1870, land was conveyed to Samuel on Little Walkers Creek by Phineas Thurston estimated for tax purposes at 200 acres.[4]

Samuel enlisted in the Confederate States Army, the 45th Infantry Regiment, Company F "The Bland County Sharpshooters" under Captain Andrew J. Grayson. He was issued clothing on December 15, 1864. Samuel was captured at Waynesboro on March 2, 1865; prisoner of war at Fort Delaware on Pea Patch Island in the Delaware River approximately 15 miles south of Wilmington, Delaware. A query was made to the Fort Delaware Society about Private Samuel Davis and in answer, "He was assigned to Prison Division 2 which was most likely one of the wooden barracks located outside of the Fort itself". Samuel took the Oath of Allegiance and was released on June 19, 1865. He was described as having gray eyes with light hair and was five feet eleven inches tall.[5] Samuel probably enlisted on May 29, 1861 in Wytheville with his brother, Rush F. Davis who was also in the 45th. The Forty-Fifth Virginia Infantry was organized on May 29, 1861, and was mustered into Confederate service a few days later. Samuel may have fought in several battles and skirmishes including: August 12, 1861 - contact at Tyree's Tavern near Big Sewell Mountain, Fayette Co., WV; April 10, 1862 - skirmish between Dublin and Pearisburg, Giles County, VA; August 5-31, 1863- operations against Averill's Raid from Winchester, Va.; through Hardy, Pendleton, Highland, Bath, Greenbrier, and Pocahontas Counties, VA and WV; December 29, 1863- engagement Mossy Creek and Talbot Station Jefferson County, TN; May 9, 1864 - engagement, Cloyd's Mountain, Cloyd family farm, Pulaski County, VA; October 19, 1864 - battle, Cedar Creek, Middletown, Shenandoah Co., and Belle Grove, VA; March 2, 1865 - engagement, Waynesboro, Augusta County, VA where Samuel was captured; March 3, 1865 - Unit participated in the evacuation of Charlottesville, VA; General Robert E. Lee surrendered on April 9, 1865 at the Appomattox Court House.

Samuel C. Davis died without a will; his land was partitioned by the Bland County court between his children and submitted to the court on November 15, 1907:[6]

"This cause came upon this day to be heard upon a bill and exhibits filed therewith, duly matured at rules, upon process duly executed, upon the bill taken for confessed as to H. N. Davis, upon the answer of the infant defendants over fourteen, Haynie King and Blanche Davis, and the answers by their guardian ad litem, Wm. C. Thomas, as required by law, and was argued by counsel. Upon consideration of which, and the court being of opinion that the heirs of S. C. Davis, deceased, are entitled to have his lands partitioned in kind; it is therefore adjudged, ordered and decreed that the following free-holders, any three of whom may act, Namely L. D. Repass, Surveyor, John C. Mustard, M. B. Allen… be the same they are hereby directed to go upon the lands of the late S. C. Davis, upon the 8th day of November, 1907, and after being duly sworn, shall partition and allot the lands in the bill mentioned to the following parties in severalty, a part

---

[1] Wythe County, VA Deed Book 20, p. 809.
[2] Pulaski County, VA Births & Deaths.
[3] Bland County, VA Deed Book 1, pg. 380.
[4] Bland County, VA Deed Book 2, p. 118.
[5] The Virginia Regimental Histories Series. 45 vols. Lynchburg: Howard, 1987.
[6] Bland County, VA Deed Book 10, p. 76.

equal to, each one interest in the whole, if this be practicable, having a due regard to the interest of all concerned, that is to say: they shall allot by metes and bounds 1/12 part thereof to the heirs of John T. Davis, deceased; 1/12 part thereof to H. N. Davis; 1/12 part thereof to Emmett Davis assignee of Martha J. Parcell; 3/12 part thereof to David C. Davis, assignee of James W. Davis, Amelia A. Davis and Bettie Corder 6/12 part thereof to R. L. Davis, ½ of which is entitled to in his own right and the remaining as assignee of J. B. Davis, S. C. Davis, Jr. Charles W. Davis, Edna D. Cassell, and Polly Davis, for this purpose they shall meet upon the premises on Friday Nov. 8th 1907."

Lot No. 1—assigned to R. L. Davis, it being 6/12 part in value of the whole tract, 1/12 of which he is entitled to by inheritance, and 5/12 by purchase—containing 170 acres.

Lot No. 2—assigned to S. D. Davis, it being 3/12 in value of the whole tract, being the part acquired by him by purchase from James W. Davis, Permelia A. Davis and Bettie Corder. This lot being assigned in three separate parcels or sections—containing 90 acres and 73 square rods.

Lot No. 3—assigned to the heirs of John T. Davis, it being 1/12 in value of the whole tract—containing 46 acres and 4 square rods.

Lot No. 4—assigned to Emmett Davis, assignee of Martha J. Parsell, it being 1/12 in value of the whole tract—containing 43 acres.

Lot No.5—assigned in two parcels or sections, it being 1/12 in value of the whole tract, to H. N. Davis—containing 43 acres and 47 square rods.

"The tract of 38 acres and 16 square rods, shown on the plat, we find in dispute as to title and therefore make no partition or allotment of it.

-:Addenda:-

Your Commissioners, while on the land, were informed by the parties that where the name "David C. Davis" appears in the Court's order, that it should be S. D. Davis, it being a mistake made in preparing the case. Therefore we use the name S. D. Davis in the assignment of Lot No. 2."

Samuel Caddell Davis

From Minnie Davis Parsell's articles, "Our family had some very dear friends who lived near us. They were the Samuel Davis family. The mother, Elizabeth, became ill and died in 1882 at the age of 50. She had a lingering illness and before she died she could not speak or raise her hands. The family had twins who were about nine years old when their mother died…When the twins were about 14 years old, Edward became sick with typhoid fever and lived only a short while….The father, Samuel Caddell Davis, married again, I do not know when. They called her "Aunt Polly"…Sammy Davis had four children who settled in Wythe County. One was Edna Doan who married Samuel Cassell of Wythe county and lived on a farm on the Fairview Road. They had three children…Then there was Jerome Bonie who married Lou Halsey of Wythe county. They live on a farm in the Fairview neighborhood. They also had three children. Samuel C. Davis married Josie Halsey of the Cove section and settled in the head of Crockett's Cove. They had a large family. Josie died before her children were grown. Sam married Miss Effie Smith. They had two sons. Another daughter, Permelia Ann, married my brother, W. T. (Billy) Davis. They moved to Wythe County and raised ten children."

Children of Samuel C. Davis and Eliza Patterson:
1. James Whitten was born on 30 October 1852 in Pulaski County and died 19 July 1928 in Bland County. He married Nancy Jane King on 26 February 1877 in Bland County. She was

the daughter of David King and Elizabeth Ann Hancock. She was born on 14 July 1859 in Wythe County and died 23 June 1899 in Bland. James and Nancy are buried in the Hidden Valley Cemetery #1.

James lived on the Bennett King land which was willed to David King and later assigned to the Nancy Jane King Davis heirs by Joseph S. King in 1913.[1]

James and Nancy's children:

1.1. <u>Meek Hoge</u> was born 13 February 1878 and died 10 July 1941 in Pulaski County. He married Ressie Clora Kitts on 23 December 1903 in Bland. Ressie was the daughter of Jacob Kitts and Cynthia Wyrick. She was born 03 December 1877 and died 29 August 1958 in Pulaski County. Meek and Ressie are buried in the Hidden Valley Cemetery #1.

Benjamin Larkin Corder bought land from Meek Hoge Davis; it was conveyed to Benjamin on June 12, 1903 "…known as the R. S. King land estimated to contain 40 acres…described in the Bland County Deed Book 4, p. 377…".[2] This land was part of the Bennett King survey conveyed to Robert King by James Washington King wife Sarah and sons, James D., William S. and Allen A. King. This conveyance was dated 18 March 1881.

On June 17, 1915, Z. S. Cecil and Sallie his wife of Augusta County; Julia C. Boyd and Edward her husband; of Aquilla, Texas; Mollie Penn and J. J. Penn; of Bluefield, West Virginia; Fannie Cecil, widow of Charles Cecil of Richmond, Virginia conveyed 110 acres on Little Walkers Creek, Pulaski County to Meek H. Davis.[3]

N. F. White conveyed 123.64 acres to M. H. Davis on January 8, 19212 and another 128.8 acres on January 2, 1928.[4]

Meek Hoge and Ressie's children:

1.1.1. <u>Everett Lawton</u> born 26 November 1904 married Kathleen Vest born 16 September 1901. Everett died on 09 April 1963 and Kathleen died January 1992. They are buried in the Stinston Cemetery, Bland County.

1.1.2. <u>James Burk</u> born 31 October 1906 and died 23 January 1962; buried in the Hidden Valley Cemetery #1.

1.1.3. <u>Fayette Floyd</u> born 21 September 1908 and died 15 August 1972 married Mary Wolfe. Fayette is buried in the Shiloh Methodist Church Cemetery, Bland County.

1.1.4. <u>Wade Hutsell</u> born 05 February 1911 and died 10 January 1980. He married Hazel Irene Faw on 12 February 1936 in Pulaski. Hazel was the daughter of Wiley Henderson Faw and Effie Goodman. Hazel was born on 21 July 1914 and died 02 April 1993. Wade died on 10 January 1980. They are buried in the Hidden Valley Cemetery #1, Bland County

1.1.5. <u>Meek Hoge, Jr.</u> born 15 September 1913 and died 20 February 1968 in Pulaski. He married Viola L. Underwood on 21 August 1936 in Pulaski. Viola was the daughter of Grover C. Underwood and Sallie Sexton. She died on 16 May 2002. They are buried in Highland Memory Gardens, Dublin, Pulaski County.

---

[1] Bland County, VA Deed Book 10, p. 76; Bland County, VA Deed Book 12, p. 243.
[2] Bland County, VA Deed Book 8, pg. 161.
[3] Pulaski County, VA Deed Book 36, p. 265.
[4] Pulaski County, VA Deed Book 58, p. 65.

- 1.1.6. Lola Bell born September 1915.
- 1.1.7. Hubert Raymond born 26 November 1919. Hubert married Ola Belle Meadows, widow of Gilbert Davis. He died 19 March 1982; buried in the Hidden Valley Cemetery #1.
- 1.1.8. Homer Lebert born 03 April 1922 and died March 1987. He married Muriel Young.
- 1.2. Frances Bell married Benjamin Larkin Corder *See Corder Family.
- 1.3. Samuel David was born on 05 November 1881 and died 22 November 1940. He married Della Rose King on 15 November 1905 in Wythe County. Della's parents were Harvey Newton King and Susanna Gray. She was born 20 November 1885 and died on 10 May 1957. Samuel and "Rose" are buried in the Hidden Valley Cemetery #1. They had one adopted son:
  - 1.3.1. Gilford Lafayette who was born 25 November 1905 and died 05 July 1966. He married Beatrice Kitts, daughter of Robert H. Kitts and Bertha J. Davis. She died on 19 March 1983. Guilford and Beatrice are buried in the Hidden Valley Cemetery #2. *See Henry Davis family.
- 1.4. Eliza Ann was born on 17 December 1883 and died 24 March 1938 in Pulaski County. She married Newton Foy White on 01 July 1910 in Bland County. This was Newton's second marriage. He was born 15 January 1857 and died 09 December 1932 in Pulaski County. Newton was the son of James Wilson White. and Martha Tynes. Newton and Eliza are buried in the Thornspring Methodist Church Cemetery in Pulaski. Newton and Eliza's children:
  - 1.4.1. Straley W. born 18 April 1911 married Lola Hylton.
  - 1.4.2. Ruby Lee born about 1914 married Harry Jackson Williams.
  - 1.4.3. Newton W. born 28 October 1915.
  - 1.4.4. Clarence W. born about 1919.
  - 1.4.5. Martha J. married Thomas Terry Dulaney, Jr.
  - 1.4.6. Julia B.
  - 1.4.7. James H.
  - 1.4.8. Lila Mae.[1]

- 1.5. Richard Floyd was born 14 January 1886 and died on 25 September 1971. He married Vernie Eliza Brunk on 29 December 1915 in Bland County. Vernie was the daughter of William Steven Brunk and Eliza Allen. She was born 11 January 1889 in Cox's Hollow, Pulaski County and died 02 November 1957. Richard and Vernie are buried in the Hidden Valley Cemetery #2. Richard and Vernie's children:
  - 1.5.1. Trinkle Whitten born 13 October 1916 married Vivian G. Chandler. He died in 1994 and is buried in the Hidden Valley Cemetery #2.
  - 1.5.2. Floyd Clayton born 12 October 1919 and died 25 September 1971. He is buried in the Hidden Valley Cemetery #2.
  - 1.5.3. James William born 15 March 1924 married 1st Ima Cox; 2nd Virginia Magdalene Spencer. He died 16 September 1978 and is buried in the Hidden Valley Cemetery #2.
- 1.6. Amey Jane was born 28 January 1889 and died 21 August 1971. She married Pearly Miller Albert on 17June 1914 in Wythe County. He was the son of Frederick H. Albert and Melvina Patterson. They divorced. Amy was listed in the 1920 Mercer County census with her sister and brother-in-law, listed as Amy Davis. Amy had one son:
  - 1.6.1. David Martin.

---

[1] 1930 Pulaski County, VA census.

1.7. Edna Catherine was born 15 September 1891. She was the second wife of Comie Albert Davis. *See Henry Davis Family

1.8. Lucy Pearl was born on 05 January 1894 and married Charles Thomas Underwood on 6 October 1916 in Pulaski. Charles was the son of Andrew Joshua Underwood and Sarah Jane Kennedy born 09 October 1885. Lucy died 07 March 1979 and Charles died 01 March 1956. They are buried in the Hunter Cemetery, Little Walkers Creek, Pulaski County. Lucy and Charles' children:
- 1.8.1. Richard Victor
- 1.8.2. Opal Virginia
- 1.8.3. Myrtle Agnes
- 1.8.4. Charlie Vivian
- 1.8.5. Alva Louise
- 1.8.6. Paul Dailey
- 1.8.7. Nina Loraine.
- 1.8.8. Charles Clifford.

1.9. Effie M. was born 20 July 1896 and died 26 August 1960. She married John Milton Underwood on 30 January 1817 in Pulaski County. He was the son of Andrew Joshua Underwood and Sarah Jane Kennedy. He was born 28 July 1880 and died 11 April 1957. John and Effie are buried in the Hunter Cemetery, Little Walkers Creek, Pulaski County.

1.10. Nannie Virginia was born March 25, 1899. She married Albert Jackson Davis. Nannie married 2nd Richard Ramage. *See Henry Davis Family

2. Jerome Bonaparte was born on 09 February 1854 in Pulaski and died in 1925 in Wythe County. He married Rachel Laura Halsey on 23 May 1881 in Wythe County. Rachel was born on 20 May 1851 in Wythe and died 01 December 1927 in Wythe. She was the daughter of Stephen J. Halsey and Sallie Cassell. Jerome and Rachel are buried in the Fairview Methodist Church Cemetery in Wythe County. Children:

2.1. George C. born 03 May 1885 and died 03 February 1910. George was working on the N & W Railroad out of Bluefield; he was working at Coaldale, West Virginia when the boiler engine blew, severely scalding George. He only lived a few days. He is buried in the Patterson Cemetery in Crockett's Cove, Wythe County.

2.2. Cora Lee was born January 1887 and died in 1981. She is buried in the Fairview Methodist Church in Wythe County. She married 1st Robert L. Myers and 2nd Mr. Wyatt.

2.3. Benjamin M. born 17 September 1888 and died 21 July 1966. He married Evelyn Maude Gregory and had two daughters:
- 2.3.1. Louise Margaret born 23 January 1913 and died 16 April 1991 in Wythe. She is buried in the Fairview Methodist Church Cemetery.
- 2.3.2. Leona Phern was born about 1915 married Roland H. Lammey in Wythe. Thelma died 13 July 2003 in Wythe County. She is buried in the Fairview Methodist Church Cemetery.

3. John Troy was born 04 December 1855 in Pulaski and died 01 September 1905. He married Mary D. Bowles the daughter of William H. Bowles and Mary Polly Austin. Mary was born 19 April 1856 in Wythe and died 25 November 1924 in Bland. John and Mary are buried in the Patterson Cemetery, Crockett's Cove, Wythe County.

On May 29, 1893, John T. conveyed 19 acres to …" Wm. S. Terry and Jenny T. Terry his wife… being a part of the land deeded to John T. Davis by Joseph Lefler and wife…".[1]

---

[1] Bland County, VA Deed Book 6, p. 414.

John conveyed land [no acreage given] to Peter C. Tickle on May 29, 1893. The part of land John bought of Joseph H. Lefler and Fransina Lefler.[1]

On July 20, 1903, "...James M. Cassell the sole heir and devisee of his father Samuel Cassell, deceased and Nannie S. Cassell, his wife, and Mrs. Sallie K. Blair, the sole devisee under the last will and testament of Frank S. Blair conveyed 350 acres to H. N. Davis and J. T. Davis being the same land conveyed by deed to Samuel Cassell, Sr. by Casper Yost...one half of which said tract of land was conveyed by said Samuel Cassell, Sr. to Crockett & Blair."[2]

On September 14, 1903 H. N. and J. T. Davis conveyed 178 acres of land to C. C. Davis being part of the Cassell tract.[3]

On May 31, 1904, 172 acres of land was partitioned between H. N. Davis and J. T. Davis by two separate deeds. H. N. Davis was to have the west end beginning on the north side of the survey and the division lines runs with the Joe Graham Branch. J. T. was to have the east end.[4]

John and Mary had children:
3.1. Victoria Agnes was born on 15 September 1875 in Bland and died 29 September 1928. She married 1st Thomas Vandergrift on 23 November 1891 in Bristol, Sullivan County, Tennessee and 2nd Henry Hampton Davis. *See Henry Davis Family. Victoria is buried in the Patterson Cemetery. Victoria had two sons with Thomas Vandergrift:
  3.1.1. Morrison born about 1895.[5]
  3.1.2. Daniel born about 1895.[6] Henry Hampton Davis and Victoria were listed in the 1910 McDowell County, West Virginia census with son Raymond (Davis), Morrison and Daniel (Vandergrift).
3.2. Henry and Victoria's children:
  3.2.1. Raymond Earl married Genoa Thelma Hamblin.
  3.2.2. Audrey Hampton married Myrtle Thelma Davis.

In September 1914, James Edward and Ollie Davis conveyed 27 ¾ acres to Morrison Vandergrift in Pulaski County on Little Creek.[7]

Morrison Vandergrift (bachelor) of Keystone, McDowell County, West Virginia conveyed to R. L. Chandler 27 ¾ acres on January 3, 1919.[8]

Morrison Vandergrift born about 1895 was listed in the 1920 Keystone, McDowell County, West Virginia census with wife Elizabeth. Was not located in the 1930 census. Morrison Vandergrift was supposedly shot and killed at a young age. Evidently, his brother, Daniel also died at a young age.

3.3. Willie Floyd was born on 17 September 1877 and died 18 April 1942. She married Charles Clinton Davis. *See Henry Davis Family.

---

[1] Bland County, VA Deed Book 6. p. 425.
[2] Bland County, VA Deed Book 10, p. 76.
[3] Bland County, VA Deed Book 8, p. 619.
[4] Bland County, VA Deed Book 8, p. 430 & 468.
[5] 1910 McDowell County, WV Census.
[6] 1910 McDowell County, WV Census.
[7] Pulaski County, VA Deed Book 35, p. 285
[8] Pulaski County, VA Deed Book 41, p. 19.

3.4. Lucy "Gussie" Augusta was born 26 October 1879 and died 29 March 1938 in Pulaski County. She married Robert Lee Chandler, the son of Hannah Chandler, on 25 May 1904 in Bland. He was born on 29 November 1879 in Bland and died 09 January 1959 in Pulaski County. Robert and Lucy are buried in the Millirons Methodist Church Cemetery, Pulaski County. Children:

    3.4.1.1. John Robert born 13 July 1905 married Wilma Lou Ritter on 23 June 1924 in Pulaski. Wilma was born 15 November 1907 and died 26 December 1970 in Chattanooga, Tennessee. John died November 1960 in Pulaski. Wilma was the daughter of Thomas Fenton Ritter and Martha Jane Johnston Bond. John and Wilma are buried in the Millirons Methodist Church Cemetery.

    3.4.2. Mary Ada born 17 August 1908 in Ashland, West Virginia married William Robert Morris King on 15 May 1929 in Pulaski. He was the son of William Davis King and Olivia Virginia Thompson. Morris was born on 16 May 1905 and died on 04 March 1987 in Leesburg, Virginia. Ada died on 28 March 1987 in Leesburg. They are buried in the Millirons Methodist Church Cemetery.

    3.4.3. Carl Davis married Ola Dare Faw on 06 August 1937 in Pulaski. Ola was the daughter of Wiley Henderson Faw and Effie Goodman.

    3.4.4. Ralph Scott was born Ashland, West Virginia 19 March 1913, married Georgia Mabel Faw on 06 August 1937 in Pulaski. Georgie was the daughter of Wiley Henderson Faw and Effie Goodman. Ralph died on 18 February 2002 in Dublin, Pulaski County. Georgia was born 04 January 1916 and died 11 July 1993 in Dublin. They are buried in the Thornspring Methodist Church Cemetery in Pulaski County.

3.5. Stuart P. was born in 1881 and died in 1944. He married Ethel Murray. She was the daughter of Thomas Murray and Delilah A. Davis Ethel was born in 1886 in Washington County, Tennessee and died in 1981. Stuart and Ethel are buried in the Goshen Methodist Church Cemetery.

Stuart and Ethel's children:

    3.5.1. Nellie May married Charles Neal Brunk, son of Walter Herbert Brunk and Nancy Cathern Banes. *See Brunk family.

    3.5.2. John Thomas married Mabel Gertrude Kitts, daughter of Robert Hutsel Kitts and Bertha Jane Davis. *See Henry Davis Family

    3.5.3. Myrtle Thelma married Audrey Hampton Davis, son of Henry Hampton Davis and Victoria Agnes Davis.

    3.5.4. Delilah married William Edward Corder son of Benjamin Larkin Corder and Frances Bell Davis. This was William Edward's second marriage. In 1930, William E. Corder is listed in Wayne County, Michigan, Taylor Township: William E. Corder age 29, wife Delila age 19, son William E. age 1 year 9 months; daughter Lula V. age 6 months; brothers Ben V. age 26, Archie C. age 21. William born West Virginia; Delilah in Virginia; the two children born in Michigan; Ben V. in Virginia and Archie in North Dakota. William and Archie working in auto factory and Ben as a carpenter. Lived on North Line Road.

3.6. Albert Terry was born on 18 May 1885 and died on 16 June 1959. He married 1st Margaret E. Williams, daughter of William Patterson Williams and Katherine Louisa Patterson. He married 2nd Annie Kate King on 16 June 192. She was the daughter of Joseph S. King and Emily Etta Pegram. He married 3rd Mattie Shelton. Margaret "Maggie" Williams was born on 18 May 1880 and died 08 May 1920 buried in the Davis Cemetery, Little Walker's Creek. Annie Kate was born 29 November 1895 and died 29 April 1947. Albert and Annie Kate are buried in the Goshen Methodist Church Cemetery.

Albert Terry bought the Jacob Kitts land which was sold to Kitts by William Collins and wife.[1]

A. T. Davis conveyed the same land to Andy W. Davis. Andy, in turn, conveyed the land to Louie Matz.[2]

Ellen Smith (Pegram) Tickle conveyed 62 acres to Albert Terry Davis on September 1, 1919 on Spur Branch.[3]

Albert and Maggie had the following children:
- 3.6.1. Roy Crockett married Nellie Pierce Bell and lived in Wythe County. Roy was born in 1906 and died 01 March 1966 and is buried in the Mountain View Methodist Church Cemetery, Smith Hollow, Wythe County. Nellie died 05 June 2002.
  - 3.6.1.1. David Elmo.
  - 3.6.1.2. Curtis Graham.
  - 3.6.1.3. Earlwood.
  - 3.6.1.4. Billy Joe.
  - 3.6.1.5. Roger Lee.
  - 3.6.1.6. Kenneth.
  - 3.6.1.7. Rufus.
  - 3.6.1.8. Edward.
  - 3.6.1.9. Sadie Marie.
  - 3.6.1.10. Betty Jean.
  - 3.6.1.11. Roy Crockett, Jr.
- 3.6.2. Mary Lou was born on 01 April 1911 and died 05 June 1985. Mary Lou never married. She is buried in the Goshen Methodist Church Cemetery.
- 3.6.3. Cranwill A. was born 07 October 1912 and died 12 October 1913. He is buried in the Davis Cemetery.
- 3.6.4. Alvah Muncy was born November 20, 1917 and died October 19, 1985. He married Mary Ann Bell. Alvah is buried in the Fairview Methodist Church Cemetery in Wythe County.

Annie Kate King Davis was the third Postmaster of Long Spur having taken charge on February 1, 1945. After Annie's death, Mrs. Clarice W. Davis assumed charge until September 8, 1948.[4]

Children of Albert Terry and Annie Kate:
- 3.6.5. Hanie.
- 3.6.6. Wayne Thornton married Norma Jean Terry.
- 3.6.7. Lewis Baxter married Clarice Neely.
- 3.6.8. Francis Irene married Oakley Neal Banes.

---

[1] Bland County, VA Deed Book 10, p. 71.
[2] Bland County, VA Deed Book 15, p. 603.
[3] Bland County, VA Deed Book 14, p. 50.
[4] National Archives and Record Administration, Washington, DC, RG 68, Site Location Reports, Long Spur Post Office.

- 3.6.9. Colleen Noal married Wayne Kenneth Banes.
- 3.6.10. Donald.
- 3.6.11. Ford Hampton married Joyce Ann Midkiff
3.7. Charles Calvin was born 25 September 1887 and died in 1929. He married Lucy Clara Davis, daughter of Comie Albert Davis and Elizabeth Ellen Carr. *See Henry Davis Family.
3.8. Hanie Genoa was born 10 January 1889 and died 02 October 1945 in Pulaski County. She married Charles Kelly King, son of John Nye King and Martha Taylor. Charles was born 10 January 1885 and died 19 July 1963. Charles and Hanie are buried in the Millirons Methodist Church Cemetery, Pulaski County. Children:
  - 3.8.1. Hanie Genoa married Edgar D. Smith.
  - 3.8.2. Mary Sue married Mr. Baumgardener.
  - 3.8.3. John Kelly, Sr. married Alma Treer.
3.9. Mary Blanche was born 06 June 1892 and died 23 May 1947 in Tampa, Florida. She married Peter Moll who was born 29 September 1877 in Spain. Peter and Mary were living in Ballast Point, Hillsborough Co, Florida in 1920 and 1930. Children taken from the 1920 Hillsborough County, Florida census:
  - 3.9.1. Charles M.
  - 3.9.2. John P.
  - 3.9.3. Virginia B.
4. Rush F. was born in 29 July 1857 in Wythe County and died about 1884 in West Virginia in a mining accident.
5. Martha Jane was born 23 February 1859 in Wythe County and died 11 June 1929 in Bland. She married Charles Lee Parsell on 26 October 1880 in Bland County. Charles was the son of John Parsell and Mary Ann Coleman. He was born 10 December 1856 in Franklin County, Virginia and died 02 March 1917 in Bland County. Charles and Martha are buried in the Goshen Methodist Church Cemetery. Children taken from the C. L. Parsell Family Bible:
  - 5.1. Annie E. born 11 August 1881, died 22 June 1920 of pulmonary tuberculosis in Smyth County, Virginia. Never married. She is buried in the State Hospital Cemetery, Plot R-16.[1]
  - 5.2. Mary E. was born 25 January 1883 and died 18 March 1886 of diphtheria. Buried in the Hamblin Cemetery, Spur Branch, Bland County.[2]
  - 5.3. Virgie E. was born 21 May 1884 and died 19 March 1886 of diphtheria. Buried in the Hamblin Cemetery.[3]
  - 5.4. Dana Lee born 22 November 1885 in Bland and died 16 January 1950 in Springfield, Clark County, Ohio. Dana never married. She is buried in the Glen Haven Memorial Gardens, Clark County, Ohio.
  - 5.5. Willie Jane was born 13 March 1888 and died 14 December 1953. Willie married Emmett Milton Davis on 01 October 1906 in Bristol, Tennessee. Emmett was the son of Hiram Newton Davis and Elizabeth Catherine Farmer. He was born 04 April 1885 and died 13 December 1955. Emmett and Willie are buried in the Goshen Methodist Church Cemetery.

    Dana Parsell, unmarried, Andrew M. Parsell and Minnie Parsell, his wife, Zena Stinson and George Stinson, her husband, all of Springfield, Ohio; Willie J. Davis and Emmett M. Davis, her husband, Ida Davis and H. H. Davis, her husband, and Charles C. Parsell

---

[1] Bonnie R. Spangler, Director, Medical Record Services, Southwestern Virginia Mental Health Institute, Marion, Smyth County, VA.
[2] Charles Lee Parsell Family Bible, Rebecca Sowers.
[3] Charles Lee Parsell Family Bible, Rebecca Sowers.

and Blanche Parsell, his wife, being all the heirs at law of C. L. Parsell and wife, deceased conveyed to Willie J. Davis "…32 acres and 125 square rods… being the same land conveyed to said C. L. Parsell by Minnie Parsell and husband by deed dated the 24th day of August, 1907…".[1] This land was later left to Charles Newton Davis by his mother, Willie Parsell Davis.

Emmett Milton & Willie Jane Davis

Emmett and Willie's children:

5.5.1. Elmer Lawrence born 12 April 1910 married Eva Ann Brunk, daughter of Walter Herbert Brunk and Nancy Cathern Banes. Elmer died 06 January 1955 in a sawmill accident on Iron Mountain in Wythe County. He is buried in the Goshen Methodist Church Cemetery. Children:
   5.5.1.1. Hughie L.
   5.5.1.2. Harold Clayton.
   5.5.1.3. Gertrude.
   5.5.1.4. Phyllis Jane.

5.5.2. Herman Milton was born 27 June 1912 and died 04 November 1975 in Roanoke County, Virginia. Herman never married. He is buried in the Goshen Methodist Church Cemetery.

5.5.3. Ernest "Sonny" Miller born 23 March 1918 married Mabel King 10 November 1945 in Pulaski. She was the daughter of Robert J. King and Grace Ward. Mabel was born 04 December 1925 and died 18 May 1999. Sonny died 14 November 1992. They are buried in the Blue Ridge Memorial Gardens, Roanoke County, Virginia. Sonny and Mabel's children:
   5.5.3.1. Shirley.
   5.5.3.2. Ernestine.

5.5.4. Virginia Era born 31 July 1920 married Homer Woodson Bailey on 08 February 1943. Homer was born 30 August 1918 and died 12 July 1992. Virginia died 10 November 1994. One daughter:
   5.5.4.1. Judy Ann.

5.5.5. Charles Newton born 08 December 1924 married Margaret Ellen Powers, daughter of Jordan Powers and Claire Long. She was born on 10 June 1927 and died in Roanoke County, Virginia on 01 May 2001. Charles died on 08 December 1988 in Bland. They had no children. Charles and Margaret are buried in the Hidden Valley Cemetery #2. Charles Newton was a World War II veteran, Private US Army.

5.5.6. Martha Elizabeth born 07 April 1927 married Harry Thomas Palmer. He was the son of Herman R. Palmer and Myrtle Ellen Dickerson. Elizabeth died on

---

[1] Bland County, VA Deed Book 18, p. 374

02 August 1995 in Portsmouth, Virginia She is buried in the Hidden Valley Cemetery #2. Tom and Elizabeth's children:
- 5.5.6.1. Susan Elaine.
- 5.5.6.2. Sharon Lawana.
- 5.5.6.3. Harry Thomas, Jr.

5.5.7. Lester Neal was born 07 April 1929 and died 06 November 1936 of a brain aneurysm. He is buried in the Goshen Methodist Church Cemetery.

5.5.8. Elsie Irene born 21 May 1932 married Jimmy Lee Cox on 30 August 1953 in York, South Carolina. He was the son of Woodie Lee Cox and Elsie Mae Roberts. Elsie died 16 February 2001. She is buried in the Goshen Methodist Church Cemetery. Child:
- 5.5.8.1. Rebecca Jane.

5.6. Andrew Miller born 02 February 1890 married Minnie Pearl Stinson on 19 July 1919 in White Gate, Bland. She was the daughter of John Stinson and Hester Ann Bussey. He married 2nd Edith R. Ridge. Andrew and Minnie moved to Springfield, Clark County, Ohio sometime before 1920. He was a World War I veteran, having served in France and receiving the Purple Heart. Andrew died 14 November 1981 in Springfield. Minnie died on 21 May 1963. He and his wife are buried in the Glen Haven Memorial Gardens, Clark County, Ohio.

Children:

5.6.1. Clyde Miller born 21 July 1920 married Ruth Mae Murry on 03 January 1940. They had two children:
- 5.6.1.1. Ralph Dewey, Sr.
- 5.6.1.2. Ruthanne.

5.6.2. Alma Pearl born 30 January 1922 married Ralph Richard Uptegraph. Their children:
- 5.6.2.1. Larry Lee.
- 5.6.2.2. Carolyn Ann.
- 5.6.2.3. Dianna Lynn.

5.6.3. Audrey Mae born 11 January 1924 married Dan Pendleton Switzer. Children:
- 5.6.3.1. Don Gary.
- 5.6.3.2. Dana.
- 5.6.3.3. Danita.

5.6.4. Ralph Lee 25 September 1925 married Edna Louise Estep. Ralph researched the Parsell/Parcell Family for many years. Their children:
- 5.6.4.1. Marc Lee.
- 5.6.4.2. Wayne Allen.
- 5.6.4.3. Cynthia Louise.
- 5.6.4.4. Julie Ann.

5.6.5. Emma Barbara born 09 July 1928 married Willard Lewis Estep. Their children:
- 5.6.5.1. Timothy.
- 5.6.5.2. Douglas Lewis.
- 5.6.5.3. Denise Louise.
- 5.6.5.4. David Richard.

5.6.6. William Wren born 29 March 1930 married Deloris Jean Bowman. Their children:
- 5.6.6.1. William Randall.
- 5.6.6.2. Richard Daryl.

5.6.6.3. Joseph Andrew.
5.6.7. Richard "Dickie" Stinson born 24 May 1932 was killed in the Korean War at Ascom City, Korea on 25 March 1953. He is buried in the Glen Haven Memorial Gardens, Clark County, Ohio.

Richard "Dickie" Stinson Parsell

MARINE HELICOPTER TRANSPORT SQUADRON 161—27 March 1953
First Marine Aircraft Wing, Fleet Marine Force
c/o Fleet Post Office, San Francisco

Mr. Andrew M. Parsell
1901 Hillside Avenue
Springfield, Ohio

My Dear. Mr. Parsell,

The untimely death of your son, Sergeant Richard S. Parsell, U. S. Marine Corps, is a source of great sorrow to me and his many friends in the squadron. Please accept our heartfelt sympathy in your bereavement.

I know you wish to learn the circumstances surrounding the death of your son, Dick was on a local test hop at our rear echelon camp located at Ascom City, Korea. He was flying with Major Doil R. Stitzel, U. S. Marine Corps. Master Sergeant Gilbert N. Caudle, Jr., U. S. Marine Corps, was also in the helicopter. They took off at 8:50 a.m. on March 25th and about 10 minutes later experienced engine failure at low altitude. In attempting to make an emergency landing under very high wind conditions, the pilot lost control of the aircraft and it crashed into the ground. All three occupants were killed instantly.

Memorial services for your son and the other two men lost in the crash was conducted this afternoon at 4:30 by the First Marine Division Protestant Chaplain at our forward echelon camp. Your son was highly thought of in the squadron, and his passing was deeply felt by its members, many of whom attended the services.

Dick's integrity and devotion to duty won for him the respect of all who knew him. Although, I realize that mere words can do little to console you. I earnestly hope the knowledge that your son is keenly missed by his friends will in some measure alleviate your sadness.

Sincerely yours,
Owen A. Chambers
Colonel, U. S. Marine Corps

5.7. Ida Augusta married Henry Hampton Davis. They had no children. *See Henry Davis Family.

5.8. Zena Gray born 20 June 1895 married George Robert Stinson on 08 July 1925 in Bland. He was the son of John Stinson and Hester Ann Bussey. Zena and Richard also moved to Clark County, Ohio. Zena died 26 October 1947. George was born on 08 April 1899 and died July 1985. They are buried in the Glen Haven Memorial Gardens. Children:
- 5.8.1. Martha born 1926 married Donald Blevins. One daughter:
  - 5.8.1.1. Nancy.
- 5.8.2. Robert born in 1928 married Norma Chapman and had three children:
  - 5.8.2.1. Thomas.
  - 5.8.2.2. Terry M.
  - 5.8.2.3. Rhonda.
- 5.8.3. Glenn Allen born 08 August 1930 married Jennie Lee Estep. One son:
  - 5.8.3.1. Rodger Allen.

5.9. Charles Cadell born 20 December 1897 married Virginia Blanche Vest 24 September 1924 in Pulaski. She was the daughter of William Vest and Ettie Woodyard. Blanch was born 18 November 1904 and died 24 March 1990 in Bluefield, West Virginia. Charles died on 11 May 1981 in Pulaski. They are buried in the Thornspring Methodist Church Cemetery, Pulaski. Children:
- 5.9.1. Raymond born 14 November 1925 married Carol Reese. Children:
  - 5.9.1.1. Mike.
  - 5.9.1.2. Liza.
  - 5.9.1.3. Thomas.
- 5.9.2. Donald Cadell born 03 August 1928 married Alice W. Goad.
- 5.9.3. William Lee born 14 March 1931.
- 5.9.4. Hazel Colleen born 06 August 1932 married Robert Pendleton. One daughter:
  - 5.9.4.1. Carol.
- 5.9.5. James Dwight married Bobbi Davis. Two sons
  - 5.9.5.1. Roger.
  - 5.9.5.2. Jeffrey.

6. Samuel Caddell, Jr. was born on 15 November 1860 in Wythe County and died 19 October 1945 in Wythe. He married 1st Josephine "Josie" Augusta Halsey on 18 December 1878 in Wythe. She was the daughter of John Trigg Halsey and Sarah E. Painter. Josie was born on 15 May 1860 and died on 13 June 1915. Samuel married 2nd Effie Mae Smith on 10 April 1920. She was the daughter of Alexander Smith and Minnie L. Brown. Effie was born April 1885 and died in 1958. She is buried in the Mountain View Methodist Church Cemetery in Smith Hollow. Samuel and Josie are buried in the Patterson Cemetery. It is noted in the 1910 census of number of children born and number of children living. Samuel and Josie had twelve children, of those twelve, only five were living at the time. Samuel and Josie's children:
- 6.1. Sallie Pearl born 11 February 1880 married John Van Buren Williams on 14 January 1904 in Wythe County. He was the son of William Patterson Williams and Katherine Louisa Patterson. John was born on 02 June 1874 in Crockett's Cove, Wythe and died on 06 April 1938 in Wythe. Sallie died on 13 October 1974. They are buried in the Fairview Methodist Church Cemetery, Wythe County. John and Sallie's children:
  - 6.1.1. Clarence C.
  - 6.1.2. John Caddell.
  - 6.1.3. Nellia Augusta.
  - 6.1.4. Elmer Graham.
  - 6.1.5. Louise W.
  - 6.1.6. Samuel P.

- 6.2. <u>Mary E.</u> born December 1882 married Steven Smith. Children:
  - 6.2.1. <u>John S.</u> born about 1908 married Mary Felty. He is listed in a Wythe County deed as the only surviving heir of Mary E. Smith.
  - 6.2.2. <u>Georgie M.</u> Died young.
- 6.3. <u>Lydia C.</u> born December 1884 died between 1900-1910, buried in unknown location.
- 6.4. <u>Terry Franklin</u> born 13 April 1887 married Lucille (maiden name unknown). Was listed in a 1946 Wythe County deed as living in New Castle, Delaware. Lucille died 23 August 1992 in Ridley Park, Pittsylvania and is buried in the West End Cemetery, Wythe County.
- 6.5. <u>Van Trigg</u> born December 1889 married Roberta Virginia Albert 28 June 1922 in Giles. He died 23 February 1956 in Giles. Roberta was born 1892 and died in 1969. They are buried in the Staffordsville Cemetery, Giles County. Children:
  - 6.5.1. <u>Van Trigg, Jr.</u> married Anna Sue Stanley in Giles.
  - 6.5.2. <u>Ruby</u> married Donald S. Johnston.
  - 6.5.3. <u>Ernest Caudell</u> married Ruby Elizabeth Johnston.
- 6.6. <u>Ernest S.</u> born 6 January 1895 and died 09 August 1905 buried in the Patterson Cemetery.
- 6.7. <u>Bessie</u> born October 1897 and died between 1900-1910 buried in unknown location.
- 6.8. <u>Samuel Caddell</u> born 15 November 1900 and died December 1975. He married Margaret Cree Sadler. She was born 20 August 1909 and died 10 June 1994. They are buried in the West End Cemetery, Wythe County. Children:
  - 6.8.1. <u>Floyd.</u>
  - 6.8.2. <u>Elvie.</u>
- 6.9. <u>Edward Thomas</u> born 12 July 1905 and died 30 November 1956 buried in the Patterson Cemetery. Married Clara Lee Cooper. They had one son, Edward Cadell born 22 August 1929 and died 30 November 1933 in Giles County. Court records indicate Edward and Clara were divorced. Daughters:
  - 6.9.1. <u>Anna Mae</u>
  - 6.9.2. <u>Janice Evelyn.</u>

Samuel and Effie's children:
- 6.10. <u>Eldridge Eugene</u> born 27 May 1922 married Hontas Yonce. Eldridge died 18 May 1992 in Wythe County. Hontas was born 18 March 1921 and died 06 June 1993. They are buried in the Mountain View Methodist Church Cemetery, Wythe County.
- 6.11. <u>Carl Junior</u> born 22 June 1925 married Rosa Melvina Corvin. She was born 28 October 1931 and died 27 September 1990. Carl died 24 August 1989. They are buried in the Mountain View Methodist Church Cemetery, Wythe County.
- 6.12. <u>Alexander</u> Caudell died at birth.
- 6.13. <u>Lucinda</u> died at birth.

7. <u>Hiram Newton</u> was born 27 January 1863 in Bland County and 30 September 1931 in Bland. He married Elizabeth Catherine Farmer on 05 March 1884 in Pulaski County. She was the daughter of Richard Farmer and Rachel Halsey. She was born 13 May 1866 in Wythe County and died 30 December 1945. Hiram and Elizabeth are buried in the Goshen Methodist Church Cemetery.

On June 16, 1913, Hiram and Elizabeth Davis conveyed ½ acre of land, south side of the road on Walkers Little Creek to H. N. Davis, E. H. Millirons, J. W. Davis, C. Calvin Davis and C. A. Davis the Board of Trustees of the Methodist Episcopal Church, South.[1]

Hiram and Elizabeth's children:

---

[1] Bland County, VA Deed Book 11, p. 598.

7.1. <u>Emmett Milton</u> was born 04 April 1885 married Willie Jane Parsell. *See Martha Jane Davis.

7.2. <u>Robert Newton</u> was born 30 June 1887 and died on 10 March 1934. He married Julia "Julie" D. King, daughter of Harvey Newton King and Susanna Gray. Julia was born on 06 December 1892 and died 28 December 1967. Robert and Julia had no children; they did raise one foster son, Brown Blankenship. Robert and Julie are buried in the Goshen Methodist Church Cemetery.

7.3. <u>Ella Augusta</u> was born 26 May 1891 and died 28 May 1991. She married Elliot W. Williams on 17 September 1919 in Bland. Elliot was the son of Albert A. Williams and Serena Dalton, born in Carroll County on 25 February 1894 and he died 15 December 1960. Elliot was a World War I veteran. Ella and Elliot were living in Crockett's Cove as listed in the 1920 Wythe County Census. They are buried in the Goshen Methodist Church Cemetery. Elliot and Ella's children:

7.3.1. <u>Kenneth.</u>
7.3.2. <u>Blanch.</u>
7.3.3.

On May 14, 1931, the Charles L. Parsell heirs conveyed to Ella A. Williams ..." two certain tracts or parcels of land situate on the waters of Spur Branch... one of which said parcels contains 54 acres and 33 poles, more or less, and being the same that was conveyed to the said C. L. Parsell, as Charles L. Parsell, by John Parsell by deed dated the 24th day of March, 1897, and of record in the Clerk's Office of the Circuit Court of Bland County, Virginia in D. B. 7, page 79, and being therein described by metes and bound, to which reference is hereby made for a more particular description of this certain tract; the other of which said tracts contains 1 ½ acres, more or less, being the same tract that was conveyed to the said C. L. Parsell, as Charles L. Parsell, by David Y. Hamblin by deed dated the 4th day of March, 1897...".[1]

7.4. <u>Eula Catherine</u> was born 18 May 1894 and died 21 May 1967. She married Robert Morehead on 16 September 1933 in Bland. Robert was the son of Gorden Andrew Morehead and Tacy Adeline Pruett. He was born 11 May 1892 and died 20 November 1961. Robert and Eula are buried in the Shiloh Methodist Church Cemetery, Bland County. One son:

7.4.1. <u>Robert, Jr.</u> married Lola Ann Tolbert.

7.5. <u>Mary Alberta</u> was born 05 January 1897 and died 01 October 1924. She married John Jesse Meadows on 30 May 1918 in Bland. *See Meadows/Pegram Family.

7.6. <u>Texie Miller</u> was born 10 October 1899 and died 26 April 1985. She married Edgar Palmer King on 12 November 1919 in Bland. Edgar was the son of Harvey Newton King and Susanna Gray. He was born 29 May 1895 and died 02 January 1958. Edgar and Texie are buried in the Bland Cemetery, Bland County. They had two children:

7.6.1. <u>Edgar Miller.</u>
7.6.2. <u>Louella.</u>

7.7. <u>Sallie Rachel</u> was born in 1903 and died 23 June 1988 in Wythe County. She married Howard Lee Smith from Wythe County. She is buried in the East End Cemetery, Wythe County. Sallie and Howard had no children.

7.8. <u>Claude Swanson</u> was born May 12, 1905 and died December 25, 1975. He married Gladys C. Davis, the daughter of Comie Albert Davis and Elizabeth Ellen Carr. *See Henry Davis Family.

8. <u>Charles William</u> was born on 17 May 1865 and died 15 October 1950. He married 1st Louisa Virginia Davis *See Henry Davis Family. Charles married 2nd Sarah "Vicey" Lavica

---

[1] Bland County, VA Deed Book 18, p. 375

Millirons on 29 October 1919 in Bland. Vicey was born 10 February 1900 and 09 October 1984. Her parents were Rufus Lee Millirons and Annie Kate King. She and Charles are buried in the "Davis" Cemetery. *See Henry Davis Family

Peter C. Tickle conveyed 85 acres to Charles W. Davis on September 12, 1896. The land run Moses Akers line on the west and with Jacob Kitts line on the south side to the middle of the creek thence with the creek to the ford we made a line fence running with that fence to the corner on the public road from that corner on the Public road so far as to give L. Lambert his thirty acres.[1]

Charles and Vicey's children:
- 8.1. Marvin Repass married Virginia Spencer Davis.
- 8.2. Miller Allen married Viola Yonce.
- 8.3. Vergie Viola married Arnold Wade Hamblin.
- 8.4. Mildred Pauline married Richard L. Matz.

9. Robert Lee was born 14 June 1867 and died 15 December 1956. Robert married Josephine "Josie" Elizabeth Burton. She was the daughter of Levi S. Burton and Emerel Smith. Josie was born in 1870 in Pulaski and died in 1941. Robert and Josie are buried in the Goshen Methodist Church Cemetery along with Josie's mother Emerel. Robert and Josie had twin daughters:
   - 9.1. Mary Lee born 15 November 1903 married 1st Martie Alfred Young on 22 March 1938 in Bland; she married 2nd Frank A. Lawrence son of Robert Ward Lawrence and Mary Elizabeth Miller. Mary died in 1989. Frank was born 1896 and died in 1971. They are buried in the Hidden Valley Cemetery #2.
   - 9.2. Martha Levell born 15 November 1903 married Govan Thedmer Hamblin on 14 November 1933 in Bland. Govan was the son of Edward L. Hamblin and Olive Virginia Millirons. Govan was born 22 August 1913 and died 27 August 1993. Martha died on 13 December 1990. *See Banes Family. Mary, Frank, Martha and Govan are buried in the Hidden Valley Cemetery #2, Bland.

At some point, Robert Lee and Josie moved to Kansas as Mary and Martha's marriage records indicate they were born in Barber County, Kansas.

10. Sarah Elizabeth "Bettie" was born 18 October 1869 and died in December, 1908 in Rugby, Pierce County, North Dakota. She married James Larkin Corder on 28 March 1889 in Bland. James was the son of Benjamin F. Corder and Julian B. Hammonds. He was born on 25 July 1855 in Giles County and died 01 April 1923. *See Corder Family
11. Permelia Ann was born 04 October 1871 and died 07 January 1928. She married William Thomas Davis. *See Henry Davis Family.
12. Edna Dove was born 24 April 1873 married Samuel Levi Cassell on 22 November 1893 in Bland. Samuel was the son of John Cassell and Elizabeth Williams. Samuel was born on 30 March 1866 and died 25 December 1921. He is buried in the Fairview Methodist Church Cemetery, Wythe County. Children:
    - 12.1. John Caddell born 11 January 1895 married Pearl G. Umberger on 25 November 1919 in Wythe. She was the daughter of Stuart R. Umberger and Minnie B. Bowles. John died in December 1973 and is buried in the Fairview Methodist Church Cemetery, Wythe County.
    - 12.2. Neta M. born about 1898.[2]

---

[1] Bland County, VA Deed Book 7, p. 31.
[2] 1910 Wythe County, VA Census.

12.3. <u>William L</u>. born about 1908.[1]
13. <u>Edward G.</u> was born 24 April 1873 and died 14 March 1885 of scarlet fever. He is buried in the Patterson Cemetery, Wythe County.

---

[1] 1920 Wythe County, VA Census.

FAW FAMILY

English, patronymic (of, relating to, or derived from the name of one's father or a paternal ancestor) derived from the Anglo-Saxon name Folki "people" common before the Conquest.[1]

Wiley Henderson Faw was born on 30 September 1889 in Ashe County, North Carolina. Wiley's parents were Pheonis Bethel Faw and Nancy E. Phillips. He married Effie Lula Goodman in North Carolina. Wiley was in Bland County by 1930. He is listed in the Mechanicsburg District with wife and children. They are buried in the Thornspring Methodist Church Cemetery in Pulaski County.

On September 4, 1933, Lee Mabry and Millie his wife conveyed 100 acres to Effie Faw…being the same tract conveyed to J. C. Truman (now deceased) by Henry L. Shinault and Virgie.[2]

Wiley bought land from J. F. Wysor and G. C. Hall…675 acres which was conveyed to T. W. Kersey, G. C. Hall by James S. Miller and wife Sallie B.[3]

Wiley sold the Little Walker Creek land in 1942 to W. H. Davis[4]; in 1944, to the Woodyard family.[5]

Biography
Wiley Henderson Faw
Submitted by Wade Arnold Davis

Wiley Henderson Faw was born in Ashe County, NC 30 Sept., 1889 and married Effie Goodman March 8, 1908. They had 12 children. They moved to Virginia in the 1920's and Virginia A. Faw was born 11 September 1926 in Bluefield, Virginia and she is the only other living relative. They lived at several places and as my mother recalled, they lived at White Gate and moved to Little Creek in about 1931. They farmed, ran a farm and sawmill and store and he was evidently a deputy sheriff then for Southwest Times gives his death in April 1946 as having been one for 15 years. They must have moved to Back Creek in 1944 to be near Roy Summers' farm as this is the date on the deed. I can remember his having returned home and suffering from inoperable cancer. A newspaper gave the death as 23 April, 1946 and included L.R. Summers along with 5 others as active pallbearers and 45 as honorary pallbearers. Another paragraph stated: "A resident of this

---

[1] *What is in Your Name?* Vitalog.net. website http://www.vitalog.net/cgi-bin/select_name.cgi
[2] Pulaski County, VA Deed Book 70, p. 224.
[3] Pulaski County, VA Deed Book 76, p. 398.
[4] Pulaski County, VA Deed Book 100, p. 291.
[5] Pulaski County, VA Deed Book 105, p. 208.

section for many years, Deputy Faw has marked himself a well-liked citizen and has served as a law enforcement agent for 15 years. During this period he also established himself successfully in the sawmill business and as merchant and farmer. His home is in the Back Creek section." Wiley and Effie's children:
1. Gilbert.
2. Beulah.
3. Clifford.
4. Hazel.
5. Mabel.
6. Ola.
7. Robert.
8. Bennie.
9. Wade.
10. Eugene.
11. Virginia.
12. Vernon.

HAMBLIN FAMILY

Either French or English, is a patronymic (of, relating to, or derived from the name of one's father or a paternal ancestor) derived from Hamo "home"; possibly contains the common French double diminutive ending -elin, contracted into –lin.[1]

To date, the first record of Mackerness Hamblin is in the Chesterfield County tax records in 1762, tithed with the family of George Coussens. In 1764, he is shown on the Lunenburg County (Cornwall Parish) tax rolls as tithable (taxable), no land, no carriages, no other family males (males became taxable at the age of 16, which would put Mackerness' birth at 1748, or earlier).

A very careful examination o f the tax records show a family unit of Thomas Hamblin/Mackerness Goode living in Lunenburg County in 1750. It identifies them as living between Sandy Creek and Bluestone Creek. A birth entry in church records identifies Thomas Hamblin and wife Phebe as parents of Peter Hamblin (born 1732). In 1764 the records shows Peter Hamblen and Mackerness Hamblin living in the same area of Lunenburg County that Thomas Hamblin and Mackerness Goode had been living in 14 years earlier. This information is the proof that indicates Thomas Hamblin as the father of Mackerness Hamblin, and solidifies the link between Mack and Peter Hamblin.

Based on tax records, it is likely that Mackerness Hamblin died in early 1815 in Franklin County, Virginia. One of Mackerness Hamblin's sons, Stephen Hamblin did live in Giles County, Virginia, for a period of time. There is no evidence that Mackerness ever lived in Giles County. At this time, evidence points to Mackerness Hamblin as a direct descendant of Captain Stephen Hamblyn, an Englishman who settled in Virginia around 1655.

Mackerness was married to Mary; some researchers believe her maiden name was Coleman. They had seven known children: Elizabeth, Edward, Thomas, Nancy, Coleman, Polly and Stephen T.

Stephen T. Hamblin was born about 1791and died May 1866 in Giles County. He 1st married Rhoda (maiden name unknown) and 2nd Sarah L. Fagg on 10 September 1840 in Montgomery County, Virginia. Stephen and Rhoda had the following children: Thomas H., David Young, Milly, Stephen W., Charlotte, Nancy, Sparrel K. and Lot I. Children by second marriage: Elizabeth, Virginia, James Henderson, Silas M., Eley, John Pierce C. and Lucy.

David Young Hamblin was born on 16 October 1818 in North Carolina and died 23 January 1903 in Giles County, Virginia. He married Nancy Heatherington on 15 February 1845 in Giles County. Nancy was born on 10 June 1824 and died 09 December 1896. David and Nancy are buried in the Hamblin Cemetery, Bearsprings, Giles County. Their children were: George Thomas born 23 January 1846 in Giles; died 09 May 1864 Cloyd's Farm, Pulaski County; Louisa Susan J. born 01 June 1851 married William H. H. Croy 06 August 1868; John M. Stafford; William J. S.; James A. Hall born 18 January 1864 married Mariah Margaret E. Williams 24 September 1884 in Giles and Harvey Tice born 08 April 1867 married Viola Alice Price 30 April 1895 in Bland county.

David Y. Hamblin was conveyed land on Spur Branch on June 4, 1876 by Samuel W. Williams being part of the Brawley tract: " … whereas by a Decree rendered on the 12th day of May 1876 by the circuit court of Bland County, Virginia in the chancery causes therein pending in the name of A. Bralley's administrator vs. A. Bralleys heirs it was adjudged, ordered and decided that

---

[1] *What is in Your Name?* Vitalog.net. website http://www.vitalog.net/cgi-bin/select_name.cgi

Samuel W. Williams as Special Commissioner should by Deed with special covenants of special warranty convey to said party of the second part that part which is mentioned in statement in writing signed by George N. Pegram and referred to in Decree and which is referred to in said writing as having been sold to said Hamblin and Wm. H. H. Croy (deed since has been partitioned by themselves). Now this deed witnesseth that for and in consideration of the premises aforesaid the said Samuel W. Williams as commissioner aforesaid doth here grant and convey to said party of the second part that entire tract or parcel of land lying on the Spur branch and waters of Walkers little creek a part of the Bralley land…".[1]

On December 14, 1878, William H. H. and Susan L. J Croy conveyed to David Y. Hamblin "…lands lying in the east end of the said Brally tract joining Mustard's lands not embraced in deeds to David Y Hamblin, John Parsell and John H. Pegram by S. D. Williams…".[2]

David Y. Hamblin and Nancy his wife conveyed to William J. Lambert, 7 acres of land on Spur Branch on January 5, 1883.[3]

On June 2, 1885, David Y. Hamblin conveyed a small tract of land to J. H. Pegram, Jno. M. S. Hamblin, William Hamblin, Samuel Davis and H. J. Kitts Trustees for the Methodist Episcopal Church South "…hold unto themselves the parties of the second part and their successors in office in trust that the said premises shall be used, kept, maintained and disposed as a place in which to erect a house of divine worship for the use of the ministry and membership of the Methodist Episcopal Church South subject to the discipline usage and ministerial appointments of said church as from time to time authorized and declared by the general conference of said Church…".[4]

David Hamblin conveyed land to Charles L. Parsell on March 4, 1897 …" the following tract of land lying in Bland County Virginia on the waters of Long Spur Branch…".[5]

David Y. Hamblin conveyed for love and affection and $1 to John M. S. Hamblin on January 17, 1900 [no acreage given] on the east end of the Brawley tract. On the same date, David Y. Hamblin conveyed to William J. S. Hamblin for love and affection 70 acres of land joining the Mustard land.[6]

It seems from the various Giles and Bland censuses, David Y. Hamblin never lived on Spur Branch. His two sons, John M. Stafford and William J. S. were the ones who settled on Spur Branch, Little Walkers Creek.

John Milton Stafford Hamblin was born 21 May 1855 in Giles County and died 02 February 1942 in Bland. He married Sarah Catherine Croy on 20 August 1876 in Giles County. Sarah was born to Lewis and Sallie Croy on 18 September 1853 in Giles and died 12 November 1921 in Bland. John and Sarah are buried in the Goshen Methodist Church Cemetery.

On the 18th of May, 1900, John and Sarah Hamblin conveyed ½ acre of land for a cemetery "That we John S. Hamblin and Sarah C. Hamblin, his wife, do designate as a place of burial for the [illegible] of Caucasian birth, One half acres of land on the top of a hill near the center of our

---

[1] Bland County, VA Deed Book 3, p. 525.
[2] Bland County, VA Deed Book 7, p. 272.
[3] Bland County, VA Deed Book 4, p. 484.
[4] Bland County, VA Deed Book 7, p. 80.
[5] Bland County, VA Deed Book 7, p. 80.
[6] Bland County, VA Deed Book 7, p. 489; Bland County, VA Deed Book 8, p. 158.

farm in Bland County on Spur Branch to be enclosed hereafter and to this end we do grant the said one half acre to William Meadows, Harry Pegram, William Hamblin, D. S. Ritter, Joseph King, Trustees of the Cemetery association of Walkers Little Creek, of Bland County together with or convenient way for a hearse and vehicles, oxen [illegible] said farm from Goshen Church to said burial place, to be held by the said Meadows in trust for the purpose aforesaid…".[1]

**John Stafford Hamblin family.
Submitted by Christine Hamblin Distelhorst.**

John Stafford and Sarah Catherine's children:
1. William Hoge born 14 August 1877 and died 25 June 1965 in Bland. He married Virgie Ethel Bond 10 May 1906 in Pulaski County. Ethel was born to James R. Bond and Martha Jane Johnston in 1889 and died in 1976. William and Ethel are buried in the Goshen Methodist Church Cemetery.
9.
Louisa McCoy conveyed 10 acres of land to William H. Hamblin on December 1, 1908.[2]

William and Ethel had three children:
   1.1. Arbie Ray married Robert Foster Chewning. Arbie and Robert are buried in the Hoge's Chapel Cemetery, Bland County. Two children:
   1.2. Raymond Alton married Lola Grace Brunk. Three sons:
      1.2.1. Leon Alton.
      1.2.2. Ronald Wade.
      1.2.3. Billy Ray.
   1.3. Roman.
2. Floyd Newton was born 23 April 1879 and died 29 October 1967 in Roanoke County. He married Margaret May Allen on 06 September 1902 in Pulaski County. She was the daughter of William Carr Allen and Lucy J. Morris. Margaret was born 27 November 1885 in Pulaski County and died 29 May 1978 in Albany, Georgia. Their children were:
   2.1. Hubert Clinton born 10 August 1903 married Helen Virginia Doss.
   2.2. Talmage Virgil born 19 October 1904; died 01 November 1904.
   2.3. Thurman Stafford born 01 April 1906 married Ola Mae McFalls.
   2.4. Curtis Floyd born 04 March 1909 married Gladiola Rebecca Hodges
   2.5. Margie Evelyn born 09 May 1912 married David J. Carter.
   2.6. James Woodrow born 21 December 1914 married Katherine Verna Deyerle.
   2.7. Mary Christine born 17 June 1917 married Thomas Bridgeman.
   2.8. Lois Elizabeth born 30 January 1921 married John Thomas Burnette.

---
[1] Bland County, VA Deed Book 7, p. 470.
[2] Bland County, VA Deed Book 10, p. 107.

   2.9.   Marguerite Alma born 20 February 1926 married Elmer Stanley Hash.
3. Della Roxie was born 16 November 1880 and died 01 January 1968. She married David Aviner Ritter on 07 January 1902 in Bland. David was born to David Spencer Ritter and Hettie Locritta Shufflebarger on 04 March 1875 in Pulaski County. He died 05 December 1962. Della and David are buried in the Goshen Methodist Church Cemetery. Children:
   - 3.1. Leonard born 22 January 1903; died 12 September 1928; buried in the Goshen Methodist Church Cemetery.
   - 3.2. Beatrice C.
   - 3.3. Virginia.
   - 3.4. Ronald.
   - 3.5. Elbert born 29 June 1909; died 31 March 1917; buried in the Goshen Methodist Church Cemetery.
4. Stewart Clayton was born 13 April 1882 and died 18 March 1946. He married Emma Josephine Clark daughter of James Alexander Clark and Elizabeth Jane Lambert. She was born 27 December 1893 in Bland. Stewart is buried at the Goshen Methodist Church Cemetery. Stewart and Emma's children:
   - 4.1. Frank.
   - 4.2. Ruby R.
   - 4.3. Verna E..
   - 4.4. Roy C.
   - 4.5. Albert C.[1]
5. Dora Ray was born 26 March 1884 and died 01 July 1962. She married Thomas B. Townley on 13 March 1921 in Bland. One daughter from the 1930 Bland census:
   - 5.1. Catherine M.
6. Frank Tyson was born 20 March 1886 and died 01 July 1962. He married Bertha King on 02 October 1912 in Pulaski County. Frank and Bertha were living in Pulaski in 1920. In 1930, they were living in Roanoke County. Children from the 1920 and 1930 census:
   - 6.1. Thelma.
   - 6.2. Violet.
   - 6.3. Lillian P.
7. Dana Rhoena was born 01 July 1888 and died 03 August 1926. She married Wiley Vincent Meadows on 02 December 1908 in Bland County. Wiley was born to James William Allen Meadows and Ida Belle Parsell on 13 September 1884; he died 12 December 1960. Dana and Wiley are buried in the Goshen Methodist Church Cemetery. Their children:
   - 7.1. Lucy Alberta married Glen Caudell Davis, son of Comie Albert Davis and Elizabeth Ellen Carr.* See Henry Davis Family.
   - 7.2. John Trenton married Lavina Elizabeth Brunk. *See Brunk Family.
   - 7.3. Charles Vinson never married.
8. Elsie Vernon was born 26 May 1890 and died in 1967 in Giles County. She married Albert Wesley Parcell on July 7, 1910 in Bland. Albert's parents were Calvin Van Doren "Kelly" Parcell and Cynthia Margaret Pegram. He was born in February 1892 and died in 1961 in Giles. They are buried in the Staffordsville Cemetery, Giles County. Children:
   - 8.1. Carl Weldon married Geneva Effie Robertson
   - 8.2. Argie Marie married John Hunter Spangler, Sr..
   - 8.3. Irvin Neil married Ernestine Elizabeth Stafford.
   - 8.4. Viola Aurelia was born 01 May 1918 and died 23 August 1918, Spur Branch, Bland County
   - 8.5. Garland Tabor married Kathrea Loretta Hale.
   - 8.6. Clayton Eldridge married Evelyn "Pat" Patterson.

---

[1] 1930 Bland County, VA Census.

- 8.7. Irene Isabelle married Aubrey Sydnor Dodson.
- 8.8. Emory Milton born 13 September 1924 and died 20 August 1925.
- 8.9. John Clifton married Gladys Lindsey.
- 8.10. Hersel Henderson married Mary Francis Burroughs.
- 8.11. Margaret Lorene "Frankie" married Harvey Green Whittaker
- 8.12. Evelyn Louise was born 16 June 1932 and died 16 June 1932.
- 8.13. Infant Daughter who died at birth 17 July 1922.
9. Hugh David was born on 18 March 1892 and died 22 December 1920. He married Ethel Letha Kitts. *See Henry Davis Family/Kitts Family

Wednesday December 23, 1920 Source: SW Times
Hughie D. Hamblin, a former service man, was so badly injured Wednesday afternoon about 4 o'clock as a result of a boiler explosion at the Kitts flouring mills at Long Spur, Bland County, that he died within 25 minutes. The victim of the explosion was fireman at the mills and was alone at the time in the boiler room, this part of the mill building being wrecked and parts of the engine strewn about for many feet. He was caught beneath some pipes and was unconscious when gotten out. No one else was hurt. The deceased was a son of J. S. and Sallie Hamblin and was born and reared in the Long Spur section of Bland County. He enlisted for service during the war and saw oversea duty, proving himself to be a gallant American soldier. Since his return home he has been employed at the mill. Besides his parents, five brothers and five sisters, he leaves a widow and one child, to whom the sympathy of his host of friends goes out in their bereavement. His age was 26 years. The funeral service will be held on Friday, burial will be held in the Long
Spur cemetery.

10. Estell Crockett was born on 11 December 1893 and died 23 March 1970. He married Lena Gray Davis on 22 July 1925 who was born to Comie Albert Davis and Elizabeth Ellen Carr on 04 May 1902 and died on 21 October 1952. See Henry Davis Family.

Lena Gray was the fourth Long Spur Postmaster assuming charge on September 8, 1948 until her death. At this time, her husband assumed charge until his retirement on December 6, 1963 at which time the Long Spur Post Office was discontinued.[1] Estell and Lena Gray are buried in the Goshen Methodist Church Cemetery *See Henry Davis Family. Estell married 2nd Minnie N. Alexander on 25 June 1966 in Pulaski County.

11. Bertie Cree was born on 13 April 1896 and died 08 November 1994. She married John Campbell Roope on 26 November 1926 in Bland. He was born on 07 December 1884 in Pulaski, the son of George W. and Cynthia M. Roope. John died 02 April 1971. John and Bertie are buried in the Goshen Methodist Church Cemetery. Children:
    - 11.1. Ralph Elwood married Nora Irene Davis.
    - 11.2. Emory Clifton married Helen Lovetta King.
    - 11.3. James Darnell married Edith Jane Davis.
    - 11.4. Fred Hensley married Edith Virgie Banes.

William J. S. Hamblin was born on 25 October 1857 in Giles County and died 27 January 1929 in Bland. He married Olleva "Ollie" E. Tabor on 12 December 1878 in Giles. Ollie was born in July 1856 in Giles and died April 1929. She was the daughter of John and Eliza Tabor. William and Ollie are buried in the Hamblin Cemetery, Spur Branch, Bland.

---

[1] National Archives and Record Administration, Washington, DC, RG 68, Site Location Reports, Long Spur Post Office.

On March 17, 1917 William J. Hamblin conveyed a small track of land to the Bland County School trustees in consideration of the educational purposes of neighborhood on Spur Branch…being reserved for school purposes. Also, conveyed ¼ acre to daughter Lillie J. Hardy[1]. On August 24, 1912, William J. S. conveyed to Edward L. Hamblin and Olevie for natural love and affection 103 acres of land on Spur Branch. It was agreed that the tract of land was to remain in the possession of Edward and said parties during their joint and separate lives.[2]

William left an additional 22 acres to Edward L. in his will and $150.00 to his daughter, Mellie Virgie Cruff.[3]

William and Ollie's children:
1. Edward L. was born 25 September 1879. He married Olive Virginia Millirons on August 22, 1903 in Bland. Edward died on 31 January 1969. Olive was the daughter of William Millirons and Julia Rose Banes. She was born 14 September 1879 in Pulaski County and died 08 May 1961. Edward and Olive are buried in the Hamblin Cemetery, Spur Branch. Their children:
    1.1. Glenord C. born 31 May 1904 and died 16 April 1975 married Margaret Stephens on 29 April 1926 in Bland. Glenord is buried is the Hamblin Cemetery, Spur Branch. They had children:
        1.1.1. Annie V. born 08 March 1927; died 14 August 1955; buried in the Hamblin Cemetery.
        1.1.2. Robert.
        1.1.3. Mary.
    1.2. Maggie Leona born 22 August 1905 married Orsen Wylie Chewning.
    1.3. Roxie M. born 22 April 1907 and died 19 March 1916 buried in the Hamblin Cemetery, Spur Branch.
    1.4. Dorothy born 12 March 1909 and died 02 February 1994; buried in the Goshen Methodist Church Cemetery. She married 1st Wiley Vincent Meadows, one son Allen Lee. She married 2nd Jerome Walter Greene.
    1.5. Genoa Thelma married Raymond Earl Davis. *See Henry Davis Family
    1.6. Garnett Lee married Janie Elizabeth Chewning
    1.7. Govan Thedmer married Martha Levell Davis. *See Samuel Davis Family.
    1.8. Charles W. was born 11 January 1916 and died 21 March 1916; buried in the Hamblin Cemetery, Spur Branch.
    1.9. Hobert born about 1919.[4]
    1.10. Arthur Edward was born February 9, 1922 and died May 11, 1955, buried in the Hamblin Cemetery. He married 1st unknown and 2nd Shirley Marie Walker.
    1.11. Ernest born about 1924.[5]

Edward conveyed for love and respect 1¼ acres to the Methodist Church South for a burial place for …"such persons as they may choose to bury there…" on May 25, 1929.[6]

On January 29, 1944, Edward conveyed a total of 125 acres to Andy Nuchols.[7]

---

[1] Bland County, VA Deed Book 13, p. 118.
[2] Bland County, VA Deed Book 12, p. 438.
[3] Bland County, VA Will Book 2, p. 161.
[4] 1920 Bland County, VA Census.
[5] 1930 Bland County, VA Census.
[6] Bland County, VA Deed Book 17, p. 322.
[7] Bland County, VA Deed Book 26, p 394.

2. <u>Nellie Virginia</u> was born 23 July 1879 [although her stone says 1879, the 1900 Bland census lists her born in 1882] married Robert Cruff on 31 August 1897 in Bland. Robert was born about 1876 to Henry D. and Lucinda Cruff in Montgomery County. Her marriage record lists her as V. N. Hamblin. She was 16 years old at the time of her marriage. Nellie died 14 January 1963; buried in the Hamblin Cemetery, Spur branch. Children from the 1910 Bland County Census:
    2.1. <u>Carolyn.</u>
    2.2. <u>Ballard.</u>
    2.3. <u>John T.</u>
    2.4. <u>Henry T.</u>
3. <u>Lilly Jane</u> was born June 1884[1]; married 1st Jacob Franklin Kitts on 20 May 1908 in Bland County. Jacob was the son of Andrew J. Kitts and Polly Leedy. He was born in November 1836 and died sometime between 1908–1910. Jacob is buried in the Goshen Methodist Church Cemetery. Lilly married 2nd Henry Ellis Hardy on 21 October 1911 in Bland. He was the son of Henry J. and Jesten Hardy. Lilly died 20 June 1959, buried in the New Dublin Presbyterian Church Cemetery, Dublin, Pulaski County, Virginia. Henry was born about 1875 in Carroll County, Virginia. Children from the 1920 and 1930 Bland County census:
    3.1. <u>Alice</u> born 22 October 1912 married Mr. Robertson. She died 23 April 1978 in Pulaski, buried in the New Dublin Presbyterian Church Cemetery.
    3.2. <u>Lottie</u> born 30 August 1914 married Frank Straley Melvin; she died 08 May 1978 and buried in the New Dublin Presbyterian Church Cemetery.
    3.3. <u>Henry J. R.</u> born about 1916.
    3.4. <u>Rachel</u> born 05 July 1918 married Albert Carter Hughett; she died 24 September 1995 and buried in the Highland Memory Gardens, Dublin, Pulaski County, Virginia.
    3.5. <u>Churchwell</u> born 13 August 1920 and died 26 June 1945, buried in the New Dublin Presbyterian Church Cemetery.
    3.6. <u>Charles</u> born 15 September 1922 and died 20 March 1994, buried in the New Dublin Presbyterian Church Cemetery.
    3.7. <u>Violet</u> born 01 September 1924, died 03 September 1924. She is buried in the Goshen Methodist Church Cemetery.
    3.8. <u>Dora</u> born 07 March 1928 and died 09 June 1988, buried in the New Dublin Presbyterian Church Cemetery.
4. <u>Ellen</u> was born about 1893; she married Samuel Sublett on 23 December 1910 in Pulaski County. She was listed in the marriage record as L. Ellen.

---

[1] 1900 Bland County, VA Census.

HANCOCK FAMILY

English origin, a patronymic (of, relating to, or derived from the name of one's father or a paternal ancestor) derived from Hann 1) a nickname for John 'gracious gift of Yahveh' or just ' gift of God or Jehovah,' from the medial syllable of the full form, Johannes; in its various national forms John has been excedingly frequent throughout Europe due to the outstanding Biblical characters John the Baptist and John the apostle, beloved disciple of Jesus, numerous popes and saints of that name; 2) if Ralf, like other Norman names beginning with R, had rhymed forms with H (such as Hick for Richard), perhaps Hancock, can be derived from Ralf used in England before the Norman Conquest, in the form Raedwulf "shield wolf," which became Radulf and then Ralf; 3) Hann can also be a short form for Henry "home rule", introduced by Normans, which became popular due to the three strong kings of this name during the twelfth and thirteenth centuries. In any case the name contains the common English diminutives -cock.[1]

Obadiah Hancock was born about 1786 and died between 1850 and 1860 per the 1850 and 1860 Wythe County census. He married Jane Bradd who was born about 1805 in Lunenburg County, Virginia. Jane died on 07 June 1853 on Little Walker's Creek, Wythe County. The death record in Wythe confirms that Obadiah and Jane lived on Little Walker's Creek in the 1850's. They were not listed as owning land during that time in the census.[2] Children from the 1850 Wythe County, Virginia Census, Wythe County marriage records and Mary B. Kegley's book, *Lost Children of Wythe County*:

1. Mary Jane was born on 16 June 1822 and died 05 March 1899 in Bland County. She is buried in the Hancock Cemetery, Little Walkers Creek, Bland. Mary never married. Her children are from various Bland county censuses and marriage records.
    1.1. Thomas S. born about 1854 and was living in Clear Fork, Tazewell County in 1880 with Louisa J. Hancock. There were two children listed, Martin L. age 1 and Mary A. age 6 months[3].
    1.2. Marcus Lee was born on 22 October 1856 and died 29 January 1938. He married Margaret Virginia Wyrick, daughter of Sanders and Nancy Wyrick, on 26 April 1877 in Bland. Margaret was born on 27 May 1856 and died 15 March 1928. Marcus and Margaret are buried in the Hancock Cemetery, Little Walkers Creek, Bland County. Marcus and Margaret's children:
        1.2.1. Effie Pearl born 21 March 1878 married Samuel Madison Corder on 23 January 1902. He was the son of James Larkin Corder and Minerva Josephine Pauley. Effie died 12 February 1934 in West Virginia.
        1.2.2. Saunders Helton born 30 December 1892 married Carrie Nellie Louisa Hancock on 19 June 1909 in Bland. She was the daughter of William Lee Hancock and Mary E. Epperson. Sanders and Carrie's children were:
            1.2.2.1. Rose Catherine married Frank Estell Collins
            1.2.2.2. Clarence.
            1.2.2.3. Ocie Evelyn married Hubert Bruce Dean.
            1.2.2.4. Robert Luther married Mary Elizabeth Corder daughter of James Larkin Corder and Mary Elizabeth Hancock.
            1.2.2.5. Huston Sanders married Beatrice Roseberry
            1.2.2.6. . Ruby Ella
            1.2.2.7. Ray
            1.2.2.8. Willard.

---

[1] *What is in Your Name?* Vitalog.net. website http://www.vitalog.net/cgi-bin/select_name.cgi
[2] Wythe County, VA Births and Deaths, Wythe County Courthouse; 1850 Wythe County, VA Census.
[3] 1880 Tazewell County, VA census.

- 1.2.2.9. <u>Carol.</u>
- 1.2.3. <u>Robert Luther</u> married Mary Elizabeth Corder. She was the daughter of James Larkin Corder and Mary Elizabeth Hancock.
- 1.2.4. <u>James W.</u> was born about 1894.
- 1.2.5. <u>Henry E.</u> was born about 1896.
- 1.2.6. <u>Robert Cecil</u> married Alma Cressell on 29 December 1926 in Pulaski County.

1.3. <u>George Washington</u> was born in 1859 and died in 1957. He married Isabelle Shrader on 02 July 1885 in Bland. She was born to Joseph and Sarah C. Shrader in 1869 and died in 1956. George was living in Clear Fork, Tazewell County in 1880 with the family of James M. Hoge living next door to Thomas Hancock.[1] George and Isabelle are buried in the Hancock Cemetery.

On January 26, 1876, Nancy Hounshell conveyed to G. W. Hancock 100 acres of land being on the east end of 605 acres patented to William Hounshell on June 30, 1843.[2]

A.T. Newberry and wife Caroline conveyed land to G. W. Hancock and John T. Farmer on November 16, 1881 [no acreage given]. This was probably the same land patented to Allen T. Newberry on December 1, 1857.[3]

On August 14, 1884, Abram Wampler and wife Polly and Joseph Shrader and wife Sarah C. conveyed land [no acreage given] to G. W. Hancock being part of the tract bought by Wampler …"known as the John Crockett entry…".[4]

John T. Farmer sold part of the A.T. Newberry land on December 23, 1890 to Samuel Williams.[5]

On February 16, 1915, Max Grief and Mrs. Laura F. Grief of Baltimore, Maryland for $1, ½ acre to George W. Burton, Stephen H. Smith and George Hancock trustees of Mitchell's Chapel Holston Methodist Episcopal Church.[6]

George and Isabell's children:
- 1.3.1. <u>Etta G.</u> was born December 1888.[7]
- 1.3.2. <u>Hattie G.</u> was born about 1889 married Stephen Alex Smith on 18 June 1905 in Bland. Stephen was born about 1876 in Wythe to John B. Smith and Sarah J. Halsey. Their children were:
  - 1.3.2.1. <u>Emma.</u>
  - 1.3.2.2. <u>William.</u>
  - 1.3.2.3. <u>Pearl.</u>
  - 1.3.2.4. <u>Robert.</u>
  - 1.3.2.5. <u>James H.</u>[8]
- 1.3.3. <u>Mary Elizabeth</u> married James Larkin Corder on 04 March 1914 in Bland. *See Corder Family.

---

[1] 1880 Tazewell County, VA Census.
[2] Bland County, VA Deed Book 4, p. 13.
[3] Bland County, VA Deed Book 4, p. 411.
[4] Bland County, VA Deed Book 5, p. 225
[5] Bland County, VA Deed Book 6, p. 139.
[6] Bland County, VA Deed Book 12, pg. 261.
[7] 1900 Bland County, VA Census.
[8] 1920 Bland County, VA Census.

1.3.4. Lucy E. was born about 1892.[1]

1.3.5. Bessie L. was born 27 November 1894 and died 01 July 1975. She married George William Collins; he was born on 16 September 1897 and died 29 January 1970. George and Bessie are buried in the Hancock Cemetery.

1.3.6. Stella Ernest was born 10 March 1897 and died 08 November 1979. Stella married Riley Harrison Hancock on 04 January 1917 in Bland. Riley was born to John Asa Hancock and Barbara Pauley on 25 June 1889 and died 03 March 1966. Riley and Stella are buried in the Hancock Cemetery. Their children are from the 1930 Bland census:

1.3.6.1. Jordan R..
1.3.6.2. Virginia E.
1.3.6.3. Barbara Belle.
1.3.6.4. Ribble J.
1.3.6.5. Martha E..

1.3.7. Samuel Roosevelt born 1903 married Annie Kate Millirons on 15 July 1925 in Bland. Annie was the daughter of Rufus Lee Millirons and Annie Kate King. Annie was born 24 June 1904 and died 19 March 1997 in Wythe County. Samuel died in 1966. They are buried in the Davis Cemetery, Little Walkers Creek.

1.3.8. Georgie Mae was born 31 August 1905 and died June 17, 1905 and died 17 June 1981 in Roanoke County, Virginia. She married Robert Newton King on 19 November 1924 in Bland and died 11 February 1971 in Montgomery County. He was the son of Joseph S. King and Emily Etta Pegram.

1.3.9. Jesse James was born 02 January 1909 and died 10 February 1994. He married Letha Virginia Ritter on 30 May 1931in Bland. Letha was the daughter of Bessie Pearl King Ritter She was born 08 August 1915 and died 18 February 1998. They are buried in the Hancock Cemetery. Their children are:

1.3.9.1. Jesse James, Jr.
1.3.9.2. Richard Lee .
1.3.9.3. Dorothy Marie.

1.3.10. Elizabeth Caroline was born in 1865 and died in 1954. She married George William Burton on 12 February 1896 in Bland. George was the son of James Thomas Burton and Mary Elizabeth Muncy; he was born in 1875 and died in 1927. George and Elizabeth are buried in the Burton Family Cemetery, Little Walkers Creek, Bland County. Their children were:

1.3.10.1. Bertha M.
1.3.10.2. Albert L.
1.3.10.3. Eva.
1.3.10.4. Charles.
1.3.10.5. George.
1.3.10.6. Thomas.
1.3.10.7. Gladys B.

2. George Washington was born in April 1830 in Wythe and buried in the Wyrick Cemetery, Bland (no dates on stone—Company A, 1st Virginia Regiment—CSA). He married 1st Julia Wyrick on 04 January 1853 and 2nd Sarah J. Pauley in 1881in Bland.

G. W. Hancock applied for a Confederate pension on July 14, 1902 in Wythe County. He served in Company A, 1st Virginia Battalion under Captain Robert Dunn and was partially

---

[1] 1920 Bland County, VA Census.

disabled due to the infirmities of old age. The pension listed him as 72 years old. George was listed as born in Campbell County, Virginia and had been a farmer all his life having lived in Wythe County for the past three years. He also listed on the application that he had joined the Confederate Army in Petersburg, Virginia and was enlisted for three years, discharged after the surrender at the Appomattox Courthouse. Witnesses for George Hancock were J. G. Sharitz and J. H. Crockett.[1]

George and Julia's children were:

2.1. Laura J. born about 1854 married John Havens on 01 January 1872 in Bland.
2.2. Marcus Walker was born in 1855 and died 30 April 1929. He married Mahala [maiden name unknown]. He married 2nd Emily Elizabeth Akers on 13 December 1910 in Bland. Emily was the daughter of Moses Akers, Jr. and Sarah P. Brawley.

Marcus Walker wrote his will on January 2, 1919. He gave son Charles W. and wife Lizzie 60 acres "east of my place". Three daughters, Laura Mae Terry, wife of Ben, Ina O. Lampert, wife of Luther and Eva T. King, wife of George W. was to have the rest of the land "being the west end". To granddaughter Hazel Marie Hancock, daughter of deceased son Andrew B. one dollar. Mae Hancock, widow of deceased son Jasper has a child of said marriage one dollar. Charles W. is to receive all the personal property.[2]

Marcus Walker and Mahala and had the following children:

2.2.1. Charles W. married Kate Lawson on 08 February 1908 in Pulaski.
2.2.2. Jasper married May Farmer. Jasper died during the influenza epidemic in 1918.
2.2.3. Laura May born in 1888 and died in 1931 married Benjamin Franklin Terry on 24 September 1904 in Bland. He was born in 1869 in Smyth County, Virginia and died in 1945. He was the son of William and Eliza Terry. Benjamin and Laura are buried in the Shrader's Chapel Cemetery. Their children from various Bland County censuses:
   2.2.3.1. Lula P.
   2.2.3.2. Fannie E. married Robert Lee Lambert on 21 May 1922 in Bland. He was the son of Mary Agnes Lambert.
   2.2.3.3. William W.
   2.2.3.4. Hazel M..
   2.2.3.5. Samuel B. married Clara French.
   2.2.3.6. Thelma G.
   2.2.3.7. Charles A.
2.2.4. Ina Olevi born about 1890 married Luther Edmond Lambert on 15 October 1905 in Bland
2.2.5. Eva Trottie was born December 1893 and died in 1931. She married George William King on 17 April 1910 in Bland. He was the son of William Thompson King and Nancy Lovica King. George was born 02 January 1883 and died in 1958. George and Eva are buried in the Shrader's Chapel Cemetery. They had one son:
   2.2.5.1. John William married Frankie Christine Elliot.
2.2.6. Andrew Ballard born 1895 married Edna Pauley, daughter of Newton Thomas Pauley and Martha Gullion. Andrew and Edna died in 1918 during the influenza epidemic.

---

[1] Library of Virginia, Richmond, Virginia, Confederate Pension Rolls, Veterans & Widows.
[2] Bland County, VA Will Book 3, p. 163.

2.3. John Asa was born about 1856 married Barbara Pauley 22 November 1881 in Bland. Barbara was born about 1857 to Jacob Pauley and Mary Jones. Their children were:
    2.3.1. Julia A. born 07 March 1883 married Harvey Blair Pauley. He was the son of Thomas G. Pauley and Telia Ann Kitts. He was born 28 June 1876 and died 05 October 195, Julia died 15 May 1952. They are buried in the Bland Cemetery, Bland County.
    2.3.2. Asa B. born November 1887[1] married Lucy (maiden name unknown) and had the following children:[2]
        2.3.2.1. Virgie.
        2.3.2.2. Hubert.
        2.3.2.3. John A.
        2.3.2.4. Wagner W.
    2.3.3. Riley Harrison born 25 June 1889 married Stella Ernest Hancock on 04 January 1917 in Bland. Riley died on 03 March 1966. Stella died 08 November 1979. They are buried in the Hancock Cemetery.
    2.3.4. Amanda Freelove born 31 May 1891 married William "Bud" Gordon Pauley, son of Gordon Paris Pauley and Sarah S. Thompson. Bud was born on 15 June 1887 and died 01 April 1953. They are buried in the Bland Cemetery.
    2.3.5. Nannie E. born April 1898.[3]
2.4. Mary Adaline was born about 1860 and married Edward Elisha Epperson, Jr. on 06 May 1881 in Bland. He was born about 1863 in Wythe to Edward Elisha, Sr. and Drucilla P. Epperson.
2.5. William Lee was born about 1861 and married Mary E. Epperson on 31 August 1882 in Bland. She was born about 1860 to Edward Elisha, Sr. and Drucilla P. Epperson. Their children were:
    2.5.1. Sidney Edward married Bessie Pearl King Ritter. *See Pegram Family.
    2.5.2. Ida M.
    2.5.3. Charles K.
    2.5.4. Carrie Nellie Louisa married Saunders Helton Hancock on 19 June 1909 in Bland. He was the son of Marcus Lafayette Hancock and Margaret Virginia Wyrick. Their children were:
        2.5.4.1. Rose Catherine married Frank Estell Collins. He was the son of John H. Collins and Gillie B. Akers. Rose married 2nd Jesse James Hancock, Sr.
        2.5.4.2. Clarence
        2.5.4.3. Ocie Evelyn married Hubert Bruce Dean.
        2.5.4.4. Robert Luther married Mary Elizabeth Corder, daughter of James Larkin Corder and Mary Elizabeth Hancock.
        2.5.4.5. Huston Sanders married Beatrice Roseberry.
        2.5.4.6. Ruby Ella.
        2.5.4.7. Ray.
        2.5.4.8. Willard.
        2.5.4.9. Carol.
    2.5.5. Cora married a Mr. Moore.
    2.5.6. Mogg .
    2.5.7. John Henry.

---

[1] 1900 Bland County, VA Census.
[2] 1920 & 1930 Bland County, VA Census.
[3] 1900 Bland County, VA Census.

- 2.6. Elizabeth Belle was born about 1862 and married Robert S. Wyrick on 01 December 1879 in Bland. He was born about 1857. Robert was the son of Asa Wyrick and Marinda Bogle.
- 2.7. Telia Agnes born about 1867 married D. P. R. Hoback on 01 November 1884.
- 2.8. Ollie W. was born about 1869. Never married. Her children were:
    - 2.8.1. Lizzie Mabel married William Nye Tickle son of Jackson Nye Tickle and Mary Ann Waggoner.
    - 2.8.2. Myrtle Nehema married William Lowe Kitts
    - 2.8.3. Bertha Louise married Daniel Crockett Pauley son of Gratton Crockett Pauley and Mary Geneva Kitts.
- 2.9. James Henry was born about 1871 married Margaret Luemma Tickle on 12 April 1894 in Bland. She was the daughter of Jackson Nye Tickle and Mary Ann Waggoner.
- 2.10. Cora born July 1873.[1]

George Washington and Sarah Pauley's children:

- 2.11. Marcia Ann born about 1877 married William Hedrick Hushour on 12 February 1894 in Bland.
- 2.12. Elexander Stinson born 21 December 1878 married Emily Lea Corder on 21 May 1903. She was the daughter of James Larkin Corder and Minerva Josephine Pauley. *See Corder Family/Akers Family.
- 2.13. Jesse Eugene born about 1890 married Lula Mae Harman and had the following children:
    - 2.13.1. Thelma J.
    - 2.13.2. William McKinley married Vena Gertrude Cassell.
    - 2.13.3. Eugene Mason married Virginia Ellen Hancock daughter of Riley Harrison Hancock and Stella Ernest Hancock.
    - 2.13.4. Ruby A. married Charles Woodrow Harman.
    - 2.13.5. Beulah married Bill Taylor.
    - 2.13.6. George E.
    - 2.13.7. Samuel C.
    - 2.13.8. Marsha E.
    - 2.13.9. Joy Kate.
    - 2.13.10. Fred Ralph.
3. Charlotte was born about 1831 in Wythe County. She married James J. Jones on 14 September 1848 in Wythe. Their children were:
    - 3.1. Sarah Ellen born about 1846 married Solomon King on 07 March 1866 in Bland. Solomon was the son of Bennett King and Bashaba Jones in Warren County, North Carolina. *See King Family.
    - 3.2. Mary Elizabeth was born about 1850 married Joshua Nye Mustard. He was the son of Joshua Mustard and Elizabeth Davis. They had children:
        - 3.2.1. James.
        - 3.2.2. Harvey Jasper.
        - 3.2.3. Lucy Lovica.
    - 3.3. Harrison H. was born 14 November 1853 on Little Walkers Creek, Wythe County.[2]
    - 3.4. Obadiah born about 1855 married Katherine Mustard on 27 January 1876 in Pulaski. She was the daughter of Joshua Mustard and Elizabeth Davis. They had children:
        - 3.4.1. James.
        - 3.4.2. Joshua.
        - 3.4.3. Delia.

---

[1] 1900 Wythe County, VA Census.
[2] Wythe County, VA Births & Deaths.

-
  -
    - 3.4.4. Rose.
    - 3.4.5. Charles Amos.
  - 3.5. Elvisia J. born about 1858 married Winton Carr on 08 July 1880 in Bland. Children from the 1900 Bland Census:
    - 3.5.1. Bell.
    - 3.5.2. Jesse R.
    - 3.5.3. Lizzie M.
    - 3.5.4. John H.
    - 3.5.5. Lillie M.
    - 3.5.6. William M.
    - 3.5.7. Lucy C.
    - 3.5.8. Burton L.
    - 3.5.9. Minnie W.
    - 3.5.10. Maude R.
    - 3.5.11. Robert S.
    - 3.5.12. Molly M.
  - 3.6. John W. born about 1861 married Eliza B. Corner on 18 September 1884 in Bland.
4. Demaricus L. born about 1832. A Lafayette Hancock is listed in the CSA records. Enlisted in Company F, 38th Infantry Regiment Virginia on 04 June 1861. Wounded on 01 July 1862 at Malvern Hill, Virginia; Hospitalized on 02 July 1862; Confined on 06 July 1863 at Fort McHenry, Maryland. Transferred on 07 July 1863 at Fort Delaware, Delaware. Transferred on 27 October 1863 at Point Lookout, Maryland. Admitted on 28 November 1863 at USA Smallpox Hospital. Point Lookout. Died of disease while a POW on 08 January 1864 in Point Lookout.[1]
5. Elizabeth Ann born about 1833 and died sometime between 1880 and 1900. She married David King on 05 June 1856 in Wythe County. David was born 08 November 1819 and died 04 April 1889. He was the son of Bennett King and Bashaba Jones. David and Elizabeth are buried in the Hidden Valley Cemetery #1 in unmarked graves. Their children were:
   - 5.1. Robert P. Hancock/King married Sarah J. Collins, daughter of James and Mary Ann Collins.
   - 5.2. Joseph S. married Emily Etta Pegram daughter of John Henry Pegram and Frances Louemma Martin. *See Pegram Family.
   - 5.3. Nancy Jane married James Whitten Davis son of Samuel Caddell Davis and Elizabeth Agnes Patterson.
6. John born about 1837.[2]
7. William born about 1839.[3]
8. Pleasant T. born about 1841 married 1st Thursa V. Wyrick on September 25, 1866. She was the daughter of Asa Wyrick and Marinda Bogle. Pleasant married 2nd Mary E. Wyrick on April 23, 1885. She was the daughter of Sanders and Nancy Wyrick. Pleasant and Thursa's children from the 1880 Bland County census were:
   - 8.1. Arbanna.
   - 8.2. Charles.
   - 8.3. Allie.
   - 8.4. Louisa.
   - 8.5. Roberta.
   - 8.6. Robert.
9. Henry born about 1843.[1]

---

[1] The Virginia Regimental Histories Series. 45 vols. Lynchburg: Howard, 1987.
[2] 1850 Wythe County, VA Census.
[3] 1850 Wythe County, VA Census.

10. <u>Alexander</u> was born about 1845.[2] Alexander enlisted in Company F, 51st Infantry Regiment Virginia on 05 May 1862. Residence was Bland County. Described as having a fair complexion, blue eyes with dark hair. He was 5 feet 8 inches tall. Prisoner of war on 02 March 1865 at Waynesboro, Virginia. Confined on 12 March 1865 at Fort Delaware, Delaware. Released on 20 June 1865 at Fort Delaware.[3]
11. <u>Virginia Ellen Bell Missouri</u> was born August 1851[4] and died after 1920. She married John Trigg Farmer on 05 April 1876 in Bland. John was the son of Richard Farmer and Rachel Halsey. He was born 31 March 1855 in Pulaski or Wythe. John died 29 September 1923 in Bluefield, Virginia. John and Virginia were living in Tazewell County, Virginia in 1920 per the 1920 Tazewell census. John and Virginia's children were:

  11.1. <u>George Hoge</u> born 12 January 1877[4] married Bertie Lee Smith.
  11.2. <u>John</u> born 08 July 1878.[5]
  11.3. <u>William Clinton</u> born about 1879.[6]
  11.4. <u>Stephen Madison</u> born July 1880 married Ollie Linkous 21 December 1903 in Pulaski County.
  11.5. <u>Charles Glenn</u> born 16 December 1882 and died 26 January 1960 in Mercer County, WV. He married Clara Ethel Covey on 27 December 1905 in Pulaski County.
  11.6. <u>Kelley Crockett</u> born April 1884[7] married Rose Linkous.
  11.7. <u>Thomas Newton</u> born July 1885[8] married Etta.
  11.8. <u>Howe Haven</u> born May 1887[9] married Ada Belle Shufflebarger on 22 March 1914 in Bland.
  11.9. <u>Woodie Lee</u> born May 1889[10] married Hubert R. Steel on 28 March 1908 in Bland.
  11.10. <u>Mamie Brown</u> born June 1891[11] married Buford Hedge on 29 December 1910 in Bland.

---

[1] 1850 Wythe County, VA Census.
[2] 1850 Wythe County, VA Census.
[3] The Virginia Regimental Histories Series. 45 vols. Lynchburg: Howard, 1987.
[4] Bland County, Virginia Births: 1861-96.
[5] Bland County, Virginia Births: 1861-96.
[6] 1880 Bland County, VA Census.
[7] 1900 Bland County, VA Census.
[8] 1900 Bland County, VA Census
[9] 1900 Bland County, VA Census.
[10] 1900 Bland County, VA Census.
[11] 1900 Bland County, VA Census.

HARRELL FAMILY

English, Welsh and Scottish, derived from the village name in Normandy Harel.[1]

William Harrell was born abt. 1740 in Frederick County, Virginia, and died 13 Aug 1822 in Wythe County, Virginia. He married Martha. She was born about 1750 in Frederick County, Virginia. The family located in Evensham (now Wytheville), Wythe County Virginia in the 1820 census pg 215. In 1784 there was land grant of 267 acres adjoining Alford's land on Harmony Creek -- granted to William Harrell. This places William in Wythe County, Virginia by 1784.

William Harrell and brother Reuben served in Captain Joseph Bowman's Company consisting of men from the lower district of Dunmoore County, during the revolutionary war. John Harrell and Enoch Harell, assumed brothers, were also in the company. Lieutenants were Joseph Denton and Thomas Allen. Served in Ltc. George Rogers Clark's Illinois Regiment.[2]

William Harrell's will:
Wythe County, Virginia Will Book 3, pages 12-13

In the name of God, I, William Harrell of Wythe County and of Virginia being weak in body but of a perfect sound and disparing? mind and memory, and calling to mind the uncertainty of life and certainty of death do make and declare this to be my last will and testament in manner and form following to wit in the first place I recommitted my soul to God, who gave it & my body to the earth to be buried in a decent manner, as to such worldly estate as it hath please God to bless me with, I give and dispose of the same in the following manner. First I direct my just debts to be paid and a fund for that purpose. I direct Seventy Dollars to be paid to Martha Harrell, my wife per annum during her life time and if that is not sufficient the boys John Harrell and Reuben Harrell is to pay a sufficiency to keep her lifetime and if they will not do it it is to be taken out of the land with all my household furniture farming tools with all my stock of cattle and sheep and the house I now live in during her life and at her death this property is to be equally divided between John Harrell and Reuben Harrell. The tract of land he now lives bounds as follows beginning at a large line on the tract of I now live and thence crossing the branch up the hill to a black oak and a hickory sapling thence crossing the hollow to the top of the ridge to two black oaks and two ? oaks thence straight on till it intersects with John Crisley live thence on a South West Course on his line to the pine tree thence along his line the several ? and corner? to Simpsons land from thence it joins with Simpsons line and corner to Peter Thrashers? land thence running with Trashers line and corner to Crocketts land then crossing the branch to Floreys corner then with Floreys line thence along Floreys line to the corner of the land I now live on thence along the line to the beginning--The said John Harrell and Reuben Harrell is to pay the heirs fifty dollars each to wit William Harrell, Elizabeth Pierce, Sarah Fulks Seventy-five dollars each I give and bequeath to my son Reuben Harrell all the rest of the land that is the tract I now live on and the balance of the tract of land I bought of Capt. ? and I give to him a small survey of twelve acres. I give to my son Reuben Harrell a large family Bible. I give and bequest to my little grand sons Monrow Harrell & Jacob Harrel son of Jacob Harrell deceased ten dollars each and to my daughter Mary Patrick or her legal heirs one dollar and to my daughter Nancy Brown or her legal heirs one dollar and to my daughter Rebeckah Axley or her legal heirs one dollar and I do hereby nominate constitute and appoint my son John Harrell and Reuben Harrell both of Wythe County my executors of this my last will and testament by me made and do declare all other wills and words and this only to be my last will and testament in witness whereof I have hereunto

---

[1] *What is in Your Name?* Vitalog.net. website http://www.vitalog.net/cgi-bin/select_name.cgi
[2] Revolutionary War Records of Virginia p. 604.(courtesy of Joyce Smith).

subscribed my name and affixed my seal this twenty seventh day of April in the year of our lord one thousand eight hundred twenty two.
Christian May, his mark   William Harrell
James Rogers, his mark
James Harrell, his mark[1]

William Harrel's son John Harrell married Sarah. They had a son, William

William Harrell married Susannah Florey 26 September 1818 in Wythe County. She was the daughter of David Florey and Maria Eva Breidinger. William died before 08 March 1833 as Susannah's children were listed in Wythe County School records during that time period. Their children were (possibly there were other children):

1. <u>Melvina</u> born June 1825[2] married Randolph Shinault. He was born July 1822[3] in Surry County, North Carolina to William Shinault and Sarah Love. Sometimes spelled Chinault and often referred to as Randal Chinault.

    On June 10, 1882, William L. Hunter and Missouri his wife conveyed 100 acres to Randolph Chinault on Little Walkers Creek..[4]

    Jesse Morris and Caroline his wife conveyed 75 acres to Randolph Shinault on August 29, 1882.[5]

    Jesse Morris and Randolph Shinault and wife Melvina conveyed 200 acres to Henrietta Harrell on September 24, 1894.[6]

    Randolph Chinault and wife Melvina conveyed 35 ½ acres to James W. Stone on March 10, 1902.[7]

    On March 12, 1908, Randolph Chinault conveyed 40 acres to Thomas B. Harrell…on line of James W. Stone part of land bought from Jesse Morris.[8]

    Randolph Shinault enlisted in Company B, 51st Infantry Regiment Virginia on July 31, 1861 in Wythe County. He was described as having a dark complexion, blue eyes with dark hair. He was 5 feet 10 inches tall. Randolph was a Prisoner of War on March 2, 1865 at Waynesboro, Virginia; confined on March 12, 1865 at Fort Delaware, Delaware. He was released on June 21, 1865.[9]

    Randolph and Melvina's children:
    1.1. <u>Sarah</u> born about 1844 married Joseph J. Morris, son of Elijah Jesse Morris and Jincey Haymore.
    1.2. <u>William</u> born about 1844.[10]

---

[1] Wythe County, Virginia Will Book 3, pages 12-13. .(Courtesy of Joyce Smith)
[2] 1900 Giles County, VA Census.
[3] 1900 Giles County, VA Census.
[4] Pulaski County, VA Deed Book 9, p. 180.
[5] Pulaski County, VA Deed Book 9, p. 181.
[6] Pulaski County, VA Deed Book 16, p. 336.
[7] Pulaski County, VA Deed Book 21, p. 458.
[8] Pulaski County, VA Deed Book 27, p. 151.
[9] The Virginia Regimental Histories Series. 45 vols. Lynchburg: Howard, 1987.
[10] 1850 Wythe County, VA Census.

1.3. David Jackson born about 1847[1] married Martha J. Merix 26 December 1872 in Giles County. David enlisted in 5th Virginia Reserves, Company G in November of 1864 in Dublin, Virginia. He applied for a Confederate Pension in Pulaski County on August 18, 1914. His place of residence was Sassin, Virginia. His disability was cancer. His wife Martha applied for a Widows Pension on 30 September 1922.[1] David died of cancer on 14 September 1922. Martha died on 07 May 1932. They are buried in the Hunter Cemetery, Little Walkers Creek. David and Martha's children were:

    1.3.1. Mary born 08 October 1872; died 08 September 1889. She is buried in the Hunter Cemetery.

    1.3.2. Helen born about 1876.[2]

    1.3.3. Ida born 02 April 1877; died 07 September 1889. She is buried in the Hunter Cemetery.

    1.3.4. Queenie M. born 28 February 1885 married Thomas B. Harrell on 19 August 1903 in Pulaski. He was the son of John H. Harrell and Henrietta Simpkins. Thomas and Queenie's children were:

        1.3.4.1. Hubert L.
        1.3.4.2. Arthur J.
        1.3.4.3. Thelma.
        1.3.4.4. Ida.
        1.3.4.5. Beulah.
        1.3.4.6. Leona.
        1.3.4.7. Ollie.
        1.3.4.8. Alva.
        1.3.4.9. Gladys.
        1.3.4.10. Emma.

    1.3.5. Vergie Lee born March 1890[1] married John Samuel Hurst, Sr. in Pulaski County.

    1.3.6. Eva born 06 January 1888; died as infant. She is buried in the Hunter Cemetery.

1.4. George Washington born about 1847 married Elizabeth Christley 20 September 1870 in Pulaski County. Applied for Confederate Pension in Wythe County; lived in Max Meadows at the time. He served with Company B, 51st Infantry. He died September 25, 1925 according to his wife Elizabeth's "Bettie" pension application filed in 1925.[3]

1.5. Mitchell born about 1855 married Louisa Akers 12 February 1874 in Pulaski County. She was the daughter of Davidson Akers and Rachel Graham.

William L. Hunter and Ethel his wife conveyed 15 acres to Mitchell Shinault on November 29, 1909 being part of the land conveyed to Hunter on February 6, 1904.[4]

On September 11, 1911, Mitchell Shinault and wife Lou conveyed the same land to Randal [Randolph] Shinault—which Randal had paid $100 for Mitchell on condition that he to secure support and maintenance for life—Mitchell had failed to do that. Mitchell was forced to deed the land to Randal.[5]

---

[1] Library of Virginia, Richmond, Virginia, Confederate Pension Rolls, Veterans & Widows.
[2] 1880 Giles County, VA Census.
[3] Library of Virginia, Richmond, Virginia, Confederate Pension Rolls, Veterans & Widows.
[4] Pulaski County, VA Deed Book 29, p. 83.
[5] Pulaski County, VA Deed Book 31, p. 436.

On April 10, 1909, Foy Combs conveys 100 acres of land on Little Walkers Creek to Henry L. Shinault (Mitchell's son) being the same that Sarah Underwood sold to Combs on March 19, 1909.[1]

Henry L. Shinault and Virgie his wife conveyed 100 acres to J. C. Truman. Dated January 18, 1912.

On July 1, 1919, D. K. Shinault and Nancy Mary conveyed 800 acres to T. T. Dulaney. This is, most likely David K., son of Mitchell Shinault.

1.6. <u>Susan</u> born about 1853 married Joseph H. Morris 11 January 1872 in Giles County. He was the son of Jesse Morris and Caroline Beller.
1.7. <u>Matilda</u> born about 1854 married George M. Whittaker 04 January 1871 in Giles County.
1.8. <u>James</u> born about 1859.
1.9. <u>Henry H.</u> born about 1864[1] married Luster A. Fink 02 September 1892 in Pulaski.
2. <u>Mitchell</u> born about 1823[2] in Virginia (most likely Wythe County) married Sarah Shinault, daughter of William Shinault and Sarah Love. She was born May 1827 in North Carolina[3]

From the book, Giles County Virginia: History-Families, Volume II:
Submitted by Myrtle Harrell Bychkowski
"Mitchell R. Harrell settled in Wythe County and married Sarah Chinault. They had ten children. Mitchell fought for the Confederacy during the Civil War. When returning home at war's end, he got within sight of his home and died before reaching it, leaving his widow and ten children. Sarah received a Civil War pension from the government (pensions for the confederacy was between $36 to $75 per year). The amount she received is uncertain.

Mitchell's (Harrell) daughter Cene A. Harrell married M. Hughes. Hughes left the Confederate Army and joined the Union Army. His family also received a Civil War pension from the government. The exact amount is uncertain, but it was between $300 to $400 per year. Mitchell's son, William Crockett Harrell, also fought in the Confederate Army.

Mitchell's daughter, Martha Ellen Harrell, married Elijah Jefferson Morris who was a well-known Methodist minister. Another daughter, Mary Maude Harrell married Gordon T. Hite. Their son operated a street car in Radford, Virginia.

Mitchell's eldest son, Stephen Ballard Harrell, married Martha Elizabeth Josephine Helton and moved to the gap of Cloyd's Mountain in Pulaski County. Fourteen children were the result of this union. Ballard and his first born son Charles Rufus (1884-1967); married to Mary Elizabeth Riddle 1915) were involved in the illegal production of whiskey. One account has the "revenuers" looking for an old white-haired man with a long white beard. In the time it took them to ask questions at the general store, Ballard had shaved his beard, put on a hat and was sitting in the rear of the store."

Sarah Harrell applied for a Confederate Widows Pension on June 19, 1888 in Giles County. Mitchell was a member of Company D, 45th Regiment, Infantry. He died in Pulaski County on May 18, 1864 of typhoid fever and chronic diarrhea. She and Mitchell were married January 27, 1847 in Pulaski County as listed on the application. She received $30 annually

---

[1] Pulaski County, VA Deed Book 28, p. 381.
[2] 1850 Pulaski County, VA Census.
[3] 1900 Pulaski County, VA Census.

from the state of Virginia. Sarah reapplied in Pulaski County on July 10, 1902; listed as living Sassin, Pulaski County. She was then entitled to $40 annually.[1]

Mitchell and Sarah's children:

2.1. James Floyd born about 1848 in Pulaski County 5 married Margaret Moye 11 May 1871 in Giles County.

2.2. William Crockett born January 1851 in Pulaski County married Miland Louisa Haskitt 05 December 1877 in Giles County.

2.3. John H. born November 1852 in Pulaski County married Henrietta Simpkins 06 October 1874 in Giles County.

2.4. Sarah J. born 30 August 1854[2]; died at age 3 months and 10 days in Pulaski County of scarlet fever.[3]

2.5. Mary M. born about 1857 in Wythe County married Gordon M. Hight 26 August 1878 in Giles County.

2.6. Stephen Ballard born 09 August 1858 in Wythe County married Martha Elizabeth Josephine Helton on 16 August 1883 in Giles County. Stephen died in 1917 and his wife died in 1956.

On January 7, 1902 Jesse Morris conveyed 50 ½ acres to S. B. Harrell (both of Giles County).[4]

S. B. Harrell and Josie his wife conveyed the same land above to E. J. Morris on December 23, 1919.[5]

Stephen "Ballard" and Josie's children:

2.6.1. Charles Rufus born 12 August 1884 in Giles County married Mary Elizabeth Riddle on 31 July 1915 in Bristol, Sullivan County, Tennessee. Mary was born 24 May 1900 in Giles County to Charles Estel Riddle and Lillie Tyretha Stafford. Charles died in 1967; Mary died January 30, 1985.

On November 27, 1911, Henrietta Harrell and J. H. Harrell conveyed land to C. R. Harrell (no acreage given)[6]

C. R. Harrell (unmarried) conveyed the same land to F. C. Combs on August 20, 1914.[7]

Charles "Rufus" and Mary's "Bess" children:
2.6.1.1. Pauline Bane.
2.6.1.2. Willard Raymond.
2.6.1.3. Elmer Elwood.
2.6.1.4. Russell David.
2.6.1.5. Hazel Irene.
2.6.1.6. Evelyn Loraine.
2.6.1.7. Arlen Woodrow.

---

[1] Library of Virginia, Richmond, Virginia, Confederate Pension Rolls, Veterans & Widows.
[2] Pulaski County, VA Births, Pulaski County Courthouse.
[3] Pulaski County, VA Deaths, Pulaski County Courthouse.
[4] Pulaski County, VA Deed Book 28, p. 548.
[5] Pulaski County, VA Deed Book 42, p. 48.
[6] Pulaski County, VA Deed Book 35, p. 198.
[7] Pulaski County, VA Deed Book 35, p. 199.

- 2.6.1.8. Myrtle Isabelle.
- 2.6.1.9. Roger Dale.
- 2.6.2. Della Maude born 01 January 1886 married Jason Hollins.
- 2.6.3. Arthur Booze born 25 December 1888 married Lennie Neal. Arthur died in 1956; buried in the Hunter Cemetery.
- 2.6.4. Lula E. born about 1890 married Creed Frank Combs on 29 January 1913 in Pulaski.
- 2.6.5. Frank J. born about 1892.
- 2.6.6. James F. born about 1893.
- 2.6.7. Martha Elizabeth born about 1898.
- 2.6.8. Elwood born July 1900.
- 2.6.9. Nola Lee born abt 1906
- 2.6.10. Elsie Marie born about 1908.
- 2.6.11. Luther Lawrence born 1900; died 1937. He is buried in the Hunter Cemetery.
- 2.6.12. Ethel May.
- 2.6.13. Emory Maxwell.
- 2.6.14. John.
- 2.7. Sena Ann born about 1860 married C. M. Hughes 29 September 1881 in Giles County.
- 2.8. Martha Ellen born 26 July 1862 married Elijah Jefferson Morris. *See Morris Family.
3. Rhoda born about 1824.
4. Elizabeth Jane "Emily" born about 1829 married Booker Richardson on 31 December 1847 in Pulaski County. Booker enlisted in Company F, 54th Infantry Regiment Virginia on 01 September 1863 at the age of 27. He was a POW on 25 November 1863 at Missionary Ridge, Tennessee; died of disease on 13 December 1863 in Nashville, Tennessee.[1] Elizabeth J. Richardson applied for a Confederate Widows Pension on March 20, 1888. She gave the details of her husband's death; explaining that he died on his way to a Union prison camp. She also gave the date and place of her marriage to Booker. She had not remarried.[2]

On July 8, 1896, E. J. Morris and Martha his wife of Giles County conveyed 31¼ acres to Emily Richardson on Little Walkers Creek.[3]

On July 8, 1896, E. J. Morris and Martha his wife of Giles County conveyed 31¼ acres to Emily Richardson on Little Walkers Creek.[4]

On February 3, 1903, Emily Richardson conveyed 31¼ acres to Thomas B. Harrell.[5]
Booker and Emily's children:
- 4.1. Ballard P. born about 1847[6] married Sarah N. Kate Mays on 10 February 1876 in Giles County.
- 4.2. Susan born about 1849.[7]
- 4.3. Nancy M. born about 1851 married James C. Dowdy on 29 May 1873 in Giles County.
- 4.4. Emily Jane born about 1853 married Andrew L. Dennis on 13 January 1876 in Giles County.
- 4.5. Nannie born about 1855.[1]

---

[1] The Virginia Regimental Histories Series. 45 vols. Lynchburg: Howard, 1987.
[2] Library of Virginia, Richmond, Virginia, Confederate Pension Rolls, Veterans & Widows.
[3] Pulaski County, VA Deed Book 17, p. 343.
[4] Pulaski County, VA Deed Book 17, p. 343.
[5] Pulaski County, VA Deed Book 22, p. 356.
[6] 1850 Wythe County, VA Census.
[7] 1850 Wythe County, VA Census.

5. Matilda born about 1830.
6. James Arthur born 20 January 1831 married Elizabeth "Bettie" Haymore on 17 January 1850 in Pulaski..

   James A. Harrell served in the 45th infantry Co. D. He enlisted April 1, 1862 in Pearisburg, Va. He was captured at Piedmont on June 5, 1864 and was taken prisoner to Camp Morton, IN. He was exchanged for another prisoner on March 4, 1865.

   Bettie Harrell applied for a Confederate Widow's Pension on 21 April 1910. She lived in Max Meadows, Wythe County. Her husband had served with the 45th Regiment, Company D under Captain Saunders. Her husband had died January 16th 1910 of bladder trouble and old age. She was 79 years old born in North Carolina but had lived in Virginia for 78 years. She was living with her daughter, Laura Harrell at the time of her application.[2]

   James and Elizabeth's children:
   6.1. Nancy Jane.
   6.2. Susan Malinda.
   6.3. William B.
   6.4. Sarah Ann.
   6.5. Louisa Frances.
   6.6. Orpha Ellen.
   6.7. Delia Elam.
   6.8. John Mitchell.
   6.9. Laura Eleanor.
   6.10. Ada Flora.
7. Nancy born about 1832 was listed in the census as idiotic.

---

[1] 1880 Giles County, VA Census.
[2] Library of Virginia, Richmond, Virginia, Confederate Pension Rolls, Veterans & Widows.

HUNTER FAMILY

English name derived from the occupational nickname for a huntsman whose work was both a necessity and a pastime for the ruling classes in the time when meat animals could not be kept well throughout the winter months.[1]

Peter Hunter was born 16 March 1776 in Louisa County, Virginia; died 21 September 1835 in Bedford County, Virginia. He married Lucy Goff on 17 August 1797 in Bedford. They had children: Absolam, Elizabeth, Peter, Lucy, Robert, Aeneas, Joseph A. William L. and Jerome.[2]

William L. Hunter was born 28 September 1816 in Bedford married Missouri Mooman on 10 May 1853 in Bedford. William served in the Civil War with the 63RD Virginia Volunteers as Captain.

"This deed made and entered into between Russell H. Cecil and Lucy A.. Cecil his wife of the sate of Kentucky, Wayne County, party of the first part and William L. Hunter of the county of Pulaski state of Virginia, the party of the second part. ...the party of the first part for and in consideration of the sum of Two Thousand five hundred dollars...land situated and being in the county of Pulaski state of Virginia and on Walkers little creek the whole of said tract containing three thousand eight hundred acres more or less...the first tract being that portion which was deeded by Russell H. Cecil by Zachariah W. Cecil by deed bearing date 20th May 1844...containing two hundred and twenty three acres...second tract containing one hundred fifteen acres...third tract being a portion of fourteen thousand five hundred acres conveyed to Russell H. Cecil by James Bane and others dated fourth of July 1842. The same three tracts herein conveyed being adjoined and connected together...the claim of Z. W. Cecil to the undivided half of the Alum Spring and half acre of land..."[3] Recorded August 4, 1859.

"Whereas, William L. Hunter the owner of one undivided moiety or half of the "Alum Springs" with one and one half acres surrounding it and Zachariah W. Cecil Jr. is the owner of the other half—of lands have never heretofore been precisely defined and settled; and all the parties being desirous to define and settle them permanently have this day agreed upon the following boundaries and descriptions ...this 29th March 1859."[4]

In 1859 William Hunter conveyed 1000 acres to William M. Miller line to Shannon's line; part of the tract conveyed to Hunter by Russell H. Cecil.

William L. Hunter conveyed 500 acres to Elizabeth J. Hunt on January 26, 1876.

Riley Harrison Hunt

Riley Harrison Hunt was a native of Franklin County, Virginia, born 30 May 1825, son of Stephen Hunt and Catharine Bird. In Giles County, Virginia, 20 September 1855, Elizabeth Jane Beller became his wife, and to them were born seven children: William Christopher, June 28, 1856 died September 12, 1875; Peter Edward, March 8, 1858, lived in Wyoming territory; George Lewis, February 15, 1860, lived in St. Louis, Missouri; James Thomas, June 21, 1862, died March 4, 1882; Margaret Permelia, February 4, 1865; Sarah Ann, November 30, 1866;

---

[1] *What is in Your Name?* Vitalog.net. website http://www.vitalog.net/cgi-bin/select_name.cgi
[2] Robert Hunter, Hunter Family Research.
[3] Pulaski County, VA Deed Book 3, p. 248.
[4] Pulaski County, VA Deed Book 3, p. 247.

Andrew B., March 31, 1860. Elizabeth J. Beller was born in Giles County, Virginia, December 19, 1835 and her parents were Peter Beller and Margaret Evaline Lucas. Riley came from Raleigh County, West Virginia, to Pulaski County in 1872, settling in Little Walkers valley.

On October 27, 1909, G. Louis Hunt (widower) of Washington County, Oklahoma conveyed 500 acres to his brother A. B. Hunt of Pulaski County.[1]

A. B. Hunt conveyed 250 acres to Etta E. Vest on April 7, 1915.[2]

On June 10, 1882, William L. Hunter conveyed 100 acres to Randolph Shinault.[3]

William and Missouri's children:
1. Robert Moorman Titus born in 1854, Port Conway, Virginia; died in 1906 Pulaski County.
2. John Walton born 1855; died in 1863.
3. William L. Jr. born 07 March 1859. He married Ethel (maiden name unknown).

On April 4, 1900, William L. Jr. sold his part of the Hunter land to R. M. T. Hunter—900 acres.[4] William L. Hunter, Jr. bought land from Bettie Shannon and Lula Weaver and husband Walter M...heirs of James King Shannon 750 acres on Walkers Little Creek—recorded on March 8, 1904.[5]

William L. Hunter and Ethel his wife conveyed 15 acres to Mitchell Shinault which was part of the Shannon land.[6]

Robert Moorman Titus Hunter (listed in court records as R. M. T. Hunter) married Queenie Victoria Hight. R. M. T. Hunter died in 1906; Queenie died in 1960. They are buried in the Hunter Cemetery, Little Walkers Creek, Pulaski County. Robert and Queenie's children were:
1. Roy born 1880 at Hunter's Alum Springs, died 1941 in Pulaski County married Nelle Beatrice Yost.
2. Ethel born 1888 in Pulaski, died 1990 in Pulaski, married Richard Cooper Kunkel on 07 June 1913.
3. Mabel born 1891 in Pulaski, died 1985 married Easton Purvis on 14 May 1913.
4. Irene married William S. Lyons on 05 June 1920.

On June 24, 1905 "...by and between R. M. T. Hunter and Queenie Hunter his wife, of Pulaski, Virginia, parties of the first part, and Hunter's Pulaski Alum Springs Company, Inc., a corporation, duly chartered under the laws of Virginia, and with its principal office at Pulaski, Virginia, party of the second part.... ...That for and in consideration of the sum of Thirty Thousand ($30,000.00) Dollars paid and to be paid as follows"...$7,000.00 to parties of the second part...the issuance to the said R. M. T. Hunter by the party of the second part of 100 shares of paid up and non-assessable capital stock of the said Hunter's Pulaski Alum Springs...of the par value of $100.00 per share and of the aggregate par value of $10,000.00...The said R. M. T. Hunter and Queenie Hunter, his wife...to grant...of title unto Hunter's Pulaski Alum Springs Company, inc...all certain tract of land known as "The Hunter's Pulaski Alum Springs

---

[1] Pulaski County, VA Deed Book 28, p. 577.
[2] Pulaski County, VA Deed Book 36, p. 33.
[3] Pulaski County, VA Deed Book 9, p. 180.
[4] Pulaski County, VA Deed Book 20, p. 133.
[5] Pulaski County, VA Deed Book 23, p. 145.
[6] Pulaski County, VA Deed Book 29, p. 83.

Property"…on the waters of Little Walkers Creek and adjoining the lands of Mrs. E. J. Hunt, John Combs heirs, John Harold [Harrell] et als and being all the property of which W. L. Hunter, Sr., died, seized and possessed, said property containing 600 acres…

…There is excepted and reserved however from the operation of this conveyance the Hunter Burying Ground, situate on said property near the Hotel and containing one acre which graveyard is situate on the Public Road through said property….

The following personal property and inventory of which was taken by T. L. Tate, General manager for the party of the second part, which property is situate in the Hotel buildings at the springs on said property and consists of hotel furnishing furniture etc. as follows—
Fifty bedsteads, 43 mattresses, 42 bedsprings, 65 dining chairs and 106 other chairs. 11 dining tables, 36 small tables, 9 washstands, 30 comforts, 30 pair blankets, 50 pair sheets, 47 counterpanns, 77 pillows, 30 mirrors, 46 lamps, 28 bowls and pitchers, 5 extra bowls, 25 alum water pitchers, 44 pair pillow cases, 27 slop buckets, 2 ice coolers, 60 teaspoons, 45 tablespoons, 88 silver forks, 93 silver knives, 11 butter knives, 1 pool table and fixtures for same, 2 cooking stoves, one lot of ten-pins and balls, 1 pair scales, office desk and furniture, and all hay and oats in the barn, also one cutting knife, forks, shovels, axes, and other utensils and articles in use in running the hotel; accepting and reserving however the farm machinery and the few pieces of furniture and other articles belonging to the said Mrs. Queenie Hunter individually, which articles are not herein entered…"

"Whereas Hunters Pulaski Alum Springs Company, Incorporated by deed of trust dated June 24 1905, Deed Book 9, page 24, conveyed to John S. Draper trustee, the property described known as Hunters Pulaski Alum Springs to secure R. M. T. Hunter the payment of $12,500 with interest. Whereas none of the bonds have been paid except the first. Whereas Hunter on June 24 1905 assigned to W. T. Graham the aforesaid bonds of $3,000 and 5,000…It is the intention of this deed to authorize, at option of the holder of the debt, as immediate sale of the property…whereas Robert C. Graham and James M. Graham being the highest bidder became purchasers paying $6,500. Dated October 1, 1909.[1]

On December 14, 1914, A. G. Woodyard bought 126.94 acres from R. C. Graham after deducting 1 acre for the Hunters graveyard. The same being parts of 600 acres conveyed to James Graham by John S. Draper, trustee.[2]

The hotel burned down in 1914.

---

[1] Pulaski County, VA Deed Book 28, p. 411.
[2] Pulaski County, VA Deed Book 35, p. 45.

JOHNSTON/JOHNSON FAMILY

Derived from the intrusive form of Johnson, patronymic (of, relating to, or derived from the name of one's father or a paternal ancestor) derived from the Biblical name John "gracious gift of Yahveh" or just "gift of God or Jehovah"; in its various national forms John has been exceedingly frequent throughout Europe due to the outstanding Biblical characters John the Baptist and John the apostle, beloved disciple of Jesus, numerous sovereigns, popes and saints of that name; 2) Scottish, derived from the place Johnston and Johnstone 'John's manor ' in Scotland.[1]

Lewis Johnston was born 17 March 1811 probably in Giles County. He married Martha Patterson on 01 June 1835 in Giles. Surety was provided by Lewis Johnston and Isaac Davis; Agnes Patterson certified daughter Martha's age. Martha's parents were William Patterson and Agnes Patton. Martha was born about 1812 and died sometime between 1870 and 1880[2]. Lewis died 08 December 1862 of fever.[3]

Addison Davis sold land to William Mustard: In January of 1852 "…by and between Addison Davis of the County of Giles and state of Virginia of the one part and William Mustard of the second and last part of the state and county aforesaid…sum of five hundred dollars…in trust for the benefit of Martha Johnston (wife of Lewis Johnston) and her heirs three several tracts or parcels of land situate, lying and being in the county of Pulaski in the state of Virginia on the waters of little Walkers creek the first part of which contains one hundred and ten acres and is bounded as follows to wit Beginning at a stake corner to the 74 acre tract the original corner down with the lines thereof…the second tract 74 acres…Beginning at two black oaks on the banks of the creek…the third contains 53 acres and was patented to said Addison Davis in the year 1848…".[4]

Lewis and Martha Patterson Johnston's children:
1. Nancy Jane born January 1838 married Nathan M. Bond 04 April 1876 in Pulaski. He was the son of James Bond and Margaret B. Mitchell; born about 1850 in Carroll County, Virginia. Nancy died in 1908 and is buried in the Bond Cemetery, Little Walkers Creek, Pulaski County. Nancy had two daughters out of wedlock. They were:
    1.1. Martha Jane N. Johnston born 13 October 1868 in Pulaski; married James R. Bond 30 June 1886 in Pulaski. He was the son of James Bond and Margaret B. Mitchell; born in Carroll County, Virginia 07 March 1858. He died 12 February 1896 and is buried in the Bond Cemetery. Martha married 2nd Thomas Fenton Ritter 09 September 1909 in Pulaski. He was the son of David Spencer Ritter and Hettie Locritta Shufflebarger. Thomas was born 24 July 1871 in Pulaski and died 07 October 1925 in Pulaski and buried in the Bond Cemetery. Martha died 10 September 1931, buried in the Bond Cemetery. James Bond and Martha Johnston's children:
        1.1.1. Victor O. born 28 September 1886 married Alma V. Pagan 15 November 1911 in Pulaski.
        1.1.2. Virgie Ethel born 1889 married William Hoge Hamblin 10 May 1906 in Pulaski.
        1.1.3. Della O. born 21 July 1890 in Pulaski.
        1.1.4. Oscar Roy born 18 March 1892 in Pulaski married Bertie White.

---

[1] *What is in Your Name?* Vitalog.net. website http://www.vitalog.net/cgi-bin/select_name.cgi
[2] 1870 and 1880 Pulaski County, VA Census.
[3] Pulaski County, VA Deaths, Pulaski County Courthouse.
[4] Pulaski County, VA Deed Book 2, p. 416.

- 1.1.5. <u>William James</u> born about 1895 married Bertha Hester Terry 17 October 1917 in Bland. She was the daughter of William Saunders Terry and Eugenia Thomas King.
- 1.1.6. <u>Lula Jane</u> born April 1896.

Children born after James R. Bond died:
- 1.1.7. <u>Abbie Elizabeth</u> born 02 January 1898 married William P. Johnston 26 December 1919 in Pulaski. Abbie died on 23 August 1993. William died before 1930. Their children:
  - 1.1.7.1. <u>Audrey Preston.</u>
  - 1.1.7.2. <u>Frank M.</u>
  - 1.1.7.3. <u>Arnold W.</u>
  - 1.1.7.4. <u>Donald L.</u>
  - 1.1.7.5. <u>Garnet R.</u>
- 1.1.8. <u>Jessie L</u>. born 01 October 1899 married Edgar Albert Banes. *See Banes Family.
- 1.1.9. <u>Wilma Lou</u> born 15 November 1907 married John Robert Chandler. *See Chandler family.
- 1.1.10. <u>Fred</u> born about 1908 per the 1930 Pulaski County census.
- 1.2. <u>Mary M. Johnston</u> born 05 March 1874.[1]
- 1.3. <u>Early Bond</u> born 01 June 1884.[2]

On March 27, 1909, Martha J. Bond was conveyed "…all that certain tract of land of which Nancy Bond (nee Johnson) died seized in December 1907 containing 65 acres[3] by decree of circuit court and entered January 4, 1909…a cause of Martha J. Bond versus Mitchell Bond and others."[4]

Martha J. Ritter (formerly Bond) to F. F. Ritter and Mrs. Abby Johnson, wife of W. P., for love and affection 65 acres corner to original Addison Davis land and Hiram Davis land. Recorded September 6, 1929.[5]

2. <u>Hugh P.</u> born 10 February 1840 married 1st Elizabeth (maiden name unknown). He married 2nd Serena Bond 15 September 1884. She was the daughter of James Bond and Margaret B. Mitchell. Hugh and Elizabeth had children Nettie and Sarah S. Hugh and Serena had children Hugh and Maude. Hugh P. died 15 March 1921. Serena Bond was born 07 May 1852 and died 15 February 1934. They are buried in the Thornspring Methodist Church Cemetery, Pulaski County. Hugh and Serena's son Hugh was born 06 July 1885 and died 16 December 1920; buried in the Thornspring Methodist Church Cemetery.

Hugh P. Johnson and Newton F. White and Clem his wife to Newton J. Morgan, Uriah Vermillion and Isaac Hudson, Trustees of Dublin District Schools 95 poles of land for a school on Little Walkers Creek. Dated August 10, 1883.[6]

Hugh enlisted in Company F, 45th Infantry Regiment Virginia on 29 May 1861, detailed as a teamster. He was sick on 15 September 1861.[7] He applied for a Confederate Pension on

---

[1] Pulaski County, VA Births and Deaths; Pulaski County Courthouse.
[2] Pulaski County, VA Births and Deaths; Pulaski County Courthouse.
[3] Pulaski County, VA Deed Book 28, p. 156.
[4] Pulaski County, VA Court Order Book 6, p. 382.
[5] Pulaski County, VA Deed Book 61, p. 524.
[6] Pulaski County Deed Book 9, p. 468.
[7] The Virginia Regimental Histories Series. 45 vols. Lynchburg: Howard, 1987.

December 7, 1905. He was suffering from rheumatism and partial loss of eyesight. He was born in Giles County and was 66 years old. During the war, he had suffered from pneumonia, typhoid fever and measles. He joined the service in May 1861 in Bland County and spent 4 years in the war. Hugh was eligible for $30 annually.[1]

3. Robert H. born about 1842.[2]
4. Wesley J. born 06 February 1842. He died 20 December 1854 from a tree falling on him at the age of 11 years, 10 months and 14 days.[3]
5. John P. born about 1844.[4]
6. James M. born 27 February 1846 married Hester Ann Flick 27 March 1866 in Giles County. Hester was born 19 August 1845, died 29 January 1904. James died 20 September 1920. Both are buried in the Thornspring Methodist Church Cemetery.

    James M. Johnson and wife Hester conveyed 45 ¼ acres to John Combs on June 16, 1873…"corner to Hiram Davis land…"[5]

7. Isaac L. born July 1850 married Sarah Elizabeth Bowles 29 December 1875 in Bland County. She was born April 1848 in Carroll County, VA and was living with James and Margaret B. Mitchell Bond in the 1850 Carroll County census. Their children:
    7.1. Alice L. born about 1876.3
    7.2. James A. born 27 August 1878 in Pulaski County.[6]
    7.3. Joseph born April 1882.
    7.4. Flora A. born February 1884.
    7.5. Isaac born 22 March 1885 in Pulaski.[7]
    7.6. Arthur born 25 March 1889 in Pulaski.[8]
    7.7. Minnie S. born about 1897.

On February 22, 1875, Isaac L. Johnston conveyed 44 ¾ acres to James Wilson White.[9]

---

[1] Library of Virginia, Richmond, Virginia, Confederate Pension Rolls, Veterans & Widows.
[2] 1850 Pulaski County, VA Census.
[3] Pulaski County, VA Deaths, Pulaski County Courthouse.
[4] 1850 Pulaski County, VA Census.
[5] Pulaski County, VA Deed Book 6, p. 357.
[6] Pulaski County, VA Births, Pulaski County Courthouse.
[7] Pulaski County, VA Births, Pulaski County Courthouse
[8] Pulaski County, VA Births, Pulaski County Courthouse
[9] Pulaski County, VA Deed Book 6, p. 180.

KING FAMILY

English, derived from the nickname for a person who played the part of king in the numerous pageants and festivals of importance in the cities and small towns during the Middle Ages, the name was also because of actual or assumed kingly qualities or appearance of the original bearer; sometimes the surname is a translation of the names with similar meaning from different European languages, e.g. German Konig.[1]

John Bennett King was born about 1790 in Ash County, NC and died between September 1 and December 14, 1857[2] in Wythe County, VA [now Bland County]. Bennett's parents were Wood King and Frances Duke.[3] He married Bashaba Jones born about 1795 in Surry County, North Carolina and died 14 August 1851.[4] She was the daughter of James Jones. Bennett was listed in the 1830, 1840 and 1850 Wythe County Census living in the area of Crockett's Cove. Bennett and Bashaba are buried in the Hidden Valley Cemetery #1 in unmarked graves.

Bennett received two land grants; the first being 175 acres dated June 30, 1846 on Walkers Little Creek, corner to John Crockett's land. The second grant was dated June 30, 1847 for 64 acres on Walkers Little Creek near Ravens Cliff and top of the Spur.

Bennett wrote his will on September 1, 1857: I Bennett King of Wythe County Virginia knowing the uncertainty of human life and being of sound mind and disposing memory for which I thank God do make this my last will and testament as follows viz: At my decease I direct that my just debts and funeral expenses be paid out of my personal estate. 1st I give and bequeath to my daughter Hannah Ritter King a bed and bedding for the same one cow and three sheep, also a home at my house while she remains unmarried. 2nd I give devise and bequeath unto my son David King and his heirs forever the eastern part of the tract of 175 acres of land upon which I now reside including the house in which I now live to be divided off by a line from a corner in the southern bounds described in the patent as a fallen white oak by a turn in a pond to a corner in the northern bounds described in the patent as a sycamore and white oak and upon condition that my daughter Hannah Ritter King as above mentioned shall have a home at my house upon the same while she remains unmarried and that my said son David King contribute to my support & much as I require of him. 3rd I give devise and bequeath unto James King infant son of my son James W. King and Sarah his wife as shall be born hereafter & their heirs forever the portion of my tract of 175 acres of land of which my son James W. King now lives to be divided of by line from the corner described in the patent as a sowerwood and white oak thence to run with a line of the part given to David King a southern course to the top of the big ridge thence westwardly along the middle of the top of said ridge to the west point thereof by a branch thence up the branch to the forks thereof thence up the eastern or right hand fork of said branch to the northern line of the patent thence with it eastwardly to the northwestern corner of David King's part the beginning and my last summers brown [illegible] and a cow which my son James W. King now has the use upon condition that my son James W. King shall contribute to much towards my support as I shall require of him. 4th I give and bequeath unto my son William G. King during his life the southwestern tract of 175 acres of land being the portion thereof not included in either off the parts thereof given to David King and children of my son James W. King and at the decease of my son William G. King I devise and bequeath unto the children of my son William G. King and their heirs forever the said portion of said tract of 175 acres which I have herein give to my son

---

[1] *What is in Your Name?* Vitalog.net. website http://www.vitalog.net/cgi-bin/select_name.cgi
[2] Wythe County, VA Will Book 9, p. 338.
[3] Rebecca Pacey, Jones Family Researcher.
[4] King Family Bible Records. Courtesy of Milt Davis.

William G. King during his lifetime under condition that my son William G. King will contribute towards my support so much as I shall require of him. 5th I give devise and bequeath unto my son Bennett King and his heirs forever my tract of 64 acres situate upon the long spur upon conditions that he settles upon it and resides upon it at the time of my decease and contributes so much toward my support as I shall require of him but if my son Bennett King shall not settle and live upon the said 64 acres unto my son David King and his heirs forever. 6th All the residue of my estate which I have not herein otherwise given I give to my son David King. 7th I hereby appoint my son David King executor of this my last will and testament. 8th I have already given to my son Solomon King and my daughters Nancy Davis and Mary Sublett all that I intend to give them. Given under my hand and seal the 1st day of September 1857.
The foregoing will was read Bennett X King
To Bennett King senr and his mark signed and acknowledged by said King in the presence of the undersigned present together at the same time
Joseph H. Holston
John H. Gibbony
The will was probated on December 14, 1857.[1]

Bennett and Bashaba's children:
1. William G. was born about 1812 in NC and died between 1888-1900 in Russell County, Virginia. He married Catherine Halsey on 02 January 1834 in Wythe. She was born about 1809 in Wythe and died 25 March 1886 in Russell County.[2] Catherine was the daughter of Stephen Halsey and Margaret Walraven.

Aug 25, 1888, "William King of Russell County conveyed land descended to him by father Bennett King to William T. King that for and in consideration that if he should stand in need of maintenance by others than John T. King.[3]

William and Catherine's children:
1.1. Cosby Jane Halsey/King was born in 1830 and died 16 November 1903 in Bland. She married Hiram Green Davis on 22 June 1848 in Wythe. Hiram was born in 1827 and died 02 November 1900 in Bland. His parents were Archibald Davis and Elizabeth Caddall. Hiram and Cosby are buried in the Red Oak Cemetery, Bland County. Cosby's descendents have always known her maiden name as Halsey. Their children were:
   1.1.1. Samuel Shelton born 05 May 1849 in Pulaski County married Sarah Ann Repass on 14 July 1881 in Bland County. Samuel died 10 March 1927 in Bland, buried in the Red Oak Church Cemetery, Bland County.
   1.1.2. John C. born about 1851.[4]
   1.1.3. Margaret Elizabeth born July 1853 married Stephen Valentine Frye on 28 February 1878 in Bland.
   1.1.4. James M. was born 27 February 1856 and died 20 October 1860.
   1.1.5. Loranzo Dow born about 1859.[5]
   1.1.6. Mary Jane born 18 November 1861 married Lafayatte Fry on 04 February 1892 in Bland.

---

[1] Wythe County, VA Will Book 9, p. 338
[2] Russell County, VA Deaths 1853-1896.
[3] Bland County, VA Deed Book 5, p. 459.
[4] 1870 Bland County, VA Census.
[5] 1870 Bland County, VA Census.

- 1.1.7. Randolph McGinnis born 06 April 1865 married Elizabeth Franklin Ingram on 21 October 1891 in Bland.
- 1.1.8. Henry B. born February 1868 never married.
- 1.1.9. Sallie born 1874 married Harman Ingram on 20 September 1896 in Bland.
- 1.2. Sarah Margaret was born about 1834 in Wythe. She married Thomas Fortner on 17 April 1851 in Wythe County. He was the son of Joseph Fortner and Elizabeth Brookman Thomas and Sarah Margaret were living in Russell County by 1870.[1] Their children:
  - 1.2.1. Joseph B.
  - 1.2.2. William Winton married Willie Jane Pegram on 03 September 1878 in Russell County. She was the daughter of John Henry and Elizabeth Pegram. *See Pegram Family.
  - 1.2.3. Elizabeth born 1855 and died 20 September 1858.[2]
  - 1.2.4. Sarah.
  - 1.2.5. Eugenia Belle married William Bennett King on 03 September 1878 in Russell County. He was the son of James Washington King and Sarah Ann Kendrick.
  - 1.2.6. John married Mary Evelyn Bush on 05 December 1888 in Wise County, Virginia.
  - 1.2.7. Mary A. married John A. Shannon on 08 November 1888 in Russell County.
- 1.3. Hester A. born about 1837 in Wythe County.[3]
- 1.4. James C. born about 1840 in Wythe County.[4]
- 1.5. John T. born December 1842 in Wythe married Sarah (maiden name unknown) and living in Russell County in 1880 and 1900. No children. William and Catherine King living with John T. in 1880.[5]
- 1.6. William Thompson was born 02 February 1846 in Wythe and died 11 March 1928. He married Nancy Lovica King 28 March 1867 in Pulaski. She was born about 1849 to Solomon King and Catherine Davis. They are buried in the Hidden Valley Cemetery #1.

William Thompson King served in the Confederate States Army in the 36th Infantry, Company G. He enlisted on March 15, 1864. He became a prisoner of war on May 9, 1864 at the Battle of Cloyd's Mountain. He was confined to Camp Chase, Ohio on May 11, 1864 and was released on March 2, 1865.[6]

William applied for a Confederate pension on October 11, 1910 at the age of 64 explaining "will be 65 February 2, 1911". He stated he was born in Wythe County, Virginia and had lived in Virginia all his life. His colonel was John McCauseland and

William T. King & Nancy Lovica King
Submitted by Sara Melton-Sumner

---

[1] 1870 Russell County, VA Census.
[2] Wythe County, VA Births & Deaths.
[3] 1850 Wythe County, VA Census.
[4] 1850 Wythe County, VA Census.
[5] 1880 Russell County, VA Census.
[6] The Virginia Regimental Histories Series. 45 vols. Lynchburg: Howard, 1987.

captain was H. C. Groseclose. He stated he enlisted in the fall of 1863 in Narrows, Giles County, Virginia and was captured at the Battle of Cloyd's Farm, impounded at Camp Chase, Ohio. William explained he was a farmer but was not able to farm at the time because of old age. Two comrades were listed who served with him in the 36th being B. H. Pauley of Bland, Virginia and Stephen Lampert of Bland, Virginia. The rest of the application is illegible.[1]

W. T. King and wife to Meek H. Davis, part of Bennett King land.

William T. King to Emily Gray for natural love and affection being of the s. side of Creek…Beginning at the mouth of Big lick Hollow with meanderings of Creek to point where Creek intersects with W T's land thence with bearings of said land on east end of King's land running into foot of Little Walker Mountain to a point in the line that intersects with King's outside line on the foot of said mountain in westward direction—being outside line of old Crockett survey…12 acres.[2] Dated December 10, 1918.

William and Nancy's children:
1.6.1. John Nye married Donnie Rogers.
1.6.2. Annie Kate born 12 September 1875 and died 17 November 1944. *See Banes Family.
1.6.3. Eugenia Thomas born May 1874 married William Saunders Terry on 24 August 1891 in Bland. William was born May 1865 in Smyth County, Virginia to William and Eliza Terry. Their children:
    1.6.3.1. James Hampton married Elizabeth Williams.
    1.6.3.2. John William.
    1.6.3.3. Bertha Hester married William James Bond. He was the son of James R. Bond and Martha J. Johnston. Bertha was widowed by 1920.
    1.6.3.4. Garnett married Lucy Clara Davis.
    1.6.3.5. Ida Kate married Carl Brown Davis.
    1.6.3.6. Otto.
1.6.4. Sallie born 25 June 1876.[3]
1.6.5. Ida Essie born about 1881 married William Curtis Haga.
1.6.6. George William born 02 January 1883 married Eva Trottie Hancock. One son:
    1.6.6.1. John William.
1.6.7. Emily Pearl born 25 June 1885 married James William Gray. James and Emily's children were:
    1.6.7.1. George W.
    1.6.7.2. Florence married Irvin Kelly Lambert.
    1.6.7.3. Hubert.
1.6.8. Rose born 23 March 1886.[4]
1.6.9. Hester J. born 24 August 1887.[5]
1.6.10. Daniel M. born November 1890.[6]

---

[1] Library of Virginia, Richmond, Virginia, Confederate Pension Rolls, Veterans & Widows.
[2] Bland County, VA Deed Book 18, p. 508.
[3] Bland County, VA Births: 1861-96.
[4] Bland County, VA Births: 1861-96.
[5] Bland County, VA Births: 1861-96.
[6] 1860 Giles County, VA Census; 1870 Wise County, VA Census.

2. <u>Nancy C.</u> born about 1819 in North Carolina married John Davis. He was the son of Abraham Davis and Sarah Moore. They had no children and were living in Giles County in 1860 and Wise County, Virginia in 1870.[1]
3. <u>David</u> born 08November 1819 in Warren County, North Carolina and died 04 April 1889. He married Elizabeth Ann Hancock on 05 June 1856 in Wythe County. Elizabeth was born about 1833 and died 04 December 1895. Her parents were Obadiah Hancock and Jane Bradd. David and Elizabeth are buried in the Hidden Valley Cemetery #1 in unmarked graves.[2]

    David and Elizabeth's children:
    3.1. <u>Robert P. King/Hancock</u> listed in the 1860 Wythe census as age 8 years old. He married Sarah J. Collins on 08 December 1871 in Bland. Sarah was the daughter of James and Mary Ann Collins. The marriage record listed Robert as Hancock and parent as Eliza A. Hancock. The census listed him as Robert King.
    3.2. <u>Joseph S.</u> born 18 August 1857 and died 06 March 1929. He married Emily Etta Pegram on 19 May 1887. *See Pegram Family.
    3.3. <u>Nancy Jane</u> born October 30, 1859 and died June 23, 1899. She married James Whitten Davis. *See Samuel Davis family.

    On December 5, 1913, Joseph and Emily King conveyed land to James W. Davis, husband of Nancy J. Davis, deceased, who was formerly Nancy J. King and the following children and heirs at law of said Nancy J. Davis, deceased, ..."namely: M. H. Davis and Ressa Davis, his wife, Frances B. Corder and B. L. Corder her husband, S. D. Davis and Della Rose Davis, his wife, Eliza A. White and N. F. White her husband, Richard F. Davis, Amy J. Davis, Edna K. Davis, Lucy P. Davis, Effie Davis and Nannie Davis…Whereas, David King was at the time of his death the owner of two tracts or parcels of land situate and lying in Bland Co, Va. one of the said tracts lying on Walkers Little Creek and supposed to contain 75 acres and the other tract lying on top of Long Spur and supposed to contain 66 acres; and said David King died and no partition of the lands was ever made between the said Joseph King and Nancy J. Davis." There was an understanding between the two parties; Nancy J. Davis was to have her share in the tract of 75 acres and Joseph S. King was to have the tract of 66 acres. The above named parties, Joseph King and the Nancy J. heirs …"are now desirous of making deeds each to the other for their respective tracts of land, in order to clear the title, and in accordance with the understanding aforesaid, as to said partition, and in accordance with the wishes of the said David King, expressed before his death…".[3]

4. <u>James Washington "Wash"</u> was born about 1820 in North Carolina and died 02 November 1890 in Russell County. He married Sarah Ann Kendrick on 24 June 1852 in Wythe. She was born 12 May 1834 in Wythe and died 28 December 1920 in Russell County.
    James and Sarah's children:[4]
    4.1. <u>William Bennett</u> born September 1855 in Wythe married Eugenia Belle Fortner, daughter of Thomas Fortner and Sarah Margaret King.
    4.2. <u>James D.</u> born about 1857 in Wythe married Esther Patrick on 27 December 1882 in Russell county.

---

[1] 1860 Giles County, VA Census; 1870 Wise County, VA Census.
[2] King Family Bible Records courtesy of Milt Davis.
[3] Bland County, VA Deed Book 12, p. 243.
[4] 1870 Bland County, VA Census; 1880-1910 Russell County, VA Census.

- 4.3. <u>Allen A</u>. born about 1859 in Wythe married Mary Alice O'Dell on 27 December 1882 in Russell.
- 4.4. <u>Elizabeth</u> born about 1860 in Wythe married 1st Roland Stableton on 06 May 1881 and 2nd William Alexander Osborn on 12 June 1884; both in Russell County.
- 4.5. <u>Mary Jane</u> born about 1868 in Bland married William H. Cook on 07 March 1889 in Russell.
- 4.6. <u>Katherine</u> born about 1870 in Bland.
- 4.7. <u>Cordelia</u> born about 1873 married Richard Scott Robinson on 25 October 1888 in Russell.
- 4.8. <u>Isabelle</u> born June 16, 1874 in Russell County[1] married Jacob A. Lyttle on 20 March 1895 in Russell.

5. <u>Hannah Ritter</u> born about 1821 in North Carolina never married. From the book, *History of Bland County (Virginia)* "Children from several families were first taught in the home of Hannah and Bennett King." She is buried in the Hidden Valley Cemetery #1 in an unmarked grave.[2]

6. <u>Solomon B.</u> born 07 July 1825 in Warren County, North Carolina and died 05 May 1901 in Pulaski County. He 1st married Catherine Davis Pendleton on 23 February 1846 in Pulaski County. She was 1st married to William G. O. Pendleton 17 October 1835 in Giles County. She had one son, James. She was born about 1819 in Giles County and died 05 December 1864 in Pulaski. Catherine's parents were William and Lovica Davis. Solomon married 2nd Sarah Ellen Jones on 07 March 1866 in Bland County. She was the daughter of James J. Jones and Charlotte Hancock. Solomon and Catherine are buried in the Millirons Methodist Church Cemetery, Pulaski County. Solomon, listed as widowed, was living with his son, Painter King in the 1900 Pulaski County census.

Solomon received a land grant in Pulaski County, Little Walker's Creek on October 2, 1854 …"On Walkers Little Creek corner to own land... corner to Lewis Jones's land." He later sold this land to Jeremiah Banes.

On April 27, 1848 in Pulaski, William Davis of Giles conveyed to Catherine King and children 134 acres of land on Little Walker's Creek for $500. The money was to insure the said William Davis a comfortable support in old age and any money owed after his death would become null and void.[3]

James Pendleton conveyed land on Little Walker's Creek to Solomon King on February 1, 1860. The land being …"vested to said Pendleton by the late will of William Davis, his grandfather…".[4]

On September 25, 1871 Harrison S. White and Mary M., his wife conveyed all right and interest in 1/7th of a certain tract containing 136 acres on Little Walkers Creek lying southwest and adjoining land of Jerry Banes.[5]

Solomon and his wife Sarah conveyed to John N. King all right and title being the undivided 1/7th interest to a tract of land containing 136 acres at the mouth of Harmon's Lick hollow corner of an entry made for William Davis—corner to "Red Pond" corner to 50 acres bought

---

[1] Russell County, VA Births 1853-1896.
[2] Hidden Valley Cemetery #1 map courtesy of Milt Davis (drawn by his father James Davis).
[3] Pulaski County, VA Deed Book 2, p.173.
[4] Pulaski County, VA Deed Book 3, p. 320.
[5] Pulaski County, VA Deed Book 5, p. 197.

by William Davis of John S. Shufflebarger to division line between King and Bane. Being same land conveyed to Catherine King and children by William Davis dated October 2, 1884.[1]

Evidently, after this conveyance or before, Solomon and wife Sarah were living in Bland County. The birth records of the children indicate they were born in Bland. Several court records and deeds also indicate they were living in Bland County. There was a long, drawn out court case involving a woman named Ellen Gills in which several Little Walkers Creek families were involved.

There was a gentleman who bought land from James Jones (Sarah's father) on June 14, 1875 by the name of "Bryl Jackson (colored)" Jackson was conveyed 100 acres of the Shelton survey.[2] Later, in 1880, Jackson conveyed the same land to Sarah King and children being James H., Sarah Ellen, Eliza V., Flora Missouri, Charley, Emily G. and Malena Etta.[3] On May 28, 1890, a court case arose concerning this land...Kegley Commissioner of Circuit Court and Sarah E. King and Solomon her husband of first part and Samuel W. Williams of the second part—Chancery cause pending in the name of Martin Williams, guardian for &c vs Solomon King and others...all that certain tract of land lying on water of Walkers Little Creek being the same land conveyed by B. Jackson (col) to the said Sarah & others on 30 September 1880...[4]

Looking at the Bland County Court records, I discovered the two above events may have been linked. On Monday, March 3, 1890-A. R. Heflin, Judge-Ellen Gills, Flora King, and Eliza King, infants over the age of 14, selected Martin Williams as their Guardian. On motion of Sarah King, Martin Williams is assigned as Guardian of Charlie King, Jennie King and Marcia King, infants under the age of 14...[5]

Thursday, November 7, 1889—Commonwealth VS Ellen Gills. Gills brought to the bar by the Sheriff, and by her attorney made motion to be admitted to bail. She, with R. N. French, James F. Grayson and W. W. Grayson, her sureties, posted bond for $1,000.00. –Wesley Jones, Lee Hancock, Samuel G. Shrader, John H. Collins, Sarah King, Marcia E. King, J. P. Shannon and R. D. Bogle, posted bond for $50.00 each, to assure their appearance at the next term of court to witness against Ellen Gills.[6]

December 2, 1889—Commonwealth VS Ellen Gills. Felony. Case continued. Ellen Gills unable to renew her bail remanded to jail. John Collins, Moses Akers. S. G. Shrader, Marcia King, Sarah King, J. P. Shannon, George Hancock, Sarah J. Hancock, Barbara Hancock, Wesley Jones, J. E. Tarter, James B. Shrader, Isabelle Jones, A. J. Grayson, C. S. Grayson and Lee Hancock, post bonds for $50 each to insure their appearance in court, to testify against Ellen Gills—Marcia King, Sarah King, J. E. Tarter, James P. Blankenship, Isabelle Jones, Lee Hancock and Harvey Blankenship post bonds for $50 to assure their appearance in court, to testify for Ellen Gills.[7]

---

[1] Pulaski County, VA Deed Book 10, p. 379.
[2] Bland County, VA Deed Book 3, p. 320.
[3] Bland County, VA Deed Book 4, p. 671.
[4] Bland County, VA Deed Book 7, p.41
[5] Bland County , VA Court Order Book 1884-1891, p. 517.
[6] Bland County , VA Court Order Book 1884-1891, p. 448.
[7] Bland County , VA Court Order Book 1884-1891, p. 490-491.

Continued on January 6, 1890. Ellen Gills. Felony. Case again continued. A rule is awarded against Isabelle Jones, William Jones, James Jones, Mrs. John Hancock and Mrs. Walker Hancock, to show cause why they should not be fined for failing to appear as witnesses against Ellen Gills.[1]

January 8, 1890—Commonwealth VS Ellen Gills. Felony. Charged with murder in the first degree. The jury was charged and then sequestered until tomorrow.4 The jury was sequestered several more times. On January 16, 1890 the jury returned with a verdict of "Not Guilty" and Ellen Gills was acquitted and discharged.[2]

There were two Gills children listed in the Pulaski County, Virginia birth records: H. Gills, male, born 27 May 1890 to William and Ellen Gills; Infant Gills, female, born 14 March 1889 to William and Ellen Gills.[3]

Solomon and Catherine's children:
6.1. Elizabeth born about 1848.[4]
6.2. Nancy Lovica married William Thompson King. *See William G. King.
6.3. Mary M. born 29 November 1849 in Pulaski and died January 14 January 1914 in Pulaski. She married Harrison Shannon White. He was born 06 August 1840 in Pulaski and died 17 March 1915 in Pulaski. Harrison was the son of John Wesley White and Mary Magdeline Plymale. Harrison and Mary are buried in the Thornspring Methodist Church Cemetery, Pulaski. Their children were
  6.3.1. John H.
  6.3.2. Mary.
  6.3.3. James.
  6.3.4. Lucy.
  6.3.5. Ernest.
  6.3.6. Charles.
6.4. John Nye was born 05 December 1851 and died 06 December 1912. John married 1st Susan L. (maiden name unknown) before 1876. He married 2nd Martha Taylor on March 27, 1878 in Pulaski. She was born in 1850 and died in 1947. Martha was the daughter of William and Elizabeth Taylor. John and Martha are buried in the Millirons Methodist Church Cemetery.

On October 4, 1900, James B. Caddall conveyed 92 acres of land to John N. King…"lying on the waters of Walker's Little Creek…beginning at the south bank of the creek corner to the Joshua Mustard tract…corner to lands of John King…".[5] The same tract of land Caddall bought from James Ingram.

John and wife Martha conveyed his 1/7 interest in 136 acres to the children of J. N. King by his wife Susan L. King on April 12, 1884.[6] *Note—The 1880 Pulaski County census lists John N. King wife Margaret S. King and son Robert J. King. In the 1900 Pulaski County census, John King is listed age 49, Martha age 40, Robert age 20, Isaac age 17; Bessie age 15; Charlie age 13, Roy age 11; Sidney age 10; Tobias age 6. No

---

[1] Bland County, VA Court Order Book 1884-1891, p. 495.
[2] Bland County, VA Court Order Book 1884-1891, p. 505.
[3] Bland County, VA Births, 1853-93.
[4] 1850 Pulaski County, VA Census.
[5] Pulaski County, VA Deed Book 20, p. 324.
[6] Pulaski County, VA Deed Book 10, p. 456.

other children have been found for John Nye King by a 1st wife Susan. Isaac was not listed in the 1880 census, therefore I believe his birth date on the headstone is incorrect. In the 1900 Pulaski census, lists Isaac's birth date as June 1882. Isaac Henry was listed in the 1910 Pulaski census with his two daughters; he was listed as age 27, widowed.

S. D. P. King conveyed to John N. King 1/7 interest of 134 acres…formerly owned by Solomon King on October 25,1885. [1](Most likely David Painter King).

John Nye King wrote his will on November 14, 1906: I, John N. King…all just debts paid…If at my decease, my son Charles Kelly has lost his leg or is otherwise totally disabled so as to make him utterly incapable of earning a living, then give said Charles Kelly ½ of all my estate including all personalty, realty, cash, bonds, notes, ect…If he is not disabled, then my estate is to be equally divided between Charles Kelly, Robert Jackson, Roy Clarence, Sidney Weldon and Tobias…To son, Isaac Henry and daughter Bessie E. Mustard the sum of $1 each…" Witnessed by R. Lee Millirons and William T. King. Probated December 11, 1913.[2]

John and Martha's children:

6.4.1. Isaac Henry "Harry" born 18 June 1876 (questionable) married Bessie May LeFew on 18 May 1904 in Bland. Isaac died 13 April 1911. Bessie was born 10 September 1883; died 02 January 1910. They are buried in the Millirons Methodist Church Cemetery, Little Walkers Creek, Pulaski. Two daughters:
    6.4.1.1. Gladys Elizabeth married Hubert Troy Allen. He was the son of William Carr Allen and Susan Sayers Morris.
    6.4.1.2. Beatrice married Vance Carl Southern son of William Southern and Maggie Vance.
6.4.2. Robert Jackson was born 1879 married Grace Ward.
    Their children were:
    6.4.2.1. Ernest
    6.4.2.2. Ruby
    6.4.2.3. Charles P.
    6.4.2.4. Dorothy M.
    6.4.2.5. Virginia E.
    6.4.2.6. Cabell W.
    6.4.2.7. Mabel.
6.4.3. Bessie Katherine born 09 July 1883; died 01 November 1960. She married Rush F. Mustard on 04 September 1906 in Pulaski. He was born 02 December 1873 in Bland and died 19 April 1947 in Pulaski. Rush was the son of William Patterson Mustard and Louisa Robinette. They are buried in the Hunter Cemetery, Little Walkers Creek, Pulaski. Their children were:
    6.4.3.1. Vance.
    6.4.3.2. Mason Manuel.
    6.4.3.3. Martha Viola.
    6.4.3.4. Naomi.
6.4.4. Charles Kelly born 10 January 1885 and died 19 July 1963 married Hanie Genoa Davis. She was the daughter of John Troy Davis and Mary D. Bowles.

---

[1] Pulaski County, VA Deed Book 11, p. 138.
[2] Pulaski County, VA Will Book 6, p. 425.

Hanie was born 10 January 1889; died 02 October 1945. Charles and Hanie are buried in the Millirons Methodist Church Cemetery. *See Samuel Davis Family.

"Uncle Kelly was logging in the mountains. A hook and rope somehow came loose from a log and struck him in the leg. I guess a horse was pulling it, because the horse drug Uncle Kelly for a considerable distance, causing multiple injuries, including to his face. He was taken to Charlottesville, which was a long distance in those days, so the injuries must have been serious. Mom said the leg never completely healed. She remembers two large holes in the back calf of one leg and that he kept them bandaged because of drainage. Eventually he had the leg amputated below the knee and wore a prosthetic leg. He had good mobility with it, though, because he was able to run the farm and the coal yard and drive a school bus. " [Suella Wolfe] *Kelly King was also a mail carrier for Little Creek. [RS]

On April 1, 1927 Kelly King donated land for a graveyard to the trustees of the Millirons Methodist Church (formerly the King Cemetery).[1]

- 6.4.5. Roy Clarence born May 1889.[2]
- 6.4.6. Sidney Weldon born about 1890 married Bertie Gray on 07 June 1911 in Pulaski.
- 6.4.7. Tobias born 22 September 1891 and died 20 January 1976. He married Nellie A. Collins. She was the daughter of John H. Collins and Gillie B. Akers Tobias is buried in the Millirons Methodist Church Cemetery. Their children were
  - 6.4.7.1. Irene.
  - 6.4.7.2. Roy Elmer.
  - 6.4.7.3. Seagle.
  - 6.4.7.4. Nina.
  - 6.4.7.5. Ernest Chaffin.
- 6.5. William Davis was born 06 October 1856 and died 07 August 1932. He married Olivia Virginia Thompson on 27 June 1881 in Bland. She was born December 1863; died 11 February 1941. She was the daughter of William and Jane Thompson. Their children were:
  - 6.5.1. Julian Bell born 08 February 1888[3] married John Jasper Davis. *See Henry Davis Family.
  - 6.5.2. Virgie born 12 July 1890.[4]
  - 6.5.3. Oscar David born 19 March 1893 married Lillie May Sutphin. Oscar died 10 June 1962. Served in the Navy, World War I. Lillie was born 24 May 1897 and died 02 February 1963. They are buried in the Millirons Methodist Church Cemetery.
  - 6.5.4. Wilbur C. born November 1886 married Grace Tucker. They had children:
    - 6.5.4.1. Helen.
    - 6.5.4.2. Myrtle.
    - 6.5.4.3. Herbert.
    - 6.5.4.4. Louise.

---

[1] Pulaski County, VA Deed Book 10, p. 456.
[2] 1900 Pulaski County, VA Census.
[3] Pulaski County, VA Births-1853-1893.
[4] Pulaski County, VA Births-1853-1893.

- 6.5.4.5. <u>Oscar Wallace</u>.
- 6.5.4.6. <u>Clifford William</u>.
- 6.5.5. <u>Mary Eula</u> born 08 January 1899 and died 03 January 1999. She married Robert Perry Millirons on 06 November 1920 in Pulaski. He was born on 16 August 1895 to William Newton Millirons and Mary Morgan. He died 15 August 1993. They had children:
  - 6.5.5.1. <u>Randolph William</u>.
  - 6.5.5.2. <u>Barbara</u>.
  - 6.5.5.3. <u>Colleen</u>
  - 6.5.5.4. <u>Karen</u>.
- 6.5.6. <u>Paris Bosang</u> was born 23 February 1902 and died 19 February 1992. He married Louise Valentine Whitt. She was born 14 February 1905 in Draper, Pulaski County; died 25 April 1993.
- 6.5.7. <u>William Robert Morris</u> was born 16 May 1905 and died 04 March 1987. He married Mary Ada Chandler. *See Samuel Davis Family.
- 6.6. <u>Harvey Newton</u> born 21 August 1859 and died 03 December 1928. He married Susanna Gray on 03 January 1883 in Pulaski. She was born 15 June 1864 and died 01 November 1938. Harvey is buried in the Bland Cemetery, Bland County. Susanna is buried in the Birtchlawn Cemetery, Giles County. Their children:
  - 6.6.1. <u>Eugene Thomas</u> born 27 November 1884[1] married Mary Veta LeFew on 20 June 1906 in Bland.
  - 6.6.2. <u>Della Rose</u> born 20 November 1885 married Samuel David Davis on 15 November 1905 in Wythe County. *See Samuel Davis Family.
  - 6.6.3. <u>Harvey L.</u> born 29 September 1887.[1]
  - 6.6.4. <u>James W.</u> born 16 March 1890.[2]
  - 6.6.5. <u>Julia D.</u> born 06 December 1892 married Robert Newton Davis. *See Samuel Davis Family.
  - 6.6.6. <u>Frances I.</u> born 06 December 1892.[3]
  - 6.6.7. <u>Edgar Palmer</u> born 29 May 1895 married Texie Miller Davis. *See Samuel Davis Family.
  - 6.6.8. <u>Arthur Jackson</u> born 24 June 1885; died 30 October 1891; buried in the Millirons Methodist Church Cemetery.
  - 6.6.9. <u>Eliza Agnes</u> born about 1897 married Ira Kelley Thompson on 31 December 1913 in Bland
  - 6.6.10. <u>Nellie Alberta</u> born 16 April 1900 married Benjamin Trigg Tickle, Sr. on 09 June 1921 in Wythe County. Benjamin was the son of George Lee Tickle and Ellen Smith Pegram. Nellie died 19 December 1966; buried in the West End Cemetery, Wythe County.
  - 6.6.11. <u>Bessie Mae</u> born about 1902.[4]
  - 6.6.12. <u>William L.</u> born about 1905.[5]
  - 6.6.13. <u>John Davidson</u> born August 12, 1909 married Willie Marie Kitts on 06 March 1929 in Bland. John died on 24 March 1993. Willie was born 05 April 1912 to William Lowe Kitts and Myrtle Nehema Hancock. Willie died on 22 February 1962. John and Willie are buried in the Bland Cemetery, Bland County.

---

[1] Pulaski County, VA Births-1853-1893.
[2] Pulaski County, VA Births-1853-1893.
[3] Pulaski County, VA Births-1853-1893.
[4] 1910 Wythe County, VA Census.
[5] 1910 Wythe County, VA Census.

6.7. David Painter born 14 October 1864 married Frances Gray on 07 September 1885 in Pulaski. Painter died on 28 February 1929; buried in the Newberry Cemetery, Bland County. Fannie died on 06 October 1944; buried in the Bland Cemetery, Bland County. They had the following children:
    6.7.1. Painter J.
    6.7.2. Lacy P. born 10 March 1889; died 19 October 1956; buried in the Bland Cemetery.
    6.7.3. Jerry.
    6.7.4. Frank born 16 April 1895; died 06 June 1930. Buried in the Newberry Cemetery.
    6.7.5. Claude.
    6.7.6. Rowena.
    6.7.7. Artie E.
    6.7.8. William.
    6.7.9. Henry Solomon born 1907 married Ida Lou Harden. Henry died in 1959. Buried in the Bland Cemetery.
    6.7.10. Van Crockett born 20 July 1902; died 19 April 1921. Buried in the Newberry Cemetery.

Solomon and Sarah Ellen's children were:
6.8. Solomon born about 1866 and was listed in the 1870 Pulaski County census but not listed in the 1880 Pulaski census. He evidently died young.[1]
6.9. James H. born about 1867.[2]
6.10. Sarah Ellen born May 1872[3] married William R. Gills on 27 April 1888 in Sullivan County, Tennessee. William was the son of Joseph J. Gills and Elizabeth Lury. They had children:
    6.10.1. Infant female born 14 March 1889.[4]
    6.10.2. H. male born 27 May 1890.[5]
    6.10.3. Mary Ellen born July 1891.[6]
    6.10.4. William A. born July 1893.[7]
    6.10.5. Effie L. born March 1895.[8]
    6.10.6. John Thomas born 31 January 1897[9] married Chloe Pearl Cole.
    6.10.7. Phillip Mathew born 27 February 1900.[10]
    6.10.8. Clora born about 1906.[11]
    6.10.9. Robert R. born about 1909.[12]
[This family still under research—RS]
6.11. Eliza V. born about 1872.[13]
6.12. Flora Missouri born 16 June 1874.[14]

---

[1] 1870 and 1880 Pulaski County, VA Census
[2] 1870 and 1880 Pulaski County, VA Census
[3] 1900 Mercer County, WV Census.
[4] Pulaski County, VA Births, Pulaski County Courthouse.
[5] Pulaski County, VA Births, Pulaski County Courthouse.
[6] 1900 Mercer County, WV Census.
[7] 1900 Mercer County, WV Census.
[8] 1900 Mercer County, WV Census.
[9] World War I Draft Registration Cards, 1917-1918 > West Virginia>Mercer County.
[10] World War I Draft Registration Cards, 1917-1918 > West Virginia>Mercer County.
[11] 1910 Mercer County,, WV Census.
[12] 1910 Mercer County,, WV Census.
[13] 1880 Pulaski County, VA Census.
[14] Pulaski County, VA Births, Pulaski County Courthouse.

6.13. Marlena E. born 27 May 1877.[1]
6.14. Charles born 29 November 1879.[2]
6.15. Emily G. born July 5, 1882.[3]
6.16. Jennie born August 1885.
7. John Bennett, Jr. born about 1828 in North Carolina married Mary Mildred Sublett on 12 June 1847 in Giles County. She was the daughter of Mathew Sublett and Frances Key. She was born about 1828. From various records, they did not live on Little Walkers Creek. John served in the Confederate States Army; enlisted 45th Infantry, Company F. on April 17, 1862 in Narrows, Giles County. He was in the Emory and Henry Hospital on March 25, 1864. Pardoned on June 13, 1865. John was described as being 6 feet tall with gray eyes and black hair. John and Mildred's children:
7.1. Frances Jane married William Paris Bogle on 18 March 1869 in Bland County.
7.2. Lucy Ann married Robert Graham Carr on 01 September 1870 in Bland.
7.3. Franklin Pierce married Sarah L. Woodyard on 20 August 1874.
7.4. Millard Fillmore married Angelina J. Franklin on 28 November 1878 in Bland.
7.5. Mary L. married Thomas A. Williams on 18 December 1879 in Bland.
7.6. John Matthew.
7.7. Laura Augusta.
8. Mary Jane married Allen W. Sublett on 10 May 1851 in Pulaski. He was the son of Mathew Sublett and Frances Key.

---

[1] Pulaski County, VA Births, Pulaski County Courthouse.
[2] Pulaski County, VA Births, Pulaski County Courthouse.
[3] Pulaski County, VA Births, Pulaski County Courthouse.

KITTS FAMILY

Kitts (Getz) is a German name derived from the pet form of Godizo "God."[1]

John Jacob Kitts (Getz) was born about 1730 in Holland married Nancy (maiden name unknown). By 1770 John Kitts had settled on 150 acres on Reedy Creek in present day Wythe County, Virginia. In about 1779 he left Virginia, crossed the Cumberland Gap, followed the Cumberland River to French Lick, which is now Nashville, Tennessee. There he received preemption rights to 640 acres about one and a half miles north of Nashville on the Cumberland River. In 1802 he died and left a will in Robertson County, Tennessee. His heirs included a wife, a son, two daughters and a grandson. When John went to Tennessee, he took with him one daughter, Mary. His second daughter, Elizabeth Kitts Blessing, and his son, Peter, remained in Virginia. Elizabeth died in Wythe County in 1825. John's son, Peter Kitts, married Elizabeth Wyrick in 1786. They moved to Grainger County, Tennessee around 1810. Peter left no will. Tradition has it that he died around 1830 and was buried in the Dyer cemetery in Rutledge, Grainger County, Tennessee. Three of Peter's sons, Henry, Jacob and Andrew, returned to Virginia to marry and raise their families.

Peter Kitts married Elizabeth Wyrick on 23 August 1786 in Montgomery County, Virginia. She was the daughter of Johann Nicolaus Wyrick and Anna Barbara Litchmere. Peter Kitts served in Hezekiah Harman's District, north of Walker Mountain and in 1797 Wythe County's Samuel Crockett's District. On 9 May 1797 he was appointed Constable in Leonard Straw's Company.[2]

Andrew J. Kitts was born about 1795 probably in Wythe County. He married Polly Leedy on 24 May 1825 in Wythe County. She was born about 1810 to John Leedy and Mary Gullian (probably same John Leedy in previously mentioned deeds of Wythe County). Andrew and Polly had thirteen children: Dulaney, Elizabeth, John David, Harvey G., James W., Telia Ann, David, Jacob Franklin, Virginia Caroline, Jane, Andrew Jackson, M. Nancy and Frances. Telia Ann married Thomas G. Pauley on 30 April 1856 in Wythe; which many of the Little Walkers Creek Pauley's descended. Virginia Caroline married Charles Russell Burton 15 October 1868 in Bland County.

Jacob Franklin 1st married Lutheria Bruce on 17 March 1864 in Bland; he married 2nd Cynthia Wyrick on 04 April 1869 in Bland and 3rd Lilly Jane Hamblin on 20 May 1908 in Bland. Cynthia was the daughter of Asa Wyrick and Marinda Bogle. Asa being a descendent of the above named Johann Nicolaus Wyrick.

Jacob Kitts
Submitted by Wade Arnold Davis

Jacob served in the Confederate Army; enlisted in the 45th Virginia Infantry, Company F on May 29, 1861 in Wytheville, Wythe County. He transferred to the 24th Infantry Regiment on December 28, 1864.[3]

Jacob applied for a Confederate pension on August 9, 1906 "by reason of old age, being past 67 years of age. He was entitled to $15.00 annually. Most of the pension application is illegible.[4]

---

[1] *What is in Your Name?* Vitalog.net. website http://www.vitalog.net/cgi-bin/select_name.cgi
[2] Betty Ross, Stone Mountain, GA.
[3] The Virginia Regimental Histories Series. 45 vols. Lynchburg: Howard, 1987.
[4] Library of Virginia, Richmond, Virginia, Confederate Pension Rolls, Veterans & Widows.

Jacob and Lutheria's child:
1. Miller White born 17 January 1866 in Bland married Emma Jane Burton on 22 December 1897 in Bland. She was the daughter of James Thomas Burton and Mary Elizabeth Muncy. Miller and Emma are buried in the Bland Cemetery, Bland County.

Jacob and Cynthia's children:

2. Franklin born about 1872; listed in the 1880 Bland census with Jacob and Cynthia. No other information, may have died young.
3. Robert Hutsel married Bertha J. Davis. *See Henry Davis Family.
4. Ressie Clora married Meek Hoge Davis. *See Samuel Davis Family.

Robert Hutsell Kitts
Submitted by Wade Arnold Davis

LAMBERT FAMILY

An English patronymic (of, relating to, or derived from the name of one's father or a paternal ancestor) name derived from the Germanic given name Lambert "land, bright," common in the Middle Ages. Often spelled Lampert in court records and censuses.[1]

Johann Heinrich "Henry" Lambert was born 01 February 1735 in Ottenberg, Rhineland, Palatinate, Germany. He married Maria Magdalina Daude 06 December 1760 in Froschen Pfalz, Bayern, Germany. She was born 08 August 1742 in Froschen Pfalz, Bayern, Germany. Henry and Maria left Germany to escape persecution of Lutherans. They sailed on the ship "Chance", arrived in America on 9 September 1765 where the family lived in New Amsterdam, New York before settling in Wythe County, Virginia. They had ten children. Henry and Maria died in Wythe County, Virginia in the early 1800's.

Henry and Maria's son, Johann Heinrich "Henry" was born October 1775 in Derry Township, Dauphin, Pennsylvania. He married Barbara Wolf 05 June 1795 in Wythe County. He died sometime between 1850 and 1860 in Wythe. Henry and Barbara had seven children.

Henry and Barbara's son, John was born 10 April 1797 in Wythe County. He married Mahala Hounshell 17 February 1840 in Wythe. She was the daughter of Henry Hounshell and Elizabeth Cline. John and Mahala had six children.

John and Mahala's son, Linsey T., was born about 1853 in Wythe and died in 1938 in Bland County. He married Sarah Elizabeth "Lizzie" Tickle on 22 March 1877 in Bland. She was the daughter of Peter C. Tickle and Mary Ann Journell. Lizzie was born October 1853[2] and died sometime after 1930. She is buried in the East End Cemetery, Wythe County. Linsey is buried in the Davis Cemetery, Little Walkers Creek, Bland County. The stone says Linsey Lampert and children—1938.

On April 6, 1891, Peter C. Tickle and wife Mary Ann conveyed 30 acres to L. T. Lampert.[3]

Linsey and Lizzie's children:
1. Mary Agnes born 05 May 1877 in Bland; died 08 April 1960. She is buried in the Davis Cemetery, Little Walkers Creek, Bland. Mary's children:
    1.1. Robert Lee married Fannie E. Terry on 21 May 1922 in Bland. Fannie was the daughter of Benjamin Franklin Terry and Laura May Hancock.
    1.2. George Cecil born 28 November 1903, died 08 April 1943. Buried in the Davis Cemetery, Little Walkers Creek.
    1.3. Irvin Kelly born 14 August 1908 in Bland married Florence Gray. Florence was the daughter of James William Gray and Emily Pearl King. Irvin died September 1971. Florence was born 25 February 1912 and died 10 October 1994. They are buried in the Hidden Valley Cemetery # 2. Their children:
        1.3.1. Alford William.
        1.3.2. Lillian Ethel.
        1.3.3. Clint.
        1.3.4. Cecil.
        1.3.5. Conway.

---
[1] *What is in Your Name?* Vitalog.net. website http://www.vitalog.net/cgi-bin/select_name.cgi
[2] 1900 Wythe County, VA Census.
[3] Bland County, VA Deed Book 6, p. 302.

- 1.3.6. Ralph Preston.
- 1.3.7. Lloyd Randolph.
- 1.3.8. Carolyn.
2. Ida born 02 July 1880[1]. Died young.
3. William A. "Bud" born 02 March 1885 married Minnie Clark 11 December 1913 in Bland. Minnie was the daughter of James Alexander Clark and Elizabeth Jane Lambert. Their children:
   - 3.1. Lula V.
   - 3.2. Lottie Jane.
   - 3.3. Genoa Violet.
   - 3.4. Arthur Alfred.
   - 3.5. Junior L.
   - 3.6. Raymond S.
4. Mary born 06 June 1890 2. Died young.
5. Female Lambert born 06 March 1892, twin; died at birth.[2]
6. Female Lambert born 06 March 1892, twin; died at birth.[3]

Lizzie Lambert was living in Wytheville by 1900,[4] listed as divorced with three daughters:
7. Effa Lambert born 01 March 1893 in Bland[5]. She died in 1924 (from Wythe County records).
8. Emily Lambert born 02 July 1895 in Bland. Name is listed as Ethel in the 1900 Wythe census. She married a Cregger.
9. Margaret Lee Lambert born May 1898[6] married Kyle Cecil. Margaret died in 1937.

It seems rumors are passed down from one generation to another (most likely embellished as time went by). It is said that Henry Davis went to Linsey Lambert and offered him a horse in exchange for his wife, Lizzie. Evidently, Linsey took Henry up on the offer. It is a fact that Henry bought a house in Wytheville and left that house to Lizzie in his will.

As written on an index card:
"Reference Note 47
I, Henry Davis, declare this my last will and testament:
First—I give and bequeath to Lizzie Lambert the following real estate and personal property namely all my real estate lying and being in the town of Wytheville and state of Virginia including the lot I bought my me and conveyed to me by M. M. Caldwell by deed of date Oct. 23. 1903—fronting on 7th street between Spring and Franklin Streets, a lot conveyed to me by Patsy and Emma Swan by deed of date Feb. 26th 1898, described as fronting on 8th street but really fronting on 7th street, a lot conveyed to me by G. R. Heufford and others trustees by deed of date June 3rd 1902 fronting on 7th street between Spring and Franklin Streets—All my household and kitchen furniture of whatever kind or description situated in my house in the town of Wytheville including sewing machine, trunks, pictures, books, & also two cows , hog, horse named Jessy, buggy, and horse wagon and jumper. All of which I have with me in Wytheville.
Second—al the rest and residue of my real and personal estate I give, devise and bequeath to my heirs at law to be divided by them as the law would divide it if I made no will.
Given under my had this 30th day of January 1906." Submitted by Juanita Bentley

---

[1] Bland County, Virginia Births: 1861-96.
[2] Bland County, Virginia Births: 1861-96.
[3] Bland County, Virginia Births: 1861-96.
[4] 1900 Wythe County, VA Census.
[5] Bland County, Virginia Births: 1861-96.
[6] 1900 Wythe County, VA Census.

Elizabeth Jane Lambert

A note about James Alexander Clark and Elizabeth Jane Lambert; Jane was the daughter of Isaac P. Lambert and Susan Rogers. Isaac and Susan were married 17 August 1848 in Wythe County. They had four children. Jane Clark's brother was William J. who married Sarah Elizabeth Meadows. William died 10 November 1887, place unknown. Jane Lambert Clark died 03 February 1923, buried in the Davis Cemetery, Little Walkers Creek. James Alexander Clark was the son of James Clark and Mahala Williams. He was born about 1854 in Greenbrier County, Virginia (now West Virginia). Jane's Lambert family was of English origin being no relation to Linsey Lambert's family.

James Alexander Clark and Elizabeth Jane Lambert were married 17 January 1882 in Bland. Their children were:
1. Rosetta born 17 October 1882.[1]
2. George A. born August 1885 married Jennie Collins
3. Minnie born 07 January 1893 married William A. Lambert.
4. Emma Josephine born 27 December 1893 married Stewart Clayton Hamblin.
5. Lula born August 1896 married William Henderson Pauley.
6. John.

---

[1] Bland County, Virginia Births: 1861-96

MEADOWS FAMILY

English; a name pertaining to landscape referring to meadow; the difference between a clearing in a wood and a small meadow is often nebulous in medieval landscape words; to our forefathers in the Middle Ages a meadow was a grassy, pasture land kept for mowing.[1]

It is believed the Meadows family descended from Ambrose Meadows/Meade of England. Ambrose was born about 1580 in England; his wife's name is unknown. He had a son Thomas Meades who emigrated to America, the Colony of Virginia in 1635. Thomas was born 24 December 1612 in Bristol, Sulfolk, England. He died 06 June 1655 in Essex County, Virginia. His will was probated June 12, 1655. His will (Record Book 2, 1637-1640, page 12) of Essex County. His wife's name was Sarah. They had children Thomas "Orphan" born about 1636; Margaret born about 1639; Joyce born about 1641; Ann born about 1643; Mary born about 1645. Thomas was mentioned in several court records as Thomas "Orphan" Meades. On August 6, 1655, Thomas Jr. (a minor) petitions the Court that he may choose a guardian, being of sufficient age. He chose William Underwood.

Thomas married Sarah Hoskins about 1658. Thomas and Sarah had three known children: John, Susannah and Mary.

John was born about 1658 married Elizabeth White. Elizabeth died on August 17, 1694. John married second unknown Awbrey. On December 10, 1695, in anticipation of a second marriage, John made a deed of gift to his seven children He is listed in court records in Essex County, Virginia as John Meador Senior. John and his family lived in Farnham Parish of Essex County, Virginia on the south side of the Rappahannock River. His will was probated November 23, 1721 in Essex County. Will: "I give to my son Thomas Meador one shilling; I give my daughter, Rachale Jodan, one shilling; to my daughter Elize Armstrong, one shilling; to my daughter Dinah Tribbile, one shilling; my desire is that my five sons shall keep their own guns without appraisal. I give to my daughter Mary Meador one gold ring. I give to my son Jones Meador a small piece of land joining upon Thomas Evan's and running up to church road that goes by my house then up a long road a small course until it comes to the fork of the branch where it began and from the fork to the first beginning and the rest of my land I give to the other four sons to be equally divided with all my houses and orchards thereon belonging and I do appoint my two sons Jobe and Jason Meador my executor. I give my son Joshua Meador one chest not to be appraised and the rest of my estate to be equally divided among my children and I do leave my two youngest sons to be of age at seventeen and I do leave my son Jonas Meador to look after them for three years and that my will not be in force 'til my decease as witness by my hand and seal this 17th day of October, 1721. Estate 3, 1717-22 C. 7283, pp. 284-5.

Thomas was born about 1680 in Essex County married Elizabeth Wood and they had ten children.

Thomas Jr. was born 1711 in Essex County and died in 1776 in Cumberland County, Virginia. He married Ann Bourne. Thomas Jr. and Ann had son Francis born 1738 and died about 1818 in Monroe County, Virginia..[2]

---

[1] *What is in Your Name?* Vitalog.net. website http://www.vitalog.net/cgi-bin/select_name.cg
[2] Deana Meadows Lewis, 4414 Durant # 62 Deer Park, Texas; Website: http://www.geocities.com/ginger77536/index.htm#TOC .

Francis Meadows came to the Blue Ridge Mountains in March 1770 and settled at the head of Hawksbill Creek in Augusta County, Virginia from Orange County. Marriage record in Orange County for Francis Meadows and Mary Kesiah Bell dated 1758. Francis is listed in the soldiers of the Revolution of Virginia in 1818 as being 80 years old and getting a pension of $80 per year.[1] He was living with his son Francis in Monroe County, Virginia.

John Meadows was born in 1782 in Orange County, Virginia and died March 1848 in Giles County. He married Elizabeth Wyant 06 March 1806 in Albemarle County, Virginia. Elizabeth died 27 November 1872 in Giles County, Walkers Creek. John and Elizabeth had thirteen children: Phillip born about 1807 married Sarah Ellis in Monroe County died in Daviess County, Missouri. They had son, Allen Parkinson Meadows. Allen married Frances Louemma Martin 23 December 1856 in Giles County. Frances was he daughter of John Martin and Elizabeth Waggoner.

Allen enlisted in the Confederate States Army, 36th Infantry Regiment, Company I on 16 April 1862 in Giles County. He died of disease on 04 November 1862.[2] Allen and Frances had three children.
1. Sarah Elizabeth born 04 September 1857 in Giles County; died between 1900-1905. She married 1st William J. Lambert on 24 December 1880 in Bland. He was the son of Isaac P. Lambert and Susan Rogers. William died on 10 November 1887. No children found from this marriage. Sarah married 2nd in Bland John Trigg Halsey on 16 September 1890. He was the son of John Trigg Halsey and Sarah E. Painter of Crockett's Cove, Wythe. John died on 05 December 1891 of Bright's Disease and buried in the Halsey Cemetery in Crockett's Cove. Sarah married 3rd David Spencer Ritter on 18 May 1893 in Bland. Sarah and David had two children:
    1.1. Huston Crockett born 19 March 1895.
    1.2. Frank Chaffin born 29 April 1896. He married Ethel Williams daughter of Alice Lee Williams
2. Mary Susan born 03 May 1859 in Giles County married James H. Overstreet on 24 January 1877 in Bland. James was born in Bedford County, Virginia to Tilmon J. Overstreet and Nancy Stanley. Mary and James later moved to the Parrot section of Pulaski County. They had three children:
    2.1. Samuel Allen born 09 October 1877 in Bland married Josie Reed 29 March 1904 in Pulaski.
        2.1.1. Bowie.
        2.1.2. James H.
        2.1.3. Mary B.
    2.2. Robert Lee born 30 August 1880 in Bland married Mary Belle Carden on 15 March 1904 in Pulaski. He died 11 November 1918 and is buried in the Highland Church Cemetery, Pulaski County. Mary Belle was the daughter of Charles Carden and Cynthia Victoria Tickle.
        2.2.1. Hattie B. married Thomas F. Mooney.
        2.2.2. Allie M.
        2.2.3. Jesse M. married Laura Tickle.
        2.2.4. Jeanette.
        2.2.5. Callie Jane married Robert Cloyd Carden.
        2.2.6. Hazel.

---

[1] Deana Meadows Lewis, 4414 Durant # 62 Deer Park, Texas; Website: http://www.geocities.com/ginger77536/index.htm#TOC.
[2] The Virginia Regimental Histories Series. 45 vols. Lynchburg: Howard, 1987.

- 2.2.7. Cecil M.
- 2.3. Cynthia born 15 August 1883[1] in Bland. Must have died young as she is not listed with them in any census.
3. James William Allen born 01 March 1863 in Giles County married Ida Belle Parsell on 24 May 1883 in Bland. Ida was the daughter of John Parsell and Mary Ann Coleman. Ida was born 01 October 1861 in Franklin County, Virginia. James died on 19 November 1917 in Bland and Ida Belle died 01 October 1945 in Bland. Ida Belle was the midwife for the Little Walkers Creek, Bland County families for many years. They are buried in the Goshen Methodist Church Cemetery.

**James William Allen & Ida Belle Parsell
Submitted by Sara Melton-Sumner**

James and Ida's children:
- 3.1. Wiley Vincent born 13 September 1884 in Bland married Dana Rhoena Hamblin on 02 December 1908 in Bland. Dana was the daughter of John M. Stafford Hamblin and Sarah Catherine Croy. He married 2nd Dorothy Hamblin, daughter of Edward L. Hamblin and Olive Virginia Millirons. Dana died 03 August 1926 and Wiley died on 12 December 1960. She died 02 February 1994. Wiley, Dana and Dorothy are buried in the Goshen Methodist Church Cemetery.
  Wiley and Dana's children:
  - 3.1.1. Lucy Alberta born 11 November 1909 married Glen Caudell Davis, son of Comie Albert Davis and Elizabeth Ellen Carr.
  - 3.1.2. John Trenton married Lavina Elizabeth Brunk, daughter of Houston Neel Brunk and Genoa Agnes Davis.
  - 3.1.3. Charles Vinson born 31 January 1917 never married. Died 13 June 2000; buried in the Goshen Methodist Church Cemetery
  Wiley and Dorothy's son:
  - 3.1.4. Allen Lee married Mary Catherine Brunk, daughter of Houston Neel Brunk and Genoa Agnes Davis
- 3.2. Lee L. born 04 September 1887 in Bland. He married Bess (maiden name unknown). Lee was living in Raleigh County, West Virginia in 1930.1 Children from the 1930 Raleigh County Census:
  - 3.2.1. Robert born about 1912.
  - 3.2.2. William born about 1914.
  - 3.2.3. Rudolph born about 1917.
  - 3.2.4. Harry born about 1921.
  - 3.2.5. May born about 1923.
  - 3.2.6. Fay born about 1925.

---

[1] Bland County, Virginia Births: 1861-96.

- 3.2.7. Charles born about 1927.
- 3.2.8. George born about 1929.
- 3.3. John Jesse born 28 May 1890 in Bland married Mary Alberta Davis on 30 May 1918 in Bland. Mary was the daughter of Hiram Newton Davis and Elizabeth Catherine Farmer. Mary was born on 05 January 1897 in Bland and died on 01 October 1924. Jesse died on 02 May 1978. Jesse never remarried; his mother, Ida Belle Parsell Meadows helped raise his children. Jesse and Mary are buried in the Goshen Methodist Church Cemetery. *See Samuel Davis Family
- 3.4. Charles William born 21 May 1892 in Bland married Mabel Johnson.
- 3.5. Albert Terry born 19 June 1895 in Bland married Laura Emily Millirons on 25 November 1915 in Bland. She was born 03 April 1898 to R. Lee Millirons and Annie Kate King Albert Terry died on 23 August 1972 and Laura died on 25 May 1973. They are buried in the Goshen Methodist Church Cemetery.

John Jesse Meadows and Mary Alberta Davis
Submitted by Sara Melton-Sumner

Their children
- 3.5.1. Earl Randolph married Pauline Bopp.
- 3.5.2. Ruby Irene married Norman Davis, son of Comie Albert Davis and Edna C. Davis.
- 3.5.3. Audrey Lee married Andrew Nucholls.
- 3.5.4. Kyle Robert married Etta Mae Roberts.
- 3.5.5. Miller Campbell married Evelyn Fellows.
- 3.5.6. Ina Juanita married James Edward Melton.
- 3.6. Hetty Naomi born 17 March 1899 and died 12 June 1900. She is buried in the Goshen Methodist Church Cemetery.
- 3.7. Ibba Erie born 15 June 1901 in Bland married Charles Bascom Jones. Ibba died February 1976 in Tazewell County.

MILLIRONS FAMILY

Christian Godfrey Muhelisen came to America from Germany to Philadelphia in 1747 on the ship Resurrection. He moved to the Valley of Virginia in 1753, purchased land on the north side of Maury River at Lexington in 1764. His wife was Mary. Children were David, William, Henry and Christopher.

David Millirons was born around 1784; he married Elizabeth Moulds. They had son John born about 1799 married Mary Polly Hypes 22 October 1821 in Botetourt County, Virginia. She was the daughter of John Hypes and Elizabeth Wimond. John Millirons died 05 May 1855 in Pulaski.[1]

On April 19, 1850 Addison Davis conveyed a tract of land to "...David Millirons and John J. Millirons lying and being in the county of Pulaski state of Virginia on the waters of Walkers Little Creek and bounded as follows to wit...corner of survey that the said Addison Davis got of his Father..."[2]

From Minnie Davis Parsell's series of articles, *A Hundred Years of Livin'*, she writes of the Millirons family, "Several miles down the valley was the Millirons Chapel. In that neighborhood lived an old couple, Mr. and Mrs. Millirons. She spent her time in a rocking chair. The Millirons Chapel was a small log building set way back off the road. They would carry her (Mrs. Millirons) in her rocker into the church. They owned their farm and had a nice dwelling house, the nicest on Little Creek at that time. The Millirons were educators. Most of them were school teachers."

John Millirons and Mary Hypes children:
1. Catherine born 13 January 1825 in Giles County married William Thomas Warner 01 March 1855 in Giles County.

    William T. Warner enlisted in the 23rd Battalion Infantry Regiment, Company D on January 28, 1863 at the age of 32 years. He was paroled on June 12, 1865. He was described as having gray eyes with auburn hair. William was 6 feet tall.[3]

    William applied for a Confederate Pension on June 5, 1900 in Giles County. He was totally disabled and incapacitated due to old age. He was 69 years old. He was given full disability pay of $30.00 annually.[4]

    Catherine applied for a Confederate Widow's Pension in Giles County on March 5, 1905. She was 70 years old and living with her son. She was entitled to $25.00 annually.[5]

2. David born 20 January 1826 married Susan Woodyard. She was born 05 February 1835 in Guilford County, North Carolina. David died 05 December 1901 in Pulaski County of kidney disease.[6] Susan died on 01 November 1911. They are buried in the old Millirons Cemetery. David enlisted in the 23rd Infantry Company. D, at the age of 24.[7] Susan Millirons applied

---

[1] 1 Pulaski County, VA Births and Deaths, Pulaski County Courthouse.
[2] Pulaski County, VA Deed Book 2, p. 320.
[3] The Virginia Regimental Histories Series. 45 vols. Lynchburg: Howard, 1987.
[4] Library of Virginia, Richmond, VA, Confederate Pension Rolls, Veterans & Widows.
[5] Library of Virginia, Richmond, VA, Confederate Pension Rolls, Veterans & Widows
[6] Library of Virginia, Richmond, VA, Confederate Pension Rolls, Veterans & Widows.
[7] The Virginia Regimental Histories Series. 45 vols. Lynchburg: Howard, 1987.

for a Confederate Widow's Pension on May 24, 1902. She explained that her husband died of bladder and kidney problems on December 5, 1901. Susan was entitled to $25.00 annually.[1]

David and Susan's children:

- 2.1. <u>Mary J.</u> born about 1857 married Hiram Martin 11 February 1875 in Pulaski County.
- 2.2. <u>William Newton</u> born 19 August 1861 married Mary Morgan 07 September 1887 in Pulaski. Mary was born 09 November 1865 and died 19 October 1952. William died 15 February 1941. They are buried in the Millirons Methodist Church Cemetery, Little Walkers Creek, Pulaski.

    On July 30, 1915, W. N. Millirons and wife Nancy M. conveyed land to the School Board of Pulaski adjoining and being an addition to a public school lot already owned by the School Board. Parties are given the right to erect and maintain a fence at their own expense.[2] No acreage given.

    On March 13, 1917, W. N. Millirons and Nannie released and conveyed land as a gift to the Trustees of Millirons Methodist Episcopal Church, South. The Trustees being T. J. Leeson, Roy Millirons and George Allen.[3] William also conveyed land to the Church on August 7, 1919.[4]

    William and Nancy's children:
    - 2.2.1. <u>Lilburn R.</u> born 27 September 1888 and died 02 August 1962. He is buried in the Millirons Methodist Church Cemetery.
    - 2.2.2. <u>Arthur B.</u> born 07 October 1890, married unknown wife and had four children.
    - 2.2.3. <u>Oscar Leroy</u> born about 1891 married Mabel B. Combs; daughter of Joseph W. Combs and Matilda K. Robertson.
    - 2.2.4. <u>Frank Wade</u> born 11 April 1893 married Launia Jackson. Frank died on 20 May 1978 and is buried in the Oakwood Cemetery in Pulaski.
    - 2.2.5. <u>Robert Perry</u> born 16 August 1895 married Mary Eula King, daughter of William Davis King and Olivia Virginia Thompson. Robert and Eula are buried in the Millirons Methodist Church Cemetery.
    - 2.2.6. <u>James Tolinger</u> born 13 March 1899 married Dorothy Spence. James is buried in the Thornspring Methodist Church Cemetery, Pulaski.
    - 2.2.7. <u>Dewey B.</u> born 12 January 1902 married Clora Kitts, daughter of Robert Hutsel Kitts and Bertha J. Davis. Dewey died in Pontiac, Oakland County, Michigan.
    - 2.2.8. <u>Fred</u> born 15 April 1905 married Gladys Vaughn. He and Gladys are buried in the Millirons Methodist Church Cemetery.
- 2.3. <u>Charles H.</u> born 15 September 1864 and died 21 July 1936. Buried in the Thompson Cemetery, Cox's Hollow, Pulaski.
- 2.4. <u>Harriet Elizabeth</u> born 25 April 1869 married Franklin Miller Thompson. He was born 20 June 1867 and died 05 August 1936. Sarah died 07 October 1960. They are buried in the Thompson Cemetery.
3. <u>John J.</u> born about 1828 married Barbara Ann Connelly. Lived in Giles County.

---

[1] Library of Virginia, Richmond, VA, Confederate Pension Rolls, Veterans & Widows.
[2] Pulaski County Deed Book 37, p. 587.
[3] Pulaski County Deed Book 38, p. 139.
[4] Pulaski County Deed Book 55, p. 427.

J. J. Millirons of Giles County applied for a Confederate Pension on July 20, 1900. He explained that he was disabled from rheumatism contracted during the "war between the states". He was not able to perform manual labor as he was 74 years of age. The doctor, A. S. Coven of Narrows, Giles county listed a chronic articulated rheumatism with deformity of the right and left knee joints, which taken with his age makes him unfit for labor. John J. served with the 23rd Battalion, Company E. He was entitled to $15.00 annually.[1]

John J. and Barbara's children were:
- 3.1. James D. born 22 September 1855, died 04 September 1876 in Giles County of diphtheria at the age of 20 years 11 months 13 days.[2]
- 3.2. Nancy S. born about 1860.[3]
- 3.3. Eliza Jane born 07 June 1863, died 12 December 1876 of diphtheria at the age of 13 years 6 months 5 days.[4]
- 3.4. John Harvey born about 1866 married Sumilda Etta Shrader 01 September 1894 in Bland County.
- 3.5. Mary A. born about 1868.[5]
- 3.6. Edna born 24 June 1875, died 09 September 1876 in Giles of diphtheria at the age of 1 year 2 months 16 days.[6]
4. Minerva born about 1833.[7]
5. Sarah born about 1835.[8]
6. Amelia Annetta born about 1837 married Guy P. Connelly 14 January 1857 in Pulaski.
7. Ann Elizabeth born about 1839 married James F. Conley 14 January 1858 in Pulaski.
8. Sally born about 1847.[9]
9. William born May 1847[10] married Julia Rose Banes. *See Banes Family.
   William enlisted in the Company. C, 54th Regiment on or about February 5, 1865 and was later a prisoner at Camp Douglas, Chicago, Illinois.[11]

Camp Douglas, originally constructed at Thirty-first Street and Cottage Grove Avenue as a Union Army training post, served as a Confederate prisoner-of-war camp. Between 1862 and 1865, the camp housed about twenty-six thousand prisoners in temporary, wooden barracks. As a result of harsh conditions, some four thousand men died at the camp; they were buried in unmarked paupers' graves in Chicago's City Cemetery, located at the southeast corner of what is now Lincoln Park. In 1867, the remains were reburied at Oak Woods Cemetery, about five miles south of the camp.

William applied for a Confederate Pension on April 20, 1888. He was 45 years of age. He explained that he was injured from a fall on the ice while on detail carrying water at Camp Douglas.. The fall resulted in breaking his leg near the hip joint. He was entitled to $15.00 annually.[12]

---

[1] Library of Virginia, Richmond, Virginia, Confederate Pension Rolls, Veterans & Widows.
[2] Giles County, VA Deaths, Giles County Courthouse.
[3] 1870 Giles County, VA Census.
[4] Giles County, VA Deaths, Giles County Courthouse.
[5] 1870 Giles County, VA Census.
[6] Giles County, VA Deaths, Giles County Courthouse
[7] 1850 Pulaski County, VA Census.
[8] 1850 Pulaski County, VA Census.
[9] 1850 Pulaski County, VA Census.
[10] 1900 Pulaski County, VA Census.
[11] The Virginia Regimental Histories Series. 45 vols. Lynchburg: Howard, 1987.
[12] Library of Virginia, Richmond, Virginia, Confederate Pension Rolls, Veterans & Widows.

MONTGOMERY FAMILY

Welsh, originally designated one who came from the ancient castle of Saint Foi de Montgomery 'hill of Gomeric or from Saint Germain de Montgomery, two places in Normandy; Roger de Montgomery accompanied the Conqueror to England.[1]

In the 1870 Pulaski census, there were several African-American Montgomery children living with different families, some of them were "house help" others were "farm laborers" and they were in the age range of being siblings. They were James born 1851, John born 1852, Larkin born 1854, Jacob born 1855, Alexander born 1856, Margaret A. born 1857 and Richard born 1858.

Larkin "Lark" Montgomery was born October 1854[2] in Pulaski County to John and Letitia Montgomery. He married Nancy Moody 14 May 1877 in Giles County. She was the daughter of Benjamin and Letitia Moody[3]. Larkin married 2nd Lucinda "Lucy" J. Peoples sometime between 1880-1890 as Nancy was listed with Larkin in the 1880 Pulaski County census. By 1900, Lucy was listed in the Pulaski County census with Larkin. Lucy was the daughter of Pharaoh and Susan Peoples[4] from Crockett's Cove, Wythe County. In the 1900 Pulaski Census, listed Larkin and Lucy as married 10 years, making their marriage year in 1890. They had 5 children with 4 living. Lucy was born September 1865 per the 1900 census.

On July 25, 1906, N. F. White conveyed 40 acres to Lucy Montgomery being part of the J. W. White farm.[5]

Larkin Montgomery and Lucy conveyed 4 ½ acres to John Dickerson on February 28, 1914.[6]

Also on February 28, 1914, Larkin and Lucy conveyed 8 acres to Mittie Peoples and her heirs.[7]

Larkin and Nancy's children taken from Pulaski County, Virginia Births-1853-93, Pulaski County Courthouse:
1. Male Infant born 01 March 1878.
2. Mettie born 15 August 1880 married Joseph Taylor Peoples on 22 December 1898 in Pulaski. Joseph was born 22 Jun 1877[8] to Pharaoh and Susan Peoples.

    N. F. White and Eliza conveyed 2 tracts of land to J. T. Peoples on October 7, 1927. Being same tracts bought from the Cecil heirs. A total of 220 acres.[9]

    Joseph and Mettie's children:
    2.1. John Huston born about 1901.
    2.2. Carrie born about 1903 married Charlie M. Banks on 24 January 1924 in Pulaski County.
    2.3. Mary Ann born about 1904.
    2.4. Joseph Larkin born 03 May 1905 married Signora Barner.

---

[1] *What is in Your Name?* Vitalog.net. website http://www.vitalog.net/cgi-bin/select_name.cgi
[2] 1900 Pulaski County, VA Census
[3] Parent's names came from Giles County, VA Marriage Records, Giles County Courthouse.
[4] Parent's names came from 1860 Wythe County, VA census.
[5] Pulaski County, VA Deed Book 29, p. 329.
[6] Pulaski County, VA Deed Book 34, p. 508.
[7] Pulaski County, VA Deed Book 34, p.522.
[8] World War I Draft Registration Cards, 1917-1918.
[9] Pulaski County, VA Deed Book 57, p. 79.

- 2.5. <u>James</u> born about 1909.
- 2.6. <u>Leonard E</u>. born about 1911.
- 2.7. <u>Mark E</u>. born about 1915.
- 2.8. <u>Edward W</u>. married 1st Edna Dickerson on 19 March 1930 in Pulaski. He married 2nd Martha Ann Spalding.
3. <u>Male Infant</u> born 16 July 1881.
4. <u>Laura</u> born 20 September 1882 married Marshall Butler on 20 February 1896 in Pulaski.
5. <u>Mary</u> born 10 February 1885.

Larkin and Lucy's children from the 1900 and 1910 census and Pulaski County Births:

6. <u>James Lawrence</u> born 08 February 1891 married Josephine Gorden.
7. <u>James</u> born 09 April 1892.
8. <u>Mary</u> born September 1895.
9. <u>Selitha</u> born February 1897.
10. <u>Ruth</u> born about 1900.
11. <u>Napoleon</u> born about 1904.
12. <u>Nancy Sylvester</u> born about 1907 married Henry Page on 19 January 1926 in Pulaski County.

MOODY FAMILY

English, derived from Old English modig "bold, impetuous, brave," applied as a nickname to the bold, brave, audacious man or soldier; it has no reference to fits of depression, the latter-day meaning.[1]

The Moody family was another African-American family who lived on Little Walkers Creek, Pulaski County.

Listed in the 1870 Pulaski County Census was Benjamin Moody age 55 and wife Letitia age 52 with children Bluford age 21, Joseph age 18, Rumbo age 14, Nancy age 13. They owned no land. Benjamin did not appear in the census until 1870, the reason, most likely, slavery. Slavery did not end until the Civil War and slaves were listed in the slave's schedules in 1850 and 1860 without names, only age and sex. Looking at the 1870 census, Benjamin and Letitia were living near William L. Hunter, the White family, Martha Johnston and the Millirons families. It is hard to deny that Benjamin Moody did not live on Little Walkers Creek in 1870 and most likely, was a slave belonging to some family in that area pre Civil War. Looking at the slave schedules, there were very few families in that area who owned slaves. The Miller family had many, as did William L. and Joseph A. Hunter and the Cecil family.

On August 2, 1883, Newton and Bettie White conveyed 40 acres to Bluford and Joseph Moody (brothers) being part of the James White farm.[2]

Benjamin and Letitia's children:
1. Bluford was born about 1845 in Pulaski; he married Matilda Wright on 26 May 1877 in Giles County. The marriage record gives his parents as Benjamin and Letitia Moody. Listed in the 1880 Pulaski census with wife Matilda and a son named Orren. Disappeared after 1880. No other information.
2. Virginia born about 1850 married Ausell Dickenson on 19 September 1867 in Giles County.
3. Nancy born about 1857 married Larkin Montgomery on 14 May 1877 in Giles County. *See Montgomery Family.
4. Joseph born about 1859 married Susie. Listed in the 1910 census as married 20 years. Had no children.

---

[1] *What is in Your Name?* Vitalog.net. website http://www.vitalog.net/cgi-bin/select_name.cgi
[2] Pulaski County, VA Deed Book 24, p. 275.

MORRIS FAMILY

Welsh, patronymic derived from Maurice, the Moorish or dark-skinned man. Morris was an early spelling of the given name now usually spelled Maurice; St. Maurice was martyred by the Romans in Switzerland in 287.[1]

Elijah Jesse Morris was born in about 1786. He married Jincey Haymore 02 November 1818 in Pittsylvania County, Virginia. They were living in Wythe County by 1850.[2] Their children were:

1. John born about 1820 married Malinda Lydia Harrell on 18 November 1837 in Patrick County, Virginia. John and Malinda had 12 children; several moved to Missouri. One son, William R. married Sarah C. Parson. Their daughter, Mary Jane married Andrew Grayson Woodyard 04 April 1894 in Pulaski County.

    When war between the States was in progress William R. Morris enlisted, in Wythe county, in Company B. Fifty-First Virginia Infantry on July 31, 1861 in Wythe County as a Sergeant. William was described as having a dark complexion, hazel eyes with light hair. He was 5 feet 3 inches tall; promoted to Full Corporal on 31 October 1862. He was listed as a prisoner of war on 02 March 1865 at Waynesboro, Virginia and confined on 12 March 1865 at Fort Delaware, Delaware. He was released on 20 June 1865 at Fort Delaware.[3] He applied for a pension on December 16, 1902 in Pulaski County. The pension listed him as living at Reed Island. William was suffering from kidney problems. He was entitled to $15.00 annually.[4]

2. Samuel born about 1822 married Rachel (maiden name unknown). Their daughter, Lucy J. married William Carr Allen 12 February 1885 in Bland County.

3. Joseph Johnson was born April 1825 married Sarah Shinault on 24 October 1864 in Giles County. Sarah was the daughter of Randolph Shinault and Melvina Harrell. Their children were:
    3.1. Susan J. born about 1866.[5]
    3.2. William J. born about 1867.[6]
    3.3. Samuel J. born about 1868.[7]
    3.4. Mary Amanda born May 1871 and died 23 November 1876.[8]
    3.5. John Bell was born 29 April 1874 married Nannie Della Combs on 19 September 1896 in Pulaski. She was the daughter of Joseph W. Combs and Matilda K. Robertson. Nannie was born 12 July 1879 and died 19 July 1966. John died 18 March 1958. They are buried in the Hunter Cemetery.
    3.6. Henry Davis born and died 22 August 1877.[9]
    3.7. Nancy M. born 22 August 1877.[10]
    3.8. Sarah Ella born 18 February 1882.[11]

4. Jesse born about 1824 married Caroline Beller.

---

[1] *What is in Your Name?* Vitalog.net. website http://www.vitalog.net/cgi-bin/select_name.cgi
[2] 1850 Wythe County, VA Census.
[3] The Virginia Regimental Histories Series. 45 vols. Lynchburg: Howard, 1987.
[4] Library of Virginia, Richmond, Virginia, Confederate Pension Rolls, Veterans & Widows.
[5] 1880 Pulaski County, VA Census.
[6] 1880 Pulaski County, VA Census.
[7] 1880 Pulaski County, VA Census.
[8] Bobby Talbert, Morris Family Research.
[9] Bobby Talbert, Morris Family Research.
[10] Bobby Talbert, Morris Family Research.
[11] Bobby Talbert, Morris Family Research.

On June 7, 1877, Jesse Morris was conveyed 300 acres by John Combs and wife Peniah "…near a line between Hunter and said Combs…".[1]

On November 9, 1893, Jesse Morris conveyed 31 ¼ acres to E. J. Morris.[2]

Jesse applied for a Confederate pension at the age of 79 on May 2, 1904 in Giles County. He was in the 51st Virginia Infantry, Company B. Most of the application is illegible. Jesse was entitled to $30.00 annually.[3]

Jesse and Caroline's children were:
4.1. Nancy J. born about 1842.[4]
4.2. Elijah Jefferson born 26 May 1846 and died 02 March 1935. He is buried in the Hunter Cemetery, Little Walkers Creek, Pulaski County. He 1st married Lucinda A. Glory probably in Missouri as his first four children were born in Missouri. Lucinda was also born in Missouri. Elijah married 2nd Martha Ellen Harrell on 24 April 1884 in Giles County. She was the daughter of Mitchell Harrell and Sarah Shinault. Elijah was a USA Civil War Veteran. He joined Company F, 13th Regiment, Tennessee Cavalry.[5] He received a United States Pension, having applied in 1883.

Regarding the 13th Tennessee Calvary:
On December 12; the 13th Tennessee Calvary was at Wytheville, Virginia; at Saltville, Virginia, December 20. In his report of the capture and burning of the salt works at Saltville, General Stoneman reported: "To Lieutenant Colonel Stacy, and the 13th Tennessee Cavalry, is due the credit of having acted the most conspicuous part." Lieutenant Colonel Stacy led the charge which captured the Confederate breastworks, and forced the evacuation of the position. The regiment got back to Knoxville on December 29, 1864, where it remained until March 18, 1865.[6]

Elijah and Lucinda's children:
4.2.1. Austin born about 1870 in Missouri.
4.2.2. Susan born about 1874 in Missouri.[7]
4.2.3. John born about 1876 in Missouri.[8]
4.2.4. Alice born 27 February 1877 in Pulaski County.[9]
4.2.5. Henry born 03 July 1878 in Pulaski County.[10]
4.2.6. Isabelle born about 1879 in Virginia.[11]
Elijah and Martha's children:
4.2.7. Amanda born 27 March 1886 in Pulaski, married Isaac Asbury Peters.
4.2.8. Charles Hicks born about 1889 married Roxie Annie Sexton on 22 April 1914 in Bland County.

---

[1] Pulaski County, VA Deed Book 9, p. 182.
[2] Pulaski County, VA Deed Book 16, p. 143.
[3] Library of Virginia, Richmond, Virginia, Confederate Pension Rolls, Veterans & Widows.
[4] 1850 Wythe County, VA Census.
[5] United States National Archives. *Civil War Compiled Military Service Records*. Ancestry.com.
[6] Nominal Roster of the 13th Tennessee Cavalry, U.S. Army 1863- 1865. Website: http://members.aol.com/jweaver301/nc/13tncav.htm.
[7] 1880 Pulaski County, VA Census.
[8] 1880 Pulaski County, VA Census.
[9] Pulaski County, VA Births, Pulaski County Courthouse.
[10] Pulaski County, VA Births, Pulaski County Courthouse.
[11] 1880 Pulaski County, VA Census.

- 4.2.9. <u>Morton</u> born about 1891. Served in World War I.
- 4.2.10. <u>Cora M</u>. born about 1893.
- 4.2.11. <u>Ethel</u> born about 1897.
- 4.3. <u>Matilda</u> born about 1848.[1]
- 4.4. <u>John Jackson</u> born about 1849 married Mary Elizabeth Akers on 17 December 1874 in Pulaski. Mary was the daughter of Davidson Akers and Rachel Graham
- 4.5. <u>Joseph H.</u> born about 1852 married Susan Shinault 11 January 1872 in Giles County. She was the daughter of Randolph Shinault and Melvina Harrell
- 4.6. <u>William Presley</u> born about 1854 in Wythe County married Jenny Dickerson. Their daughter Alice Gish married Samuel Hubert Parsell 15 April 1900 in Pulaski County. Samuel Hubert was the son of John Parsell and Mary Ann Coleman. William's 2nd daughter, Susan married Samuel Hubert's son by his first wife, Leslie W.
- 4.7. <u>Vilena</u> born 26 March 1856[2] She died at 13 days old of croup.[3]
- 4.8. <u>Susan Sayers</u> born 09 April 1858 in Wythe married William Carr Allen 22 May 1886 in Pulaski. *See Allen Family.
- 4.9. <u>Samuel</u> born about 1861.
- 4.10. <u>James A</u>. born December 18638 married Mary C. Robinett on 03 December 1885 in Bland County.
5. <u>Tabitha</u> born about 1831.[4]
6. <u>Susan</u> born about 1833[5] married John Washington Lawson on 24 November 1853 in Wythe County.

---

[1] 1850 Wythe County, VA Census.
[2] Pulaski County, VA Births, Pulaski County Courthouse.
[3] Pulaski County, VA Deaths, Pulaski County Courthouse.
[4] 1850 Wythe County, VA Census.
[5] 1850 Wythe County, VA Census.

PARCELL-PARSELL FAMILY

The Parcell family was researched by Ralph Lee Parsell who was born in Springfield, Clark County, Ohio to Andrew Miller Parsell and Minnie Pearl Stinson. Much of his research is cited in this family history. Much of it is not documented; accuracy is not guaranteed.

Richard Parcell married Sarah Love, possibly in Pennsylvania. One theory accounts the marriage of Richard and Sarah in the Valley of Virginia during the Revolution. A brother Morgan was mentioned in Ralph Parsell's research. Ralph believed Morgan was a brother to Richard. Looking at the traveling preachers during that era, a traveling preacher by the name of Edward Morgan traveled in a around the area of Montgomery County, Virginia during the Revolutionary era. Also during that time, a Sarah Love became an orphan and is mentioned in the very early Montgomery County records. Is it possible that Brother Edward Morgan married Sarah and Richard Parcell?
Richard Parcell was probably born in Carlisle, Cumberland County, Pennsylvania. He moved with his wife Sarah 1st to Rockbridge County, Virginia, and after 1800 onward to Franklin County, Virginia. In the 1810 Franklin County census, he is listed with his wife, five children under 10, two children between 10 and 16 and two children between 16 and 26. There is a court order to Sarah Parcell (Richard's widow) dated 3 June 1816, summoning her to appear in Franklin County Court on the first Monday of July to take on herself the administration of the estate of her deceased husband.[1] It seems nine children were listed in the 1810 census; Richard was listed as 45 and upwards and Sarah of 26 and under 45.

Richard and Sarah had seven known children being John, Sr. born about 1790; Rachel born about 1792 married William Lavinder; Joel born about 1794 married Drusilla Law; James born about 1800 married Delilah Hodges; William born about 1802 married Lucy White; Anna born about 1805 married Elisha Hodges; Sarah born about 1810 married Jonathan Davis.

John Parcell, Sr. was born about 1790 married Jane Ashworth on 16 January 1819 in Franklin County. She was the daughter of John H. Ashworth and Susannah Brizendine. John is listed in the 1820 Franklin County census as follows: 1 male under 10, 1 male of 26 and under 45, 1 female of 15 and under 26, 1 male slave under the age of 14. John died 23 July 1852 in Franklin County. Jane died between 1870-1872 in Franklin County.

John, Sr. and Jane had eight children being John, Jr.; Mary A. born 1821 married Hardin Shumate, she died 11 April 1854 in Franklin County; Isaac born January 1824 married Mary Malinda Pyrtle, he died 17 October 1865 in Franklin County; Peter born 1827 married Nancy A.T. Houseman; Christopher Columbus born 1831, died 19 November 1859 in Franklin County; Elizabeth born 1831 married Chapman Coleman; William born March 1834 married Martha D. Vaughn, moved to Washington Territory (died Raymond, Washington); Benjamin F. born 11 October 1838 married Lucy Jane Hunt, moved to Washington Territory (died Raymond, Washington).

John, Jr. born 14 December 1819 in Rocky Mount, Franklin County married Mary Ann Coleman on 10 December 1845 in Franklin County. She was the daughter of Samuel Coleman and Priscilla Beheler. Mary was born 10 January 1823 and died 20 December 1889[2]. She is buried in the Hamblin Cemetery, Spur Branch, Little Walkers Creek, Bland County. John is buried on the mountain near the location he lived. John and Mary were listed in the 1850-1870 Franklin County census. By 1876 (or earlier), John and Mary were in Bland County.

---

[1] Parcell Family, Ralph L. Parsell.
[2] Charles Lee Parsell Family Bible. Owner--Rebecca Sowers.

On the 4th day of June 1876, a deed was entered at the Bland Courthouse for John Parcell from the heirs of A. Brawley. Samuel W. Williams acted as special Commissioner, conveying the land to John Parcell. George N. Pegram gave written proof that John Parcell had paid for the land. This being a "parcel of land lying on the waters of the Spur Branch on little Walkers creek being a part of the A. Brawley lands". No acreage was given.[1]

On March 24, 1897, John Parsell conveyed land to Charles L. Parsell "in consideration of the parental love toward the said Charles L. Parsell...beginning corner between Charles Parsell & Calvin in a division line between the same parties... at the Sulphur Spring...division line between Wm Hamblin & Charles Parsell thence it leaves the division line thence with a newly made line between Charles Parsell and David Y. Hamblin...passing white oak in the low gap by the Crockett path...containing 54 acres".[2]

On April 12, 1897, John Parsell conveyed land to Calvin Parsell..."that in the consideration of the parental love toward the said Calvin Parsell". Containing 2 tracts, 100 acres and 15 acres.[3]

John Parcell enlisted as a private on April 17, 1862 at the age of 43 in Company A, 57th Infantry Regiment Virginia. He was discharged on May 24, 1862 because of his age. He reenlisted as a Private on December 1, 1863 in Franklin County, Virginia in Company K, "The Old Dominion Guards", 9th Infantry Regiment Virginia; Hospitalized on June 11, 1864. John was described as having a fair complexion, blue eyes with sandy hair. He was 6 feet 2 inches tall.[4]

During the War Between the States, close to 2,000 men served in the ranks of the 9th Virginia Infantry. On April 10, 1865, General Robert E. Lee issued General Order number 9. The great Army of Northern Virginia was no more. Only 40 members of the 9th Virginia Regiment were present at Appomattox to participate in the surrender proceedings.[5]

John applied for a Confederate Pension on May 3, 1903 (which disputes his death date of 28 January 1903). He said he had joined the 9th Virginia Infantry, Company K (Pickett's Division) in Norfolk, Virginia. John's age at the time was 84 years. He listed that he had lived in Bland County for 28 years and that he was totally disabled. John was suffering from erysipelas (a skin disease) which was found in 1867 in the service. Dr. D. A. Miller examined John in Bland County and agreed with the diagnosis.[6]

John and Mary's children:
1. Elizabeth born in 1846 in Franklin County married Thomas Simpkins 11 June 1874 in Giles County. Elizabeth died in 1898; buried in the Staffordsville Cemetery, Giles County.
2. Samuel Hubert born in 1848 in Franklin County married 1st Louisa Bird on 03 November 1870 in Franklin County. Louisa died on 12 June 1896 in Franklin. Samuel moved to Giles County and later married Alice Gish Morris on 15 April 1900 in Pulaski County. She was the

---

[1] Bland County, VA Deed Book 3, p. 601.
[2] Bland County, VA Deed Book 7, p. 79.
[3] Bland County, VA Deed Book 7, p. 621.
[4] The Virginia Regimental Histories Series. 45 vols. Lynchburg: Howard, 1987.
[5] Buck-Thompson, Cynthia M. *The 9th Regiment Virginia Volunteers*. http://pw1.netcom.com/~buck1755/9thregiment.htm.
[6] Library of Virginia, Richmond, Virginia, Confederate Pension Rolls, Veterans & Widows.

daughter of William Presley Morris and Jenny Dickerson. Samuel died in 1912, buried in the Pearis Cemetery, Bluff City, Giles County. Alice died in 1938.

3. <u>William Wise</u> born 1854 in Franklin County married Margaret Ellen Lindsey on 21 November 1877 in Giles County. William died 21 August 1940 and Margaret died 22 December 1933. They are buried in the Wesley's Chapel Cemetery, Giles County.
4. <u>Charles Lee</u> born 10 December 1856 in Franklin County married Martha Jane Davis on 26 October 1880 in Bland County. *See Samuel Davis Family.

On March 4, 1897, David Y. Hamblin conveyed land on Spur Branch, Little Walkers Creek to Charles Lee Parsell. No acreage given.[1]

The heirs of C. L. Parsell and wife, now deceased conveyed 32 acres and 125 square rods to Willie J. Davis on May 14, 1931. Dana Parsell, unmarried, Andrew M. Parsell and Minnie Parsell; Zena Stinson and George Stinson all of Springfield, Ohio; Willie J. Davis and Emmett M. Davis, Ida Davis and H. H. Davis, Charles C. Parsell and Blanche Parsell—all the heirs at law of C. L. Parsell and wife.[2]

On the 14th of May 1931, the C. L. Parsell heirs (as stated above) conveyed land to Ella A. Williams it being the same that was conveyed to the said C. L. Parsell, as Charles L. Parsell, by John Parsell by deed dated the 24th day of March, 1897, and of record in the Clerk's Office of the Circuit Court of Bland County, Virginia in D. B. 7, page 79, and being therein described by metes and bound, to which reference is hereby made for a more particular description of this certain tract; the other of which said tracts contains 1 ½ acres, more or less, being the same tract that was conveyed to the said C. L. Parsell, as Charles L. Parsell, by David Y. Hamblin by deed dated the 4th day of March, 1897…[3]

5. <u>Ida Belle</u> born 01 October 1861 in Franklin County married James William Allen Meadows on 24 May 1883 in Bland County. *See Meadows Family.
6. <u>Calvin Van Doren "Kelly"</u> born 24 May 1863 in Franklin County married Cynthia Margaret Pegram on 28 November 1887 in Bland County. *See Pegram Family.

On October 29, 1929, Calvin Parsell and wife Cynthia M. conveyed land to Lillie J. Hardy. Two tracts conveyed to Calvin by his father. Another tract which was conveyed to the said Calvin Parsell by John Q. Dickinson and wife deed dated on the 2nd day of April, 1919. A total of 126 acres.[4]

7. <u>Tobias Daniel</u> born 26 May 1869 in Franklin County married Minnie Bell Davis 16 June 1891 in Bland County. *See Henry Davis Family

---

[1] Bland County Deed Book 7, p. 80.
[2] Bland County Deed Book 18, p. 374.
[3] Bland County, VA Deed Book 18, p. 375.
[4] Bland County, VA Deed Book 18, p. 130.

PAULEY FAMILY

Thomas G. Pauley was born 30 May 1833 in Wythe County to John Pauley and Mary Polly Grayson; he married Telia Ann Kitts on 30 April 1856 in Wythe County. She was the daughter of Andrew J. Kitts and Polly Leedy. Telia was born 10 October 1833 in Wythe County; she died between 1902 and 1910. Thomas died on 28 February 1911. He is buried in the Burton Family Cemetery, Little Walkers Creek, Bland County. Thomas served in Jackson's Virginia Artillery CSA.

Thomas Pauley Family
Submitted by Karen Fallin

On February 8, 1902, Telia A. Pauley and husband conveyed land to Nannie Dillow for love and affection…being the same land that was conveyed to Telia by S. W. Williams on September 11, 1894.[1]

Thomas Pauley left Julia Margaret Ann and her son, William Henderson 50 acres on the east end of his farm running north-south with right of way over this 50 acres to lead to the Bland Turnpike at some convenient point. All other property pass to all other children and wife Telia Ann Pauley Executrix Julia Margaret. Witness: D. A., W. D. and G. G. Smith.[2]

Thomas and Telia's children:
1. Creed Franklin born 14 March 1857 in Wythe County married Lettia Martelia Kitts on 02 February 1881 in Bland County. She was the daughter of John D. and Jane Kitts.
2. Harold M. born 23 December 1858 in Wythe County.
3. Jasper H. born 22 September 1860 in Wythe County.
4. Rachel C. born 15 May 1862 in Bland County married John E. Thompson on 21 November 1885 in Bland County.
5. Sylvia J. born 22 November 1863 in Bland County.
6. Julia Margaret Ann born 11 January 1866 in Bland County married John Fortner on 30 September 1905 in Bland. Julia had a son out of wedlock:
    6.1. William Henderson born 02 December 1894 in Bland. He married Lula Clark on 10 June 1920 in Bland. She was the daughter of James Alexander Clark and Elizabeth Jane Lambert.

---

[1] Bland County, VA Deed Book 11, p. 108.
[2] Bland County, VA Will Book 2, p. 48.

7. <u>Newton Thomas</u> born 20 December 1867 in Bland County married Martha Gullion on 02 February 1893 in Tazewell County. They had children:
   - 7.1. <u>Edna Mae</u> married Andrew Ballard Hancock. He was the son of Marcus Walker and Mahala Hancock. Edna and Andrew died in 1918 during the influenza epidemic.
   - 7.2. <u>Thompson Effie Rose</u> born December 1893.[1]
   - 7.3. <u>Maude E</u>. born January 1896.[2]
   - 7.4. <u>Edith J</u>. born December 1898.[3]

Newton Pauley Family
Submitted by Karen Fallin

Samuel W. Williams and wife Maggie conveyed 80 acres to Newton Pauley on April 18, 1901 being part of 100 acres patented to Allen T. Newberry on December 1, 1857.[4]

On January 29, 1906, Martin Hill and wife Elizabeth conveyed their land to Newton Pauley with the condition that he (Newton) would care for and maintain the Hills in sickness and health during their natural lives, provide a comfortable home at their dwelling house where Hill now resides—provide clothing, food, medical attention and a Christian burial. The land was located between Poplar Spring Branch to the east and the Raleigh Grayson Turnpike the west.[5] Note—This land was in and around the area of Carnot—most being on the Raleigh Grayson Turnpike.

Mrs. Martha Pauley was the first Postmaster of Carnot (transcription of original application)[6]:
Sir:
With reference to the proposed establishment of a post office at the point named below, and in order that the office, if established, may be accurately represented upon the post-route maps, it is requested that you furnish accurately the information called for below and prepare a sketch according to instructions on opposite side of paper, which should be returned to this Division as soon as possible.

---

[1] 1900 Bland County, VA Census.
[2] 1900 Bland County, VA Census.
[3] 1900 Bland County, VA Census.
[4] Bland County, VA Deed Book 9, p. 287.
[5] Bland County, VA Deed Book 9, p. 288.
[6] National Archives and Record Administration, Washington, DC, RG 68, *Site Location Reports, Carnot Post Office*.

Respectfully,
Fourth Assistant Postmaster General

Proposed post office, <u>Freestone</u> (marked out and written after) <u>Carnot. County: Bland, Virginia</u>
(stamped)
The name proposed for the post office is (blank)
If the town, village, or site of the post office be known by another name other than that of the post office, state the other name here: <u>Little Creek.</u>

The post office would be situated in the <u>South</u> part of <u>Seddon</u> Township County of <u>Bland</u>, State of <u>Virginia.</u>

The name of the nearest creek is <u>Little Walkers Creek</u> and the post office building will be a distance of <u>30 yards</u>, on the <u>South side of it.</u>
The name of the nearest office on the same route as this proposed post office is Bland and its distance is <u>10 miles</u>, by the traveled road, in a <u>N.</u> direction from the site of the proposed office.

The name of the nearest office on the same route, on the other side, is <u>Wytheville</u> and its distance is <u>11 miles</u>, in a <u>S.</u> direction from the site of the proposed office.

The name of the nearest office not on the same route as this proposed post office is <u>Longspur</u> and its distance is 12 miles, by the traveled road in a <u>N. E.</u> direction from the site of the proposed post office.

The post office would be about <u>1 mile</u>, air-line distance <u>N</u> direction from the nearest point of my county boundary.
(*Signature of applicant for Postmaster*)

Mrs. Martha Pauly
(*Date*) April 2, 1915

Mrs. Frances B. Corder took over the Carnot Post Office on June 27, 1929.[1]

8. <u>James Roach</u> born 06 November 1869 in Bland County married Molly Lampert.
9. <u>John A</u>. born 24 February 1872 in Bland County married Mary J. Shaw.
10. <u>Nancy Gray</u> born 08 June 1874 in Bland County married Rush Dillow on 29 August 1898 in Bland.
11. <u>Harvey Blair</u> born 28 June 1876 in Bland County married Julia A. Hancock. She was the daughter of John Asa Hancock and Barbara Pauley.
12. <u>Mary J.</u> born May 1879.[2]

---

[1] National Archives and Record Administration, Washington, DC, RG 68, *Site Location Reports, Carnot Post Office*.
[2] 1900 Bland County, VA Census.

PEGRAM FAMILY

George Pegram was born 17 August 1806 in Guilford County, North Carolina. He married Wilicia "Willie" Harrison on 01 September 1827 in Guildford County. George and Willie Pegram had nine children:

1. Calvin Washington born 28 June 1828 in Guilford County married Elizabeth Bragg.
2. John Henry born 22 April 1832 in Guilford County.
3. George Newton born 31 October 1834 married Susannah Louisa Brawley, daughter of Anselm Brawley and Susannah Hutsell.
4. Elizabeth "Betsy" Jane born March 1838 married Daniel McTheney 29 December 1856 in Giles County, Virginia.
5. Pinkney N. born about 1839.
6. Parthenia born in 1843.
7. Thomas L. born about 1842.
8. Albert Gilmore born about 1846.
9. Martin Jackson born about 1849.

John Henry Pegram was married three times. First to Elizabeth (maiden name unknown). The were listed in the 1860 Fayette County, Virginia (now West Virginia) census. Elizabeth died 06 October 1861 in Bland County. One daughter was born to this union, Willie Jane born 08 January 1861in Bland County. John married 2nd Almira A. Bogle 29 July 1862 in Bland County. She was the daughter of James Bogle and Susan Kennison. She, evidently died shortly after they were married and there were no children born of this union. John married 3rd Frances Louemma Martin Meadows on 10 January 1869 in Giles County. John Henry and Frances were listed in the 1870 Giles County census. Frances Martin was a widow when she married John. She first married Allen Parkinson Meadows on 23 December 1856 in Giles County. He was the son of Phillip Meadows and Sarah Ellis. After she married John, these children were listed in the census with the surname Pegram resulting in much confusion among Pegram researchers. Frances' children were raised by their step father, the only real father they ever knew. John Pegram died on 21 May 1909 in Bland; Frances died on 23 May 1911. They are buried in the Goshen Methodist Church Cemetery.

This deed made and entered into this the 4th day of June 1876. Between Samuel W. Williams Special Commissioner of the first part and John H. Pegram of the second part. Witnesseth that whereas by a decree rendered on the [blank] Day of May 1876 by the Circuit court of Bland County, Virginia in the chancery cause therein pending in the name of A. Brawley Administrators and A. Brawleys heirs amongst other things it was adjudged, ordered and decreed that Samuel W. Williams as Special Commissioner should by deed with covenants of Special warranty convey to said party of the second part that part of the real estate in the bill and proceedings mentioned described in statement in writing signed by George N. Pegram and referred to in said decree as having been sold by said George N. to said John H. Pegram.[1]

John Pegram conveyed 175 acres to Joseph Stafford on September 8, 1882.[2]

---

[1] Bland County, VA Deed Book 3, Pg. 444
[2] Bland County, VA Deed Book 4, p. 422.

Joseph E. Stafford and Susan S. his wife conveyed 50 acres to Henry J. Overstreet on March 24, 1885.[1]

Henry J. Overstreet conveyed the above land to James H. Overstreet on August 2, 1888 in return for the care and maintenance of said Henry and their mother, Nancy A. Overstreet. Henry agreed to give said James the balance of the purchase money and all household and kitchen furniture.[2]

John conveyed 56 ½ acres on Spur Branch to Ellen S. Pegram Tickle on September 8, 1892.[3]
On March 30, 1893, John conveyed 160 acres to James W. Meadows "… on Spur Branch east by the lands of John Hamblin & north by the Big Survey; west of William Brunk and Emily King…". To Emily E. King, 11 acres on the same day.[4]

John Henry Pegram was in the 8th Virginia Calvary according to his pension application; most likely under Captain William Neel Harman of Bland. Enlisting in the Confederate service on August 8, 1861, Captain William Neel Harman spent the month of September helping to outfit and prepare his company, the Bland Rangers, for cavalry field service, a unit that was apparently designated as Company F, 8th Virginia Cavalry, in late December.

John also enlisted in the Confederate States Army, 45th Infantry Regiment, Company F, (the Bland County Sharpshooters) on June 1, 1863 in Lewisburg, Virginia. He is listed as being in the in Emory and Henry Hospital on March 23, 1864.[5]

On May 18, 1900 John H. Pegram applied for a Confederate pension. He explained that he was partially disabled from a rupture while serving with Company F, 8th Virginia Calvary. He also listed that he had also served with the 45th Regiment. John was entitled to $15.00 annually.[6]

Daughter of John Henry and Elizabeth Pegram:
1. Willie Jane born 08 January 1861 in Bland County, married William Winton Fortner 03 September 1878 in Russell County, Virginia. He was the son of Thomas Fortner and Sarah Margaret King. Willie died 09 November 1942 in Russell. William was born 18 September 1854 in Wythe County, now Bland County. He died 18 October 1931 in Russell. From a Fortner descendent, it was handed down through the family that Willie Jane lived with a relative in Russell County when she was 12 or 13 years old.

John and Frances' children:
2. Cynthia Margaret was born 13 January 1870. She married Calvin Van Doren "Kelly" Parsell on 28 November 1887 in Bland County. Kelly was born on 24 May 1863 in Franklin County, Virginia to John Parsell and Mary Ann Coleman. Cynthia died 26 March 1956 in Giles County; Kelly died 09 October 1937 in Giles County. They are buried in the Davis Cemetery, Clendenin, Giles County. Their children:
   2.1. John W. born September 1888 in Bland County.
   2.2. Robert Clinton born 21 January 1890 in Bland County married Mary Cowan.
   2.3. Albert Wesley born February 1892 married Elsie Vernon Hamblin on 07 July 1910 in Bland County. She was the daughter of John M. Stafford Hamblin and Sarah Catherine

---
[1] Bland County, VA Deed Book 5, p.. 44.
[2] Bland County, VA Deed Book 6, p. 263.
[3] Bland County, VA Deed Book 6, p.. 33.
[4] Bland County, VA Deed Book 6, p. 409.
[5] The Virginia Regimental Histories Series. Published in 1987.
[6] Library of Virginia, Richmond, Virginia, Confederate Pension Rolls, Veterans & Widows.

Croy. Albert died in 1961 in Giles County. Elsie was born 26 May 1890 in Bland and died in 1967. They are buried in the Staffordsville Cemetery, Giles County.

2.4. Mary Francis born 14 October 1893 and died 25 August 1980 in Giles County. She married Andrew William Davis, son of Charles William Davis and Louisa Virginia Davis. Andrew was born on 11 March 1894 and died 29 December 1961 in Giles County. They are buried in the Birtchlawn Cemetery, Giles.

2.5. Martha Ethel born July 1896 married Wise L. Davis on 26 November 1913 in Bland. Wise was the son of James Edward Davis and Ollie E. Byrd.

2.6. Tobias born January 1898 married Anna Mustard.

2.7. Price H. born in 1903 in Bland County.

2.8. Everett C. born 1907 in Bland; died 1973 in Giles. Buried in the Cedar Grove Cemetery, Giles.

2.9. Effie G. born 08 October 1909 married Adda J. Parcell.

3. Emily Etta born 13 September 1872 in Bland married Joseph S. King on 19 May 1887 in Bland. Joseph was the son of David King and Elizabeth Ann Hancock. He was born on 18 August 1857 in Wythe County and died 06 March 1929. Emily died on 01 April 1959. They are buried the Goshen Methodist Church Cemetery. Their children:

3.1. Bessie Pearl born 19 January 1888 in Bland married David Spencer Ritter sometime around 1904 or 1905. David died on 19 November 1911. Buried in the Goshen Methodist Cemetery. Their children were:

3.1.1. Margaret Elizabeth born 02 April 1905 married James P. Ashley.

3.1.2. Sanders Spencer born 12 July 1907 in Bland.

3.1.3. Claude Swanson born 06 April 1909.

Children born after David Ritter died:

3.1.4. Letha Virginia born 08 August 1915 in Bland; married Jesse James Hancock, Sr. on 30 May 1931 in Bland.

3.1.5. Lorene W. born about 1913

3.1.6. Charles born about 19191 in Bland.

3.1.7. Mary Etta Hancock born about 1925 married Ernest Hamblin, son of Edward L. Hamblin and Olive Virginia Millirons.

3.1.8. Elva Mae Hancock born 24 May 1933.

Bessie evidently married Sidney Edward Hancock after 1930 as Bessie is listed in the 1930 Bland census as Bessie Ritter, widowed and all children were listed as Ritter. Bessie died 04 January 1949; Sidney Edward Hancock died 06 February 1944. They are buried in the Goshen Methodist Church Cemetery.

3.2. Willie J. born 11 April 1889 in Bland.[1]

3.3. John D. born 19 February 1891 in Bland; died 19 June 1959. He is buried in the Goshen Methodist Church Cemetery. Served in World War I.

3.4. Eliza M. born June 1892 in Bland.[2]

3.5. Franklin P. born 05 August 1893.[3]

3.6. Annie Kate born 29 November 1895 in Bland married Albert Terry Davis on 16 June 1920 in Bland.

3.7. Robert Newton born 28 May 1899 in Bland married Georgie Mae Hancock on 19 November 1924 in Bland. She was the daughter of George Washington Hancock and

---

[1] Bland County, VA Births: 1861-96.
[2] 1900 Bland County, VA Census.
[3] Bland County, VA Births: 1861-96.

Isabelle Shrader. He died in Montgomery County on 11 February 1971. Georgie died 17 June 1981 in Roanoke County, Virginia.

- 3.8. Charles Caxton born 11 July 1902 in Bland, married Tessie Robertson. Charles died on 25 November 1990 in Wythe County. Tessie died 20 October 2001 in Wythe. They are buried in the Patterson Cemetery, Crockett's Cove, Wythe County.
- 3.9. Eugene L. born about 1904 in Bland County.[1]
- 3.10. Frances born 15 September 1906 in Bland; married William Moses Millirons on 12 August 1930 in Bland. He was the son of Estell Hoge Millirons and Ella Augusta Akers. Frances died on 19 April 1993 and William died 19 August 1938. They are buried in the Davis Cemetery on Little Walkers Creek, Bland.
- 3.11. Ora Lee born about 1909 married Alford R. Kitts son of Robert Hutsel Kitts and Bertha J. Davis.
- 3.12. Violet Etta born 09 December 1912 in Bland married Phillip Astor Davis on 11 April 1934 in Bland. He was the son of Charles Calvin Davis and Lucy Clara Davis. Violet died 02 December 1986 and Phillip died on 23 August 1968. They are buried in the Goshen Methodist Church Cemetery.
- 3.13. Nora E. born about 1914 in Bland.[2]

Joseph King received 66 acres on Spur Branch from the Nancy Davis heirs. Being the same land as their father David King inherited from his father, Bennett King.[3]

4. Ellen Smith born 27 October 1873 in Bland married George Lee Tickle on 16 January 1890 in Bland. He was the son of Jackson Nye Tickle and Mary Ann Waggoner. He was born in 29 April 1869 in Bland and died 11 March 1938 in Sullivan County, Tennessee. Ellen died 29 November 1944 in Tennessee. They are buried in the Oak Hill Cemetery, Kingsport, Tennessee. Their children:
- 4.1. Rose Leona born 11 October 1890 married George Greever Smith. They are buried in the Mountain View Methodist Church Cemetery, Wythe County.
- 4.2. John Nye born 16 February 1892 died of disease during WWI.[4]
- 4.3. Benjamin Trigg born 05 May 1893 married first Nellie Alberta King, daughter of Harvey Newton King and Susanna Gray. He married second Cecil Thelma Davis Millirons. He is buried in the West End Cemetery, Wythe County.
- 4.4. Charles Grant born 04 September 1894 married Anna Jane Hoback. He is buried in the West End Cemetery, Wythe County.
- 4.5. Josie Agnes born 30 Oct 1896 in Bland. Died in Bland County.
- 4.6. Isaac Newton born 16 September 1898 in Bland married Anna Dillon Lambert in Bland. Buried in the Oak Hill Cemetery, Kingsport, Tennessee.
- 4.7. Emma Lee born 25 January 1900 in Bland married Andrew Maiden Hoback. They are buried in the West End Cemetery, Wythe County.
- 4.8. Arthur Lee born 25 January 1900 in Bland. Died 25 January 1900 in Bland.
- 4.9. Stella Elizabeth born 16 October 1901 in Bland married Walter Henry Hoback. Died in Pulaski.
- 4.10. Lola Maud born 21 June 1903 in Bland married Jesse Ernest Kitts in Bland. She is buried in the Bel Air Memorial Gardens, Bel Air, Maryland.
- 4.11. Georgie Myrtle born 28 February 1905 in Bland married Hubert Nello Harden in Bland. She died in Dalton, Georgia.

---

[1] 1910 Bland County, VA Census.
[2] 1920 Bland County, VA Census.
[3] Bland County, VA Deed Book 12, p. 243
[4] Virginia Military Dead: Library of Virginia, Richmond, Virginia.

4.12. <u>Robert Brown</u> born June 1906 in Bland married Norma Jean Kyker. Died in Candian City, Oklahoma.

4.13. <u>Theodore Samuel</u> born 18 September 1908 married Amber Hildreth Staton. He died in Cabell County, West Virginia.

4.14. <u>Patrick Henry</u> born 04 Mar 1910 in Bland married Ethel Catherine Peterson. He died in Nevada City, California.

4.15. <u>Stonewall Jackson</u> born 03 July 1913 in Pulaski County married first Thelma and second Mary Lou Tickle. Died in Parke County, Indiana.

On September 1, 1919 Ellen Smith Tickle and husband conveyed 62 acres to A. T. Davis.[1]

---

[1] Bland County, VA Deed Book 14, p. 50.

RITTER FAMILY

German, 1) designated a military servant to the king or great baron, he was mounted soldier owing loyalty to his liege lord bound to fight in his quarrels; 2) patronymic derived from the nickname which called attention to noble birth or exalted rank, means "knight."[1]

David Spencer Ritter was born in June 1842 to George Ritter and Margaret Carper. He married Hettie Locritta Shufflebarger sometime before 1864. Hettie died on 28 October 1892 in Pulaski County; buried in the Wysor Cemetery, Dublin, Virginia. David moved to Bland County sometime in 1893 as he married Sarah Elizabeth Meadows on 18 May 1893 in Bland County. Sarah died between 1900-1904, most likely in Bland County. David married 3rd Bessie Pearl King probably in 1904. Bessie was the daughter of Joseph S. King and Emily Etta Pegram.

William S. Brunk and his wife Nancy C. conveyed 50 acres to David S. Ritter on October 7, 1893.[2]

James H. Overstreet and wife Mary S. and Henry J. Overstreet conveyed 50 acres to David S. Ritter on August 19, 1897.[3]

David Ritter Enlisted in Company F, 54th Infantry Regiment Virginia on 09 September 1861 at the age of 17. Furloughed on 22 February 1864 (30 days). Deserted on 01 November 1864.

David Ritter applied for a Confederate Pension on May 26, 1900 in Bland County and again in 1909. He listed that he was in Company F, 54th Infantry (enlisted Newbern, VA) and had served faithfully for 4 years. He also stated that he had suffered from exposure during the war. In 1900 he was entitled to $15.00 annually.[4] J. S. Hamblin and J. A. Meadows were witnesses.

In 1950, Junior Neel Brunk bought the Ritter land from the Ritter heirs—being a total of 100 acres.[5]

David and Hettie's children:
1. William Jackson born 22 December 1864 married Daisy Drawbond.
2. George Washington born 12 May 1866 married Sarah Catherine Waddell.
3. Cora Lee born 21 March 1868 married Sanders C. Farris.
4. Addie Lou born 04 December 1869 married Edwin Thomas Shufflebarger.
5. Thomas Fenton born 24 July 1871 married Martha Jane N. Johnston Bond.
6. Nellie May born 08 March 1873 married Addison Burke Davis.
7. David Aviner born 04 March 1875 married Della Roxie Hamblin *See Hamblin Family.
8. John Lewis born 20 October 1879.
9. Edward born 01 August 1881 married Alice Gray Davis. *See Henry Davis Family
10. Allie Ann born 18 February 1884 married Eugene Edward Brunk; married 2nd Robert Perry.
11. James Ernest born 03 December 1885 married Alice Blackwell.
12. Infant born 23 October 1892—stillborn.[6]

All above children were born in Pulaski County.

---

[1] *What is in Your Name?* Vitalog.net. website http://www.vitalog.net/cgi-bin/select_name.cgi.
[2] Bland County Deed Book 6, pg. 548.
[3] Bland County, VA Deed Book 7, p. 223.
[4] Library of Virginia, Richmond, Virginia, Confederate Pension Rolls, Veterans & Widows.
[5] Bland County, VA Deed Book 33, p. 168, 169.
[6] Pulaski County, VA Births, Pulaski County Courthouse.

David and Sarah's children:
13. Huston Crockett born 19 March 1895 in Bland County.
14. Frank Chaffin born 29 April 1896 in Bland County married Ethel May Williams.
David and Bessie's children:
15. Margaret Elizabeth born 02 April 1905 in Bland married James P. Ashley.
16. Sanders Spencer born 12 July 1907 in Bland married Verna Alice Testerman.
17. Claude Swanson born 06 April 1909 in Bland married Gladys Williams.

TICKLE FAMILY

Mary Ann Journell & Peter Conrad Tickle
Submitted by Don E. Halsey

English, designated the original bearer who came from Tickhill "Tica's hill" in the West Riding of Yorkshire.[1]

Daniel Tickle married Sarah Elizabeth Lineberry on 22 November 1819 in Guilford County, North Carolina. They were in Southwest Virginia by 1850. Peter Conrad Tickle was born to Daniel and Sarah in March 1830[2] in Orange County, North Carolina. He married Mary Ann Journell on 18 November 1852 in Pulaski. Mary's parents were William Journell and Margaret Honaker. She was born 18 April 1830 in Montgomery County and died 26 February 1914 in Pulaski County. Peter died on 13 February 1903 in Pulaski County.

Peter C. Tickle served with Company F, 36th Virginia Regiment during the Civil War. He was described as 5 feet 4 inches tall, fair complexion, gray eyes and auburn hair.[3]

His wife, Mary Ann applied for a Confederate Widows Pension on March 14, 1903. Her application gave her husbands date of death as 13 February 1903; she explained that her husband fell dead in the field. Mary received $28.00 annually.[4]

John Troy Davis conveyed land [no acreage given] to Peter C. Tickle on May 29, 1893. The same land John bought of Joseph H. Lefler and Fransina Akers Lefler.[5]

On April 6, 1891, Peter C. Tickle and wife Mary Ann conveyed 30 acres to L. T. Lampert.[6]

Peter C. Tickle conveyed 85 acres to Charles W. Davis on September 12, 1896. The land run on Moses Akers line on the west and with Jacob Kitts line on the south side to the middle of the creek thence with the creek to the ford we made a line fence running with that fence to the corner

---

[1] *What is in Your Name?* Vitalog.net. website http://www.vitalog.net/cgi-bin/select_name.cgi.
[2] 1900 Pulaski County, VA Census.
[3] Submitted by Don E. Halsey..
[4] Library of Virginia, Richmond, Virginia, Confederate Pension Rolls, Veterans & Widows.
[5] Bland County, VA Deed Book 6. p. 425.
[6] Bland County, VA Deed Book 7, p. 31.

on the public road from that corner on the Public road so far as to give L. Lambert his thirty acres.[1]

Peter and Mary's children:
1. Sarah Elizabeth "Lizzie" was born October 1853[2] in Smyth County[3] married Linsey T. Lambert on 22 March 1877 in Bland County. *See Lambert Family.
2. John H. born about 1854[4] in Giles County[5] married Sarah A. Caves on 28 December 1880 in Pulaski County.
3. Margaret Ann born 11 March 1856 in Pulaski County married James William Banes on 24 October 1876 in Bland County. See Banes Family.
4. Cynthia Victoria born 25 February 1858 in Pulaski County married Charles W. Carden on 20 September 1879 in Pulaski County.
5. Elizabeth Jane born 03 July 1860 in Pulaski County married John H. Caves.
6. Peter H. born about 1862 in Bland County[6] married Rosa Collins on 10 September 1884 in Bland , she was the daughter of James and Mary Ann Collins. *See Collins Family.
7. Sylvia Caledonia born 30 November 1864 in Giles County[7] married Thomas Jefferson Halsey on 07 April 1884 in Bland County. He was the son of Stephen J. Halsey and Sallie Cassell.
8. Harriett Emily born 11 November 1866 in Bland[8] married William Ribble Patterson 13 May 1885 in Bland County. He was the son of James Harvey Patterson and Nancy Jane Davis.
9. Ella Catherine born 11 January 1870 in Pulaski8 married John Jasper Bland 26 August 1892 in Bland County.
10. Josephine born 07 September 1871 in Bland married William Alexander Hamilton on 20 November 1894 in Bland County.
11. William H. born 17 August 1875 married Addie Kimbleton on 26 September 1900 in Pulaski County.

---

[1] Bland County, VA Deed Book 7, p. 31.
[2] 1900 Wythe County, VA Census.
[3] Bland County, VA Marriage Records, Bland County Courthouse.
[4] 1870 Bland County, VA Census.
[5] Pulaski County, VA Marriage Records, Pulaski County Courthouse.
[6] Bland County, VA Marriage Records, Bland County Courthouse.
[7] Bland County, VA Marriage Records, Bland County Courthouse.
[8] Bland County, VA Marriage Records, Bland County Courthouse.

UNDERWOOD FAMILY

English, derived from the place name meaning beneath the wood.[1]

Joshua Underwood was born about 1810 in North Carolina. He 1st married Charlotte Wilson 17 March 1823 in Guilford County, North Carolina. He marred 2nd Delitha Keens 24 October 1845 in North Carolina (undocumented). Joshua and Charlotte had 5 known children. One of them, Laura A. Underwood born 29 January 1842 Guilford County married William Green Tickle 12 November 1868 in Giles County. They are buried in the Thornspring Methodist Church Cemetery in Pulaski County. Joshua and Delitha's children:

1. Andrew Giles born 01 January 1847 in Guilford County, North Carolina married Sarah Jane Kennedy on 23 December 1869 in Pulaski County. Sarah was the daughter of John Kennedy and Mary Deaton. She was born in 1851 and died on 18 September 1910. Andrew died 18 February 1908. They are buried in the Hunter Cemetery, Little Walkers Creek, Pulaski County.

On December 27, 1901, Mrs. Mary H., Julie A., James A. and Sallie B. Miller conveyed part of a tract of land to A. G. Underwood; being part of a tract conveyed to William Miller by William L. Hunter. No acreage given.[2]

William and Elizabeth Underwood, Clara Woodyard and husband A. S. Woodyard, Aggie Combs and Robert her husband and Sallie Underwood conveyed the above land to Charlie, Grover and John Underwood in exchange for the care and maintenance for their mother, Sallie and to provide a comfortable home during her natural life at present homeplace. No acreage given. Dated April 14, 1908.[3]

On March 19, 1909, Sarah Underwood, widow, conveyed land to Foy C. Combs being part of the land conveyed to Sarah by Mrs. Mary A. Miller and others.[4]

Andrew and Sarah's children:
1.1. Robert Lee born 15 January 1874 married Myrtle Combs on 07 October 1902 in Pulaski. She was born on 26 February 1881 to Joseph W. Combs and Matilda K. Robertson Robert died on 23 July 1905; Myrtle died on 19 February 1912. The are buried in the Hunter Cemetery. See Combs Family.
1.2. Agnes born 26 March 1876 married James Robert Combs. He was born 19 November 1899 to Joseph W. Combs and Matilda K. Robertson. *See Combs Family.
1.3. Clara born 13 October 1877 married Albert Sidney Woodyard on 12 September 1900 in Pulaski. He was born in June 1870 to Newton Woodyard and Bethia White. Albert died October 1946; Clara died on 29 June 1908. Albert and Clara's Children:
    1.3.1. Lee T. married Jeanette Fowler.
    1.3.2. Dolly G. married Arnold E. Johnson. Dolly was born 02 October 1903 and died 12 June 1933; buried in the Hunter Cemetery.
    1.3.3. Trinkle.
1.4. William born about 1879 married Elizabeth L. (maiden name unknown).
1.5. John Milton born 28 July 1880 married 1st Nellie G. Combs on 29 November 1904 in Pulaski County; Nellie was the daughter of Joseph W. Combs and Matilda K.

---

[1] *What is in Your Name?* Vitalog.net. website http://www.vitalog.net/cgi-bin/select_name.cgi.
[2] Pulaski County Deed Book 21, p. 402.
[3] Pulaski County Deed Book 27, p. 161.
[4] Pulaski County Deed Book 28, p. 149.

Robertson. Nellie died in 1914. John married 2nd Effie M. Davis on 30 January 1917 in Pulaski. She was the daughter of James Whitten Davis and Nancy Jane King. John Milton died on 11 April 1957, Effie died on 26 August 1960. They are buried in the Hunter Cemetery, Little Walkers Creek. John and Effie had no children. John and Nellie had two daughters:

    1.5.1. Jennie
    1.5.2. Lucille

1.6. Charles Thomas was born on 09 October 1885 married Lucy Pearl Davis on 10 October 1916 in Pulaski County. She was born 05 January 1894 in Bland County to James Whitten Davis and Nancy Jane King. Charles died on 01 March 1956; Lucy died on 07 March 1979. They are buried in the Hunter Cemetery. Charles and Lucy's children:

    1.6.1. Richard Victor.
    1.6.2. Opal Virginia.
    1.6.3. Myrtle Agnes.
    1.6.4. Charlie Vivian.
    1.6.5. Alva Louise.
    1.6.6. Paul Dailey.
    1.6.7. Nina Loraine.
    1.6.8. Charles Clifford.

1.7. Grover C. born 09 May 1892 married Sallie Sexton. Had daughters:
    1.7.1. Viola married Meek Hoge Davis, Jr.
    1.7.2. Georgie .
    1.7.3. Ruby.

2. Charlotte born about 1849 in North Carolina.[1]
3. George W.[2] born 12 August 1849 in Guilford County, North Carolina married Sarah Ann Akers on 11 January 1872 in Pulaski. She was born on 28 November 1854 in Pulaski County to Davidson Akers and Rachel Graham. Their children were:

    3.1. William Joshua born 18 November 1872 in Pulaski married Malinda Dowdy 05 October 1893 in Pulaski County. She was born on 27 July 1877 in Pulaski to James C. Dowdy and Nancy M. Richardson. William died on 14 April 1958; Malinda on 02 January 1949. They are buried in the Sunrise Burial Park, Fairlawn, Pulaski County.
    3.2. George Stuart born 09 January 1875 married Helen Dowdy.
    3.3. Bettie Mae born 16 November 1877 in Pulaski married James Andrew Robertson on 17 October 1894 in Pulaski County.
    3.4. David Pierce born 06 August 1880 married Della Williams. She was the daughter of James J. Williams and Amanda J. Akers.
    3.5. Jordan born 13 May 1885; died 17 January 1886 in Pulaski County.
    3.6. Luli B. born 22 January 1889 married Hubert Hurst on 14 January 1904 in Pulaski County.
    3.7. Sidney Queen[3]. born 20 July 1892 married Mary A. Vest.

4. Nancy born about 1853[4] in North Carolina.
5. Susan born March 1858[5] in North Carolina married William A. Burgess on 04 November 1879 in Pulaski County.

---

[1] 1850 Guilford County, NC Census.
[2] George W. Underwood information submitted by Bobby Talbert, e-mail: Westgatebo@aol.com.
[3] World War I Draft Registration Cards, 1917-1918, Pulaski County, Virginia.
[4] 1860 Giles County, VA Census.
[5] 1900 Pulaski County, VA Census.

WHITE FAMILY

Of English origin, 1) applied to a person with light hair or complexion; 2) sometimes derived from Old English given name, Hwita "white"; 3) sometimes translation from different languages with the meaning "white"; 4) English and German, referred to the white-haired gentry.[1]

John Hunter White married Nancy Copley possibly in Montgomery County on 08 June 1793. No marriage record has been found for John and Nancy in Montgomery County but it is possible they did marry there. John and Nancy had children: John Wesley, James Russell, Sally, William, David, Rachel, Achilles, Horatio and Jemima.

John Wesley was born about 1798[2] in Virginia married Mary Magdeline Plymale. John was listed in the 1840 Pulaski County census with 1 male under 5, 1 male 5-10, 1 male 5-15, 1 male 40-50, 1 female under 5, 1 female 5- 10, 2 females 5-15, 1 female 30-40, no slaves. In the 1860 Pulaski County census John was living in the Little Walkers Creek community as he was neighbors with Zachariah W. Cecil and William L. Hunter. John and James White were the only Whites listed in the 1860 Pulaski County census. John Wesley was still living in 1880 in Pulaski County with his daughter Sophina. He was age 73 and daughter was age 45.

John and Mary had the following children:
1. <u>James Wilson</u> born about 1824 married Martha Tynes. No marriage record has been found for James and Martha; her maiden name was discovered in the census. In the 1850 Pulaski County census, Paulina Tines was living with James and Martha White. In the 1860 Pulaski County census Mary S. Tynes and daughter Josephine (age 1) are living with James and Martha. Martha was born about 1824, Paulina born about 1829 and Mary born about 1837. William Thomas Mustard, son of Joshua Mustard and Elizabeth Davis married a Paulina Tynes. Most likely the same person as the Tynes surname is rare in the Southwest Virginia region.

    In the 1870 Pulaski County census Mary Tynes was living with James W. and Martha White with her children Victoria, Virginia N. and Beatrice.

    On May 25, 1860, Z. W. Cecil and Mary his wife conveyed land on Little Walkers Creek to James W. White. No acreage given.[3]

    Isaac L. Johnson conveyed 44 ¼ acres of land on Little Walkers Creek to James Wilson White on October 27, 1873.[4]

    On February 3, 1875, Joseph A. White and H. Shannon White partitioned the land held by Isaac L. Johnson which was transferred by deed dated October 27, 1873.[5]

    Zachariah W. Cecil conveyed 40 acres of land on Little Walkers Creek to the J. W. White heirs on January 24, 1878 on the south side of Walkers Big Mountain to upper end of Zachariah to the 100 acres of J. W. White land and William Miller.[6]

---

[1] *What is in Your Name?* Vitalog.net. website http://www.vitalog.net/cgi-bin/select_name.cgi.
[2] 1850 Pulaski County, VA Census.
[3] Pulaski County, VA Deed Book 3, p. 328.
[4] Pulaski County, VA Deed Book 6, p. 180.
[5] Pulaski County, VA Deed Book 6, p. 207.
[6] Pulaski County, VA Births, Pulaski County Courthouse.

James and Martha's children:
1.1. John Wesley born 18 September 1848 married Mattie M. Lyons on 12 October 1880 in Pulaski. John died on 19 July 1938, buried in the Hunter Cemetery, Little Walkers Creek.

John and Mattie's children:
1.1.1. Benjamin born 10 September 1888 in Pulaski.[1]
1.1.2. Harrison William born about 1889[2] married Minnie Thompson. They had children:
    1.1.2.1. Mary Edith married Bernie Kitts.
    1.1.2.2. Myrtle L.
    1.1.2.3. Gladys M.
    1.1.2.4. David H.
    1.1.2.5. Kellas Marvin.
    1.1.2.6. Violet J.
    1.1.2.7. Hubert Wallace
    1.1.2.8. Glenna B.
    1.1.2.9. James Clayton.
    1.1.2.10. Reba G.
1.1.3. Robert born 06 November 1890 in Pulaski.[3]
1.1.4. Bertie born about 1891.[4]
1.1.5. June born about 1896.[5]
1.1.6. Myrtle born about 1897.[6]
1.1.7. John born about 1899.[7]
1.1.8. Pearl born about 1903.[8]
1.1.9. Lester born about 1905.[9]

1.2. Mary M. born abt 1849.[10] Listed in the 1880 Pulaski County census as single. Listed in the 1880 census with her children (listed race as Mulatto).
1.2.1. Mary S. born about 1873.
1.2.2. Thomas born about 1875.
1.2.3. James born about 1878.
1.2.4. Edna born April 1880.

1.3. Nancy L. born about 1854.[11]
1.4. Newton Foy born 15 January 1857 married 1st Jemina C. Stone on 19 September 1881 in Pulaski. She was the daughter of James Steven Stone and Rhoda Hurst. Jemina died/divorced about 1890. Newton married 2nd Eliza Ann Davis on 01 July 1910 in Pulaski. She was the daughter of James Whitten Davis and Nancy Jane King. Newton died 09 December 1932; Eliza died 24 March 1938. They are buried in the Thornspring Methodist Church Cemetery in Pulaski.

---

[1] Pulaski County, VA Births, Pulaski County Courthouse.
[2] 1910 Pulaski County, VA Census.
[3] Pulaski County, VA Births, Pulaski County Courthouse.
[4] 1910 Pulaski County, VA Census
[5] 1910 Pulaski County, VA Census
[6] 1910 Pulaski County, VA Census
[7] 1910 Pulaski County, VA Census
[8] 1910 Pulaski County, VA Census
[9] 1910 Pulaski County, VA Census
[10] 1850 Pulaski County, VA Census.
[11] 1860 Pulaski County, VA Census.

Nancy J. White conveyed her interest in two tracts of land to Newton White on January 3, 1878...bounded by Cecil and Miller.[1]

Mary M. White conveyed her interest in father's land to Newton White on January 3, 1878.[2]

John W. White to Newton White, same as above.[3]

N. F. White conveyed 40 acres to Bluford and Joseph Moody (brothers) being part of the James White farm on August 2, 1883.[4]

William L. Hunter (Jr.) conveyed land to N. F. White on April 9, 1904. No acreage given.[5]

On July 25, 1906, N. F. White conveyed 40 acres to Lucy Montgomery being part of the J. W. White farm.[6]

On May 22, 1908, N. F. White conveyed land to John B. Morris being a part of a tract of land conveyed by William L. Hunter (Jr.).[7]

N. F. White conveyed land to G. S. Underwood on May 22, 1908 being part conveyed to White by W. L. Hunter.[8]

N. F. White conveyed 123.64 acres to M. H. Davis on January 8, 1921[9] and another 128.8 acres on January 2, 1928.[10]

N. F. White and Eliza conveyed 2 tracts of land to J. T. Peoples on October 7, 1927. Being same tracts bought from the Cecil heirs. A total of 220 acres.[11]

In the 1880 Pulaski County census, Mary Tynes was living with Newton White, listed as Aunt. She had children Virginia N., Beatrice and Lanna.

Newton and Jemina's children:
1.4.1. Maude born 06 August 1882 in Pulaski.[12]
1.4.2. Virginia A. born 27 October 1883 in Pulaski.[13]
1.4.3. Ruth born 23 June 1885 in Pulaski.14
1.4.4. Blaine Chester. born 01 October 1886 in Pulaski.[14]

---

[1] Pulaski County, VA Deed Book 7, p. 28.
[2] Pulaski County, VA Deed Book 7, p. 29.
[3] Pulaski County, VA Deed Book 7, p. 30.
[4] Pulaski County, VA Deed Book 24, p. 275.
[5] Pulaski County, VA Deed Book 37, p. 498.
[6] Pulaski County, VA Deed Book 29, p. 329.
[7] Pulaski County, VA Deed Book 37, p. 493.
[8] Pulaski County, VA Deed Book 37, p. 493.
[9] Pulaski County, VA Deed Book 23, p. 216
[10] Pulaski County, VA Deed Book 58, p. 65.
[11] Pulaski County, VA Deed Book 57, p. 79.
[12] Pulaski County, VA Births, Pulaski County Courthouse.
[13] Pulaski County, VA Births, Pulaski County Courthouse.
[14] World War I Draft Registration Cards, 1917-1918: Pulaski County, Virginia.

- 1.4.5. Rhoda P. born 24 January 1888 married Albert Sidney Woodyard on 12 May 1909 in Pulaski. He was the son of Newton Woodyard and Bethia White. Albert was born June 1870 and died October 1946. Rhoda died 08 September 1972. They are buried in the Hunter Cemetery, Little Walkers Creek.
  Albert and Rhoda's children:
  - 1.4.5.1. Roxie married Garnett Whitt.
  - 1.4.5.2. Albert.
  - 1.4.5.3. Robert married Lelia Morris, daughter of John Bell Morris and Nannie Della Combs.
  - 1.4.5.4. Ray H. married Marie Linkous.
  - 1.4.5.5. Ernest Clowers.
  - 1.4.5.6. Lela Hazel.
  - 1.4.5.7. William.
  - 1.4.5.8. Randolph.
  - 1.4.5.9. David A.
- 1.4.6. Rosa born October 1889.[1]
- 1.4.7. Male Infant born 25 August 1890.[2]
- 1.5. Jemima born June 1865. Jemima was listed in the 1880 Pulaski County census living with Simon Johnson and family; listed as orphan.

2. Nancy born about 1831[4] married Valentine Fink on 05 April 1855 in Pulaski County. Valentine and Nancy's children:
   - 2.1. William H. born 21 February 1856.[3]
   - 2.2. Maggie P. born 09 July 1860.[4]
   - 2.3. George W. born 24 November 1864.[5]
   - 2.4. Bertha born 26 April 1867.[6]

3. Bethia born about 1835[7] married Newton Woodyard on 03 September 1870 in Pulaski County. He was born about 1809 in Guilford County, North Carolina. He died 03 September 1885 in Giles County.[8] Newton and Bethia's children
   - 3.1. Albert Sidney born June 1870 married 1st Clara Underwood on 12 September 1900 in Pulaski. She was born 13 October 1877 to Andrew Giles Underwood and Sarah Jane Kennedy. Clara died on 29 June 1908, buried in the Hunter Cemetery. Albert married 2nd Rhoda P. White, daughter of Newton Foy White and Jemina C. Stone. See Newton White above.
     - 3.1.1. Lee T. married Jeanette Fowler.
     - 3.1.2. Dolly G. born 02 October 1903 married Arnold E. Johnson. Dolly died on 12 June 1933, buried in the Hunter Cemetery,
     - 3.1.3. Trinkle.
   - 3.2. Ettie Emily born 1872 married William Morris Vest born 1874 in Giles County to Calvin Likens Vest and Catherine Stinson. Ettie died in 1935 and William died in 1950. They are buried in the Hunter Cemetery.

---

[1] Pulaski County, VA Births, Pulaski County Courthouse.
[2] Pulaski County, VA Births, Pulaski County Courthouse.
[3] Pulaski County, VA Births, Pulaski County Courthouse.
[4] Pulaski County, VA Births, Pulaski County Courthouse.
[5] Pulaski County, VA Births, Pulaski County Courthouse.
[6] Pulaski County, VA Births, Pulaski County Courthouse.
[7] 1850 Pulaski County, VA Census.
[8] Giles County, VA Death Record, Giles County Courthouse.

A.B. Hunt conveyed 250 acres to Etta E. Vest on April 7, 1915…adjoining R. C. Graham, A. G. and A. S. Woodyard.

William and Ettie's children:
- 3.2.1. Emery C. born September 1896 in Giles County.[1]
- 3.2.2. Albert Grayson born 08 January 1897 in Giles County.[2]
- 3.2.3. Calvin born November 1899 in Giles County.[3]
- 3.2.4. Newton R. born about 1901 in Giles County.[4]
- 3.2.5. Virginia Blanche born 18 November 1904 married Charles Cadell Parsell on 24 September 1924 in Pulaski. *See Parsell Family.
- 3.2.6. Martin H. born about 1907.[5]
- 3.2.7. Ruby born about 1910.[6]
- 3.2.8. Jackson born 18 June 1913 in Pulaski County married Myrtle M. Morris on 13 March 1937 in Pulaski. Myrtle was the daughter of John Bell Morris and Nannie Della Combs.
- 3.2.9. Helen born 08 March 1916 in Pulaski married Sam E. Stevens on 27 March 1937 in Pulaski.

3.3. Andrew Grayson born 01 April 1875 married Mary Jane Morris on 04 April 1894 in Pulaski. She was the daughter of William Riley Morris and Sarah C. Parson. Andrew died on 13 March 1945; Mary died 17 August 1930. They are buried in the Hunter Cemetery.
- 3.3.1. Rhoda born February 1895.[7]
- 3.3.2. Annie F. born January 1896.[8]
- 3.3.3. Bessie Owens born 17 September 1898 married Albert Asa Allen on 03 March 1918 in Pulaski. He was the son of William Carr Allen and Susan Sayers Morris. *See Allen Family.
- 3.3.4. William M. born May 1900.[9]
- 3.3.5. Ted born about 1903.[10]
- 3.3.6. Jenny B. born about 1905.[11]
- 3.3.7. Wade Hampton born 26 May 1907, died 26 March 1931. He is buried in the Hunters Cemetery.
- 3.3.8. Lessie born about 1915.[12]

4. George W. born about 1837.[13]
5. Sophina born about 1839.6[14] Living with father in 1880. Living with nephew, Newton Foy White in the 1900 Pulaski County census.
6. Harrison Shannon born 06 August 1840 married Mary M. King She was born on 29 November 1849 to Solomon B. King and Catherine Davis. See King Family.

---

[1] 1900 Giles County, VA Census
[2] 1900 Giles County, VA Census
[3] 1900 Giles County, VA Census
[4] 1910 Giles County, VA Census.
[5] 1910 Giles County, VA Census
[6] 1910 Giles County, VA Census
[7] 1900 Giles County, VA Census.
[8] 1900 Giles County, VA Census
[9] 1900 Giles County, VA Census
[10] 1910 Giles County, VA Census
[11] 1910 Giles County, VA Census
[12] 1930 Pulaski County, VA Census.
[13] 1850 Pulaski County, VA Census.
[14] 1850 Pulaski County, VA Census.

Harrison enlisted in Company F, 54th Infantry Regiment Virginia on 09 September 1861. he was sick on 01 January 1862 at Prestonburg, Virginia; wounded on 30 January 1863 at Kelly's Store, Virginia and hospitalized on 31 January 1863 at Charlottesville, Virginia. Returned on 30 September 1864.[1]

Harrison White applied for a Confederate Pension on April 2, 1888 in Pulaski County. He was a member of Company F, 54th Virginia Regiment. On or about January 30, 1863, he was wounded at the fight at Kelley's Farm (Isle of Wright County or near Suffolk). He explained that he was wounded "in the right leg just below the knee joint, necessitating amputation". The wound was caused by a minnie ball entering the right leg from the front. The leg was amputated 3 inches above the knee. Harrison was 47 years old. He received $30 annually for total disability.[2]

7. Mary S. born about 1842.[3]
8. Dianna born about 1844[4]. Dianna had children:[5]
   8.1. Nancy E. born about 1874.
   8.2. Lockard S. born about 1877.
   8.3. Andrew R. born April 1880.
9. Eliza born about 1846.[6]
10. Martha P. born about 1849.[7]
11. Joseph Absolam K. born 01 February 1854[8] married Lucinda Woods on 28 July 1876 in Pulaski County. Joseph moved from Pulaski County, Virginia to Greene County, Tennessee between 1885 and 1888. Later about 1907, they moved to Iowa, thinking that they could do better at farming there. Joseph however became dissatisfied with Iowa and returned to Tennessee. Lucinda did not want to leave Iowa, so Joseph left without her. Later in Tennessee he married M. Lizzie Shouse.

---

[1] The Virginia Regimental Histories Series. 45 vols. Lynchburg: Howard, 1987.
[2] Library of Virginia, Richmond, Virginia, Confederate Pension Rolls, Veterans & Widows.
[3] 1850 Pulaski County, VA Census.
[4] 1850 Pulaski County, VA Census.
[5] 1880 Pulaski County, VA Census
[6] 1850 Pulaski County, VA Census.
[7] 1850 Pulaski County, VA Census.
[8] Pulaski County, VA Births, Pulaski County Courthouse.

MISCELLANEOUS PHOTOGRAPHS

DAVIS SCHOOL

Davis School dated late 1800's to early 1900's. Students are unknown. Teacher most likely R. Lee Millirons. (Picture courtesy of Robert Millirons). Submitted by Christine Hamblin Distelhorst.

SPUR BRANCH SCHOOL

Spur Branch School—Goshen Church seen right hand side in the back of the school. Students unknown.
Submitted by Juanita Bentley & Christine Hamblin Distelhorst.

PULASKI COUNTY LITTLE WALKERS CREEK SCHOOL

1st row, left to right: Joe Banes, George Allen, Asa Allen, Ed Thompson, Perry Millirons, Ossie White, Charles White and Frank Millirons. 2nd row: Luther Millirons, Hugh Millirons, Frank Fink, Roy Millirons, Lilburn Millirons, Belle King, Mrs. Roop, Mr. Roop, Pearl Millirons, Eliza Millirons, Annie Banes, Josie Banes, Nancy Banes, Grace Stuart and Lillie Bond.
3rd row: Esker Stuart, Early Fink, Hoge Millirons, Maggie Allen, Cynthia Stuart, Alice Allen, Grace White and Bessie King.
Submitted by Sarah Melton Sumner.

GOSHEN CHURCH

Goshen Church dated August 29, 1903.
Submitted by Clayton Parcell

HENRY DAVIS' SAWMILL

Submitted by Juanita Bentley

EMMETT DAVIS

Submitted by Rebecca Sowers

SPUR BRANCH--POSSIBLY SCHOOL CHILDREN
Date Unknown

Submitted by Juanita Bentley

A FAMILY REUNION/CHURCH GATHERING
R. L. D. possibly Robert Lee Davis

Submitted by Rebecca Sowers

BIBLIOGRAPHY

BOOKS

Bland County Centennial Corporation. *History of Bland County (Virginia)*. 1st ed. Radford, Virginia: Commonwealth Press. 2nd ed. Tazewell, Virginia: Clinch Valley Printing Company, Inc. Copyright 1992.

Brunk, Ivan W. *Jacob's Ladder: A Supplement to The Progeny of Jacob Brunk I, The Will-maker*. 1982, Sarasota, Florida.

Giles County Historical Society, Research Committee. *Giles County, Virginia History—Families*. Seventh Printing, 2000. Marceline, Missouri: Walsworth Publishing Company.

Halsey, Richard J. *One Branch of the Halsey Family*. Springfield, Missouri: 1967. Second Edition.

Kegley, Mary B. *Early Adventurers on Western Waters, Volume III, Part 1 and 2*. Marceline, Missouri: Walsworth Publishing Company. Copyright 1995.

Kegley, Mary B. *Southwest Virginia Tax Assessments, 1815*. Wytheville, Virginia: Kegley Books. Copyright 1991.

The Virginia Regimental Histories Series. 45 vols. Lynchburg: Howard, 1987.

CENSUS RECORDS

Bland County, Virginia. 1870-1930.
Cumberland County, Virginia. 1930.
Daviess County, Missouri. 1850.
Fayette County, Virginia. 1860.
Giles County, Virginia. 1810-1930.
Guilford County, North Carolina. 1850.
Knox County, Kentucky. 1870.
Mercer County, West Virginia. 1900-1930.
Orange County, North Carolina. 1820-1840.
Pulaski County, Virginia. 1840-1930.
Raleigh County, West Virginia. 1930.
Russell County, Virginia. 1880-1910.
Tazewell County, Virginia. 1880-1930.
Wayne County, Michigan. 1930.
Wythe County, Virginia. 1810-1930.

COURT RECORDS

Bland County, Virginia. Wills, Marriages, Deeds, Land Grants. Births, Confederate Pension Records. Bland County Courthouse, Bland, Virginia. Library of Virginia Website, Richmond, Virginia.

Giles County, Virginia. Marriages, Deaths. Giles County Courthouse. Pearisburg, Virginia.

Montgomery County, Virginia. Land Grants. Montgomery County Courthouse, Christiansburg, Virginia. Library of Virginia Website, Richmond, Virginia.

Pulaski County, Virginia. Wills, Marriages, Deeds, Land Grants. Births, Deaths, Confederate Pension Records. Pulaski County Courthouse, Pulaski, Virginia. Library of Virginia Website, Richmond, Virginia.

Russell County, Virginia. Marriages, Births, Deaths.

Wythe County, Virginia. Wills, Marriages, Deeds, Land Grants, Births, Deaths, Confederate Pension Records. Wythe County Courthouse, Wytheville, Virginia. Library of Virginia Website, Richmond, Virginia.

PUBLISHED MANUSCRIPTS

Brackin, Henry B. Jr. MD. *The Akers Family.* Privately Published. Copyright 2000.

NONPUBLISHED FAMILY MANUSCRIPTS

Corder, Estelle. *Corder Family Research.*

Crockett, J. D. *Crockett Family Research.*

Hamann, Lee. *The Allen Family of Little Creek (A Genealogy of the Family of John Allen, Son of Carr, resident of the Little Creek Area of Northern Pulaski County, Virginia).* February 1992. [Courtesy of George Allen.]

Hunter, Robert. *Hunter Family Research.*

Parsell, Ralph Lee. *Parcell Family Research.*

Sowers, Rebecca. *Davis and Farmer Family Research.*

Talbert, Bobby. *Underwood and Morris Family Research.*

WEBSITES AND ONLINE DATABASES

Ancestry.com. World War I Selective Service System Draft Registration Cards, 1917-18 [database online] Provo, UT: Ancestry.com, 2002. National Archives and Records Administration. World War I Selective Service System Draft Registration Cards, 1917-1918. M1509, 4,277 rolls. Washington, D.C.: National Archives and Records Administration (varied dates).

Buck-Thompson, Cynthia M. *The 9th Regiment Virginia Volunteers.* <http://pw1.netcom.com/~buck1755/9thregiment.htm>. (14 October 2002).

Centers for Disease Control and Prevention. *Pandemics and Pandemic Scares in the 20th Century.* <http://www.cdc.gov/od/nvpo/pandemics/flu3.htm#9>. (12 September 2003).

Confederate Pension Rolls, Veterans and Widows. The Library of Virginia.
<http://ajax.lva.lib.va.us/F/?func=file&file_name=find-b-clas10&local_base=CLAS10> [online database] (varied dates).

Fridley, Beth, compiler. Provo, Utah: Ancestry.com, 2000. *Bland County, Virginia Births: 1861-96*. [database online]. <http://www.ancestry.com/search/locality/dbpage.htm?t=2&c=49&co=0&y=0&dbid=5275>. Original data: Bland County, Birth Records, 1861-96. Richmond, Virginia: Library of Virginia. (varied dates).

Frisch, Karen. *Childhood Diseases in the Victorian Age, Part II: The Victims*. Ancestry.com. <http://www.ancestry.com/library/view/news/articles/5675.asp>(01 August 2003).

Lewis, Deana Meadows, *Descendants of Ambrose Meadows*. <http://www.geocities.com/ginger77536/index.htm#TOC%20> (06 March 2002).

National Archives and Records Administration. *Civil War Pension Index*. [database online] Provo, UT: Ancestry.com, 2000. Data indexed and imaged from National Archives and Records. Administration. *General Index to Pension Files, 1861-1934*. T288, 544 rolls. Washington, D.C.: National Archives and Records Administration. (21 April 2003).

Nominal Roster of the 13th Tennessee Cavalry, U.S. Army 1863- 1865. <http://members.aol.com/jweaver301/nc/13tncav.htm>. (21 April 2003).

Social Security Death Index Interactive Search. Rootsweb.com. <http://ssdi.genealogy.rootsweb.com/cgibin/ssdi.cgi> [online database] (varied dates).

United States National Archives. *Civil War Compiled Military Service Records* [database online] Provo, UT: Ancestry.com, 1999-. (21 April 2003).

Virginia Land Office Patents and Grants/Northern Neck Grants and Surveys. The Library of Virginia. <http://ajax.lva.lib.va.us/F/?func=file&file_name=find-b-clas30&local_base=CLAS30> > [online database] (varied dates).

Virginia Military Dead. The Library of Virginia. <http://www.lva.lib.va.us/whatwehave/mil/vmd/index.asp> [online database] (varied dates).

What is in your Name?. vitalog.net. <http://www.vitalog.net/cgi-bin/select_name.cgi> [online database] (varied dates).

World War I History Commission Questionnaires. The Library of Virginia. <http://ajax.lva.lib.va.us/F/?func=file&file_name=find-b-clas13&local_base=CLAS13> [online database] (varied dates).

GOVERNMENT DOCUMENTS

National Archives and Record Administration, Washington, DC, RG 68, *Site Location Reports, Long Spur Post Office*.

National Archives and Record Administration, Washington, DC, RG 68, *Site Location Reports, Carnot Post Office*.

ABOUT THE AUTHOR

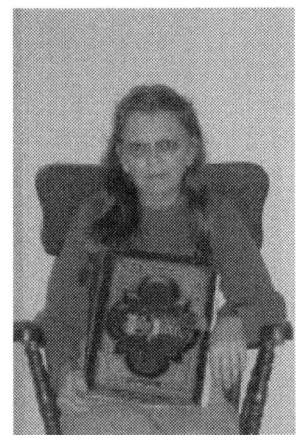

Rebecca "Becky" Cox Sowers was born on 05 October 1953 in Pulaski, Virginia to Jimmy Lee Cox and Elsie Irene Davis. She grew up in her grandfather, Emmett Davis' homeplace on Little Creek. Becky attended the Spur Branch School during her first two years of school. In 1963, she was transferred to Pulaski, attending Northwood Elementary. Becky graduated from Pulaski High School in 1972. She attended New River Community College in Dublin, Virginia from 1993-1996 receiving two associate degrees in Industrial Instrumentation and Electrical Technology.

Becky's interest in historical and genealogical research began in 2000 beginning with her research on the Davis and Parsell families. In researching her families, she realized there was no significant historical information on the community of Little Walkers Creek. Facing many hours of research, she traced the land records; beginning with the original land grants of that area, visiting the Montgomery, Wythe, Pulaski, Giles and Bland County courthouses looking for land records, wills, marriages and other pertinent records. This book is the result of three years of research.

Becky now makes her home in Pulaski, Virginia. You may contact her at 1014 Floyd Lane, Pulaski, VA 24301 or e-mail bsowers@verizon.net.

Becky with her dog, Rusty—October 1960.
Submitted by Rebecca Sowers

INDEX

2

24th Infantry Regiment 146

6

63RD Virginia Volunteers 127

A

Adams
   Robert 9
African-American 42, 158, 160
Akers
   Amanda J. 180
   Amos 29, 32, 33, 37
   Ann. 29
   Blackburn 29
   Catherine 33
   Catherine (widow) 32
   Dandridge 23, 29, 30, 32, 33, 37
   David Crockett 64
   Davidson 30, 122, 163, 180
   Davis 29, 32, 33
   Dora Alice 31, 35
   Elizabeth 29, 30
   Ella Augusta 35, 51, 68, 173
   Emeline 29, 31, 32, 33
   Emily Elizabeth 35, 115
   Emma V. 64
   Francina Julia 30, 35
   Fransina 29
   Gillie B. 33, 66, 116
   Gordon F 31
   John 29, 30, 32
   Julia M. 50
   Julian N. 34
   Katherine 29
   Louisa 122
   Maggie L. 64
   Margaret Melvina 32
   Martha 32
   Mary Catherine 29, 30
   Mary Elizabeth 163
   Mary Lizzie 64
   Mildred Ann 29, 32, 65
   Missouri 32, 33
   Moses ... 18, 23, 29, 30, 32, 33, 35, 37, 53,
      65, 66, 101, 139, 177
   Moses, Jr. 23, 33, 37, 115
   Moses, Sr. 23, 29, 33
   Octava 29, 30
   Parthena 32, 33
   Paulina 61
   Pearl R. 64
   Rachel 33
   Sallie P. 32, 37
   Sarah Ann 180
   W. B. 30
   William 29
   William B. 29
   William C. 64
   William D. 29, 32
   William II 29
   William III 29
   William McKinley 64
   Willie 64
   Wm. D. 32, 33
Albert
   Frederick H. 89
   Pearly Miller 89
Alexander
   Minnie N. 109
Alford 120
   John 19, 20
   Peggy 19
Allen 60
   Benjamin Franklin 40
   Benjamin Franklin Frank 40
   Carr 39
   Charles Edward 40
   Eliza 52, 89
   George 156
   George Julian 64
   Hubert Troy 41, 141
   Ida Catherine 41
   James Franklin 40
   James H. 40, 41
   Jesse McKinley 41
   John 39
   John A. 41
   Joseph L. 40
   Juliet 8
   Laura Ellen 54
   Liza 61
   M. B. 86
   Madison 44
   Margaret 39
   Margaret May 41, 107
   Martha Alice 41

Mary Magdalene ... 40
  Samuel Walice ... 41
  Sarah A. ... 40
  Susan ... 40
  Susan S. ... 40
  Thomas ... 120
  W. C. ... 40
  W. J. ... 40
  William ... 39
  William C. ... 40
  William Carr ... 62, 107, 161, 163
  William Carson ... 40
  William Jackson ... 41
  William W. C. Carr ... 39
Allen Cemetery ... 40
Allford ... 16
Allison
  George B. ... 31
Altizer
  Catherine ... 29, 65
  John ... 29
Alum Spring ... 13, 127
Alum Springs ... 127
Amburn
  Ada Mary ... 75
  David ... 75
  Doris ... 75
  Edward ... 75
  Katherine ... 75
  Preston S. ... 75
  Preston S. Jr. ... 75
  W. E. ... 75
Andrews
  Curtis ... *78*
Arthur
  Lennie Neal ... 125
Ashley
  James P. ... 172
Ashworth
  Jane ... 164
  John H. ... 164
Assistant Postmaster ... 82
Austin
  James Young ... 42
  Mary Polly ... 90
Averill's Raid ... 86
Axley
  Rebeckah ... 120

B

Back Creek ... 7

Baiery Bottom ... 7
Bailey
  Homer Woodson ... 95
  Judy Ann ... 95
Bain
  Dorothy S. ... 46
  J. Walter ... 46
Baker
  Isaac ... 15
  Sally ... 15
Bane
  Alice Bell ... 46
  Arthur Clifford ... 46
  Brady Edward ... 46
  Carl William ... 46, 53
  Earl ... 46
  Elizabeth A. ... 44
  Ellen M ... 46
  Ethel D. ... 46
  Frances Nellie ... 46
  George Harrison ... 46
  Harrison L. ... 46
  Hubert Lee ... 46
  James ... 13, 127
  James W. ... 44
  Jeremiah ... 44
  Jesse ... 13
  John ... 13
  John Harvey, Jr. ... 46
  John Harvey, Sr. ... 46, 53
  John Robert ... 46
  Lillie Sue ... 46
  Lottie Ellen ... 46
  Mabel V. ... 46
  Nancy C. ... 44
  Nettie Frances ... 46, 53
  Rachel Madeline ... 46
  Robert A. ... 46
  Robert Andrew ... 46
  Sally ... 44
  Sarah ... 44
Banes
  Andrew ... 47
  Ann May Annie ... 44
  Annie ... *81*
  Bernard ... 48
  Carolyn Aileen ... 37
  Charles J. Jerry ... 47
  Charley ... 48
  Chester ... 48
  Cynthia Jane ... 45

Daisy 46
Edgar Albert 36, 48, 131
Edith Virgie 47, 109
Edna Jane 44
Elizabeth 43
Elizabeth A. Bettie 44
Ellis Wilber 48
Ernest Dreyton 37, 48
Ethel 47
George 43
Harrison 48
James William 48, 178
James William Bill 45
Jeremiah 11, 43, 52, 138
Jerry 48, 138
Josephine Alice Josie 48
Julia Rose 35, 48, 110, 157
Lula 48
Margaret 47, 48
Mary 48
Missouri 55
Nancy Catherine 52, 53
Nancy Cathern 47, 49, 69, 92, 95
Nancy Cook 43, 85
Nellie Gray Banes 47
Oakley Neal 48, 93
Sarah 8, 43, 48
Sarah Davis 44
Shurley 48
Wayne Kenneth 48, 94
William David 47
William Joe Dreyton 47
Willie Missouri 45
Banes branch 10
Banes/Leeson Cemetery 44, 48
Banks
 Charlie M. 158
Barber
 Rebecca 67
Barger 8
Barner
 Signora 158
Barton
 John Quincy 40
Baskerville
 John B. 12
Bateman
 Margaret 45
 Nancy 20
Batte
 Henry 4

Thomas 4
Baumgardener 94
Beasley Cemetery *80*
Becklehimer
 Elizabeth 32
 John 30, 32
 Martha 30
Beheler
 Priscilla 164
Bel Air Memorial Gardens 173
Bell
 Mary Ann 93
 Mary Kesiah 152
 Nellie Pierce 93
Belle Grove 86
Beller
 Caroline 39, 123, 161
 Elias 60
 Elizabeth Jane 127
 Peninah 39
 Penninah Jane 60
 Peter 128
Belspring 53
Bertha Mineral Company 40
Beverley
 Robert 2
big Mountain 44
Big Mountain 44
Big Spring 18
Big Survey 31, 171
Biography
 Dr. Thomas Walker 5
 Emma Louella Millirons 58
 Robert Lee Chandler 57
 Wiley Hnederson Faw 103
Bird
 Catharine 127
 James H. 67
 Louisa 165
Birtchlawn Cemetery *78*, 172
Blackburn
 Elizabeth 29
 Susanna 29
Blackwell
 Alice 175
 Mary Ella 40
Bland
 John Jasper 178
 Richard 6
Bland Cemetery ...68, *79*, 100, 116, 143, 144
Bland Turnpike 167

Blankenship
   Donald L. 76
   H. J. 76
   Harvey 139
   James P. 139
   Robinette Brown 76
   Robinette Brown, Jr. 76
Blessing
   Elizabeth Kitts 146
Blevins
   Donald 98
   Nancy 98
Blue Ridge Memorial Gardens 95
Bluestone Creek 105
Bluestone River 9, 16
Bogle
   Almira A. 170
   George William 22
   James 170
   John 23
   John Jr 22
   Joseph Longstreet 22
   Lucinda Catherine 22
   Luemma Isobel 22
   Margaret Susanna. 22
   Marinda 117, 118
   R. D. 139
   Sarah Elizabeth 22
   Victoria Jane 22
Bond
   Della O. 130
   James 130, 131
   James R. 48, 107, 130, 136
   Jessie L. 48, 131
   Lula Jane 131
   Martha J. 131
   Martha Jane Johnston 92
   Martha Jane N. Johnston 56, 175
   Mitchell 131
   Nathan M. 130
   Oscar Roy 130
   Serena 131
   Victor O. 130
   Virgie Ethel 54, 107, 130
   William James 131, 136
Bond Cemetery 130
Bopp
   Pauline 154
Borden
   Benjamin 2
Bourne

   Ann 151
Bowles
   Annie 76
   Charles S. 31
   Ella M. 76
   Joseph Shannon 32
   Marcus Lafayette 76
   Mary D. *79*, *81*, 84, 90, 141
   Minnie B. 101
   Sarah Elizabeth 132
   William H. 90
Bowls
   Jacob 67
   Susannah 67
Bowman
   Deloris Jean 96
   Joseph (Captain) 120
Bowyer
   Charles A. 20
Boyd
   Edward 88
   Julia C. 88
   Nancy Jane 13
   Nannie C. 42
   Thomas I. 42
Bradd
   Jane 112, 137
Bragg
   Elizabeth 170
Bralley
                      A.105
   Susan 23
Bralley tract 23
Brally tract 106
Brawley 105
                    A.21, 165, 170
   Adams 22
   Anselm 21, 22, 23, 30, 33, 170
   Barbara 22
   Elizabeth 22
   Elizabeth H 22
   George T. 22
   Hannah Smyth 22
   James 22, 23
   John 22
   John Smyth 22
   Jonathan 22
   Julia 22
   Julia Ann 22
   Louisa 22
   Margaret Emily 23

Martha. 22
Mary 22
Samuel Guy 22
Sarah 30, 66
Sarah P. 23, 33, 115
Susannah Brawley 23
Susannah Hutsell 23
Susannah Louisa 170

Breidinger
Maria Eva 121

Bridgeman
Thomas 107

Brizendine
Susannah 164

Brock
R. A. (Dr) 39

Brookman
Catherine 13
Elizabeth 135
Mary 13

Brown
Minnie L. 98
Nancy 120
Salatha *82*

Bruce
J. Henderson 15
Lutheria 146

Brunk
Agnes May 46, 53
Albert 47, 78
Bertha Jane 45, 54, 55
Bertie L. 53
Betty Marie 54
Beulah Virginia 47
Charles Neal 47
Christopher 52
Clara Elizabeth 47, 69
Clarence Herbert 47
Dorothy M. 53
Edith 53
Edna 53
Edward 54
Elizabeth 53
Elizabeth Lizzie Cora 52
Ernest B. 53
Ethel 53
Eugene B. 53
Eugene Edward 52, 175
Eva Ann 47, 95
Floyd 47
Francis Catherine 47

Genoa Bell 47, 49
George 47
George Thomas 46, 53
George Washington 52
Hannah M. 52
Hazel Naomi 54
Houston N. 54
Houston Neel 54, *78*, 153
Irene E. 53
Jacob 52
John 52
John Griffith 52
John T. 53
John William 53
Junior N. 54
Junior Neel 54, 175
Lavina Elizabeth 54, 108, 153
Linda 53
Lola Grace 54, 107
Louise C. 53
Lula Ann 54
Marvel 54
Mary Catherine 50, 54, 153
Mary Louisa 52
Nancy 48
Nancy Ann 52
Nancy C. 175
Neal 92
Nellie L. 53
Opal Belle 54
Otis Roy 46, 53
Ralph C. 53
Raymond E. 53
Robert Bruce 54
Robert Kelley 53, *78*
Samuel Neal 53
Sara Lavina 52
Thomas Repass 47
Vance Clayton 54
Vernie Eliza 54, 89
Viola Agnes 54
W. H. 38
W. S. 54
Walter 35, 53
Walter Herbert 47, 49, 53, 69, 92, 95
William 53, 171
William S. 54, 175
William Steven 52, 54, 89

Buchanan
Raymond 75
Robert E. 75

Victor 76
Burgess
    Polly 44
    William A. 180
Burk
    Elizabeth Betsey 85
Burnette
    John Thomas 107
Burton
    Albert L 114
    Bertha M. 114
    Charles 114
    Charles Calvin 45, 54, 55
    Charles Russell 146
    Daisy 45
    David 45
    Della 45
    Emma Jane 147
    Eva 114
    Fradela 13
    Frank 45
    George 114
    George W. 113
    George William 114
    Gladys B. 114
    Ida L. 68
    Irene 54
    James Andrew 68
    James Thomas 114, 147
    Jerry 45
    John 45
    Josephine Elizabeth Burton 50
    Josephine Josie Elizabeth 101
    Levi S. 45, 101
    Mary J. 68
    Miller T. 68
    Mitchell M. 45, 55
    Nancy 13
    Nannie L. 68
    Robert 45
    Samuel Vance 68
    Thomas 68, 114
    Vernie 45
    William 45
    Willie M. 48
Burton Cemetery 68
Burton Family Cemetery 114, 167
Bush
    Betty 8
Bussey
    George 22

Hester Ann 22, 96, 98
James 22
Sarah F. 22
Thompson H. 22
Butler
    Marshall 159
    Mildred 30
Byrd
    John 74
    Ollie E. 74, 172
    Susan 74

C

Caddall
    Elizabeth 85, 134
    James B. 10, 140
    Sarah 15
Caldwell
    Daisy Virginia 82
    Hannah Ruth 52
Cameron
    Larnie Belle 31
Camp Douglas, Chicago 49
Camp Douglas, Chicago, Illinois 157
Camp Morton, IN. 126
Cannaday
    Gladys 50
Carden
    Charles 152
    Charles W. 53, 178
    David Cloyd 45
    Ellen Lee 46, 53
    Everett Oral 45
    Hannah 67
    Lillian Helena 45
    Lottie Jane 45
    Mary Belle 45, 152
    Robert Andrew 45, 46
    Robert Cloyd 45, 152
    Vergie Bell 45
    Virginia Bell 46, 53
    Willie A 45
Carnot 49
Carnot Post Office 68, 169
Carpenter
    Comie 79
    Edgar 79
    Ernest 79
    Geraldine 79
    Lorene M. 79
    Raymond 79

Ruby *79*
Carper
　Margaret 175
Carr
　Bell 118
　Burton L. 118
　Elizabeth 73, *78*
　Elizabeth Ellen 94, 100, 108, 109, 153
　Elizabeth Nannie Ellen *78*
　Jack 73
　Jesse R. 118
　John 13
　John H. 118
　John J. *78*
　Lillie M. 118
　Lizzie M. 118
　Lucy C. 118
　Maude R. 118
　Minnie W. 118
　Molly M. 118
　Robert Graham 145
　Robert S. 118
　William C. 13
　William M. 118
　Winton 118
Carter
　David J. 107
Carver
　Lucreasey 47
Cassell
　Edna D. 87
　J. G. 67
　James M. 91
　John 101
　John Caddell 101
　Nannie S. 91
　Neta M. 101
　Sallie 90, 178
　Samuel 17, 87, 91
　Samuel Levi 101
　Vena Gertrude 117
　William L. 102
Cassell tract 91
Catron
　Virginia 46
Caves
　John H. 178
　Sarah 47
　Sarah A. 178
Cecil 183
　Charles 88

Charles W. 13
Estelle Ann 13
Fannie 88
Giles S. 13
James T. 13
Kyle 149
Lou N. (Mrs.) 42
Lucy A. 13, 127
Mary 181
Mary A. (Mrs.) 42
Mary Ann 13
Russell 13
Russell H. 13, 127
Sallie 42, 88
　Z. 21
Z. S. 42, 88
Z. W. 127, 181
Zachariah 7, 10
Zachariah W. 13, 127, 181
Zachariah W., Jr. 127
Zachariah White Sr 13
Zachariah, Jr. 13
Cecil family 160
Cecil heirs 158
Cedar Creek 86
Cedar Grove Cemetery, Giles 172
Chandler
　Carl 74
　Carl Davis 57, 92
　Cornelia 85
　Ellen 56
　George 56
　Hannah 36, 92
　Hannah C. 56
　James H. 56
　James William 36, 57
　John Robert 54, 56, 92, 131
　Margaret 56
　Mary 56
　Mary Ada 57, 92, 143
　Nicholas 56
　R. L. 74, 91
　Ralph 74
　Ralph Scott 57, 92
　Reba Lee 36, 57
　Richard 56
　Robert Lee 36, 56, 74, 92
　Vivian G. 54, 89
Chapman
　Norma 98
Charlottesville, VA 86

Chewning
   Janie Elizabeth 50, 110
   Orsen Wylie 50, 110
   Robert Foster 107
Chinault
   Sarah 123
Christley
   Elizabeth 122
Chumbley
   S. C. 73
Church Of Jesus Cemetery 53
Clark
   Elizabeth J. 66
   Emma Josephine 108, 150
   George A. 150
   George Rogers 120
   James 150
   James Alexander 108, 149, 150, 167
   Jane Lambert 150
   John 150
   Lula 150, 167
   Minnie 149, 150
   Rosetta 150
Clinch River 9, 16
Cline
   Elizabeth 148
Cloyd family farm 86
Cloyd's Mountain 8, 13
Coburn
   Waucella Mae 36
Cole
   Chloe Pearl 144
Coleman 105
   Chapman 164
   Mary Ann *81*, 94, 153, 163, 164, 171
   Samuel 164
Collins
   Berta M. 34
   Bertha 32
   Callie 32
   Cary 33
   Charles 32
   Charles E. 34
   Christopher P. 32, 33
   Crockett 32
   Cynthia Lou 32
   David H. 34
   Della Geraldine 34
   Dolly B. 66
   Edmond 32, 65
   Elizabeth 32, 65
   Emma 32
   Estell 32
   Ethel Mae *79*
   Frances 34
   Frank Estell 34, 112
   George William *79*, 114
   Gillie 66
   Harvey 32
   Harvey Lee 34
   Hester 33
   James 17, 32, 33, 65, 66, 118, 137, 178
   James C. 66
   Jennie 150
   John 66, 139
   John H. 33, 34, 66, 116, 139
   John 32
   Josie 66
   Kelley J. L. 34
   Madison R. 32
   Margaret M. 32
   Martha 33
   Mary Ann 32, 33, 65, 118, 137, 178
   Mary J. 34, 66
   Melvina 33
   Mildred 32, 33
   Mildred C. 32
   Minnie Caldonia 65
   Nancy 32, 66
   Nellie A. 34
   Nina 34
   Rosa 66, 178
   Sarah 34
   Sarah J. 65, 118, 137
   Sheffey Margaret Frances 34
   Stuart M. 66
   Thelma 33
   Walter 32
   William 93
   William C. 33
   William L. 32, 65
   William P. 66
   William 32
   Wm. L. 33
   Woodrow Wilson 78
Combs
   Aggie 63, 179
   Argie Bell 64
   C. F. 62
   Cam 63
   Charles C. 61
   Charles W. 63

Creed Frank	62, 125
Dicie	63
Dorothy	63
Eliza J.	39
Eliza J. C.	62
Evelyn	63
Everett	61
F. C.	124
Foy	123
Foy C.	179
Foy Crockett	63
Foy Crockett, Jr.	63
Frank	63
G. E.	63
George Edward	63
Georgiana	60, 61, 64
H. E.	39
Harry Genett	63
Henry	64
Herbert D.	62
Infant female	62
J. W.	61, 62
James	61, 62
James Robert	179
Jeremiah	60, 62
Jessie Savella	63
Joe W.	60, 61
John	39, 60, 61, 62, 64, 129, 132, 162
John W.	60, 61, 62
Joseph	60
Joseph W.	60, 62, 63, 156, 161, 179
Lee Roy	63
Lena	62
Lizzie J.	61
Lucinda	63
M. J.	39, 40, 61
Mabel B.	63, 156
Mandeville Jackson	61
Mary Alva	63
Mary Ann	62
Mary Arabella	64
Mary E.	62, 63
Melinda	60
Myrtle	63, 179
Nancy	60, 61
Nancy Ann	62
Nannie Della	62, 161, 184, 185
Nellie G.	63, 179
Neta Morgan	64
Nettie	61
Nettie M.	60
P. R.	62
Paulina C.	64
Peniah	162
Robert	63, 179
Robert V.	63
Robert Wesley	63
Sarah	60
Virgie Bell	61
Virginia	62
W. C.	62
William	60
William Cam Cameron	62
William Hix	62
William J.	61
William R.	61
William Victor	62, *81*
Zedekiah (often called Zadoc)	60
Company A, 57th Infantry Regiment	165
Company D 45th Regiment	126
Company D 23rd Battalion Infantry Regiment	155
Company F 45th Virginia Infantry	146
Company F 54th Infantry Regiment	30, 31
Company F, 45th Infantry Regiment	131
Company F, 54th Infantry Regiment	125
Company G. 36th Infantry	135
Company K, "The Old Dominion Guards", 9th Infantry Regiment	165
Company M. 2nd Tennessee Volunteer Infantry USA	76
Company. D 23rd Infantry	155

Conley
James F.	157

Connelly
Barbara Ann	156
Guy P.	157

Cook
Madona	61
Nancy	43
William H.	138

Cooper
Clara Lee	99

Copley
Nancy	181

Corder
Alvie Garland	36, 68
Amy Ruth	69
Archie C.	68, 92
B. L.	137
Ben V.	92
Benjamin	67

Benjamin F. 67, 101
Benjamin Larkin 36, 47, 54, 68, *79*, 88, 89, 92
Benjamin Victor 68
Bettie 87
Cora Ethel 68
Dewey Wayne 36
Edna Augusta 36
Edna Bell 68
Edward 67
Edward I 67
Edward II 67
Elias 67
Emily Lea 35, 69, 117
Fayette Francis 47, 69
Frances B. 137
Frances B. (Mrs.) 169
Francis Bell Davis 68
Garland Lee 36
George 70
Grace 70
James 67, 69
James L. 37
James Larkin 67, 68, *79*, 101, 112, 113, 116, 117
John 67
John Roach 69
Louella 69
Lula V. 92
Mary Elizabeth 70, 112, 113, 116
Mary J. 67
Meek D. 69
Mollie N. 69
Robert Wiley 36
Roger Allen 36
Sallie A. 67
Sallie E. 69
Samuel Madison 69, 112
Samuel Richard 68
Samuel Snow 67
Sarah Davis 69
Virgie D. 69
Walter T. 69
William 67
William B. 67
William E. 92
William Edward 54, 68, 92
Corner
   Eliza B. 118
Cove 87
Coven

A. S. 157
Covey
   Clara Ethel 119
Cowan
   Mary 171
Cox
   Dollie 77
   Ima 54, 89
   Jimmy Lee 96
   Juanita B *77*
   Rebecca Jane 96
   William Edward *77*
   William Walker *77*
   Wilma May *77*
   Woodie Lee 96
Crawford
   Jack 36, 57
Cregger 149
Cressell
   Alma 113
Crisco
   Adam McKinley *80*
   Andrew Wayne *80*
   Calvin Orrin *80*
   McKinley Adam *80*
Crisley
   John 120
Crockett 18, 33, 120
   Col. 21
   J. H. 115
   James 15
   Jane 19
   Jean Armstrong 19
   John 9, 14, 15, 16, 17
   John C. 15, 21, 29, 86
   Joseph N. 15
   Margaret 14, 15, 16, 17
   Margaret T. 14
   Mary 47
   Samuel 14, 17, 19
   Thompson S. 15
   W. G. 21
   William G. 15
Crockett & Blair 91
Crockett Cemetery 14
Crockett path 165
Crockett survey 136
Crockett's Cove 152, 158
Crow
   Agnes 7
Croy

Lewis 106
Sallie 106
Sarah Catherine .41, *80*, 83, 106, 153, 172
Susan L. J 106
William H. H. 105, 106
Wm. H. H. 106
Cruff
　Ballard 111
　Carolyn 111
　Henry D. 111
　Henry T. 111
　John T. 111
　Lucinda 111
　Mellie Virgie 110
　Robert 111
Culpeper
　Thomas (Lord) 2
Curtice
　Claib 21
Curtis (Rev) 38

D

Dalton
　Gomez *81*
　Serena 100
Daniel
　Temperance 39
Darst
　Elizabeth M. 11
　Mary K. 11
Daude
　Maria Magdalina 148
Davidson
　Ivan Hope 68
Davis 40, 72, 93
　A. T. 93, 174
　Abraham 85, 137
　Ada Ann 75
　Addison ...9, 10, 11, 18, 44, 130, 131, 155
　Addison Burke 175
　Agnes 75
　Agnes Ruth 68
　Aileen Gayle *77*
　Albert Jackson *79*, 90
　Albert Terry 48, 92, 93, 172
　Aletta *80*
　Alexander Caudell 99
　Alice Gray 84, 175
　Alicia *77*
　Allie Belle *79*
　Alvah Muncy 93
　Alvin Howard *77*
　Amelia A. 87
　Amey Jane 89
　Amie *79*
　Amy J. 137
　Andrew W. *78*
　Andrew William 172
　Andy W. 93
　Angelina 71
　Anna Mae 99
　Archibald 85, 134
　Arthur Adam *78*
　Aryce Selma 75, 77
　Audrey Hampton 84, 91, 92
　Benjamin M. 90
　Bertha J. *79*, 82, 89, 147, 173
　Bertha Jane 92
　Bessie 99
　Bessie A. 76
　Betty Jean 93
　Betty Lou 76
　Beulah *79*
　Billy Joe 93
　Blanche 86
　Bobbi 98
　C. A. 71, 73, *79*, 99
　C. C. 38, 71, 73
　C. Calvin 99
　Cadwell *80*
　Carl Brown *79*, 136
　Carl Junior 99
　Carlton Albert *80*
　Carol Jean *77*
　Carolyn 75
　Catherine 135, 185
　Cecil Thelma 49, *81*
　Charles 35
　Charles C. 73, 78
　Charles Calvin *79*, 83, 94, 173
　Charles Clinton 49, *81*, 91
　Charles Newton 95
　Charles W. 87, 101, 177
　Charles William 47, 49, 53, 54, 77, 100, 172
　Charlie Ray *79*
　Christine. 34
　Clarence L. *80*
　Clarice W. (Mrs.) 93
　Clarina 83
　Claude Swanson *79*, *80*, 100
　Clevell *77*

Clifford 77	Elwood *77*
Clyde 50	Emily Jane *79*
Colleen Noal 48, 94	Emmett 87, 189
Coma 73	Emmett M. 94, 166
Coma A. 73	Emmett Milton 47, 94, 100
Comie Albert *78*, 90, 94, 100, 108, 109, 153, 154	Ernest Caudell 99
	Ernest S. 99
Cora Lee *77*	Ernest Sonny Miller 95
Cranwill A. 93	Ernestine 95
Curtis Graham 93	Estel Vance 75, 77
Daniel 50, 75	Eugene 77
Darce Benjamin *77*	Eula Catherine 100
David 75, *77*	Euvada 83
David C. 87	Eva 24
David Elmo 93	Everett Lawton 88
Debbie 76	F. V. 71, 73, 74
Delilah 92	Fabious Victor 75, 76
Delilah A. 92	Fayette Floyd 88
Della 83	Florence 76
Della Rose 137	Floyd 99
Donald 94	Floyd Clayton 54, 89
Donald Alvin Mauyer *77*	Ford Hampton 94
Doris *78*	Frances Bell 36, 47, 54, 68, *79*, 89, 92
Dorothy M. 47, *78*	Francis Irene 48, 93
E. M. *79*	Frank *78*
Earl Bowman 81	Franklin *80*
Earlwood 93	Fred Pierce 77
Eavie E. *77*	Garland Pierce 77
Edith Jane *80*, 109	Genoa Agnes 54, 153
Edith Virginia 76	George C. 90
Edna C. *78*, 90, 154	George M. 34
Edna Doan 87	Gerald *80*
Edna Dove 101	Gertrude 95
Edna K. 137	Gilbert Frazier *80*
Edna Margaret 75	Gilford David 83
Edward 87, 93	Gilford Lafayette 83, 89
Edward Cadell 99	Gladys C. *79*, *80*, 100
Edward G. 102	Glen Caudell *80*, 108, 153
Edward T. 99	Gregory 76
Effie 137	H. H. 71, 94, 166
Effie Ethel 53, *78*	H. N. 86, 87, 91, 99
Effie M. 90, 180	H.H. 73
Eldridge Eugene 99	Hanie 93
Eliza Ann 89, 182	Hanie Genoa 94, 141
Elizabeth 9, 73, 85, 99, 117, 181	Harald Clayton 95
Elizabeth Betsey 21	Helen *80*
Ella Augusta 100	Henry 10, 18, 21, 71, 72, 73, 149
Ellen *80*	Henry B. 135
Elmer Lawrence 47, 95	Henry Hampton 50, 84, 91, 92, 97
Elsie Irene 96	Henry Samuel Little Henry 76
Elvie 99	Herman Milton 95

Hiram 6, 8, 19, 20, 39, 44, 60, 99, 131, 132
Hiram Green 85, 134
Hiram H. 8, 9, 85
Hiram Newton *80*, 94, 99, 154
Homer Lebert 89
Hubert C. *78*
Hubert Raymond 89
Hughie L. 95
Ida 94, 166
Ina Augusta *78*
Infant (2) 77
Infant son *81*
Irene 77
Isaac 85, 130
Isaac J. 44
Isaac Newton 34, 85
J. E. 10, 71, 73, 74
J. J. 71, 73
J. T. 91
J. W. 99
Jacob 35
Jacob H. 34, 50, 53
James 19, 20, 85
James Edward 56, 74, 91, 172
James Robert 83
James W. 87
James Whitten 54, 68, *78*, *79*, 87, 118, 137, 180, 182
James William 54, 89
Janice Evelyn 99
Jasper Hampton 73, *81*
Jerome Bonaparte 85, 90
Jerome Bonie 87
John 24, 85, 137
John C. 134
John Jasper 84, 142
John T. 31, 87, 90
John Thomas 83, 92
John Troy *79*, *81*, 84, 90, 141, 177
John W. 34
Jonathan 164
Joseph Donald *77*
Judith Elaine 57
Judy 83
Julia 35, 75
Julia A. 53
Julian 35
Juliet 9
Juliet G. 9
Kathleen 77
Kenneth 93
Kyle C. *81*
L. V. (Mrs.) 71
Larry Benjamin *77*
Lee Earl, Jr. *77*
Lee Earl, Sr. 77
Lena Gray *80*, 109
Leona Phern 90
Lester Neal 96
Lewis Baxter 57, 93
Linda Jane 75
Lockie L. 77
Lois Katherine *79*, *80*
Lola Bell 89
Loraine *80*
Loranzo Dow 134
Loretta 35
Louisa V. 73
Louisa Virginia 47, 53, 54, *77*, 100, 172
Louise Alberta 50
Louise Margaret 90
Lovica 21, 43, 138
Lucien B. 9
Lucille 75
Lucinda 99
Lucy Augusta Gussie 56
Lucy Clara *79*, 83, 94, 136, 173
Lucy Gussie Augusta 92
Lucy P. 137
Lucy Pearl 90, 180
M. H. 88, 137, 183
Macie *78*
Margaret *78*
Margaret Elizabeth 134
Margaret Naomi *81*
Marie *80*
Martha 9, 85
Martha Elizabeth 95
Martha Jane 84, 94, 166
Martha Levell 50, 101, 110
Marvin 37
Marvin Repass 101
Mary 24, 85
Mary Alberta *81*, 154
Mary Ann 75
Mary Blanche 94
Mary E. 99
Mary Jane 134
Mary L 34
Mary Lee 101
Mary Lou 93

Meek H.	88, 136
Meek Hoge	68, 88, 147
Meek Hoge, Jr.	88, 180
Michael	*77*
Mildred	83
Mildred Pauline	101
Millard Floyd	75
Miller Allen	101
Miller Daniel	34
Minnie Alberta	*78*
Minnie Bell	*81*, 166
Miranda Elizabeth	*80*
Myrtle Thelma	84, 91, 92
Nancy	18, 85, 134, 173
Nancy J.	137
Nancy Jane	85, 178
Nancy Jane King	88
Nannie	137
Nannie Virginia	*79*, 90
Naomi Katherine	54
Nellie May	47, 92
Nellie P.	76
Nora Irene	109
Norman	154
Ollie	91
Ollie E.	10, 74
Paul Preston	*81*
Peggy	83
Permelia	85
Permelia A.	87
Permelia Ann	87, 101
Permelia Ann Nellie	75
Phillip Astor	*79*, 173
Phyllis Jane	95
Polly	87
Polly (Aunt)	87
R. L.	87
Rachel	19, 20, 32
Rachel Kennison	20
Ranald Lee	*81*
Randolph McGinnis	135
Raymond Earl	50, 84, 91, 110
Raymond Elwood	50
Ressa	137
Richard F.	137
Richard Floyd	54, 89
Robert Elwood	*77*
Robert Lee	50, 101
Robert Newton	100, 143
Robt. G.	43
Roger Lee	93
Ronald W	76
Rosaline	50
Roxie Mae	75
Roy Crockett	93
Roy Crockett, Jr.	93
Ruby	99
Ruby V.	*77*
Rufus	93
Rush F.	85, 86, 94
Russell James	76
Russell James, Jr.	76
Ruth Agnes	*79*
S. C.	*79*, 86
S. C. Davis, Jr	87
S. D.	87, 137
Sadie Marie	93
Sallie	135
Sallie Pearl	98
Sallie Rachel	100
Sallie S.	34
Sally	9
Sally E.	9
Saml. C.	72
Sammy	87
Samuel	106
Samuel C.	21, 23, 30, 44, 87
Samuel Caddell	49, 75, *77*, 85, 87, 99, 118
Samuel Caddell, Jr.	98
Samuel David	89, 143
Samuel Shelton	134
Sarah	43, 52
Sarah Elizabeth	67
Sarah Elizabeth Bettie	101
Sharon	*77*
Shelby Jean	*77*
Shirley	95
Stuart P.	47, 83, 84, 92
Susan	74
Susan Elizabeth	71
Terry C., Jr.	34
Terry Chaffin	34, 50
Terry Franklin	99
Texie Miller	100, 143
Therman O.	*77*
Thomas Dayton	83
Trinkle Whitten	54, 89
Van Trigg, Jr.	99
Vance Calvin	*79*, 83
Vergie Viola	101
Victoria Agnes	50, 91, 92
Violet Virginia	62, *81*

Virginia Era 95
Virginia Spencer 101
W. H. 103
W. T. 73
W. T. (Billy) 87
Wade Hutsell 88
Wallace Green *81*
Wayne Thornton 93
Wayne William *78*
Wesley *80*
William. 8, 10, 11, 21, 43, 44, 71, 85, 138.
See
William B 76
William Thomas 75, 101
Willie Floyd 49, *81*, 91
Willie J. 94, 166
Willie Parsell 95
Wilma *81*
Wise L. 74, 172
Wm. 10
Zelda Mae 75
Davis Cemetery 30, 33, 35, 36, 49, *77*, 92, 93, 101, 114, 148, 150, 173
Davis Cemetery, Clendenin, Giles 171
Davis School 187
Dean
    Hubert Bruce 112
Deaton
    Mary 179
Dennis
    Andrew L 125
Denton
    Joseph 120
Dewey 35
Deyerle
    Katherine Verna 107
Dickenson
    Ausell 160
Dickerson
    Edna 159
    Jenny 163, 166
    John 158
    Myrtle Ellen 95
Dickinson
    John Q. 166
Dillow
    Nannie 167
    Rush 169
Dodson
    Aubrey Sydnor 109
Doss

    Helen Virginia 107
Dowdy
    Helen 180
    James C 125, 180
    Malinda 180
Draper
    George 4
    Jane 19
    John 19
    John (Jr) 18
    John S. .... 74, 129. *See*
Draper survey 9
Draper's Mountain 12
Draper's path 16, 18
Drawbond
    Daisy 175
Drinnon
    James 85
Drummand.
    Madelene 46
Duke
    Frances 133
Dulaney
    T. T. 8, 123
    Thomas Terry, Jr. 89
Duncan 53
Dunn
    Robert (Captain) 114
Dunn's road 16
Dyer cemetery 146

E

East End Cemetery 100, 148
East river 9
East River 16
Eaton
    W. F. (Captain) 38
Elkins
    Elizabeth 29
    Lydia 29
Elliot
    Frankie Christine 115
Ellis
    Sarah 152
Epperson
    Drucilla P. 68, 116
    Edward Elisha, Jr. 116
    Edward Elisha, Sr. 68, 116
    John Henry 68
    Mary E. 112, 116
Estep

Betty 47
David Richard 96
Denise Louise 96
Douglas Lewis 96
Edna Louise 96
Jennie Lee 98
Timothy 96
Willard Lewis 96
Evan
    Thomas 151
Evensham 120

F

Fagg
    Sarah L. 105
Fairview Methodist Church Cemetery 75, 76, 90, 93, 98, 101
Fairview neighborhood 87
Fairview Road 87
Fanning
    Akalis 9
Farley
    Lenza 45
Farmer
    Charles Glenn 119
    Elizabeth Catherine *80*, 94, 99, 154
    Florence 35
    George Hoge 119
    Howe Haven 119
    John 119
    John T. 113
    John Trigg 119
    Kelley Crockett 119
    Mamie Brown 119
    May 115
    Parthena 30
    Richard 99, 119
    Stephen Madison 119
    Thomas Newton 119
    William Clinton 119
    Woodie Lee 119
Farris
    Sanders C. 175
Faw
    Bennie 104
    Beulah 104
    Clifford 104
    Eugene 104
    Georgia Mabel 57, 92
    Gilbert 104
    Hazel 104
    Hazel Irene 88
    Mabel 104
    Ola 57, 104
    Ola Dare 92
    Pheonis Bethel 103
    Robert 104
    Vernon 104
    Virginia 104
    Wade 104
    Wiley Henderson 57, 88, 92, 103
Fellows
    Evelyn 154
Felty
    Lois 76
    Martin Luther 76
    Mary 99
    Mary Ellen 76
Ferrin spring 11
Fink
    Bertha 184
    George W. 184
    Luster A. 123
    Maggie P. 184
    Valentine 184
    William H. 184
Fletcher
    Aldora 74
    Charles W. 74
    Chas W. 10
    George 41
    Joseph Walford 41
    Madison Allen 41
Flick
    Hester Ann 132
Florey 120
    David 121
    Susannah 121
Foote
    Sylvanus 7
Fortner
    Elizabeth 135
    Eugenia Belle 135, 137
    John 135, 167
    Joseph 135
    Joseph B. 135
    Mary A. 135
    Sarah 135
    Thomas 135, 137, 171
    William Winton .... 171. *See*
Fowler
    Jeanette 179, 184

Margaret 71
Samuel L. 71
Franklin
Andrew J. 71
Angelina J. 145
French
Clara 115
R. N. 139
French and Indian War 14
Fry
Joshua 2
Lafayatte 134
Frye
Stephen Valentine 134
Fulks
Sarah 120

G

George
Yeardley, Governor 2
Gibboney
James M. 12
Gibbony
John H. 134
Gibbs
Ann Wiggington 43
Giles
William Branch 6
Gills 140
Clora 144
Effie L. 144
Ellen 139, 140
H.140, 144
Infant 140
Infant female 144
John Thomas 144
Joseph J. 144
Mary Ellen 144
Phillip Mathew 144
Robert R. 144
William 140
William A. 144
William R. 144
Gilmer
George (Dr.) 5
Gleason
Evelyn *77*
Rosalee *77*
Thomas W *77*
Vergie *77*
William G. *77*

Gleaves
James T. 14, 16
Malvina 14
Robert H. 14, 15
Glen Haven Memorial Gardens 75, 76, 94, 96, 97
Glendy
Mary M. 12
Nancy 12
William J. 12
Glory
Lucinda A. 162
Goad
Alice W. 98
Bertha 46
Goff
Lucy 127
Goode
Mackerness 105
Goodman
Effie 57, 88, 92, 103
Effie Lula 103
Gorden
Josephine 159
Goshen Church 107
Goshen Methodist Church Cemetery. 45, 47, 48, 52, 54, 55, 68, 71, 74, 76, 78, *79*, *80*, 81, 82, 83, 84, 92, 93, 94, 95, 96, 99, 100, 101, 106, 107, 108, 109, 111, 153, 154, 170, 172, 173
Graham
James 129
James M. 129
R. C. 129, 185
Rachel 30, 122, 163, 180
Robert C. 129
W. T. 129
Grandview Memory Gardens 36, 69
Gray
Bertie 142
Emily 136
Florence 136, 148
Frances 144
George W. 136
Hubert 136
James William 136, 148
Susanna 89, 100, 143, 173
Grayson
A. J. 139
Andrew J. (Captain) 86
C. S. 139

212

James F.	139
Mary Polly	167
W. W.	139

Greenbrier County 22

Greene
- Jerome Walter 50, 110

Gregory
- Evelyn Maude 90

Grief
- Laura F. (Mrs.) 113
- Max 12, 53, *79*, 113

Griffith
- Emma 22

Grimes
- Priscilla 85

Groseclose
- H. C. 136

Gullian
- Mary 146

Gullion
- Martha 115, 168
- William 31

H

Haga
- Bertha 62
- William Curtis 136

Haganan
- Geertje Charity 67

Hale
- Aileen *81*
- Kathrea Loretta 108

Hall
- Allen 60
- Ervin *79*
- Ervin Blake *79*
- G. C. 103
- John D. 60
- Walter *79*
- Walter Wirt *79*

Halsey 65
- Carl Cecil 76
- Carl Cecil, Jr. 76
- Catherine 134
- Elizabeth Ann 17
- Gladys Louise 76
- James William 76
- John Trigg 17, 98, 152
- Josephine Josie Augusta 98
- Josie 87
- Lou 87
- Rachel 99, 119
- Rachel Laura 90
- Sarah 85
- Sarah J. 113
- Stephen 17, 23, 134
- Stephen J. 90, 178
- Stephen, Junior 65
- Thelma Irene 76
- Thomas 76
- Thomas Jefferson 178
- Thomas Reed 76

Halsey Cemetery 152

Halsey/King
- Cosby Jane 134

Hamblin
- Albert C. 108
- Alma Mae 80
- Annie Mae. 36
- Annie V. 110
- Arbie Ray 107
- Arnold Wade *80*, 101
- Arthur Edward 50, 110
- Augusta Gray 36
- Barbara. 50
- Bertie Cree 109
- Billy Ray 107
- Carlos M. 50
- Charles W. 110
- Charlotte 105
- Clinton *80*
- Coleman 105
- Curtis Floyd 107
- Dana Rhoena 54, *80*, 108, 153
- David Y. 23, 100, 105, 106, 165, 166
- David Young 105
- Della Roxie 108, 175
- Dora Ray 108
- Dorothy 50, 110, 153
- Edgar Albert. *80*
- Edward 105, 110
- Edward L. 50, 84, 101, 110, 153, 172
- Eleanor *80*
- Eley 105
- Elizabeth 105
- Ellen 111
- Elsie Vernon 108, 171
- Ernest 50, 110, 172
- Estell Crockett *80*, 109
- Estell Lewis *80*
- Floyd Newton 41, 107
- Frank 108

Frank Tyson 108
Garnett Lee 50, 110
Genoa Thelma 50, 84, 91, 110
George Thomas 105
Glenord C. 50, 110
Govan Thedmer 50, 101, 110
Harvey Tice 105
Hobert 50
Hubert Clinton 107
Hugh David 82
J. S. 175
James A. Hall 105
James Henderson 105
Jno. M. S. 106
John 106, 171
John Crockett 36
John M. S. 106
John M. Stafford 41, *80*, 105, 153, 171
John Milton Stafford 106
John Pierce C. 105
John Robert 83
John S. 106
Judas 50
Lena Bell *80*
Lena Gray 109
Leon Alton 107
Leonard Hensley *80*
Lillian P. 108
Lilly Jane 111, 146
Lois Elizabeth 107
Lot I. 105
Louisa Susan J. 105
Lucy 105
Mackerness 105
Maggie Leona 50, 110
Margie Evelyn 107
Marguerite Alma 108
Mary 110
Mary Christine 107
Milly 105
Nancy 105
Naomi Adeline *80*
Nellie Virginia 111
Olevie 110
Peter 105
Polly 50, 105
Raymond Alton 54, 107
Robert 110
Roman 107
Ronald Wade 107
Roxie M. 50, 110

Roy C. 108
Ruby R. 108
Sarah 106
Sarah C. 106
Silas M. 105
Sparrel K. 105
Stephen 105
Stephen T. 105
Stephen W. 105
Stewart Clayton 108, 150
Sylvia 50
Thelma 108
Thomas 105
Thomas H. 105
Thurman Stafford 107
Vanessa Gail. 36
Verna E. 108
Violet 108
Virginia 105
W. 72
William 106, 107, 110
William H. 107
William Hoge 54, 107, 130
William J. S. 50, 105, 106, 109, 110
Wm 165
Yvonne 50
Hamblin Cemetery 50, 94, 109, 110, 111, 164
Hamblin Cemetery, Bearsprings 105
Hamblyn
   Stephen (Captain) 105
Hamilton
   Kelly Orson 66
   Tim 21
   William Alexander 178
Hammonds
   Julian B. 67, 101
Hancock
   Albert Mitchell 69
   Alexander 119
   Allie 118
   Amanda Freelove 116
   Andrew B. 115
   Andrew Ballard 115, 168
   Annie Elizabeth 35, 69
   Arbanna 118
   Asa B. 116
   Barbara 139
   Barbara Belle 114
   Bertha Louise 117
   Bessie L. *79*, 114

Beulah...117	Jordan R...114
Carol..113, 116	Joy Kate..117
Carrie Bell (Mrs.)....................................69	Julia A..116, 169
Carrie Nellie Louisa 34, 70, 112, 116	Lafayette..118
Charles..118, 172	Larry M...50
Charles K..116	Laura J..115
Charles W..115	Laura May....................................115, 148
Charlotte..........................21, 117, 138	Lee...139
Clarence..112, 116	Lizzie..115
Cora...116, 117	Lizzie Mabel..117
Demaricus L..118	Lorene W..172
Dorothy Marie......................................114	Louisa..118
Effie Pearl..69, 112	Louisa J..112
Elexander Stinson...................35, 69, 117	Lucy E..114
Eliza A..65	Mae..115
Elizabeth Ann...............88, 118, 137, 172	Mahala...168
Elizabeth Belle......................................117	Marcia Ann..117
Elizabeth Caroline................................114	Marcus L..69
Elva Mae...172	Marcus Lafayette.................................116
Etta G..113	Marcus Lee..112
Eugene Mason......................................117	Marcus Walker....................35, 115, 168
Eva Trottie....................................115, 136	Marsha E..117
Fred Ralph..117	Martha E..114
G. W...16, 113, 114	Martin L...112
George.....................................15, 113, 139	Mary Adaline.......................................116
George E...117	Mary Elizabeth 67, 112, 113, 116
George Larkin..69	Mary Etta.......................................50, 172
George W. (Jr)..15	Mary Jane..112
George Washington..35, 50, 69, 113, 114, 172	Mogg..116
Georgie Mae................................114, 172	Myrtle Nehema............................117, 143
Hattie G..113	Nannie E..116
Hazel Marie..115	Naomi Isabell..50
Henry..118	Obadiah..112, 137
Henry E..113	Ocie Evelyn.................................112, 116
Hubert...116	Ollie W...117
Huston Sanders.............................112, 116	Pleasant T...118
Ida M..116	Ray...112, 116
James Henry...117	Ribble J..114
James Lewis...50	Richard Lee..114
James W..113	Riley Harrison 114, 116, 117
Jasper..115	Robert...118
Jesse Eugene..117	Robert Cecil...113
Jesse James..114	Robert Luther................70, 112, 113, 116
Jesse James, Jr......................................114	Robert P..65
Jesse James, Sr.....................................116	Roberta...118
John..118	Rome..83
John (Mrs.)...140	Rose Catherine................34, 112, 116
John A..116	Ruby A...117
John Asa...............................114, 116, 169	Ruby Ella......................................112, 116
John Henry...116	Samuel C..117
	Samuel Roosevelt..........................50, 114

Sarah J. 139
Saunders Helton 34, 70, 112, 116
Sidney Edward 50, 116, 172
Stella Ernest......................... 114, 116, 117
Telia Agnes 117
Thelma J. 117
Thomas S. 112
Virgie 116
Virginia E. 114
Virginia Ellen 117
Virginia Ellen Bell Missouri 119
Wagner W. 116
Walker (Mrs.) 140
Wilber W. 69
Wilbur Weeden 69
Willard 116
Willard 112
William 118
William Lee 112, 116
William McKinley 117
Hancock Cemetery 112, 113, 114
Hancock/King
   Robert P. 118
Harden
   Hubert Nello 173
   Ida Lou 144
Hardy
   Alice 111
   Charles 111
   Churchwell 111
   Dora 111
   Henry Ellis 111
   Henry J. 111
   Henry J. R. 111
   Jesten 111
   Lillie J. 110, 166
   Lottie 111
   Rachel 111
   Violet 111
Harell
   Enoch 120
Harman
   A. Z. 18
   Charles Woodrow 117
   John 23
   Lula Mae 117
   Orlevia 72
   W. A. 73
   W. N. 18, 72
   William Neel (Captain) 171
Harman's Lick hollow 8
Harmon
   Peggy 44
Harmon's Lick hollow 138
Harmony Creek 120
Harold
   John 129
Harrel
   Jacob 120
Harrell
   Ada Flora 126
   Alva 122
   Arlen Woodrow 124
   Arthur Booze 125
   Arthur J. 122
   Ballard 62
   Bettie 126
   Beulah 122
   C. R. 124
   Cene A. 123
   Charles Rufus 123, 124
   Delia Elam 126
   Della Maude 125
   Elizabeth Jane Emily 125
   Elmer Elwood 124
   Elsie Marie 125
   Elwood 125
   Emma 122
   Emory Maxwell 125
   Ethel May 125
   Frank J. 125
   Gladys 122
   Hazel Irene 124
   Henrietta 121, 124
   Hubert L. 122
   Ida 122
   J. H. 124
   James 121
   James Arthur 126
   James F. 125
   James Floyd 124
   John 120, 121, 125
   John H. 122
   John Mitchell 126
   Josie 124
   Laura 126
   Laura Eleanor 126
   Leona 122
   Louisa Frances 126
   Lula E. 62, 125
   Luther Lawrence 125
   Malinda Lydia 161

Martha	120
Martha Elizabeth	125
Martha Ellen	123, 162
Mary M.	124
Mary Maude	123
Matilda	126
Melvina	121, 161, 163
Mitchell	123, 162
Mitchell R.	123
Monrow	120
Myrtle Isabelle	125
Nancy	126
Nancy Jane	126
Nola Lee	125
Ollie	122
Orpha Ellen	126
Pauline Bane	124
Reuben	120
Rhoda	125
Roger Dale	125
Russell David	124
S. B.	124. *See*
Sarah	123
Sarah Ann	126
Sarah J.	124
Stephen Ballard	123, 124
Susan Malinda	126
Thelma	122
Thomas B.	121, 122, 125
Willard Raymond	124
William	120, 121
William B.	126
William Crockett	123, 124

Harrell Family 120

Harris
- Minnie *77*

Harrison 43
- Wilicia Willie 170

Hash
- Elmer Stanley 108

Havens
- Beatrice 35
- John 18, 115

Hayes
- Mary C. 85
- Samuel C. 85

Haymore
- Elizabeth Bettie 126
- Jincey 121, 161

Hearns old path 17

Heatherington
- Nancy 105

Hedge
- Buford 119

Heflin
- A. R. 139

Helm
- George 9, 16, 17

Helton
- Martha Elizabeth Josephine 123, 124

Helvey
- John Chrisman 35

Henderson
- Amy 9
- Mary Ann 14
- Nehemiah 9

Hendrick 23

Henry Davis' Sawmill 189

Hezekiah Harman's District 146

Hidden Valley Cemetery #1 ...68, 69, 79, 88, 89, 118, 133, 135, 137, 138

Hidden Valley Cemetery #2 ...53, 54, 83, 89, 95, 96, 101

Highland Memory Gardens 69, 88, 111

Hight
- Gordon M. 124
- Queenie Victoria 128

Hill
- Charles J. 66
- Cora J. 66
- Elizabeth 16, 66, 168
- Jenny 66
- Lucy E. 66
- Martin 16, 66, 168
- Mary 66
- Maxwell 66
- Stephen 66

Hite.
- Gordon T. 123

Hoback
- Andrew Maiden 173
- Anna B. Bessie 46
- Anna Jane 173
- D. P. R. 117
- Peyton 69
- Walter Henry 173
- William Odell 76

Hodges
- Delilah 164
- Elisha 164
- Gladiola Rebecca 107

Hoge 10

James 19, 20
James M. 113
Joseph .... *See*
Martha 22
Hoge's Chapel Cemetery 107
Hoiliman
   J. H. 71
Holbrook
   G. L. 42
   Irene 42
   Irene E. 13
Holiday
   Jackson 30, 32
   Octavia 32
Hollins
   Jason 125
Hollinsworth
   Saml. 7
Holloway
   Susannah 75, 76
Holston
   Joseph H. 134
Honaker
   Henry (Sr) 10
   Margaret 177
Hoskins
   Sarah 151
Hounshell
   James H 17
Hounshell 22
   Henry 148
   James H. 18, 19, 22, 24
   Mahala 148
   Mary 76
   Nancy 16, 113
   William 15, 16, 113
Houseman
   Nancy A.T. 164
Howe
   Daniel 7, 9, 13
   John D. 7, 11
   Joseph 7, 11
   Julia 13
Hudgins
   Mary Lucy 67
Hudson
   Isaac 131
Hughes
   M. 123
Hughett
   Albert Carter 111

Hungate
   Emmett Granville 45
Hunt
   A.B. 128, 185
   Andrew B. 128
   E. J. (Mrs.) 129
   Elizabeth J. 127
   G. Louis 128
   George Lewis 127
   James Thomas 127
   John Walton 128
   Lucy Jane 164
   Margaret Permelia 127
   Peter Edward 127
   Riley Harrison 127
   Sarah Ann 127
   Stephen 127
   William 75
   William Christopher 127
   William L. Jr. 128
Hunter
   William L. 179
Hunter
   Absolam 127
   Aeneas 127
   Elizabeth 127
   Ethel 122, 128
   Irene 128
   Jerome 127
   Joseph A. 127, 160
   Lucy 127
   M. 21
   Missouri 121
   Peter 127
   Queenie 128
   Queenie (Mrs.) 129
   R. M. T. 61, 62, 128, 129
   Robert 127
   Robert Moorman Titus 128
   Roy 128
   W. L. , Sr. 129
   William 21, 60
   William L..8, 60, 121, 122, 127, 128, 160,
      181, 183
   William L. , Jr. 128
   William L. Jr. 128
Hunter Burying Ground 129
Hunter Cemetery 41, 61, 62, 63, 90, 122,
   125, 128, 141, 161, 162, 179, 182, 184,
   185
Hunter's Pulaski Alum Springs 128

Hunter's Pulaski Alum Springs Company, Inc. 128
Hunters Pulaski Alum Springs Company 129
Hurst
    Hubert 180
    John Samuel, Sr. 122
    Rhoda 182
Hushour
    William Hedrick 117
Hutsell
    Elizabeth 22
    George 24
    Jacob 22, 24
    Johann George 23
    Johann Matthaus 24
    Johann Peter 24
    Johannes 24
    Ludwig 24
    Ludwig (Lewis) 24
    Margaret 24
    Susanna 24
    Susannah 22, 30, 33, 170
Hutzel
    George 23
Hylton
    Dorothy Jenett 46
    Lola 89
Hypes
    Frank Montgomery 46
    John 155
    John Monroe 45
    Mary Polly 155
    Rachael Magelene 46

I

Infantry
    36th, Company C 61
Infantry Company F 54th Virginia 48
Ingles
    John 4
    Thomas 4
    William 4
Ingram
    Elizabeth Franklin 135
    Harman 135
    James 140
    James C. 10

J

J. B.
    Davis 87
J. H.
    Pegram 106
J. W. White heirs 181
Jackson
    B. 139
    Bryl 139
    Launia 156
James White farm 160
Jefferson
    Peter 2, 5
    Thomas 5
Joe Graham Branch 91
John Crockett entry 113
John Crockett's land 133
Johnson
    Abby (Mrs.) 131
    Arnold E. 179, 184
    Elizabeth 60
    Hester 60, 132
    Hugh 131
    Hugh P. 131
    Isaac L. 181
    James 39
    James M. 60, 132
    Lewis 10
    Mabel 154
    Nancy 39, 40
    Sarah 39
    W. P. 131
Johnston
    Alice L. 132
    Arthur 132
    Clarence *82*
    Donald S. 99
    Flora A. 132
    Hugh 131
    Hugh P. 131
    Isaac 132
    Isaac L. 132
    James A. 132
    John P. 132
    Joseph 132
    Lewis 10, 21, 130
    Martha 10, 130, 160
    Martha J. 136
    Martha Jane 48, 107
    Martha Jane N. 130
    Maude 131
    Minnie S. 132
    Nancy Jane 130
    Nettie 131

Robert H. 132
Ruby Elizabeth 99
Sarah S. 131
Wesley J. 132
Johnston Family 130
Jones
   Bashaba 117, 133
   Charles Amos 118
   Charles Bascom 154
   Delia 117
   Elvisia J. 118
   Harrison H. 117
   Henry Newton 53
   Isabelle 139, 140
   James 17, 117, 133, 139, 140
   James J. 21, 117, 138
   John 17
   John A. 17
   John W. 118
   Joshua 117
   Lewis 11, 44, 138
   Mary 116
   Mary Elizabeth 21, 117
   Nancy 17
   Obadiah 21, 117
   Rose 118
   Sarah Ellen 117, 138
   Wesley 139
   William 140
Jones survey 17
Jordan
   Adison 38
Jordan's
   William J. (Captain) 37
Journell
   Mary Ann 45, 66, 148, 177
   William 177

K

Keens
   Delitha 179
Keffer
   Elizabeth W. 52
   George Washington 52
Kelly
   Missouri 30
Kelly's Store 186
Kendrick
   Sarah Ann .... 137. *See*
Kennedy
   John 179

Sarah Jane 63, 90, 179, 184
Kennison
   Mark 85
   Rachel 85
   Susan 170
Kent
   David 21
Kersey
   T. W. 103
Key
   Frances 145
Kid
   Ruth 31
Kimbleton
   Addie 178
   Mary 46
King
   Allen A. 68, 88, 138
   Annie Kate 47, 48, 49, *81*, 92, 101, 114, 136, 154, 172
   Arthur Jackson 143
   Artie E. 144
   Beatrice 74, 141
   Bennett 18, 68, 88, 117, 134, 136, 138, 173
   Bennett (Sr) 17
   Bennett (Sr.) 18
   Bertha 108
   Bessie 74, 140
   Bessie Katherine 141
   Bessie Mae 143
   Bessie Pearl 50, 172, 175
   Cabell W. 141
   Catherine 8, 138, 139
   Charles 10, 145
   Charles Caxton 173
   Charles Kelly 94, 141
   Charles P. 141
   Charley 139
   Charlie 139, 140
   Claude 144
   Clifford William 143
   Cordelia 138
   Cosby Jane 85
   Daniel M. 136
   David 18, 21, 23, 65, 88, 118, 133, 137, 172, 173
   David Painter 141, 144
   Della Rose 89, 143
   Dorothy M. 141
   Edgar Miller 100

Edgar Palmer .... 100. *See*
Eliza 139
Eliza A. 65
Eliza Agnes 143
Eliza M. 172
Eliza V. 139, 144
Elizabeth 138, 140
Emily 171
Emily G. 139, 145
Emily Pearl 136, 148
Ernest Chaffin 34, 142
Eugene L. 173
Eugene Thomas 143
Eugenia Thomas *79*, 131, 136
Eva T. 115
Flora 139
Flora Missouri 139, 144
Frances 36, 173
Frances I. 143
Frances Jane 145
Frank 144
Franklin P. 172
Franklin Pierce 145
George W. 115
George William 115
Gladys 74
Gladys Elizabeth 41, 141
Hanie Genoa 94
Hannah Ritter 18, 133, 138
Harvey L. 143
Harvey Newton 89, 100, 143, 173
Haynie 86
Helen 142
Henry Solomon 144
Herbert 142
Hester A. 135
Hester J. 136
Ida Essie 136
Irene 34, 142
Isaac 140
Isaac Henry .... 41, 74. *See*
Isaac Henry Harry 141
Isabelle 138
J. B. 61
J. N. 140
James 18, 133
James C. 135
James D. 68, 88, 137
James H. 139, 144
James W 143
James W. 18, 133

James Washington 88, 135
James Washington Wash 137
Jennie 139, 145
Jerry 144
John 140
John Bennett 133
John Bennett, Jr. 145
John D. 172
John Davidson 143
John Kelly, Sr. 94
John Matthew 145
John N. 138, 140, 141
John Nye 34, 94, 136, 140, 141
John T. 134, 135
Joseph 107, 137, 173
Joseph S. 36, *79*, 83, 88, 92, 114, 118,
                               137, 172, 175
Joseph Sidney 34
Julia D. 143
Julia Julie D. 100
Julian Bell 84, 142
Katherine 44, 138
Kelly 142
Lacy P. 144
Laura Augusta 145
Louella 100
Louise 142
M. N. 74
Mabel 95, 141
Malena Etta 139
Marcia 139
Marcia E. 139
Margaret S. 140
Marlena E. 145
Martha 140
Mary Eula 143, 156
Mary Jane 138, 145
Mary L. .... *See*
Mary M. 140, 185
Mary Sue 94
Millard Fillmore 145
Myrtle 142
Nancy C. 137
Nancy Jane ..54, *78*, *79*, 87, 118, 137, 180,
                               182
Nancy L. 32
Nancy Lovica 49, 115, 135, 140
Nellie Alberta 143, 173
Nina 142
Nina. 34
Nora E. 173

Ora Lee 83, 173
Oscar David 142
Oscar Wallace 143
Painter 138
Painter J. 144
Pansy F. 84
Paris Bosang 143
R. S. 68, 88
Robert 15, 65, 88, 140
Robert J. 95, 140
Robert Jackson 141
Robert Newton 172
Robert S. 14
Rose 136
Rowena 144
Roy 140
Roy Clarence 141
Roy Elmer 34, 142
Ruby 141
S. D. P. 141
Sallie 136
Sarah 18, 68, 88, 133, 138, 139
Sarah E. 139
Sarah Ellen 139, 144
Sarah Margaret 135, 137, 171
Seagle 34, 142
Sidney 140
Sidney Weldon 141, 142
Solomon 11, 18, 23, 44, 117, 134, 135,
138, 139, 141, 144
Solomon B. 138, 185
Susan L. 140
Tobias 34, 56, 140, 141
Van Crockett 144
Violet Etta *79*, 173
Virgie 142
Virginia E 141
W. T. 136
Washington 23
Wilbur C. 142
William 32, 134, 144
William Bennett 135, 137
William Davis 57, 84, 92, 142, 156
William G. 18, 133, 134
William Robert Morris 57, 92, 143
William S. 68, 88
William T. 31, 32, 134, 136, 141
William Thompson 49, 115, 135, 140
Willie J. 172
Wood 133
King Charles II 2

King Family 133
King/Hancock
   Robert P. 137
Kinion Place 10
Kitts
   Alford R. 83, 173
   Andrew 146
   Andrew J. 111, 146, 167
   Andrew Jackson 146
   B. J. (Mrs.) 71
   Beatrice 83, 89
   Bernie 182
   Bertha J. (Mrs.) 73
   Clora 83, 156
   David 146
   Dulaney 146
   Elizabeth 146
   Ethel Letha *79*, 82
   Eunice A. 83
   Fay Rena 84
   Frances 146
   Franklin 147
   Geneva 83
   H. J. 106
   Harvey G. 146
   Henry 146
   Jacob 31, 32, 88, 93, 101, 146, 177
   Jacob Franklin 82, 111, 146
   James W. 146
   Jane 146, 167
   Jesse Ernest 173
   John 146
   John D. 167
   John David 146
   Lettia Martelia 167
   Lute 82
   M. Nancy 146
   Mabel Gertrude 83, 92
   Madeline 83
   Mary Geneva 34, 117
   Mary Jane 31, *78*
   Miller White 147
   Peter 146
   Ressie Clora 88, 147
   Robert H. 73, 89
   Robert Hutsel *79*, 82, 92, 147, 173
   Ruth 83
   Telia Ann 116, 146, 167
   Viola 31
   Viola E. Lee 83
   Virginia Caroline 146

Kitts
   William Lowe 117, 143
   Willie Marie 143
Kitts (Getz)
   John Jacob 146
Kitts Family 146
Kunkel
   Richard Cooper 128
Kyker
   Norma Jean 174

L

Lachy
   Julia E. 13
Lackey
   Julia (Mrs.) 42
Lambert
   Alford William 148
   Anna Dillon 173
   Arthur Alfred 149
   Carolyn 149
   Cecil 148
   Clint 148
   Conway 148
   Effa 149
   Elizabeth Jane 108, 149, 150, 167
   Emily 149
   Female 149
   Genoa Violet 149
   George Cecil 148
   Ida 149
   Irvin Kelly 148
   Isaac P. 150, 152
   James Edward 51
   Johann Heinrich Henry 148
   John 148
   Junior L. 149
      L. 101, 178
   Lillian Ethel 148
   Linsey 149
   Linsey T. 148, 178
   Lizzie 149
   Lloyd Randolph 149
   Lottie Jane 149
   Lula V. 149
   Luther Edmond 115
   Margaret Lee 149
   Mary 149
   Mary Agnes 115, 148
   Mary Tarter 51
   Ralph Preston 149
   Raymond S. 149
   Robert Lee 115, 148
   Sarah E. 72
   W. J. 72
   William A. 150
   William A. Bud 149
   William J. 106, 150, 152
   Wm 72
Lammey
   Roland H. 90
Lampert
   Ina O. 115
   L. T. 148, 177
   Luther 115
   Molly 169
   Stephen 136
Larton 73
Laugon
   Oscar 8
Laura
   Tickle 152
Lavinder
   William 164
Law
   Drusilla 164
Lawrence
   Frank A. 101
   Robert Ward 101
Lawson
   John Washington 163
   Kate 115
   Martha 77
Layton
   Robert C. 67
Ledford
   James Vernon 45
Lee
   Robert E. (General) 86
Leedy
   John 15, 16, 17, 146
   John M. 18
   Polly 15, 111, 146, 167
Leeson
   Alma Mildred. 45
   Freda 45
   Garnett 44
   T. J. 156
   Thomas J. 44, *81*
   Vance G 44
   Violet 45
LeFew
   Bessie May 41, 141

223

  J. M. 74
  Mary Veta 143
Leffler
  Ellen C. 31
Lefler
  Aaron Maize 30
  Ada 31
  Alma Marie *78*
  Bessie 31
  Beulah Mae *78*
  Bowen C. 35
  Claude William 31, *78*
  Claude, Jr. *78*
  Damon Cassell *78*
  David Houston 31
  Edward S. 35
  Ella 31
  Francina 32
  Fransina 33, 91
  Fransina Akers 177
  Garland 31
  Genoa B. 35
  George P. 31
  Harvey Kent 31
  Helen Virginia *78*
  Henry S. 35
  Henry Sidney 31, 35
  Ida Gray 31
  Isaac 32, 33
  Issac Maize 31
  James M. 31
  James O. 35
  James Thomas *78*
  Joseph 32, 33
  Joseph E. 31
  Joseph H. 30, 35, 91, 177
  Leila A. 31
  Leslie Brown 31
  Lucy M. 31
  Luther Green 31
  Margaret Irene *78*
  Mary Beatrice *78*
  Mary L. 31
  Mary Lou 31
  Mary M. 35
  Ollie G. 31
  Raymond Isaac *78*
  Sallie F. 35
  Sherman 31
  Stuart. 31
  Thomas Reed 31, *78*

  William Dennis *78*
  William J. 31
Leonard Straw's 146
Leslie 53
  John Gorden 47
Lindsey
  Gladys 109
  Margaret Ellen 166
Lineberry
  Sarah Elizabeth 177
Linkous
  Marie 184
  Ollie 119
  Raymond *81*
  Rose 119
Litchmere
  Anna Barbara 146
Little Hiram Davis's path 18
Little Walkers Creek 13
Long
  Claire 95
long spur 18
Long Spur 17, 19, 49, 73
Long Spur Branch 106
Long Spur Postmaster 109
Lord Fairfax 3
Love
  Sarah 121, 123, 164
Lucas 83
  Margaret Evaline 128
Lury
  Elizabeth 144
Lusk
  John 67
  Mary 67
Lux
  Darby 67
Lyons
  Mattie M. 182
  William S. 128
Lyttle
  Jacob A. 138

M

Mabry
  Lee 103
  Millie 103
Martin
  Augustus 12
  Buford R. 53
  David *80*, 89

  Elizabeth 12
  Frances Louemma 118, 152
  Henrietta E. 61
  Hiram 156
  John 152
Masfield
  Thomas 48
Mason
  Annie L. 47
  Hazel V. 47
  Ida. 47
  Leonard 47
  Lillie 47
  Lula D. 47
  Mary 47
  Nellie 48
  Robert 47
  Silas D. 47
  Susie 47
Matherly
  Bandy 46
  Carl 46
Mathews
  Ruby 50
Matz
  Louie. 93
  Richard L. 101
May
  Christian 121
Mays
  Sarah N. Kate 125
McCauseland
  John 135
McCorkle, Captain 67
McCoy
  Buford Marion 46
  Louisa 107
McCulloch 12
McCulloh
  Robert 7, 10
McCulloh survey 11
McCullough
  Robert 13
McDowell
  James 24
McFalls
  Ola Mae 107
McGavock
  Hugh 9, 16
McGavock.
  Hugh 9

McMeans
  Carrie Belle 69
McTheney
  Daniel 170
Meades
  Ann 151
  John. 151
  Joyce 151
  Margaret 151
  Mary 151
  Susannah 151
  Thomas 151
  Thomas Jr. 151
  Thomas Orphan 151
Meador
  Jason 151
  John. 151
  Jonas 151
  Jones 151
  Mary 151
  Thomas 151
  Thomas Jr. 151
Meadow
  Jobe. 151
Meadows 7, 107
  Albert Terry 49, *80*, 154
  Allen Lee 50, 54, 110, 153
  Allen Parkinson 152
  Audrey Lee 154
  Charles 154
  Charles Vinson 108, 153
  Charles William 154
  Earl Randolph 154
  Fay 153
  Frances Louemma Martin 170
  Francis 151
  George 154
  Harry 153
  Hetty Naomi 154
  Ibba Erie 154
  Ida Belle Parsell 154
  Ina Juanita 154
  J. A. 175
  James W. 171
  James William Allen 49, 108, 153, 166
  John. 152
  John Jesse *81*, 154
  John Trenton 54, 108, 153
  Kyle Robert 154
  Lee L. 153
  Lucy Alberta *80*, 108, 153

Mary Edith	*81*
Mary Susan	152
May	153
Miller Campbell	154
Ola Belle	*80*, 89
Phillip	152
Robert	153
Ruby Irene	*80*, 154
Rudolph	153
Sarah Elizabeth	150, 152, 175
Wiley Vincent	50, 54, *80*, 108, 110, 153
William	107, 153
Meadows Family	151

Meadows/Meade
- Ambrose ... 151

Mechanicsburg Cemetery ... 75

Melton
- James Edward ... 154

Melvin
- Frank Straley ... 111
- Stanford ... 23

Meranda
- Charles Richard ... 75

Meriwether
- Mildred Thornton ... 5
- Nicholas ... 5

Merix
- Martha J. ... 122

Methodist Episcopal Church South ... 106

Midkiff
- Joyce Ann ... 94

Miller ... 183
- D. A. (Dr.) ... 165
- David ... 13
- Hattie ... 12
- James A. ... 11, 12, 179
- James S. ... 103
- John K. ... 11, 12
- Julie A. ... 179
- Mary ... 12
- Mary A. (Mrs.) ... 179
- Mary Elizabeth ... 101
- Mary H. (Mrs.) ... 179
- Orlena ... 12
- Sallie B. ... 103, 179
- Sebastian W. ... 11
- Thomas ... 12
- William ... 7, 8, 10, 11, 12, 39, 40, 179
- William M. ... 11, 127

Miller family ... 160

Millirons ... 13

Amelia Annetta	157
Ann Elizabeth	157
Annie Kate	50, 114
Arthur B.	156
Augusta Delphine	36, 48
Barbara	143
Catherine	155
Cecil Thelma Davis	173
Charles H.	156
Christopher	155
Clarence Hicks	36
Colleen	143
David	9, 21, 39, 155
Delphine	36
Dewey B.	83, 156
Dolly Marie	37, 48
Donnie Sue	37
Douglas	36
E. H.	38, 99
Edgar Hampton	49, *81*
Edna	157
Edward	83
Eliza Jane	157
Elizabeth Ellen	51
Ella A.	35, 37
Emma Louella	36, 56
Estell Hoge	35, 51, 68, 173
Estil Stinson	35
Frank Wade	156
Franklin Hicks	63
Fred	156
George Edward	50
George Lewis	47, 49
George William	35
Glenn	64
Gordon M.	37
Harriet Elizabeth	156
Harry Zelmer	36
Henry	155
Howard P.	37
Howard Paul	35
Howard Preston	35, 69
Hugh Lagner	51
J. J.	157
James D.	157
James Hicks	36
James Tolinger	156
John	9, 51, 155
John Daniel	50
John Harvey	157
John J.	9, 155, 156

Joseph Hampton 50
Julia Rose 50
Karen 143
Laura Emily 49, *80*, 154
Lelia Pearl 36, 51, 68
Lilburn R. 156
Louella 37
Malcolm Mac 36
Mary A. 157
Mary J. 156
Mason Vance 36
Meek Gordon 35
Minerva 157
Nancy M. 156
Nancy S. 157
Nannie 156
Olive Virginia .. 50, 84, 101, 110, 153, 172
Opal. 64
Oscar Leroy 63, 156
R. L. 53
R. Lee 33, 49, 141, 154
Randolph William 143
Raymond 64
Robert Lee Jr 50
Robert Perry 143, 156
Rosa Evelyn 51
Rosa Rosie Evelyn 36
Roy 156
Rufus Lee 47, *81*, 101, 114
Rufus Lee R. Lee 49
Sally 157
Sarah 157
Sarah Vicey Lavica 49, 101
Thomas Martin Luther 51
W. N. 48, 156
Walter Pug Vance 36
William 35, 38, 40, 48, 110, 155, 157
William Moses 36, 173
William Newton 83, 143, 156
Wythe Monroe 51
Millirons Cemetery 155
Millirons Chapel 155
Millirons families 160
Millirons Methodist Church 40, 142
Millirons Methodist Church Cemetery 156
    aka King Cemetery 35, 56, 57, 92, 94,
        138, 140, 141, 142, 143, 156
Millirons Methodist Episcopal Church,
    South 156
Minnie Davis Parsell 82
Mitchell

Margaret B. 130, 131
Mitchell's Chapel Holston Methodist
    Episcopal Church 113
Moll
    Charles M. 94
    John P. 94
    Peter 94
    Virginia B. 94
Monocacy, Maryland 23
Montgomery 158
    Alexander 158
    Elizabeth Martha 14
    Jacob 158
    James 158, 159
    James Lawrence 159
    John 158
    Larkin 158, 160
    Larkin Lark 158
    Laura 159
    Letitia 158
    Lucy 158, 183
    Male Infant 158, 159
    Mamie 68
    Margaret A. 158
    Mary 159
    Mettie 158
    Nancy Sylvester 159
    Napoleon 159
    Richard 5, 158
    Ruth 159
    Selitha 159
Montgomery Family 158
Moody
    Benjamin 158, 160
    Bluford 160, 183
    Joseph 160, 183
    Letitia 158, 160
    Nancy 158, 160
    Orren 160
    Rumbo 160
    Virginia 160
Mooman
    Missouri 127
Mooney
    Thomas F. 152
Moore 116
    Sarah 85, 137
Morehead
    Gorden Andrew 100
    Julian M. 85
    Robert 100

  Robert, Jr. 100
Morgan 164
  Edward 164
  Mary 83, 143, 156
  Newton J. 131
Morris
  Alice 162
  Alice Gish 163, 165
  Amanda 162
  Austin 162
  Caroline 121
  Charles Hicks 162
  Cora M. 163
  Delia B. 62
  E. J. 124, 125, 162
  Edith 62
  Elijah Jefferson 123, 162
  Elijah Jesse 121, 161
  Ethel 163
  Fanny 62
  Glen 62
  Harris H. 62
  Henry 162
  Henry Davis 161
  Isabelle 162
  James A. 163
  Jesse 39, 60, 121, 123, 124, 161, 162
  John 161, 162
  John B. 183
  John Bell 62, 161, 184, 185
  John Bell, Jr. 63
  John Jackson 163
  Joseph H. 123, 163
  Joseph J. 121
  Joseph Johnson 161
  Lelia 62, 184
  Lucy J. 39, 107, 161
  Martha 125
  Mary 62
  Mary Amanda 161
  Mary Jane 161, 185
  Matilda 163
  Morton 163
  Myrtle M. 62, 185
  Nancy J. 162
  Nancy M. 161
  Rachel 39
  Robert 12
  S. M. B 61
  Samuel 39, 161, 163
  Samuel J. 161
  Sarah Ella 161
  Susan 162, 163
  Susan J. 161
  Susan S. 39
  Susan Sayers 163
  Tabitha 163
  Vilena 163
  William A. 61
  William Presley 163, 166
  William R. 161
  William Riley 185
Morris. 41
Mossy Creek 86
Motley
  Lucinda 63
Moulds
  Elizabeth 155
Mountain View Methodist Church Cemetery
  .... 85, 93, 98, 99, 173
Moxley
  Leonard 46
Moye
  Margaret 124
Moyer
  Michael 65
Muhelisen
  Christian Godfrey 155
Muncy
  Mary Elizabeth 68, 114, 147
Muncy Cemetery 68
Munsey
  Sarah 21
Murray
  Ethel 47, 83, 84, 92
  Thomas 92
Murry
  Ruth Mae 96
Musser
  Cherrie Elizabeth 41
Mustard
  Anna 172
  Bessie E. 141
  Betsey 10
  Elizabeth 21, 43
  Elizabeth Davis 21
  Harvey Jasper 117
  Harvey R. 10, 23
  Henry 23
  J. H. 23, 72
  J. J. 72
  J. T. 23

James 21, 117
James H. 21, 23
James Harvey 21
Jno. C. 73
John 10, 21
John C. 86
John J. 21
John T. 23
Joshua . 9, 10, 20, 21, 71, 72, 86, 117, 140, 181
Joshua Nye 21, 117
Katherine 21, 117
Lavica 10, 21
Lucy Lovica 117
Mariah 10, 74
Martha Viola 141
Mason Manuel 141
Minerva Jane 21
Naomi 141
Nye 72
Rush F. 141
Sarah 21
Thomas 23
Vance 141
W. 21
William 10, 130
William P. 71
William Patterson 141
William Thomas 21, 181
Wm. N. 15
Mustard land 106
Mustard's lands 106
Myers
   Robert L. 90

N

N & W Railroad 90
Nancy
   Bond (nee Johnson) 131
Neely
   Clarice 57, 93
New Dublin Presbyterian Church Cemetery
   111
Newberry 18
   A.T. 113
   Allen T. 18, 113, 168
   Betty 83
   Carl Miller 83
   Caroline 113
   W. C. 18
Newberry Cemetery 144

Newgate Prison 67
Norris
   Mary 56
Nucholls
   Andrew 154
Nuchols
   Andy 110
Nye
   A. J. 71

O

O'Dell
   Mary Alice 138
Oak Hill Cemetery 173
Oakwood Cemetery 156
old Crockett survey 18
Osborn
   William Alexander 138
Overstreet
   Allie M. 152
   Bowie 152
   Callie Jane 152
   Callie Jeanette 45
   Cecil M. 153
   Cynthia 153
   Hattie B. 152
   Hazel 152
   Henry J. 171, 175
   J. H. 54
   James 9, 15, 19
   James C. 19
   James H. 152, 171, 175
   Jeanette 152
   Jesse M. 152
   Mary B. 152
   Mary S. 175
   Nancy A. 171
   Robert Lee 45, 152
   Sally 15
   Samuel Allen 152
   Tilmon J. 152

P

Pagan
   Alma V. 130
Page
   Henry 159
Painter
   Sarah E. 98, 152
Palmer
   Harry Thomas 95

    Harry Thomas, Jr. 96
    Herman R. 95
    Sharon Lawana 96
    Susan Elaine 96
Parcell
    Adda J. 172
    Albert Wesley 108
    Anna 164
    Argie Marie 108
    Benjamin F 164
    Carl Weldon 108
    Charles Lee 166
    Christopher Columbus 164
    Clayton Eldridge 108
    Elizabeth 164, 165
    Emory Milton 109
    Evelyn Louise 109
    Garland Tabor 108
    Hersel Henderson 109
    Infant Daughter 109
    Irene Isabelle 109
    Irvin Neil 108
    Isaac 164
    James 164
    Joel 164
    John 165
    John, Jr. 164
    John, Sr. 164
    Margaret Lorene "Frankie" 109
    Martha J. 87
    Mary A. 164
    Peter 164
    Rachel 164
    Richard 164
    Sarah 164
    T.. B. (Mrs.) 71
    William 164
    William Wise 166
Parsell
    Albert Wesley 171
    Alma Pearl 96
    Andrew M. 94, 166
    Andrew Miller 96, 164
    Annie E. 94
    Audrey Mae 96
    Blanche 95, 166
    C. L. ....……95, 100, 166
    Calvin 165, 166
    Calvin Kelly 74, *78*
    Calvin Van Doren Kelly 108, 166, 171
    Charles 18, 165
    Charles C. 94, 166
    Charles Cadell 98, 185
    Charles L. 100, 106, 165, 166
    Charles Lee *82*, 84, 94, 166
    Clyde Miller 96
    Cynthia Louise 96
    Cynthia M. 166
    Dana 94, 166
    Dana Lee 94
    Donald Cadell 98
    Effie G. 172
    Emma Barbara 96
    Ernest Victor *82*
    Everett C. 172
    Hazel Colleen 98
    Ida Augusta 84, 97
    Ida Belle 49, 108, 153, 166
    James Dwight 98
    Jeffrey 98
    John .23, 94, 100, 106, 153, 163, 165, 166,
            171
    John Henry *82*
    John W. 171
    John William *81*
    Joseph Andrew 97
    Julie Ann 96
    Laura Elizabeth *82*
    Leslie W. 163
    Lester Guy *82*
    Lewis Russell *82*
    Liza 98
    Marc Lee 96
    Martha Ethel 74, 172
    Martha J. 87
    Mary E. 94
    Mary Francis *78*, 172
    Mike 98
    Minnie *82*, 94, 95, 166
    Minnie Davis 73, *77*, 83, 87
    Nina Leecester *82*
    Paul Mason 82
    Price H. 172
    Ralph Dewey, Sr. 96
    Ralph Lee 96, 164
    Raymond 98
    Richard Daryl 96
    Richard Dickie Stinson 97
    Robert Clinton 171
    Roger 98
    Ruthanne 96
    Samuel Hubert 163

  Thomas 98
  Tobias *82*, 172
  Tobias Daniel 166
  Tobias Daniel, Jr *82*
  Tobias Tobe Daniel *81*
  Viola Aurelia 108
  Virgie E. 94
  Visa Alma..*82*
  Wayne Allen...96
  William Lee 98
  William Randall 96
  William Wren 96
  Willie Jane 47, 94, 100
  Zena Gray 98
  Zular Bell..*82*
Parson
  Sarah C. 161, 185
Patrick
  Esther 137
Patterson
  Agnes...130
  Amanda 44
  Elizabeth Agnes............49, 75, *77*, 118
  Evelyn Pat 108
  Isaac 16, 19
  James 16, 17, 19, 24, 85
  James Harvey 24, 85, 178
  Jane 85
  Katherine Louisa 92, 98
  Martha 130
  Melvina..89
  William 9, 16, 130
  William Ribble 178
Patterson Cemetery...84, 85, 90, 98, 99, 102, 173
Patton 74
  Agnes...130
  Ellis 75
  Flossie...75
  Henshell..75
  Hubert...75
  J. R. 74
  James (Colonel).......................................4
  Margaret 75
  Mary 74
  Russell 21
Pauley
  B. H. 136
  Barbara 114, 116, 169
  Cleo S. 34
  Creed Franklin....................................167

  Daniel Crockett...................................117
  David Henry Carl 34
  Edith J..168
  Edna 115
  Edna Mae 168
  Garnet C..34
  Gordon Paris 116
  Gratton Crockett 34, 117
  Harold M. 167
  Harvey Blair 116, 169
  Jacob 116
  James Roach 169
  Jasper H. 167
  John..167
  John A..169
  John G..18
  Julia Margaret 167
  Julia Margaret Ann 167
  Margaret 34
  Martha (Mrs.) 168
  Mary J. 169
  Maude E. 168
  Minerva...67
  Minerva Josephine......................112, 117
  Nancy Gray...169
  Newton 16, 168
  Newton Thomas..........................115, 168
  Rachel C. 167
  Sarah J. 114
  Sylvia J. 167
  Telia A. 167
  Telia Ann 167
  Thomas 167
  Thomas G. 116, 146, 167
  Thompson Effie Rose 168
  Vivian G 34
  William Bud Gordon 116
  William Henderson.....................150, 167
Peak Creek 12, 85
Pearis Cemetery 166
Peck
  Christopher 12, 13
  Jacob 11, 12, 13
  James B..52
  William 13
Peery
  Robert 53
Pegram
  Albert Gilmore....................................170
  Calvin Washington 170
  Cynthia Margaret......74, *78*, 108, 166, 171

Elizabeth 135
Elizabeth Betsy Jane 170
Ellen Smith 143, 173
Emily Etta ... 36, *79*, 83, 92, 114, 118, 137, 172, 175
George 170
George N. 23, 106, 165, 170
George Newton 23, 170
Harry 107
John 23, 170
John H. 106, 170
John Henry 118, 135, 170, 171
Martin Jackson 170
Parthenia 170
Pinkney N. 170
Thomas L. 170
Willie Jane 135, 170, 171
Pegram Family 170
Pendleton
  Carol 98
  Catherine Davis 138
  James 138
  Robert 98
  William G. O. 138
Penn
  J. J. 88
  Mollie 88
Peoples
  Carrie 158
  Edward W. 159
  J. T. 158, 183
  James 159
  John Huston 158
  Joseph Larkin 158
  Joseph Taylor 158
  Leonard E. 159
  Lucinda Lucy J. 158
  Mark E. 159
  Mary Ann 158
  Mittie 158
  Pharaoh 158
  Susan 158
Perry
  Robert 175
Peters
  Isaac Asbury 162
Peterson
  Ethel Catherine 174
Pfaffenhofen, Germany 23
Philadelphia, Pennsylvania 23
Phillips
  Nancy E. 103
Phipps
  Thomas Rhea 37
  Wilma Beatrice 36
Photo
  Emmett Milton & Willie Jane Davis 95
  Estell Hoge Millirons & Ella Augusta Akers 35
  Henry Davis Margaret Fowler 71
  John Stafford Hamblin family 107
  Lelia Millirons & Alvie Corder 36
  Moses Akers Jr. 33
  Richard Dickie Stinson Parsell 97
  Robert Kitts & Bertha Davis 82
  Samuel Caddell Davis 87
  Susannah Holloway and Fabious Davis 76
  William T. King & Nancy Lovica King 135
Pickett's Division 165
Pierce
  Elizabeth 120
Plymale
  Mary Magdeline 140, 181
Poff
  Lebran *82*
Pollard
  Robert 9, 10, 16
Pond" 138
Poplar Spring Branch 16, 168
Porter
  Catherine 56
Porterfield
  A. H. 72
  Arthur J. 71
Post Master of Carnot 69
Powers
  Hickman 10
  Jordan 95
  Margaret Ellen 95
Price
  Viola Alice 105
Pruett
  Tacy Adeline 100
Pulaski
  Casimir 6
Pulaski Alum Springs 13
Pulaski Alum Springs Company, inc 128
Pulaski County Little Walkers Creek School 188
Purdy
  Robert Lee 46

Pyrtle
- Mary Malinda 164

R

Raines
- Letitia 71
- Rebecca Louise 51

Raleigh Grayson Turnpike 16, 168

Ramage
- Richard 90

Ravens Cliff 18, 133

Red Oak Cemetery 134

Reed
- Josie 152

Reed Creek 12

Reedy Creek 146

Reese
- Carol 98

Regiment
- 54th Infantry 37

Repass
- L. D. 73, 86
- Sarah Ann 134

Richardson
- Ballard P. 125
- Booker 125
- Emily 125
- Emily Jane 125
- Nancy M. 125, 180
- Nannie 125
- Susan 125

Riddle
- Charles Estel 124
- Mary Elizabeth 123, 124

Ridge
- Edith R. 96

Rife
- Thomas 75

Rigney
- Larry Warren 36, 57

Ring.
- Gussie 31

Ritter
- A. J. (Mrs.) 71
- Addie Lou 175
- Alice (Mrs.) 73
- Allie Ann 52, 175
- Beatrice C. 108
- Bessie Pearl King 114, 116
- Claude Swanson 172
- Cora Lee 175
- D. S. 107
- David 54
- David Aviner 108, 175
- David S. 52, 175
- David Spencer 52, 84, 108, 130, 152, 172, 175
- Edward 84, 175
- Elbert 108
- F. F. 131
- Frank Chaffin 152
- Fred 131
- George 175
- George Washington 175
- Howard 84
- Huston Crockett 152
- Infant 175
- James 84
- James Ernest 175
- John Lewis 175
- Lawson 84
- Leonard 108
- Letha Virginia 114, 172
- Macy V. 84
- Margaret Elizabeth 172
- Nellie May 175
- Richard 84
- Ronald 108
- Sanders Spencer 172
- Thomas Fenton 56, 92, 130, 175
- Virginia 108
- Wendell H. 84
- Wilber S. 84
- Wilma Lou 54, 56, 92, 131

Ritter (formerly Bond)
- Martha J. 131

Ritter Family 175

Roark
- Virginia Myrenthia Vergie' 77

Roberts
- Elsie Mae 96
- Etta Mae 154
- William 43

Robertson 111
- Clemens 83
- Geneva Effie 108
- Irene 53
- James Andrew 180
- Matilda K. 62, 156, 161, 179, 180
- Tessie 173

Robinett
- Mary C. 163

Robinette
   Louisa 141
Robinson 8
   Jennie 32
   Louisa 12, 13
   Richard Scott 138
Rogers
   Benjamin 22
   Donnie 136
   James 121
   John 22
   Susan 150, 152
Roope
   Cynthia M. 109
   Emory Clifton 109
   George W. 109
   John Campbell 109
   Ralph Elwood 109
Rorrer
   W. T. 21
Rosa Melvina
   Corvin 99
Roseberry
   Beatrice 112, 116
Roy Clarence 142
Runions
   John D. 40
Runyan
   Mary Bell 45, 46
Runyon
   Isaac 67
   Rebecca 67
   Richard 67
Rutherford
   J. B. 21
   J. B. C. 21
Rutter
   William Jackson 175

S

Sadler
   Margaret Cree 99
Sailing
   John 4
Samuel Crockett's District 146
Sands
   Martha Esther 34, 41
Sandy Creek 105
Sassin 124
Saunders (Captain) 126
Sayers
   James 11
   John S. 6
Scaggs
   Susannah 29
Schweinhardt
   Anna Maria Magdalena 23
Seddon school District 15
Setliff
   Chester 83
Sexton
   Roxie Annie 162
   Sallie 88
Shank
   Nancy Ann 52
Shannon 18, 40, 127, 128
   Bettie 8, 128
   J. P. 139
   James 9
   James King 8, 128
   John A. 135
   Juliet H. 8
   Mary Haven 8, 11
   Samuel 7, 8
   Thomas 7, 8
   Thomas S. 8
Shannon Cemetery 8
Sharitz
   J. G. 115
Shaw
   Mary J. 169
Shell
   Hazel Maxine 77
Shelton 65
   Elsey 17, 65
   Madison 17, 65, 66
   Mattie 92
Shelton survey 139
Shepherd
   Harvey 6
Shewey.
   Gladys 41
Shifford
   Ralph A. 44
Shiloh Methodist Church Cemetery . 88, 100
Shinault
   D. K. 8, 123
   David Jackson 122
   Eva 122
   George Washington 122
   Helen 122
   Henry H. 123

Henry L. 123
Ida 122
James 123
Lou 122
Mary 122
Matilda 123
Mitchell 122, 123, 128
Nancy Mary 8, 123
Queenie M. 122
Randal [Randolph] 122
Randolph 121, 128, 161, 163
Sarah 123, 161, 162
Susan 123, 163
Vergie Lee 122
Virgie 123
William 121, 123

Shinualt
   Melvina 121
   Sarah 121
   William 121

Shofflebarrier [Shufflebarger
   Elijah 7

Shouse
   M. Lizzie 186

Shrader
   Eliza J. 15
   Henry 15
   Isabelle 50, 113, 173
   James B. 139
   James Brown 15
   Joseph 15, 113
   Mary J. 15
   Nannie Belle 54
   S. G. 139
   Samuel G. 139
   Samuel Gleaves 15
   Sarah C. 15, 113
   Sumilda Etta 157

Shrader's Chapel Cemetery 115
Shrader's Chapel Cemetery 115

Shufflebarger
   Abraham 7
   Abram 8
   Ada Belle 119
   Edwin Thomas 175
   Hettie Locritta 52, 84, 108, 130, 175
   John 8, 16
   John S. 139
   Margaret 8

Shumate
   Hardin 164

Sifford
   Earl Kenneth 45
   James Harvey 45
   Verland R. 46
Sifford Cemetery 46, 84
Simmerman
   John A. 17
Simpkins 13
   Henrietta 122, 124
   John 13
   Thomas 165
Simpsons 120
Sink.
   George Lewis 47
Smith
   Alexander 98
   Bertie Lee 119
   D. A. 167
   Daniel 5
   Effie 87
   Effie Mae 98
   Emerel 101
   Emma 113
   G. G. 167
   George Greever 173
   Georgie M. 99
   Howard Lee 100
   James H. 113
   John 22
   John B. 113
   John Frank 41
   John S. 99
   Lydia C. 99
   Pearl 113
   Robert 113
   Sally *81*
   Sarah 22
   Stephen Alex 113
   Stephen H. 113
   Steven 99
   W. D. 167
   William 113
Smyth
   Hannah 22
Smythers
   William Anderson 71
Southern
   Vance 141
   Vance Carl 141
   William 141
Sowers

Nancy 29
Spackner
    Gertrude 41
Spalding
    Martha Ann 159
Spangler.
    John Hunter, Sr. 108
Spanish American War 76
Spence
    Dorothy 156
Spencer
    Virginia Magdalene 54, 89
spring 11
Spur 18
Spur branch 17, 18, 19, 106
Spur Branch 18, 19, 24, 93, 106
Spur Branch School 187
Srader
    Sarah C. 15
St. John Cemetery 67
St. Luke's Lutheran Church Cemetery 32, 75, 76
Stableton
    Roland 138
Stafford
    Ernestine Elizabeth 108
    Flora L. 41
    John M. 83
    Joseph 170
    Joseph E. 52, 171
    Kenneth *80*
    Lillie Tyretha 124
    Susan S. 171
Staffordsville Cemetery 99, 108, 165, 172
Stanley 47
    Anna Sue 99
    Nancy 152
Staton
    Amber Hildreth 174
Steel
    Hubert R. 119
Stephens
    Margaret 50, 110
Sterns
    Franklin 12
Stevens
    Sam E. 185
Stinson
    Catherine 184
    George 94, 166
    George Robert 98

    Glenn Allen 98
    John 22, 96, 98
    Martha 98
    Minnie Pearl 96, 164
    Rhonda 98
    Robert 98
    Rodger Allen 98
    Terry M. 98
    Thomas 98
    Zena 94, 166
Stinston Cemetery 88
Stoever
    John Casper (Reverend) 23
Stone
    Alice 63
    James Steven 182
    James W. 121
    Jemina C. 182, 184
Stoots
    Margaret 71
Stouffer
    Anna Maria 52
Stowers
    Cynthia E. 51
Straw
    Leonard 9
Stuart
    Ann 39
Sublett
    Allen W. 23, 145
    Mary 18, 134
    Mary Mildred 145
    Mathew 145
    Samuel 111
Suiter
    George W. 23
Sulphur Spring 165
Summers 85
    L.R. 103
Sunrise Burial Park 180
Surface
    Saphronia 85
Suthers
    . Launia (Ms) 40
    Charles R. 40
Sutphin
    Lillie May 142
Sutton
    John 18
Swinney
    Red 31

Switzer
- Dan Pendleton 96
- Dana 96
- Danita 96
- Don Gary 96

T

Tabor
- Eliza 109
- John 109
- Oleva E. 50
- Olleva Ollie E. 109

Tade
- Peggy 56

Talbot Station 86

Tarter
- J. E. 139

Tate
- T. L. 129

Taylor
- Bill 117
- Elizabeth 140
- Martha 34, 94, 140
- William 140

Terry
- Ben 115
- Benjamin Franklin 115, 148
- Bertha Hester 131, 136
- Charles A. 115
- Eliza 115, 136
- Fannie E. 115, 148
- Garnett *79*, 136
- George William 136
- Hazel M. 115
- Ida Kate *79*, 136
- James Hampton 136
- Jenny T. 90
- John William 136
- Laura Mae 115
- Lula P. 115
- Norma Jean 93
- Otto 136
- Samuel B. 115
- Thelma G. 115
- William 115, 136
- William Saunders *79*, 131, 136
- William W. 115
- Wm. S. 90

The Hunter's Pulaski Alum Springs
- Property 129

Thomas
- Fairfax (Lord) 2
- Wm. C. 86

Thompson
- A. N. 15
- Calvin Gleve 48
- Ester 14
- Franklin Miller 156
- Ira Kelley 143
- Jane 142
- John E. 167
- Josie 48
- Minnie 182
- Olivia Virginia 57, 84, 92, 142, 156
- Sarah S. 116
- William 142

Thompson Cemetery 156

Thornspring Methodist Church Cemetery 51, 78, *81*, 89, 92, 98, 103, 131, 132, 140, 156, 179, 182

Thurston 10, 44, 86
- Phineas 12, 44

Tickle
- Arthur Lee 173
- Benjamin Trigg 173
- Benjamin Trigg, Sr. 143
- Charles Grant 173
- Charles L. 47
- Cynthia Victoria 53, 152, 178
- Daniel 177
- Elizabeth Jane 178
- Ella Catherine 178
- Ellen S. Pegram 171
- Ellen Smith 174
- Ellen Smith Pegram 93
- Emma Lee 173
- George Lee 143, 173
- Georgie Myrtle 173
- Harriett Emily 178
- Isaac Newton 173
- Jackson Nye 117, 173
- James 66
- John H. 178
- John Nye 173
- Josephine 178
- Josie Agnes 173
- Lola Maud 173
- Margaret Ann 45, 178
- Margaret Luemma 117
- Mary Ann 148, 177
- Mary Etta 76
- Mary Lou 174

Nela 76
Patrick Henry 174
Peter 31
Peter C. 91, 101, 148, 177
Peter Conrad 45, 66, 177
Peter H. 66, 178
Robert Brown 174
Robert T. 45
Rose Leona 173
Sarah Elizabeth Lizzie 148, 178
Stella Elizabeth 173
Stonewall Jackson 174
Sylvia Caledonia 178
Theodore Samuel 174
William 66
William Green 179
William H. 178
William Nye 117
Tines
Paulina 181
Townley
Catherine M. 108
Thomas B. 108
Trashers 120
Treer
Alma 94
Trent
Ruth 76
Tribbile
Dinah 151
Trigg
Daniel (Captain) 29
R. C. (Colonel) 38
Stephen 67
Trolinger
Henrietta 12
Henry C. 12
Truman
J. C. 103, 123
Trustees of Dublin District Schools 131
Tucker
Grace 142
Turnpike 16
Tynes
Beatrice 181, 183
Josephine 181
Lanna 183
Martha 89, 181
Mary 181, 183
Mary J. 40
Mary S. 181
Paulina 21, 181
Victoria 181
Virginia N. 181, 183
Tyree's Tavern 86

U

Umberger
Pearl G. 101
Stuart R. 101
Underwood
Agnes 63, 179
Alva Louise 90, 180
Andrew Giles 179, 184
Andrew Joshua 63, 90
Bettie Mae 180
Charles Clifford 90, 180
Charles Thomas 90, 180
Charlie 179
Charlie Vivian 90, 180
Charlotte 180
Clara 179, 184
David Pierce 180
Elizabeth 179
G. S. 183
George Stuart 180
George W. 180
Georgie 180
Grover 179
Grover C. 88, 180
Herbert 63
Jennie 63, 180
John 179
John Milton 63, 90, 179
Joshua 179
Laura A. 179
Lucille 63, 180
Luli B. 180
Myrtle Agnes 90, 180
Nancy 180
Nina Loraine 90, 180
Opal Virginia 90, 180
Paul Dailey 90, 180
Richard Victor 90, 180
Robert L. 63
Robert Lee 179
Ruby 180
Sallie 179
Sarah 123, 179
Sidney Queen 180
Stella 63
Susan 180

    Viola 180
    Viola L. 88
    William 151, 179
    William Joshua 180
United States Government 53
Unknown
    Awbrey 151
    Bess 153
    Elizabeth 131, 170
    Elizabeth L. 179
    Etta 119
    Judith 71
    Louisa J. 65
    Lovica 85
    Lucille 99
    Lucy 116
    Mahala 115
    Martha 120
    Mary 105, 155
    Mary Ann 65
    Mary Magdalene 52
    Minnie 47
    Nancy 146
    Phebe 105
    Rachel 161
    Rhoda 105
    Sarah 121, 135, 151
    Susan L. 140
    Susannah 67
    Susie 160
    Thelma 174
Uptegraph
    Carolyn Ann 96
    Dianna Lynn 96
    Larry Lee 96
    Ralph Richard 96

V

Vance
    Maggie 141
Vandergrift
    Daniel 91
    Elizabeth 91
    Morrison 56, 74, 91
    Thomas 91
    Victoria Agnes Davis 84
Vanmeter
    John 2
Vaughn
    Luther Vivian 54
    Martha D. 164

Vaught
    Virginia Bessie Mabel 46
Vermillion
    Uriah 131
Vest
    Albert Grayson 185
    Calvin 185
    Calvin Likens 184
    Emery C. 185
    Ethel 63
    Etta E. 128, 185
    Helen 185
    Jackson 62, 185
    Kathleen 88
    Martin H. 185
    Mary A. 180
    Newton R. 185
    Ruby 185
    Virginia Blanche 98, 185
    William 62, 98
    William Morris 184

W

W. White farm 158
Waddell
    Sarah Catherine 175
Waggon Road… 7
Waggoner
    Elizabeth 152
    Mary Ann 117, 173
Wagner
    J. A. (Dr.) 38
Walker
    Shirley Marie 110
    Susan Preachy 5
    Thomas 5
    Thomas (Dr.) 4, 5
Walkers Creek 12, 24
Walkers little creek 106
Walkers Little Creek 14
Walraven
    Margaret 17, 134
Wampler 113
    Abraham 14
    Abram 15, 18, 33, 113
    Mary 14, 15
    Polly 113
Ward
    Grace 95, 141
    Rufus 46
Warf

Sarah Gertrude 45
Warner
   William T. 155
   William Thomas 155
Washington
   George 5, 67
   William H. 51
Watts
   Elizabeth *82*
Waynesboro 86
Weaver
   B. J. 8
   Lula 128
   Lula Shannon 8
   W. M. 8
   Walter M. 8, 128
Web
   Kenny *82*
Weeks
   Catherine 12
   Robert 12
Wellman
   Hannah 67
   John 67
Wesley's Chapel Cemetery 81, *82*, 166
West End Cemetery 69, 99, 173
Wheeler
   Turner Bascom 64
White
   Achilles 181
   Andrew R. 186
   Benjamin 182
   Bertie 130, 182
   Bethia 179, 184
   Bettie 160
   Blain Chester 183
   Charles 140
   Clarence W. 89
   Clem 131
   David 181
   David H. 182
   Dianna 186
   Edna 182
   Eliza 158, 183, 186
   Eliza A. 137
   Elizabeth 151
   Ernest 140
   George 30, 32, 33
   George W. 185
   Gladys M. 182
   Glenna B. 182

H. Shannon 181
Harrison S. 138
Harrison Shannon 140, 185
Harrison William 182
Horatio 181
Hubert Wallace 182
J. W. 39
James 140, 182, 183
James Clayton 182
James H. 89
James Russell 181
James W. 11, 21, 181
James Wilson 89, 132, 181
Jemima 181, 184
John 11, 182
John H. 140
John Hunter 181
John W. 183
John Wesley 140, 181, 182
Joseph A, ... 181
Joseph Absolam K. 186
Julia B. 89
June 182
Kellas Marvin 182
Lester 182
Lila Mae 89
Lockard S. 186
Lucy 140, 164
Martha J. 89
Martha P. 186
Mary 33, 61, 140
Mary C. 32
Mary Edith 182
Mary M. 138, 182, 183
Mary S. 182, 186
Maude 183
Myrtle 182
N. F. 88, 137, 158, 183
Nancy 184
Nancy E. 186
Nancy J. 183
Nancy L. 182
Newton 160, 183
Newton F. 131
Newton Foy 89, 182, 184
Newton W. 89
Pearl 182
Rachel 181
Reba G. 182
Rhoda 62
Rhoda P. 63, 184

Robert 182
Rosa 184
Ruby Lee 89
Ruth 183
Sally 181
Sophina 185
Straley W. 89
Thomas 182
Violet J. 182
Virginia A. 183
William 181
White family 160
Whitt
   Garnett 184
   Louise Valentine 143
Whittaker
   George M. 123
   Harvey Green 109
William Christians' Company 14
William Harrell 120
Williams
   Albert A. 100
   Alice Lee 152
   Blanch 100
   Clarence C. 98
   Della 180
   Elizabeth 101, 136
   Ella A. 100, 166
   Elliot W. 100
   Elmer Graham 98
   Ethel 152
   Harry Jackson 89
   James J. 180
   John 85
   John Caddell 98
   John Van Buren 98
   Kenneth 100
   Louise W. 98
   Maggie 33, 168
   Mahala 150
   Margaret E. 92
   Mariah Margaret E. 105
   Martin 139
   Mary J. T. 62
   Nellia Augusta 98
   S. D. 106
   S. W. 167
   Samuel 113
   Samuel P. 98
   Samuel W. 23, 33, 105, 139, 165, 168, 170
   Thomas A. 145

William Patterson 92, 98
Willis
   Nettie Ann 47
Wills
   Nancy 60
   Phoebe R. 64
Wilson
   Charlotte 179
   Luther Hubert 54
Wimond
   Elizabeth 155
Winegardner
   Robert 75
Wolf
   Barbara 148
Wolf Creek 9, 16
Wolfe
   Everett C. 54
   Hazel Davidson 54
   Hoge Harvey 54
   Mary 88
Wood
   Abraham 4
   Elizabeth 151
Wooden
   John 22
Woods
   Lucinda 186
Woodyard 103
   A. G. 129, 185
   A. S. 179, 185
   Albert 184
   Albert Sidney 63, 179, 184
   Almarine 71
   Andrew Grayson 41, 161, 185
   Annie F. 185
   Bessie Owens 41, 185
   Cecil 62
   Clara 179
   David A. 184
   Dolly G. 179, 184
   Ernest Clowers 184
   Ettie 62, 98
   Ettie Emily 184
   Jenny B. 185
   Lee T. 179, 184
   Lela Hazel 63, 184
   Lessie 185
   Newton 179, 184
   Randolph 184
   Ray H. 184

Rhoda 185
Robert 62, 184
Roxie 184
Sarah L. 145
Sidney 62
Susan 155
Ted 185
Trinkle 179, 184
W. H. 11
Wade Hampton 185
William 184
William M. 185
Wright
　Matilda 160
Wyant
　Elizabeth 152
Wyatt 90
Wygal
　James 12
　John 85
　Joseph 12
　Thomas B. 21
　Tom B. 21
Wynn
　Nick 21
Wyrick
　Asa 117, 118
　Cynthia 82, 88, 146
　Elizabeth 146
　Johann Nicolaus 146
　Julia 114
　Margaret Virginia 112, 116
　Mary E. 118
　Nancy 112
　Robert 18
　Robert S. 117
　Sanders 112, 118
　Thursa V. 118
Wyrick.
　Julia 35
　Margaret Virginia 69
Wysor
　Eve 12
　J. F. 103
Wysor Cemetery 175
Wythe
　George 6

Y

Yonce
　Hontas 99
　Samuel Joseph 51
　Viola 101
Yost
　Casper 17, 91
　Nelle Beatrice 128
Young
　Isaac 42
　James 42
　Kate 42
　Lillie Mae 42
　Lucy 42
　Malinda 42
　Martha 42
　Martie Alfred 101
　May 42
　Mollie 42
　Muriel 89
　Percy Lee 42
　Sarah Peggy 42

www.ingramcontent.com/pod-product-compliance
Lightning Source LLC
Chambersburg PA
CBHW081214230426
43666CB00015B/2727